Praise For *Saviors and Survivors*

"Mahmood Mamdani . . . is one of the most penetrating analysts of African affairs. In *Saviors and Survivors: Darfur, Politics, and the War on Terror*, he has written a learned book that reintroduces history into the discussion of the Darfur crisis and questions the logic and even the good faith of those who seek to place it at the pinnacle of Africa's recent troubles. . . . [An] important book."

—Howard W. French, *New York Times*

"Say 'Darfur' and horrific images leap to mind: Janjawiid, rape, genocide. But most of us would be hard-pressed to explain the violence there, beyond the popular notion that it's ethnic cleansing of Africans by Arabs. Columbia University scholar Mahmood Mamdani's brilliant new book, *Saviors and Survivors*, explains why this assumption is faulty, and why it's foiling peace efforts."

—Katie Baker, *Newsweek*

"Mahmood Mamdani . . . demonstrates just how politically charged the word 'genocide' has become and how many shady agendas it can serve, even among those purporting to act in the name of universal values. . . . His extensively documented study of the political and media circus that came to surround the hitherto uncelebrated province of Darfur is a vivid demonstration of the predictably calamitous results of outsiders meddling in places whose history, politics, and culture they can hardly be bothered to read up on."

—Benjamin Moser, *Harper's Magazine*

"Very few books on the Darfur crisis have provided such a good analysis of what is happening in the region, and very few voices have attempted to understand the crisis in its local, regional, and international context. Very few books have attempted to discuss the crisis in its historical and geopolitical context. In reality, discovering such an insightful book is like finding a needle in the sea."

—*Al-Quds Al-Arabi* (London)

"Whatever one thinks about *Saviors and Survivors,* the study and practice of contemporary Sudanese politics, humanitarian concerns, peacemaking, and peacekeeping have received a jolt to the present paradigms that may get us all thinking at a new level of depth. Let's hope that it will be lessons learned, and not repeated, and congratulations to Dr. Mamdani for the clarity and courage to challenge conventional 'wisdom.'"

—Richard Lobban, *Sudan Studies Association Newsletter*

"There are three reasons why this book's perspective on the Sudan-Darfur conflict may be of considerable value to readers interested in African politics and international relations. First, *Saviors and Survivors* is unique in that it presents an African-centered perspective on the Sudan-Darfur crisis in the context of the study of international relations, geopolitics, and the War on Terror. Second, it draws attention to African regional, epistemological, and ideological perspectives on the crisis. Third, it tackles the bogeyman of African politics—the national-ethnic question in the context of cultural pluralism. . . . Hidden in the middle of *Saviors and Survivors*'s controversial thesis critiquing international interventionism is Mamdani's scholarly genius. The book scrutinizes, critically analyzes, deconstructs, and reconstructs the deep historical transformations that constitute the underbelly of the continent's post-colonial citizenship structures."

—*African Affairs* (London)

"Mamdani's book is by far the most exhaustive study of the conflict and is carried out with an impressive display of investigative prowess and referencing. . . . This study is reassuring in its learned dependence on a great variety of sources and an admirable depth of research. Indeed, the reader will discover that Darfur is not quite the mysterious and unknown place that we have tended to imagine. . . . It is to be hoped that this book is widely read and debated."

—John C. Caldwell, *Population and Development Review*

"[A] sweeping history of Darfur . . . Mamdani argues that calling the events in Darfur genocide is inaccurate and irresponsible. . . . He believes that the West's concern with Darfur is a preferred distraction from the failed U.S. occupation in Iraq, offering Western citizens a means to reclaim the moral high ground. . . . [P]rovide[s] valuable historical and cultural background to recent events in Darfur and the sure-to-continue scholarly debate on genocide."

—Veronica Arellano, *Library Journal*

SAVIORS
AND
SURVIVORS

Darfur, Politics, and the War on Terror

Mahmood Mamdani

DOUBLEDAY

New York   London   Toronto   Sydney   Auckland

DD

DOUBLEDAY

DOUBLEDAY and the DD colophon
are registered trademarks of Random House, Inc.

Originally published in hardcover in the United States by Pantheon Books,
a division of Random House, Inc., New York, in 2009.

Library of Congress Cataloging-in-Publication Data
Mamdani, Mahmood, [date]
Saviors and survivors : Darfur, politics, and the War
on terror / Mahmood Mamdani.
Includes bibliographical references and index.
1. Darfur (Sudan)—History.   2. Sudan—History—Darfur Conflict,
2003–   3. Sudan—History.   4. Sudan—Politics and government.
5. Darfur (Sudan)—Politics and government.   6. Sudan—Ethnic
relations.   7. Darfur (Sudan)—Ethnic relations.   I. Title.
DT159.6.D27M36 2008
8510404'3—dc22   2008027317

ISBN 978-0-385-52596-1

First Paperback Edition

To those who seek to make an independent African Union,
and especially to

Abdulqadir Mohammed,
Sam Ibok,
Salim Ahmed Salim,
and
Alpha Oumar Konaré

Who understood that only those who are able to safeguard their
independence can dare to pursue a path of reform

CONTENTS

Part III: Rethinking the Darfur Crisis

ACKNOWLEDGMENTS

When I went to Sudan in 2003, I could not have imagined that it would be the beginning of an incredibly rewarding five-year-long journey. This acknowledgment is an opportunity to thank those family, friends, and colleagues, without whose solidarity I doubt I would have been able to complete it.

I was lucky to have two old and dear Sudanese friends who were then resident in Khartoum: Mohamed el Gaddal, historian at the University of Khartoum, and Abdelrahman Abu Zayd, a colleague at Makerere University in 1972 and, subsequently, vice chancellor of a number of universities in Sudan. Both took time to introduce me to a wide of range of intellectuals and activists. Alas, both passed away before this book was finished.

I was also lucky that a friend from my days in Dar es Salaam, Jyoti Rajkudalia, was working with World Food Programme in Khartoum and knew the ins and outs of the international developmental bureaucracy in Sudan. To Jyoti, who was my host in 2003, and to Nazar and Hanan, who welcomed me into their home time and again over years, and to Samia Ahmed and Mohamed, who I turned to every time I needed a guiding hand in the world of NGO activism, my deepest thanks.

The Sudanese are a generous people, and particularly so once they are convinced that you do not have a hidden agenda. Many helped me with their time and contacts as I tried to identify and connect with various tendencies—whether in the academy or in political parties, or in the world of Darfuri politics—even when they were not always wholly comfortable with my line of inquiry and the tentative conclusions I seemed to draw from findings. It is difficult to recall every helping hand, but there were some who helped me so willingly and unselfishly that I developed a habit of turning to them every time I was stuck: Salah Hasan at Cornell; and in Sudan, Mohamed al-Amin el Tom; Siddiq R. Umbadda; Atta el-Batahani; Adlan A. Hardallo; Amal Hamza; Farouk M. Ibrahim; Ali Saleiman; Nasredeem Hussein Hassan; Salah Shazali; Dr. Eltayeb Hag Ateya, director, Peace Research Institute; and Professor Yusuf Fadl Hasan, the doyen of Sudanese history; Mansour Khalid of SPLA; and Abdulqadir Mohammed of the African Union.

Every endeavor has its infrastructure, and research is no exception. I am grateful for the generous technical assistance of a number of librarians: Yuusuf Caruso, the Africa librarian at Columbia University; Abdul Fattah at Graduate College Library, University of Khartoum; Abbas Azzain at Sudan Library; Khalda at Sudan Records Office; and Jane Hogan at Sudan Archive of Durham University. Professor Ash Amin, executive director of the Institute of Advanced Studies, Durham University, of which I was a fellow for a short but invaluable period in 2008, was thoughtful and gracious in meeting my needs. A number of research assistants helped me identify sources and gather information: Amel al-Dehaib at the University of Khartoum; and Brenda Coughlin, Anders Wallace, Rebecca Yeh, and Sarah Kim at Columbia University.

Most important of all, I have benefitted from invaluable interlocutors and guides: Tim Mitchell at Columbia University; Jay Spaulding at Kean University; Bob Meister at the University of California, Santa Cruz; Tomaz Mastanak at the University of California, Santa Clara; Abdelwahib el-Affendi at the University of London; Noah Soloman at the University of Chicago; and, above all, members of my study group in New York City: Talal Asad, Partha Chatterjee, David Scott, and Carlos Forment. They read at least one draft, sometimes several, and made invaluable suggestions, some of which I eagerly embraced and incorporated into the manuscript. Without their solidarity, writing would have been a lonely exercise.

It is a pleasure to thank my editor at Pantheon, Shelley Wanger, for her valuable guidance and generous support.

The funding for this research came from several sources: the Ford Foundation, the Guggenheim Foundation, and the African Union. I thank them here, and explain the precise nature of their assistance in the introduction.

Finally, I take this opportunity to thank those who tolerated me under trying conditions. My eighty-six-year old father, who spends the warmer parts of the year with us, has learned to endure long periods of rude silence from his eldest son, as we sit and read in the same room. My wife, Mira, has been a constant source of inspiration and support, as she teaches one and all how to combine work and family, life and love; and our rapidly growing son, Zohran, continues to look with curiosity and concern at the world his parents' generation made.

I dedicate this book to those who inspired the African Union's work in Darfur. Unsung and unacknowledged, they had the foresight, tenacity, and vision to work for a tomorrow in which Africa may be able to identify and correct its own problems. They understood that the right of reform can only belong to those who are able to safeguard their independence.

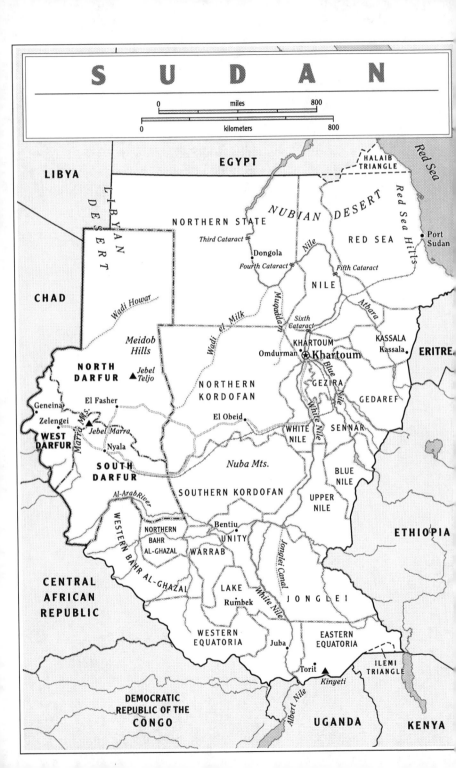

Saviors and Survivors

Introduction

THE SAVE DARFUR MOVEMENT claims to have learned from Rwanda. But what is the lesson of Rwanda? For many of those mobilized to save Darfur, the lesson is to rescue before it is too late, to act before seeking to understand. Though it is never explicitly stated, Rwanda is recalled as a time when we thought we needed to know more; we waited to find out, to learn the difference between Tutsi and Hutu, and why one was killing the other, but it was too late. Needing to know turned into an excuse for doing nothing. What is new about Darfur, human rights interventionists will tell you, is the realization that *sometimes* we must respond ethically and not wait. That time is when genocide is occurring.

But how do we know it is genocide? Because we are told it is. This is why the battle for naming turns out to be all-important: Once Darfur is named as the site of genocide, people recognize something they have already seen elsewhere and conclude that what they know is enough to call for action. They need to know no more in order to act. But killing is not what defines genocide. Killing happens in war, in insurgency and counterinsurgency. It is killing with intent to eliminate an entire group—a race, for example—that is genocide.

Those who prioritize doing over knowing assume that genocide is the name of a consequence, and not its context or cause. But how do we decipher "intent" except by focusing on *both* context and consequence? The connection between the two is the only clue to naming an action.

We shall see that the violence in Darfur was driven by two issues: one local, the other national. The local grievance focused on *land* and had a double background; its deep background was a colonial legacy of parceling Darfur between tribes, with some given homelands and others not; its immediate background was a four-decades-long process of drought and desertification that exacerbated the conflict between tribes with land and those without. The national context was a *rebellion* that brought the state into an ongoing civil (tribal) war.

The conflict in Darfur began as a localized civil war (1987–89) and turned into a rebellion (beginning in 2003). That Darfur was the site of genocide was the view of one side in the civil war—the tribes with land who sought to keep out landless or land-poor tribes fleeing the advancing drought and desert. As early as the 1989 reconciliation conference in Darfur, that side was already using the language of "genocide"—and indeed "holocaust." But that charge was made against the coalition of tribes they fought, and not against the government of Sudan. In spite of this important difference, that language has come to inform the view of those who blew the whistle—genocide—at the U.S. Holocaust Memorial Museum in 2004 and was translated into a unanimous resolution of both houses of the U.S. Congress that year.

Observers noted the exceptional brutality with which both sides fought the civil war. This derived in part from the zero-sum nature of the conflict: the land conflict was about group survival. If the stakes were already high, the lethal means to wage this bitter conflict were provided by external powers. In the opening phase, these deadly weapons came from adversaries in the Cold War over Chad: Colonel Muammar al-Qaddafi of Libya and the anti-Libyan triad (Reaganite America, France, and Israel); with the onset of rebellion, the government of Sudan stepped in to wage a brutal counterinsurgency, just as the managers of the War on Terror set about framing the government as genocidaire while shielding the insurgents in the name of justice.

There have been two international reports on the post-2003 violence in Darfur. The first was by the U.N. Commission on Darfur (2005) and the second from the prosecutor of the International Criminal Court (2008). Neither paid attention to the land question that has fueled the two-decades-long civil war in Darfur. Instead, they focused on those who had contributed to further militarizing the conflict. But even that focus was partial, limited to the government of Sudan; it was silent about the role of regional and international powers in exacerbating and militarizing the conflict over the Cold War and the subsequent War on Terror.

The U.N. Commission concluded "that the Government of Sudan has not pursued a policy of genocide," for the element of "genocidal intent" was missing. It derived the government's lack of genocidal intent from the context of the violence: "it would seem that those who planned and organized attacks on villages pursued the intent to drive the victims from their homes, primarily for purposes of counter-insurgency warfare."[1] In contrast, when the prosecutor of the International Criminal Court charged the president of Sudan, Omar Hasan Ahmad al-Bashir, with genocide, he focused on the *consequences* of the violence, not its *context*.

Let us compare deaths related to violence in two places: Darfur and Iraq. The Darfur insurgency began in 2003, the same year as the United States invaded Iraq. I discuss estimates of the number of "excess deaths" (that is, deaths beyond what would ordinarily be expected) in Darfur in chapter 1, but, briefly, the estimates for the period during which the violence was horrendous (2003–4) range from 70,000 to 400,000. Compare this with three available estimates of excess deaths in Iraq following the U.S. invasion in 2003.* The lowest comprehensive estimate, from the Iraqi Health Ministry survey, published in *The New England Journal of Medicine,* is of 400,000 Iraqi deaths, of which 151,000 are said to be "violent deaths." A middling estimate is from the British medical journal *The Lancet*: an estimated 654,965 excess deaths, of which 601,027 are said to be violent. The highest estimate comes from a survey by Opinion Research Business, an independent polling agency located in London: 1,033,000 violent deaths as a result of the conflict. The first two estimates cover the period from the 2003 invasion to June 2006. The third survey extends to August 2007.[2]

Not only are the figures for Iraq far higher than those for Darfur, ranging from a low of 400,000 to a high of 1,033,000, but the proportion

---

* I have not included the estimate of 86,425 to 94,290 "documented civilian deaths from violence" by Iraq Body Count—an organization that records only war-related violent deaths reported by at least two approved international media sources—because of its highly selective nature.

of violent deaths in relation to the total excess mortality is also far higher in Iraq than in Darfur: 38 percent to nearly 92 percent in Iraq, but 20 to 30 percent in Darfur. So why do we call the killing in Darfur genocide but not that in Iraq? Is it because, despite the wide disparity in the number of excess deaths, whether violence-related or violent, victims and perpetrators belong to different races in Darfur but not in Iraq? That is what many assume, but the facts do not bear this out.

Those who blew the whistle on Darfur in 2004 have continued to argue, for almost four years, that the violence in Darfur is racially motivated, perpetrated by "light-skinned Arabs" on "black Africans." In the chapters that follow, I suggest that this kind of framing of the violence continues the error that came out of the colonial tradition of racializing the peoples of Sudan.

This book invites the reader to rethink Rwanda in light of Darfur. Rather than a call to act in the face of moral certainty, it is an argument against those who substitute moral certainty for knowledge, and who feel virtuous even when acting on the basis of total ignorance.

Indeed, the lesson of Darfur is a warning to those who would act first and understand later. Only those possessed of disproportionate power can afford to assume that knowing is irrelevant, thereby caring little about the consequences of their actions. Not only is this mind-set the driving force behind the War on Terror, it also provides the self-indulgent motto of the human rights interventionist recruited into the ranks of the terror warriors. This feel-good imperative can be summed up as follows: as long as I feel good, nothing else matters. It is this shared mind-set that has turned the movement to Save Darfur into the humanitarian face of the War on Terror.

In contrast to those who suggest that we act the minute the whistle blows, I suggest that, even before the whistle blows, we ceaselessly try to know the world in which we live—and act. Even if we must act on imperfect knowledge, we must never act as if knowing is no longer relevant.

Save Darfur activists combine a contemptuous attitude toward knowing with an imperative to act. Trying hard *not* to be "good Germans," they employ techniques of protest politics against their own government—and now the government of China—and turn a deaf ear to experts who they claim only complicate the story with so many details as to miss the main point. Instead, they rely on the evidence of their eyes and avoid any discussion of context. But by letting pictures and interviews do the talking, they have opened an entire movement to "the CNN effect." If "good Germans" were taught to trust their leaders first and ask questions later, the good souls mobilized to save Darfur are taught to trust pictures above all else and ask questions later. Above all, they strip Darfur—and the violence in Darfur—of context.

I put Darfur as well as Rwanda in a national, African, and global context, which over the past century has been one of colonialism, the Cold War, and the War on Terror.* In 2001, I wrote a book on the Rwanda genocide in which I warned against conferring an ethic of impunity on those who resist genocide. Such impunity led to the killing of some of the millions who died in Congo between 1998 and 2002. Equally, I warned against turning Nuremberg into a paradigm for victors' justice and employing it as a response to the Rwanda genocide. For a continent where a relentless pursuit of justice in the postindependence period had all too often turned into vengeance, a more relevant paradigm would be that of survivors' justice. Based on South Africa's transition to a postapartheid society, it would seek to reconcile rather than to punish, to look forward rather than backward.

Calling the violence in Darfur genocide has had three consequences. First, it has postponed any discussion of context while imposing the view of one party in the 1987–89 civil war in the name of stopping the "genocide." Second, it has conferred impunity on these same partisans by casting them as resisters to genocide. Finally, the description of the violence as genocide—racial killing—has served to further racialize the conflict and give legitimacy to those who seek to punish rather than to reconcile.

---

* The Rwanda genocide unfolded at the same time as the elections marking the transition to a postapartheid South Africa—during the first half of 1994. At a meeting of African intellectuals called in Arusha later that year to reflect on the lessons of Rwanda, I pointed out that if we had been told a decade earlier that there would be reconciliation in one country and genocide in another, none of us could have been expected to identify the locations correctly—for the simple reason that 1984 was the year of reconciliation in Rwanda and repression in the townships of South Africa. Indeed, as subsequent events showed, there was nothing inevitable about either genocide in Rwanda or reconciliation in South Africa.

Thus, the movement to save Darfur, which initially had the salutary effect of directing world attention to the horrendous violence in Darfur in 2003–4, must now bear some of the blame for delaying reconciliation by focusing on a single-minded pursuit of revenge as punishment.

There is an important difference between Rwanda and Darfur. Rwanda was the site of genocide. Darfur is not. It is, rather, the site where the language of genocide has been turned into an instrument. It is where genocide has become ideological.

Contemporary Sudan is Africa's largest country, with a land area roughly the size of western Europe. This vast colony was first put together in the early nineteenth century under Turco-Egyptian rule. The *Turkiyya,* as the colonial administration was called, brought three different territories under its control: The first two were the Sultanate of Funj in central Sudan and that of Dar Fur to its west, and the third was the southern periphery, which both sultanates had over the centuries turned into a reserve for the capture of prized booty, mainly slaves and ivory.

The two sultanates—Funj and Dar Fur—make up the bulk of northern Sudan and encompass its two major ecological zones. Central Sudan is watered by the Nile River year-round and, for that reason, is known as *riverine* Sudan. The river's two main tributaries, the Blue and White Nile, flow into Sudan from Ethiopia and Uganda, respectively, and meet in Khartoum (a word that means "the elephant's trunk") before flowing north into Egypt. Despite the Nile, this country comprises two halves, one desert or semidesert and the other (except for 1 percent mountainous terrain) savanna with varying degrees of rainfall.[3]

In contrast to riverine Sudan, the provinces to the west (Darfur and Kordofan) depend exclusively on rains for their supply of water. Though Darfur is a part of Sudan politically, its geography is similar to that of its three neighbors: Chad, Libya, and the Central African Republic. A shared geography has also made for a common way of life and history, particularly with Chad.

Darfur, the westernmost province of Sudan, is roughly the size of France. The historical memory of the Darfuris is anchored in the Sultanate of Dar Fur. Created in 1650, this sultanate remained an independent power until its colonization by the Turkiyya for a decade toward the end of the nineteenth century and then by Britain in the early twentieth century. British colonization took place in two stages. In the first phase, starting in 1898, Darfur remained a nominally independent state; in reality, though, it was a semidependency of Britain. Full colonization followed in 1922, when Darfur was incorporated into the Anglo-Egyptian colony of Sudan. Historians distinguish between the sultanate and the province that became part of colonial Sudan, the former being the Sultanate of Dar Fur and the latter the province of Darfur.

If the Nile is the lifeblood of central Sudan, the heart of Darfur is the striking and verdant Jebel Marra mountain range (*jebel* means "mountain"). Consisting of a series of extinct volcanoes, the range is about seventy miles long and thirty miles wide and rises as high as ten thousand feet, splitting the province on roughly a north-south line into almost equal halves. Historically, the Jebel Marra marked the limit of cultural influence from the Nile in the east and provided the base from which the sultans of Dar Fur spread their rule to the west. In the 1940s, when the Sahelian drought hit the region and the desert began to move southward, a full one hundred kilometers in four decades, many of the inhabitants of the Sahel—nomads and settled peoples—began to move, some south, others east, all in the direction of the Jebel Marra, which is flanked on its southern side by the Al-Arab River (itself a tributary of the White Nile) and is thus the one certain source of sustenance in an increasingly arid land. Just as the drought knew no borders, those affected by it also shed their sense of borders, whether between countries or between tribal homelands, as they groped for ways to survive.[4]

The province of Darfur is made up of three geographic zones, ranging from the tropical green of Jebel Marra to the arid desert in the far north. Centered on the main crater in the southwest corner of Jebel Marra, where there are two lakes—one of salt water and the other of freshwater—is among the most lush vegetation in Sudan. Here, temperate crops, such as apples, grapes, strawberries, and sweet oranges, abound. Rainfall is heavy, and there is little danger of crop loss through drought. A number of great *wadis* (seasonal streams) drain from the watershed of the mountain range on its western side. The wadis provide a steady water supply, encouraging permanent settlement and continuous development. Though these streams are periodic, their beds supply water year-round to areas cultivated after floods and to lands that draw water from surrounding wells. Regular floods deposit rich alluvial soil on terraced banks of major wadis, such as Wadi Azum to the southwest and Wadi Barei to the west, making them ideal for agriculture. No wonder the areas around Jebel Marra and in Dar Massalit in the western region of Darfur, between the highlands and the border with Chad, are among the richest agricultural lands in Sudan, where farmers grow grains for domestic use and fruits (mangoes, oranges) for markets.

The second geographic zone in the province is the *qoz,* or the southern savanna region. This vast flat and sandy region of dunes extending across central and southern Darfur and neighboring Kordofan supports a wide variety of vegetation, from grass to trees, and many food crops, both rainwater-fed and irrigated, from citrus trees to bulrush millet, tobacco and cotton, and even tomatoes and melons. The rainfall in the central *qoz* is sufficient to support agriculture through the runoff that collects in transient surface drainage systems. With a relatively regular rainfall and seasonal watercourses, the *qoz* is home to both permanent settlement and cattle herding.[5]

To the far north lies the waterless desert. It accounts for fully one-third of Darfur's territory. Only the southern fringe of the desert enjoys periodic rains. In this transition zone between savanna and the desert lies a third zone of sparse and variable rainfall. This is the Sahel, which extends from Senegal eastward to Sudan, forming a narrow transitional band between the arid Sahara to the north and the humid savanna to the south. The ecology of this semiarid zone is marked by a prolonged dry spell, of from eight to eleven months every year. This is an important browsing and grazing area for both camels and sheep and is the home of nomadic camel pastoralism. For as long as its inhabitants can remember, the Sahelian belt has been spotted with baobab and acacia trees and sparse grass cover. But since the late twentieth century, it has been subjected to desertification and soil erosion caused by a combination of natural climate change and human activity.[6]

Corresponding to this natural habitat—highlands, savanna, and the

Sahel[7]—are distinctive ways of life. Rain-watered hand-hoe agriculture is practiced in the central highlands; cattle nomadism prevails in the southern savanna and camel nomadism in the northern and northeastern parts of the province.[8] Camels and cattle occupy different ecological zones. Camels will not survive in land that is wet or muddy or where they may fall prey to biting flies. Thus, the nomads of Darfur have lived in two different belts: the camel belt up north on the edge of the Sahara and the cattle belt to the south on the edge of the rain-watered equator. One single fact illustrates the difference between cattle and camel nomadism: Cattle graze, but camels browse. Unlike cattle, which usually feed on grasses and harvest remnants, camels largely look to trees for nourishment. Unlike cattle nomads, camel nomads are constantly on the move and establish their camps far from villages, preferring to exploit the extended tree bands in lowland areas. From the viewpoint of farmers, camel breeders tend to practice overcutting while grazing. All in all, cattle nomads typically have a symbiotic relationship with sedentary farmers, whereas relations between camel nomads and sedentary groups are likely to be more strained.[9]

Until the Sahelian drought of the 1960s, each nomadic group had its own discrete cycle of movement, either within the belt that borders mud and flies in the south or along the semidesert in the north. The need to access different types of land in different seasons dictated the nature of water, grazing, and cultivation rights, with joint rights over grazing and surface water but individual ownership of gardens and wells. Constant movement made for a constantly fluctuating relation to political power, leading to a process that involved splitting, migrating, and resettling both among and within kin-based groups. This is why close kinship relations did not necessarily translate into close political alliances, whether at the highest or lowest levels.

The Baggara (which means "cattlepeople" in Arabic) are Arabic-speaking cattle nomads who live in both Sudan and Chad.[10] The "Baggara belt" extends from the White Nile in the east to Lake Chad in the west, lying just south of the old sultanates of Funj, Dar Fur, Wadai, Baguirmi, and Bornu. Centered on the tenth parallel north, the belt consists of broadly similar weather, soil, and vegetation features and is particularly suited to nomadic cattle keeping. The area is inhabited by many groups, Arab and non-Arab, pastoral and agricultural, but the Baggara are characteristic of it and the most numerous. In contrast, the camel nomads of the north are known as the Abbala.

The countries of the Sahel zone suffered devastating drought and famine in the early 1970s and then again in the 1980s. In Sudan, the worst impact was felt in the central and northern states, particularly in Northern Kordofan, Northern state, North Darfur and West Darfur, and the Red Sea and White Nile states. The most severe drought occurred in 1980–84 and was accompanied by widespread displacement and localized famine. A comparison of different parts of the African Sahel confirms that drought did not automatically translate into famine. Similarly, a comparison of the worst-affected parts of northern Sudan—such as Kordofan and Darfur—confirms that famine, too, did not inevitably lead to armed conflicts. The ecological crisis is an important backdrop in understanding the ethnicized conflict in Darfur, but it cannot by itself explain this tragic outcome. To understand such an outcome, we need to focus on the institutions and forces through which power and people—in Darfur, Sudan, the Sahelian region, and the international community (a post–Cold War nom de guerre for the Western powers)—intervened in response to the crisis. There is no doubt that several tensions underlie the spiraling conflict in Darfur. Together, they spread out like ripples: from the local to the national to the regional to the global. Local tensions arise from the colonial system and the nationalist failure to reform it; regional and global tensions arise from the Cold War and the War on Terror.

I first went to Sudan in the mid-1970s, when I was a young lecturer at the University of Dar es Salaam and one of the Eritrean rebel movements invited a comrade and me to visit their bases. Sudan was but a way station on this journey: We flew from Dar es Salaam to Khartoum; rode in a creaky, dust-filled bus from the capital to the border town of Kassala; and then took a Toyota Land Cruiser—which had already become the favorite transport of rebels in semiarid zones—across the border to the vicinity of Agordat in Eritrea. I recall marveling that although we could see no road, the driver of the Land Cruiser found his way across the desert like the captain of a ship navigating at sea.

My next trips to Sudan were not until 2003, the year the armed insurgency in Darfur began raging full-force. I spent the first of my two visits that year meeting Sudanese intellectuals, both within and outside the university, hoping to map the outlines of the Sudanese debate on Sudan. During the second visit, I shifted my attention from intellectuals to political parties and rebel groups.

My preoccupation with Sudan has intensified since 2003 and has involved more visits to Sudan and to Darfur. Three different sponsorships have helped make these visits possible: the Ford and Guggenheim Foundations and the African Union. I was a recipient of a Ford Foundation research grant in 2003–5 and a Guggenheim grant during 2007–8. The Ford grant made possible earlier visits and the Guggenheim additional visits to Sudan and the United Kingdom for archival work (at the National Archives in Khartoum and the Sudan Archive at Durham University in the United Kingdom) and to Darfur for interviews. It was during one such visit in 2006 that I made contact with the Darfur-Darfur Dialogue and Consultation (DDDC) office in the African Union. The DDDC had been set up as a result of a provision in the Abuja agreement that mandated it to promote consultation with and among different groups in Darfur so as to nurture an internal reflection on how to move beyond a conflict-ridden present. The opening phase involved meetings in three states of Darfur: West Darfur (Zalingei), South Darfur (Nyala), and North Darfur (El Fasher). In each of these locations, separate day-long meetings were held with representatives of five different groups: traditional leaders (consisting of the hierarchy of chiefs in the native administration), political parties (both government and opposition), representatives of IDPs (internally displaced persons) from different camps, local community-based organizations, and academics and intellectuals (each of the three states of Darfur has a university with a center that specializes in conflict resolution). The leadership of the DDDC asked me to act as a consultant to the process. My job was to read background documents, attend the meetings, listen to the proceedings, and point out which issues and which points of view had been left out of the discussion or needed fuller articulation. It was a job ideally suited to thinking through the Darfur crisis from multiple vantage points.

The more I focused on contemporary issues, the more I became conscious of key assumptions that underlie contemporary discussions on Darfur, and the more I was led to think through—academics would say, problematize—these assumptions. My way of examining an assumption was to unravel its genealogy: When and in what context did it come into being, and how does it facilitate or obscure an understanding of contemporary realities? Over time, this reflection gave my exploration an increasingly historical character.

The historical part of this book is an attempt to think through four key assumptions—regarding tradition, tribe, race, and locality. In chapter 3 ("Writing Race into History"), I point out the key assumption that drove colonial history-writing: that the people of Sudan are best identified as members of different races, termed "Arab" and "Zurga" ("black") earlier and "Arab" and "African" more recently. I examine the remarkable continuity between two kinds of historiographies—colonial and nationalist—both of which see Sudan's history as an interaction between Negroid "natives" and Arab "settlers." This process, known as "Arabization," is said to have produced a hybrid race—the Arabs of Sudan—and civilized it. To show the limitations of this—official—history, I lean on local histories, mostly done by historically inclined anthropologists and political scientists. They suggest an opposite conclusion—that there is no single history of "Arabization" or Arabs in Sudan. Even the Arabs of riverine Sudan—of the Funj Sultanate—came from multiple places: Some were immigrant Arabs, but most were locals; some were slave masters, and many were former slaves. In Dar Fur, however, the sultanate was not an Arab power, and slavery was not an Arab institution. If anything, slavery in Dar Fur was a Fur-driven institution in which the Baggara, the cattle nomads of the south, were junior partners; the northern camel nomads (the Abbala), however, who would later provide part of the fodder for the Janjawiid-led counterinsurgency in the 2003–4 conflict, had no part in it. If many former slaves in riverine Sudan later assumed the identity of their former masters, becoming Arabs, most former slaves in Darfur became Fur. The contrast between the Arabs of the riverine north and the Arabs of Darfur is, however, even sharper. To appreciate the great gulf that separates the settled riverine Arabs from the nomadic Arabs of western Sudan (Kordofan and Darfur) is to understand a cardinal political fact of Darfur: If Darfur was marginal in Sudan, the Arabs of Darfur were marginal in Darfur. In other words, the Arabs of Darfur were doubly marginalized.

A widespread assumption among historians of Sudan/Darfur and its political class is that the colonial period benignly reproduced the key ingredient in the tradition of Darfur—tribal identity—by reproducing a tribal system of property (*dar*) and a tribal system of governance (native administration). In chapter 4 on the Sultanate of Dar Fur and chapter 5 on the colonial period, I show that the sultanate was actually moving away from tribal forms of property and governance and that the thrust of colonial policy was to abort this movement and retribalize Darfuri society.

In chapter 6 ("Building Nation and State in Independent Sudan"), I bring together the discussion of both tradition and race to drive home a single conclusion: At the heart of the crisis of Sudanese nationalism has been the failure to think through the colonially crafted divide, at once conceptual and institutional, that counterposes modernity to tradition and racializes the discussion of (tribal) identity.

It is unfortunate that the assumptions built into the "official" historiography, both colonial and nationalist, have been uncritically reproduced in much of the current literature on the conflict in Darfur. These works thus present the history of both Sudan and Darfur as one of settler rule over natives.[11] I point out that neither the Sultanate of Funj nor that of Dar Fur was a settler state. Even the Funj "Arabs"—the combination of merchants and religious leaders who subordinated the royalty to regents they appointed in the late eighteenth century, and proclaimed themselves "Arabs"—were not settlers. As native as the rest of the population, they were first categorized as a settler race in the twentieth century through a British colonial census.

The final issue to be examined concerns locality. It arises from the assumption that local problems have exclusively or even mainly local origins. I argue otherwise: The political tensions that produced the civil war starting in 1987 and rapidly militarized its conduct were the product of a regional and global dynamic that calls for a regional solution and a global acknowledgment of responsibility. This regional dynamic was set in motion by the Cold War and is currently being reinforced by the attempt to insert Africa into the War on Terror. As I show in chapter 7 ("The Cold War and Its Aftermath"), the most intractable conflicts in Africa today—those in the Great Lakes region or the Mano River complex—are similarly embedded in a regional dynamic and call for a regional solution.

It is after rethinking key assumptions—about tradition, race, tribe, and locality—that I return to the core concern of this book: political violence in Darfur. The big difference between violence in Darfur and in the south of Sudan in an earlier era is that the conflict in Darfur began as a civil war in which the government was originally not involved. The war began as an internal Darfuri affair in 1987–89; the government got involved only after the Islamist coup of 1989, and the national opposition parties joined the fray in 2002–3. Despite the racialized ideology that drove the civil war in its opening phase, the mobilization for and conduct of the civil war took place through tribal institutions. Apart from government forces, the war has all along been fought by tribal militias and tribally mobilized rebel movements. At no point has this been a war between "Africans" and "Arabs." As I show in part three ("Rethinking the Darfur Crisis"), the effect of the drought was filtered through colonially crafted institutions, which divided Darfuri society into two groups: tribes with *dars* (tribal homelands) and tribes without. The more drought and desertification devastated entire groups, the greater was the tendency for tribes without homelands to be set against those with homelands.

The conflict unfolded along two axes. Each pit tribes looking for land (a homeland) against those with land. The difference was that whereas the adversary tribes along the north-south axis were usually "Arab" and "non-Arab," those along the south-south axis were "Arab" on both sides. The work of the Save Darfur movement—and the media in its wake— has had the effect of obscuring the south-south axis in the conflict so as to present the violence as genocide unleashed by "Arab" perpetrators against "African" victims.

The conclusion returns to the discussion in chapter 1: the many ways in which the mobilization around Darfur ("save Darfur") has sought to reinforce the War on Terror. One needs to bear in mind that the movement to save Darfur—like the War on Terror—is *not* a peace movement: it calls for a military intervention rather than political reconciliation, punishment rather than peace.

In the final analysis, the problem of Darfur calls for a triple solution: a regionally negotiated peace, reform of power in the nation-state of Sudan, and reform of land and governance systems within Darfur.

PART I

The Save Darfur Movement and the Global War on Terror

1

Globalizing Darfur

WAR MAY BE SERIOUS BUSINESS, but you would never know it from the casual manner in which African wars tend to be reported in the Western media. Africa is usually the entry point for a novice reporter on the international desk, a learning laboratory where he or she is expected to gain experience. Reporting from Africa is a low-risk job: Not only are mistakes expected and tolerated, but often they are not even noticed. When it comes to mainstream media, there are no Africa specialists.

As a rule African tragedies happen in isolation and silence, under the cover of night. This was true of the Angolan war, which ended in 2002, and it remains true of the continuing wars in eastern Congo. When corporate media does focus on Africa, it seeks the dramatic, which is why media silence on Africa is often punctuated by high drama and why the reportage on African wars is more superficial than in-depth. The same media that downplays the specificity of each African war is often interested in covering only war, thereby continually misrepresenting the African continent. Without regard to context, war is presented as the camera sees it, as a contest between brutes. No wonder those who rely on the media for their knowledge of Africa come to think of Africans as peculiarly given to fighting over no discernible issue and why the standard remedy for internal conflicts in Africa is not to focus on issues but to get adversaries to "reconcile," regardless of the issues involved.

From Silent Slaughter to an Epic Tragedy

A British author and journalist has written of her failed attempts to pub-
licize the human slaughter that accompanied the renewed fighting in
Angola in November 1998.[1] Known as Angola's fourth war, it was said to
be "more brutal than any phase in the country's conflict history since
1975": There were reports of "mass graves," of "the Angolan army using
napalm," and of "hundreds of thousands of people" dying of hunger.
Human Rights Watch estimated that, in the two years that followed
October 1992, 3 percent of the Angolan population—about 300,000
people—died as a direct result of the conflict. Then the United Nations
reported that up to 1,000 people were dying every day in Angola between
May and October 1993, "more than in any conflict in the world."[2]

    Another example of silent death is the Democratic Republic of the
Congo (DRC). In 2006, UNICEF issued a "child alert" on the Democratic Republic of the Congo. The report documented that "1200 people
die each day in the DRC" due to the conflict and that "over half of them
are children." On the basis of four mortality surveys conducted between
1998 and 2004, the International Rescue Committee estimated that
"about 3.9 million people have died as a result of the conflict between
August, 1998 and April, 2004." If the statistics seem convenient, easy to
remember—1,200 die each day, 4 million in eight years—it is surely
because they are rounded off for easy recall. Those who gather statistics
on emergency situations will tell you that the numbers should not be
relied on for mathematical accuracy but should merely be regarded as
indicators of the *scale* of the disaster. Their object is to wake up, even to
alarm, those used to being assailed by advertising and news media—
constantly breaking news—on a daily basis. For that reason, the
UNICEF report tried to compare the Congo tragedy to contexts more
familiar to its readers. At least two comparisons stand out. The first was
a parallel with the tsunami: "Put differently the number of dead every
six months was equivalent to the toll exacted by the 2004 Indian
tsunami." The second was a comparison with the world's most populous
country, China, and an entire continent, Latin America: "Each year,
more children under five die in DRC than in China (a country with 23
times the population) or in all the countries of Latin America com-

bined." According to UNICEF, "The DRC is currently witnessing the world's deadliest humanitarian crisis since World War II."[3]

Congo, like Angola, is the norm. Darfur is the exception. With Darfur, media reports on Africa entered the arena of grand narratives. What used to be seen as meaningless anarchy—in which men, sometimes women, and increasingly, children, fight without aim or memory; in which wars can go on endlessly, even for decades; in which there are no clear stakes and no discernible outcomes; and in which it is difficult even to distinguish among protagonists—has now become invested with an epic significance. Why the contrast between the relative silence that greets most African wars and the global publicity boom around the carnage in Darfur?

Those disturbed by evidence of silent slaughter around Africa, such as the English journalist Lara Pawson, have focused on silence as the price exacted by Western corporations with an interest in these locations.[4] Pawson points out that about 8 percent of U.S. oil imports have come from Angola, before and after 2002. The war may have led to the death of 3 percent of Angola's population, but it did not halt the flow of oil to the United States, even if the oil fields in question had to be protected by Cuban soldiers. She points to Congo, where a U.N. panel of experts highlighted the role of up to eighteen British-based companies in the plundering of Congo's minerals, the revenue from which fueled the conflict in the eastern part of the country. The U.N. Security Council advised governments to follow up investigations into the biggest of these companies, such as Anglo American and Barclays Bank, advice the British government continues to ignore, citing a lack of adequate evidence. A 2005 Human Rights Watch report alleged that AngloGold Ashanti, part of the mining giant Anglo American, had developed links with mercenaries and warlords in order to gain access to gold-rich mining areas in eastern Congo. These accusations notwithstanding, Lara Pawson reminds us, Anglo American's chairman, Sir Mark Moody-Stuart, was invited to join U.K. prime minister Tony Blair's Commission for Africa and played a leading role on it.

Interest in oil is also an important dimension of U.S. involvement in the Darfur-Chad region and U.S.-China contention in Sudan. U.S. oil exploitation in the southern Doba region of Chad had begun in June 2000 when Exxon Mobil Corporation led a consortium in a $3.7-billion project that began exporting oil in October 2003 via a one-thousand-kilometer-long buried pipeline through Cameroon to Kibri, on the Gulf of Guinea.[5] The World Bank provided loans with the proviso that local use of oil revenue be monitored internationally. In December 2005, the Chadian parliament modified the law, calling for a relaxation in the international monitoring of local oil revenue. Under instructions from its new president, Paul Wolfowitz, who was eager to endorse U.S. policy in Darfur no matter the cost, the World Bank had no hesitation about reaching an accommodating new agreement in June 2006.

The economic factor may explain the silence of power in the face of some human catastrophes (Congo, Angola, Uganda) but cannot by itself explain the opposite phenomenon: popular outrage, as in the case of Darfur. The most important factor that distinguishes Darfur from any other African tragedy—Congo, malaria, AIDS—is that Darfur has become the core concern of a *domestic* social and political movement in the United States, one whose scale recalls the antiwar movement of the late 1960s and early 1970s. Spearheaded by an army of college and high school students, the Save Darfur movement has evolved into an *internal* American phenomenon. At the heart of this remarkably successful campaign is one interreligious umbrella organization, the Save Darfur Coalition (SDC).

On February 26, 2003, some three hundred insurgents calling themselves the Darfur Liberation Front (DLF) seized the town of Gulu, capital of Jebel Marra Province in the state of West Darfur. The government's response was a brutal counterinsurgency. Seventeen months later, Darfur exploded into the global media when the U.S. Congress passed a resolution declaring that the government of Sudan had committed genocide in Darfur.

The chain of events leading to the congressional proclamation began with a "genocide alert" from the management committee of the United States Holocaust Memorial Museum (USHMM) in Washington, D.C.; according to *The Jerusalem Post*, the alert was "the first ever of its kind, issued by the U.S. Holocaust Museum."[6] The point is worth stressing: not Rwanda but Darfur was the subject of the museum's first alert. The meeting that laid the foundation for the Save Darfur Coalition took place on July 14, 2004, at the City University of New York (CUNY). It was organized by Jerry Fowler, then director of the Committee on Conscience at the U.S. Holocaust Memorial Museum, and Ruth Messinger of American Jewish World Service (AJWS), the two organizations whose joint efforts created the Save Darfur Coalition.[7] This is how the Save Darfur Coalition described that meeting and its subsequent phenomenal growth in a 2007 search letter for a new executive director: "Following an impassioned speech by Nobel Laureate Elie Wiesel, participating organizations signed a Unity Statement and Call to Action. Since then, the growth of the Coalition has been extraordinary. In three years, the name, 'Save Darfur,' has become the brand for the Darfur anti-genocide movement." By 2007, the coalition had grown into an alliance of "more than 180 faith-based, advocacy and humanitarian organizations" claiming a "130 million person network" with "a rapidly growing activist list of nearly 1 million concerned citizens." Armed with an e-mail subscriber list of more than 1 million addresses and "an annual budget of approximately $14 million . . . derived primarily from foundation grants and individual contributions," SDC claimed to work "every week" through 30,000 key activists spread "over one thousand community coalitions."[8] Save Darfur claims to be an advocacy group, very much in the manner of the nineteenth-century Anti-slavery League. Like the Anti-slavery League, Save Darfur's object is also to shape (U.S. and Western) government policy through public pressure, which is presumably why no meaningful part of its annual budget goes to help the needy in Darfur. Save Darfur employs a staff of more than thirty, but its publicity campaign is really guided by an advertising agency hired for that purpose. The ad agency was M + R Services, based in Washington, D.C. The importance of the agency for the work of SDC can be gauged from a single fact: after the SDC board fired its executive director, David Rubenstein in spring 2007, and before it appointed Jerry Fowler in mid-January 2008, the president of M + R Services, Bill Wasserman, served as interim executive director of SDC.*

On June 24, 2004, Representative Donald Payne, a Democrat and a leading member of the Congressional Black Caucus, and Senator Sam

---

* This should be enough to raise questions about conflict of interest involved in the board hiring a consultant as the manager of its organization. See, http://www.mrss.com/ and http://www.mrss.com/savedarfur.html, both accessed on August 5, 2008.

Brownback, a conservative Republican, introduced concurrent resolutions in the House and Senate declaring that genocide was occurring in Darfur. In less than a month, on July 22, 2004, the House and Senate passed their respective resolutions unanimously.

Somewhat reluctant to fall in line was Colin Powell, the U.S. secretary of state. Five days after the resolution on genocide was introduced in Congress, on June 30, Powell was in Khartoum, returning from Darfur, and was interviewed by Michele Norris on National Public Radio:

MS. NORRIS: Why is the Administration reluctant to call this genocide?

SECRETARY POWELL: Well, why would we call it genocide when the genocide definition has to meet certain legal tests? It is a legal determination. And based on what we have seen, there were some indicators but there was certainly no full accounting of all indicators that lead to a legal indication of genocide, in accordance with the term of the genocidal treaties. That is the advice of my lawyers.
. . .

MS. NORRIS: . . . And for some, the reluctance to label this a genocide hearkens back to Rwanda.

SECRETARY POWELL: It isn't a reluctance. It isn't a reluctance that, based on the evidence that is available, it doesn't meet the tests of the evidence of genocide. It isn't reluctance. I can assure you that if all the indicators lined up and said this meets what the treaty test of genocide is, I would have no reluctance to call it that. And the fact that we have not called it—have not called it that is not based on reluctance. This is not Rwanda ten years ago; it is Sudan now.[9]

But in the days that followed, Powell obliged, presumably under pressure. Darfur was one of two pivotal presentations that Colin Powell would make on critical issues of war and peace during his tenure as secretary of state. The other was on Iraq. Testifying before the Senate Foreign Relations Committee on September 9, 2004, Powell claimed that "genocide has been committed in Darfur and that the Government of Sudan and the Jingaweit [Janjawiid] bear responsibility—and . . . genocide may still be occurring."[10] Could it be that in Darfur too—as indeed in Iraq—his judgment was shaped more by the force of the pressure brought to bear on him than the weight of the evidence before him? Darfur was one of the rare issues on which the U.S. Congress and the executive branch were able to achieve a unanimity of views. It was also the first time one government had accused another of genocide.

The Numbers Debate

Soon after the vote in the U.S. Congress, in August 2004, the World Health Organization (WHO) released its findings on levels of mortality in Darfur. The figures presented a direct challenge to the official U.S. line. First, WHO estimated the mortality level in Darfur at 50,000 in the eighteen months of the crisis beginning in February 2003. Although it later revised the figure to 70,000, the figure was nonetheless far lower than in several other contemporary crises. This is how the International Rescue Committee compared mortality figures for different post–World War II catastrophes in its 2006 article on deaths from violence in the Congo conflict: "These data show that the Congolese conflict has been the world's most deadly since the end of World War II and that the death toll far exceeds those of other recent crises, including those in Bosnia (estimated 250,000 dead), Rwanda (800,000), Kosovo (12,000) and Darfur in Sudan (70,000)."[11] Second, WHO argued that most of the dead were not direct victims of violence. Death due to violence was marked within one specific age group—"among adults between 15 to 49 years of age"—but not across age groups. This finding alone challenged the hypothesis of genocide. In fact, the study noted that "the main cause of death reported during the survey was diarrhea," reflecting "poor environmental sanitation."[12] From this followed the main recommendation of the study: "Additional efforts are needed to improve environmental health (access to clean water and latrines)."[13] This is not to claim that there was no relationship between the violence and deaths from diarrhea. Given that fighting certainly delayed and sometimes deliberately obstructed the provision of emergency relief, many of these deaths could be attributed indirectly to violence—but not all; as the United Nations' own environmental agency would later point out, the drought had preceded the violence by decades. Overall, the findings suggested that the high level of mortality in Darfur was the result of two separate if connected causes: rapid environmental degradation and political violence.

Around the time Congress unanimously resolved that "genocide" was occurring in Darfur—in July/August 2004—the U.S. Department of State put together a research team comprised of officials from State and USAID and members of the CIJ (Coalition for International Justice) and the American Bar Association to conduct interviews in refugee camps in Chad. Circumstantial evidence points to the conclusion that the U.S. government's decision to launch an alternative study was politically motivated. Its executors seemed to be in such haste that they did not even wait for the findings of the WHO study, even though its findings were more far more representative than data CIJ gathered from refugee camps in Chad.[14] In addition, the very language used to describe the CIJ study suggested that it was politically charged and driven: The study group was called the "Atrocity Mission," and its findings were termed "Atrocity Statistics."

The Bush administration based its declaration of genocide on these findings. The same findings, which were later published by CIJ in April 2005, claimed that 396,563 people had died in Darfur since the conflict began. It was a figure both the U.S. State Department and most humanitarian and human rights groups would seize upon to underscore the urgency of an international response.[15] WHO issued an updated estimate the following month: This put total deaths for the six-month period from March through September 2004 at between 45,000 to 80,000, and excess deaths between 35,000 and 70,000. A WHO affiliate, the Centre for Research on the Epidemiology of Disasters (CRED), calculated the number of excess deaths from September 2003 through January 2005 at 118,142. Apparently not satisfied with the accuracy of the CIJ-released figures from the Chad Study it had financed, the State Department compiled its own estimate, "for internal policymakers," of excess deaths. Covering a slightly longer period, from March 2003 through January 2005, it estimated excess deaths of between 63,000 to 146,000.[16] This revised estimate continued to define the low end of how many had died in Darfur in the phase of the conflict that began in February 2003.

It is not the State Department's low-end internal estimate but the high-end findings from its earlier study that have provided the baseline for most international reporting in the West, from the March 2005 British parliamentary estimate of 300,000 dead[17] to the September 21, 2006 U.N. News Service report that "UN officials estimate over 400,000 people have lost their lives."[18] The number 400,000 soon became the official U.N. figure.[19] One notable source, however, took pains to navigate a middle ground between the two extremes. This was the new U.S. deputy secretary of state for Africa, Robert Zoellick. During his trip to Sudan in 2005, Zoellick put the State Department's estimate of deaths in Darfur at between 60,000 and 160,000. We shall soon see that this reflected estimates from the Department of State's own internal study. Outraged that this "dramatically understates the true scale of the killing," a *Washington Post* editorial traced this revised estimate to the original WHO study. It then proceeded to question the credibility of the WHO study, repeating CIJ claims, in effect, point by point: "Last year it [the WHO] reported that 70,000 people had died. . . . WHO's estimate referred only to deaths during a 7-month phase of a crisis that has now been going on for 26 months. It referred only to deaths from malnutrition and disease, excluding deaths from violence. And it referred only to deaths in areas to which WHO had access, excluding deaths among refugees in Chad and deaths in remote rural areas." *The Post* was wrong on all counts: WHO estimates were based on a six-month period but were *not* limited to it; the estimates did *not* exclude deaths from violence; and finally, they were *not* limited to test sites but extrapolated from these to the entire country. *The Washington Post* then offered the alternative CIJ estimate of "closer to 400,000" as being nearer to the truth. *The Post* went on to point out the real damage done by Zoellick's low estimates: "International partners are likely to drag their feet unless they are forced to confront the full horror of the killings." And for that reason, it advised: "Next time he should cite better numbers." The editorial left little doubt as to what it meant by "better numbers."[20]

These "better numbers" have come from various individual human rights entrepreneurs. One of them is Professor John Hagan of Northwestern University, one of the two lead authors of the CIJ study. When *The Washington Post* criticized low figures from Zoellick, it cited as evidence Hagan's estimate that 140,000 people had died violently or gone missing since the start of the conflict, with another 250,000 people having died of malnutrition and disease, putting the total of violent and nonviolent deaths at 390,000.[21]

If Hagan was the most authoritative of the individual entrepreneurs, Dr. Eric Reeves, a professor of literature at Smith College, was the most prolific. Reeves gave a running tally of the dead in Darfur in his blog, usually on a weekly basis but sometimes several times a week. Just consider his tally for the years 2004, 2005, and 2006. Reeves provided a steadily climbing body count for the year 2004: from 10,000 on February 1[22] to 30,000 four days later (February 5),[23] to 50,000 three months later (May 12),[24] to 80,000 in another month (June 11).[25] His mortality estimates for the second half of 2004 were even more dramatic: 100,000 (June 28),[26] 120,000 (July 6),[27] 150,000 (July 21),[28] 180,000 (August 13),[29] 200,000 (August 27),[30] 300,000 (October 12),[31] 335,000 (November 16),[32] 370,000 (December 12),[33] and 400,000 on December 29.[34]

Inexplicably, Dr. Reeves began to lower his estimate of the number of dead in 2005. Having announced that the level of mortality in Darfur had reached 340,000 on February 10,[35] he then lowered it to 300,000 a week later (February 17).[36] On July 14, Dr. Reeves grudgingly admitted that his lower figure was a response to lower estimates released by WHO.[37]

Dr. Reeves began the year 2006 with a mortality estimate of 400,000 (January 14),[38] which he upped to 450,000 (May 20)[39] and then to 500,000 (June 24).[40] This figure was repeated—"some 500,000" (November 26)—five months later, but with no discussion of whether the more or less constant figure over five months meant that violence-related deaths had more or less ceased.[41] Then followed a second drop in estimates, to 400,000 (May 11).[42] This time, Reeves provided no explanation for why his estimate of the deaths had gone down by a fifth in a year, from "as many as 500,000" on June 24, 2006, to 400,000 on May 2, 2007. We shall soon see that this drop followed a sharp criticism of

Reeves, Hagan, and the Save Darfur Coalition by a U.S. government agency for using sloppy methods and releasing unreliable data.

Another seemingly indefatigable crusader on Darfur was *New York Times* op-ed columnist Nicholas Kristof. At last count, Nick Kristof had written more than thirty columns about Darfur; for his continuing and relentless coverage of Darfur, he eventually received a Pulitzer Prize. Kristof made six highly publicized trips to Darfur, the first in March 2004 and the sixth two years later. Anyone keeping a tally of the death toll in Darfur as reported in the Kristof columns would find their rise, fall, and rise again truly bewildering: Starting with a projection of 320,000 dead (June 16, 2004), the estimate was scaled down to between 70,000 and 220,000 (February 23, 2005), then upped to "nearly 400,000" (May 3, 2005), only to come down yet again to 300,000 (April 23, 2006).[43] If rising numbers reflected rising mortality levels, what could possibly explain declining numbers? The fact that the figures were given each time with equal confidence but with no attempt to explain their basis was even more puzzling. Was Kristof, like Reeves, experiencing a stiff learning curve, or was he simply making adjustments in response to the changing mood internationally? Perhaps it was both, as became clear when the U.S. Government Accountability Office (GAO) intervened in the numbers debate.

In 2006, the Government Accountability Office, a U.S. Government agency whose mandate is to audit other government agencies—one may say, keep them honest (its "core values" are "accountability, integrity, and reliability")—undertook a review of six sources of data on mortality in Darfur. These comprised sources of three low-end estimates (WHO; a Belgium-based WHO-affiliated research organization called Centre for Research on the Epidemiology of Disasters, or CRED; and an internal study by the Department of State) and three high-end studies (the Atrocities Documentation Team study led by Hagan, estimates by Reeves writing in his blog, and a third set of figures by a European human rights activist named Jan Coebergh). The GAO convened twelve experts in collaboration with the National Academy of Sciences and asked them to assess the scientific validity of each study. GAO reported these findings to Congress in November 2006. To begin with, it cast doubt on the reliability of the Atrocities Documentation Team's findings: "A number of experts noted problems in the design, sampling, and data collection in the Atrocities Documentation Team's survey of Chad refugees."[44] It then proceeded to question the validity of all three high-end studies: "Most of the experts reported the least confidence in three estimates that reported the highest number of deaths." It explained that these experts "cited several methodological shortcomings . . . including the use of problematic data and application of unrealistic assumptions about the levels of mortality over time and affected populations."[45] The GAO proceeded to give a devastating critique of assumptions, source data, and extrapolations behind the findings of the two most prolific high-end researchers associated with Save Darfur: Hagan and Reeves. Nine of the experts found Hagan's *source data* "generally" or "definitely" unsound, the number of experts registering this view being ten in the case of Reeves. Ten said Hagan's *assumptions* were "somewhat" or "very unreasonable," and eleven said so with regard to Reeves. Eleven said Hagan's *extrapolations* were "somewhat" or "very inappropriate," and all twelve said so in reference to Reeves.[46]

In contrast, the experts declared the highest confidence in the study by the Belgium-based WHO affiliate, the Centre for Research on the Epidemiology of Disasters. CRED estimated 118,142 "excess deaths," which it "attributed to violence, disease and malnutrition because of the conflict during this period" (September 2003 to January 2005). Of these, 35,000 were "deaths due to violence." Given that desertification and drought preceded the conflict, the report left unanswered an important question: How many deaths from disease and malnutrition were due to drought and how many due to the conflict? GAO's concluding recommendation could not have been more critical of the high-end studies: "To safeguard the U.S. government's credibility as a source of reliable death estimates, GAO recommends ensuring greater transparency regarding the data and methods used for such estimates."[47] When asked to comment on the GAO's findings and recommendations, the Department of State agreed wholeheartedly: "The Department of State endorses these recommendations and supports efforts to increase transparency, address gaps in data, and improve the quality of further death estimates."[48]

The difference between both houses of Congress passing the genocide resolution—unanimously—on July 22, even before the Atrocities Documentation Team had gathered data, and Secretary Powell's testimony on September 9 and President Bush's statement that same day was that the latter two were evidence driven. But now that the GAO had brought into question the methods used by the Atrocities Documentation Team and made clear that the results of the State Department's internal study—"to provide information for internal policymakers"—sharply contradicted all high-end mortality claims in the public domain,[49] every branch of the U.S. government seemed to have fallen in line in the short space of two months. Still, differences remained: If Congress was the most open to Save Darfur lobbying, the State Department resisted it.

What impact did the GAO's verdict and the improving situation in Darfur have on Save Darfur campaigners? In a review of studies of mortality in Darfur, one that he copublished with Alberto Palloni in the journal *Science*,[50] Hagan revised his estimates of mortality in Darfur sharply downward, from around 400,000 to a range between 170,000 and 255,000. But even these figures were claims about total deaths, not excess deaths over what would normally be expected.[51] In contrast to John Hagan, Eric Reeves showed evidence of no more than a hiccup, continuing to give mortality estimates of 400,000 and higher in his blog.

There has been no further field study in Darfur of the type that WHO carried out in September 2004 (and the follow-up study after that). This means there is no basis for comprehensive mortality estimates for Darfur after June 2005. But there are field reports from U.N. agencies, including WHO. When I asked Fabienne Hara, director of political affairs at the U.N. mission in Khartoum, Sudan, about the validity of post-2005 mortality figures on Darfur, she replied:

> There was a dispute in the U.N. system whether or not to publish numbers. A decision was taken in 2005 not to publish numbers. Pronk [Jan Pronk, U.N. special representative of the secretary-general in Sudan] was not sure of their validity. We have seen how numbers got politicized. In Congo, the ratio of those who died of violence was 10 percent of the 4 million dead in four years. We may find a similar case here. There was not so much direct combat, not the kind of mas-

sive killing on the scale claimed by [the] Save Darfur Coalition. . . . Some embassies estimate the numbers killed at
60,000 to 70,000, no more.[52]

Ramesh Rajasingham, head of the United Nations Office for the
Coordination of Humanitarian Affairs (UN-OCHA) in Sudan, agreed:
"No NGO has [the] capacity to give a global figure. If an NGO gives a
figure for Darfur, it is a political figure. Save Darfur Coalition has no
understanding of the situation on the ground. . . . We never give out a
figure. Jan Egeland [head of UN-OCHA] did; his figures, too, were politically motivated." The only agency in a position to give a global figure, he
thought, was USAID, which has its "own figures and has a capacity to
analyze data and to gather it on the ground."[53] Interestingly, as we have
seen, USAID kept its own internal tally of mortality in Darfur; meant
"for internal policymakers," it was not only separate but it was also significantly lower than the findings of the atrocities mission it had earlier
financed.

For precisely these reasons, there is no single publicly available and
reliable global estimate of the numbers who have died since the dip in
the level of fighting in early 2005. The best one can get are impressionis-
tic responses from those whose work is to monitor the situation on the
ground over the long term. When I asked Immanual de Solva, humanitarian coordinator for Sudan, also assistant secretary-general and head
of the World Food Programme, to estimate the number of violent
deaths after mid-2005, his response was nine thousand per year.[54] Asked
the same question, Ramesh Rajasingham of UN-OCHA responded,
"The excess death is ten thousand."[55] He was referring to the overall
figure, and not just per year.

All agree that there has been a dramatic drop in mortality rates in
Darfur starting in 2005. These reports point to the development of
political violence in Darfur in two phases. The first phase was from February 2003 to the end of 2004, a time when Darfur was the site of a brutal counterinsurgency. Whatever estimates we accept of the level of
deaths in that period, there is no doubt that the numbers of dead were
far too high, unnecessary, and unjustifiable—whether from a military or
a moral point of view. The second phase began in 2005, when mortality
rates began to decline dramatically. Professor Debarati Guha-Sapir,
director of CRED, wrote a letter to the editor of the *Financial Times*

(London) that "during 2006, mortality in Darfur decreased below emergency levels."[56] Julie Flint of the London-based *Independent* gathered field reports from U.N. agencies for an overview of mortality figures for 2005–6, reporting that U.N. sources in Sudan regarded the mortality rate as having dipped so low in 2005 that the figures no longer justified considering the situation in Darfur an emergency; they also estimated civilian deaths in the last half of 2006 to average two hundred per month. Alex de Waal, who runs a blog on Darfur for the Social Science Research Council of New York, concluded in a recently coauthored book: "From February 2005, known violent deaths ran at approximately a hundred a month, increasing to between two and three hundred in 2006 and 2007."[57] As Julie Flint of *The Independent* pointed out, "The Darfur of 2007 is not the Darfur of 2004." She reported that "mortality levels among those reached by relief are marginally better than they were before the war and, remarkably, lower than they are in the suburbs of Khartoum," even lower than in southern Sudan, where "children have higher death rates and lower school enrollment" than they do in Darfur.[58] When fighting erupted between government of Sudan forces and JEM (Justice and Equality Movement) insurgents in Jebel Moon in early 2008, the London-based *Guardian* reported this as the first upsurge in violence "in more than eighteen months."[59]

Ironically, the first international outcry arose at almost the same time as the dramatic reduction in the level of fatalities. Though the number of deaths fluctuated from month to month and place to place, the general level of fatalities remained low. Yet international media reports did not acknowledge this development, and the international outcry did not subside. To get a sense of the gulf between ground-level reports and claims made by the Save Darfur campaign, one need only recall that Eric Reeves was writing of a mortality rate "very likely more than 10,000 conflict-related deaths per month" on September 29, 2006, just when U.N. sources in Darfur were estimating civilian deaths at an average of 200 a month, no longer an emergency.[60]

The rhetoric of the Save Darfur movement in the United States escalated as the level of mortality in Darfur declined. When Senator Hillary Clinton called for a "no flight zone that is militarily enforced over Darfur," English journalist Julie Flint wrote in a *New York Times* op-ed that "Mrs. Clinton is reading from an outdated script": "During the height of the conflict in 2003–04, the worst violence in Darfur was caused by

coordinated ground and air attacks against villages accused of supporting the rebels. But this year it has been caused by battles on the ground
between Arab militias fighting one another over land and by attacks by
rebels now aligned with the government. Not once this year has there
been aerial bombing 'before, during and after' these offensives, as Mrs.
Clinton claimed. Today, stopping military flights wouldn't make much
of a difference to the Darfurian people."[61] The escalating rhetoric was
followed by U.S. sanctions and the introduction of U.N. troops. A growing chorus of voices under the Save Darfur umbrella called for more
international sanctions and a no-fly zone over Darfur.

How does one explain a situation in which mortality figures in Darfur had dipped below emergency levels but the campaign for a military
intervention to save Darfur was getting shriller and louder by the day—
and continuing to mobilize increasing public support? An important
part of the explanation lies in the fact that the press followed the lead of
the powerful Save Darfur movement, failing in its duty to inform the
public of matters of vital public interest. In particular, the press failed to
probe the validity of the designation of genocide for the violence in Darfur and to provide space for a debate on it. There was, in fact, more of a
debate on the question in U.S. government circles than in the press. This
much became clear in the exchange that followed the testimony of the
president's special envoy to Sudan, Andrew S. Natsios, to the Senate Foreign Relations Committee, which held a hearing on Darfur on April 11,
2007.

Natsios began his testimony by warning against the growing infatua-
tion with a military solution to the conflict in Darfur: "We believe the
only way to deal with this is ultimately a negotiated settlement, because
over the long term, we have to have some kind of an agreement between
the people who live there, who have been at war with each other, . . . one
side with support of the government of Sudan, for the economy and the
social structure and the social fabric of the province to be put back
together again." Natsios then went on to disabuse his audience of the
simplistic notion that this was a race war with Arab perpetrators targeting African victims:

> The government has lost control of large parts of the
> province now. And some of the rapes, by the way, that are

going on are by rebels raping women in their own tribes. We know in one of the refugee camps, it's now controlled by the rebels, formally. There have been terrible atrocities committed by the rebels against the people in the camps. . . . And there are acts of barbarity against people. Some of them are now being committed by rebels. . . . So I think it's a very bad idea to assume this is all Africans versus all Arabs. That is simply not true, and it may make peace harder if people think the bad guys are all the Arabs and the good guys are all of the African tribes. That's simply not the case.[62]

Finally, Natsios went on to confirm that "the death rates in the camps are well below emergency levels," that "the principal people getting killed right now are one Arab tribe fighting with other Arab tribes." Otherwise, he pointed out, it is Darfur that is peaceful and Chad that is the heart of the violence in the region: "Some of the worst atrocities are being committed in Chad now, not in Darfur."

The Senate committee was not prepared for a script other than genocide when it came to Darfur. The more aggressive of the senators tried to get Natsios to recant allegations of rebel atrocities, demanding that he join them in repeating verbatim the allegation of genocide as if it were a pledge of allegiance.

SEN. MENENDEZ: You know, I want to ask you a question. Do you still stand by what you were quoted in the *Georgetown Voice,* saying that the ongoing crisis in Darfur is no longer a genocide situation?

MR. NATSIOS: Senator, I actually—there was a retraction of that by the newspaper the following week. I actually looked at my statement. Very clearly, I did not say that at the—there were three mistakes. And the *Georgetown Voice,* which is a [inaudible] student newspaper—

SEN. MENENDEZ: So would you now tell the committee, what is the situation in Darfur? Is it a genocide?

MR. NATSIOS: Darfur—Senator, right now there is very little fighting in Darfur.

SEN. MENENDEZ: That does not mean that we do not have an ongoing circumstance of genocide.

MR. NATSIOS: Senator, could I finish?

SEN. MENENDEZ: The question is, do you consider—

MR. NATSIOS: Senator.

SEN. MENENDEZ: Answer my question.

MR. NATSIOS: I am answering your question.

SEN. MENENDEZ: I have a limited amount of time, Ambassador.

MR. NATSIOS: Yes.

SEN. MENENDEZ: So I ask you to be specific and answer my question.

MR. NATSIOS: I'm answering your question.

SEN. MENENDEZ: Do you—you can't answer it if you haven't heard it.

Do you consider the ongoing situation in Darfur genocide? Yes or no?

MR. NATSIOS: What you just—

SEN. MENENDEZ: Yes or no?

MR. NATSIOS: Senator, please, what you just read did not take place in Darfur. It took place in Chad.

SEN. MENENDEZ: I didn't refer to that. I was asking you, yes or no?

MR. NATSIOS: There is very little violence in Darfur right now.

SEN. MENENDEZ: Ambassador, what is the difficulty in my question? What do you not understand?

MR. NATSIOS: Senator, I just answered your question.

SEN. MENENDEZ: Is the circumstances in Darfur today a continuing genocide? Yes or no?

MR. NATSIOS: Senator, there is very little fighting between the rebels and the government, and very few civilian casualties going on in Darfur right now. I just told you the answer.

SEN. MENENDEZ: Ambassador, I'm not asking whether diminished fighting. I'm asking whether the situation in Darfur today is a genocide. Yes or no?

MR. NATSIOS: Senator, the situation is very volatile.

SEN. MENENDEZ: All right.

MR. NATSIOS: There are periods of killings which could be construed as genocide that took place last fall and earlier this year.

. . .

SEN. MENENDEZ: Let me just say, I've got the corrected *Georgetown* version here, and you are quoted in the corrected version as saying, "The term genocide is counter to the facts of what is really occurring in Darfur."

MR. NATSIOS: No—no, Senator, I did not say that. But that—

SEN. MENENDEZ: That's the corrected version.

MR. NATSIOS: —Look, that's not the point. The fact of the matter is, Senator, there's terrible—

SEN. MENENDEZ: Well, I hope that this administration views what is happening in Darfur as genocide.

MR. NATSIOS: There is terrible violence—

. . .

SEN. BIDEN: Is the—are the atrocities that are being carried out sanctioned by, cooperated with or a blind eye being turned by Khartoum not significantly greater than the atrocities that are occurring at the hands of the rebels?

MR. NATSIOS: There is no equivalency whatsoever, Senator.

SEN. BIDEN: Well, I wish you'd stop talking about it.

MR. NATSIOS: Well, I'm talking about it, Senator, because the rebels think they can get away with this.

SEN. BIDEN: Well, I'm—look—

MR. NATSIOS: It's getting worse, and what's happening is no one's saying anything about it because it's politically sensitive. We can't let any civilians—

SEN. BIDEN: No, no, it's not politically sensitive. I mean, why—we went through this exercise a couple years ago in coaxing out of the administration the word "genocide." Why won't you just say, is genocide still the operative word?

MR. NATSIOS: Yes.
    SEN. BIDEN: It is. So genocide is being committed—
MR. NATSIOS: Yes.
    SEN. BIDEN: —in Darfur.
MR. NATSIOS: Yes.
    SEN. BIDEN: All right. All right, now—[63]

Not surprisingly, the senators succeeded in extracting the "pledge of allegiance" from a loyal public servant. But not for long. Andrew Natsios resigned as Presidential Special Envoy to Sudan on December 21, 2007.

The dramatic decline in mortality rates was brought about by two developments. One was the work of the international NGOs (INGOs). Their main contribution was to lessen the direct effects of the relentless thirty-year drought in Darfur and the indirect effects (malnutrition and disease) of the five-year civil war and the counterinsurgency. Their ability to dramatically reduce mortality rates vindicated those researchers who had always claimed that the main cause of excess mortality in Darfur is the drought. The second development was the work of the African Union (AU), which was able to radically reduce deaths from political violence. Whereas the contribution of INGOs is almost universally celebrated, the work of the African Union has been almost universally derided. The African Union's weak financial and resource capacity has been evident to one and all, making it heavily dependent on external material support, functioning more as a nongovernmental than an intergovernmental organization—as if it were the biggest African NGO on the ground. Perhaps this is why many have found it difficult to fathom the African Union's strength, which flows from the fact that, unlike Save Darfur and the INGOs, which take pride in seeing their work as moral rather than political, the AU leadership fused moral fervor with a political vision. The African Union did not see its work in Darfur as a purely humanitarian intervention from the outside but as one guided by humanitarian *and* political objectives. Speaking before the South African parliament, President Thabo Mbeki said the African Union's "strategic framework" was based on two considerations: "to protect the civilian population" *and* "to find an inclusive political solution."[64] As we shall see, the United Nations claimed to share the former objective but not quite the latter.

The African Union Intervention and the United Nations

The African Union's involvement in Darfur began just over a year after the start of the insurgency, in April 2004, when it brokered the N'Djamena Humanitarian Ceasefire Agreement between the Sudanese government and the rebel movements.[65] The result was the establishment of the African Union Mission in Sudan (AMIS), which started with a group of 60 observers in June 2004 and expanded to 3,605 by the end of the year—450 observers, 2,341 soldiers, and 814 police officers—coming from nine countries in all.[66] A Joint Assessment Mission, led by the African Union with participants from the United Nations, the European Union, and Canada, followed in March 2005.[67]

One member of the Joint Assessment Mission was Major General Henry Anyidoho from Ghana, who had been U.N. deputy force commander in Rwanda at the time of the genocide. I met him in Khartoum in May 2007 and asked what he thought of the African Union Mission in Sudan. "I got to Darfur in January 2005," he said. "I found out they were doing an incredibly good job. First, the rebel movements were still intact, so it was easy to deal with the government and the two rebel movements. Second, the Janjawiid were pretty well under control. Third, the cease-fire agreement was being observed."[68] This positive view was shared by Refugees International, a member of the Save Darfur Coalition, which carried out a study of AMIS in November 2005 and was otherwise loath to acknowledge any improvement in the general situation in Darfur.[69]

The African Union's main accomplishment was political. It had established a political basis for peace by negotiating a Declaration of Principles and getting all the insurgent factions and the government of Sudan to sign it on July 5, 2005, in Abuja. Though the parties held to different versions of what they had signed, that declaration remains to date the only political template for peace in Darfur. Three months later, the two main rebel movements had splintered into more than twenty. As the rebels began to split, the political agreement underlying the cease-fire unraveled. Fighting resumed, and the inadequacy of AMIS's mandate became apparent. There were demands that the force be expanded so that armed peacekeepers could protect not only unarmed observers, who were supposed to monitor the cease-fire, but also civilian victims of the conflict.

But the African Union's real dilemma was political: It had in good faith accepted Western guarantees that if Africa provided the bodies on the ground, Western donors would provide the necessary equipment and funds. Despite promises, these hopes were soon dashed. Western donor support began to lag just as the going got tough for the African Union. The N'Djamena Humanitarian Ceasefire Agreement had involved a formal collaboration between the African Union, the United Nations, and leading Western powers. According to Anyidoho, "Canada was to provide aircraft and maintenance, the U.K. vehicles, the U.S. camps, and the EU [pay for] soldiers and police."[70] Donors eager to be seen pledging money early in 2005 were reluctant to release it once the mission ran into difficulties. The United States had promised $50 million to support AMIS at the donors' conference in May 2005 but didn't deliver. By November of the following year, Congress had removed the funds from the 2006 Foreign Operations Appropriations Bill.[71] Around the same time, the European Union announced that salaries would be paid only on a quarterly basis and demanded proper financial accountability before releasing funds for the next quarter. When the paperwork didn't arrive, the European Union suspended the provision of funds. In the entire history of war, it would be difficult to think of a similar response, one that stopped the flow of funds to soldiers on the ground because of alleged corruption in the bureaucracy. For one thing, any power would be aware that withholding funds would leave its own soldiers literally stranded in a theater of war.

It seems fair to conclude that a coordinated effort was under way to discredit the African Union's presence so as to clear the way for "blue-hatting" African soldiers—literally replacing African Union hats with blue U.N. hats. "AU has not been paid for four months as we speak; that means a potential for mutiny. Who has ever waged a war depending on another man's pocket? Donors call the shots," Anyidoho told me. "The AU force has not been paid since January 2007. It is short of aviation fuel from time to time. Donors have provided the AU with commercial, not military, helicopters, so the pilots must decide whether or not to go to an area."[72] In July 2007, when I next visited Sudan, the AU force still hadn't been paid. Not surprisingly, there was growing demoralization and lack of discipline in AU ranks. How were the soldiers making ends meet? I asked around. In the soldiers' mess where I often ate lunch, I could see evidence of the buddy system: U.N. personnel using their meal tickets to buy lunch for buddies in the African Union. When I asked about how the soldiers were surviving, no one was willing to be quoted, but rumors were rife of all kinds of unsavory practices, from sex rings to liquor bootlegging.

The African Union itself quickly became a target both for the belligerents and for anybody agitated by the conflict—including the media, the INGOs, and the IDPs they had come to "save." Throughout the second half of 2005, several rebel factions made attempts to murder or kidnap AU soldiers. According to Refugees International, a rebel splinter group kidnapped nearly forty AMIS troops in West Darfur; four Nigerian AMIS troops and two of its civilian contractors were killed when they intervened in an attack, reportedly by the SLA (Sudan Liberation Army), on another contractor; the next day, a JEM (Justice and Equality Movement) splinter group kidnapped an entire AMIS patrol of eighteen, including its American monitor, in Nana, near Tine in West Darfur. "The AU has become part of the conflict," Mohamed Saley, the leader of the JEM splinter group that allegedly abducted the AMIS patrol in October 2005, told Reuters at the time. "We want the AU to leave and we have warned them not to travel to our areas."

AMIS responded ineptly to this combination of problems and pressures. It had almost no appreciation of the critical role of spin in shaping public opinion in modern Western democracies and had neither a public relations office nor a legal department. Instead of presenting its version of events in a convincing way, it resorted to bureaucratic strategies, such as issuing a short press release whenever circumstances called for it. Refugees International reported incredulously that when it asked for "a brochure describing their mission, officers handed RI a printed copy in English and Arabic of the Declaration of Principles . . . with photos of the signatories."[73]

Throughout 2005 and 2006, precisely when mortality levels in Darfur were falling dramatically, there was a major public campaign, involving Save Darfur and key Western governments, to have the African Union replaced by the United Nations. At first glance, this was rather puzzling, since it would seem that the African Union's success would point to a different solution: reinforcing the African Union rather than replacing it. To understand why the big powers were reluctant to reinforce the work of the African Union in Darfur, one must keep in mind that the African Union and the United Nations came to be sites of two very different, even contradictory, initiatives.

No other government had followed suit when the United States declared in 2004 that genocide was occurring in Darfur. The European Parliament publicly hedged its bets when it cast an extraordinary vote of 566 to 6 claiming that the conflict in Darfur was "tantamount to genocide."[74] On September 23, 2004, Nigerian president Olusegun Obasanjo, then the chair of the African Union, visited U.N. headquarters in New York. At a press conference there, he was asked about the violence in Darfur: Was it genocide or not? His response: "Before you can say that this is genocide or ethnic cleansing, we will have to have a definite decision and plan and program of a government to wipe out a particular group of people, then we will be talking about genocide, ethnic cleansing. What we know is not that. What we know is that there was an uprising, rebellion, and the government armed another group of people to stop that rebellion. That's what we know. That does not amount to genocide from our own reckoning. It amounts to of course conflict. It amounts to violence."[75]

The United Nations acceded to American pressure by creating an International Commission of Inquiry on Darfur in October 2004. The Security Council asked the five-person commission to report within three months on "violations of international humanitarian law and human rights law in Darfur by all parties" and specifically to determine "whether or not acts of genocide have occurred." Among the members of the commission was the chief prosecutor of South Africa's Truth and Reconciliation Commission (TRC), Dumisa Ntsebeza. In its report, submitted on January 25, 2005, the commission concluded that "the Government of the Sudan has not pursued a policy of genocide . . . directly or through the militias under its control." But the commission did find that the government's violence was "deliberately and indiscriminately directed against civilians." Indeed, "even where rebels may have been present in villages, the impact of attacks on civilians shows that the use of military force was manifestly disproportionate to any threat posed by the rebels." These acts, the commission concluded, "were conducted on a widespread and systematic basis, and therefore may amount to *crimes against humanity*" (italics added). Yet, the commission insisted, they did not amount to acts of genocide: "The crucial element of genocidal intent appears to be missing. . . . It would seem that those who planned and organised attacks on villages pursued the intent to drive the victims from their homes, primarily for purposes of counterinsurgency warfare."[76]

At the same time, the commission assigned secondary responsibility to rebel forces—namely, members of the Sudan Liberation Army and the Justice and Equality Movement—which it held "responsible for serious violations of international human rights and humanitarian law which may amount to *war crimes*" (italics added). If the government stood accused of "crimes against humanity," rebel movements were accused of "war crimes." Finally, the commission identified individual perpetrators and presented the U.N. secretary-general with a sealed list that included "officials of the government of Sudan, members of militia forces, members of rebel groups and certain foreign army officers acting in their personal capacity." The list named fifty-one individuals.[77]

The commission's findings highlighted three violations of international law: (a) a disproportionate response, conducted on (b) a widespread and systematic basis, and (c) targeting entire groups (as opposed to identifiable individuals) but without the intention to eliminate them as groups. It is for this last reason that the commission ruled out the finding of genocide. Its less grave findings of "crimes against humanity" and "war crimes" are not unique to Darfur but fit several other situations of extreme violence: in particular, the U.S. occupation of Iraq, the Hema-Lendu violence in eastern Congo, and the Israeli invasion of Lebanon. As noted, among those in the counterinsurgency accused of war crimes were "foreign army officers acting in their personal capacity"—that is, mercenaries, presumably recruited from armed forces outside Sudan. The involvement of mercenaries in perpetrating gross violence has also been seen during the occupation in Iraq, where they go by the name of "contractors" and where their numbers have rapidly swollen to around 180,000.

The language of the commission's findings was important. For one thing, if the violence against civilians were termed "genocide," it would make it mandatory and therefore also legitimate for the big powers to intervene to stop the "genocide." Even calling the violence "a crime against humanity" or "a war crime" had definite, though lesser, legal implications. Already, soon after Congress passed the genocide resolution, the United States had pressured the U.N. Security Council for a resolution, which it got (number 1556, adopted July 30, 2004) with thirteen votes in favor and two abstentions (China and Pakistan). This is how Colin Powell explained the significance of the resolution to the Senate Committee on Foreign Relations at its hearing on September 9, 2004: "This resolution, 1556, demands that the government of Sudan take action to disarm the Jingaweit militia and bring leaders to justice. It warns Khartoum that the Security Council will take further actions and measures, which is the U.N. term for sanctions. Measures is not a softer word. It includes sanctions and any other measures that might be contemplated or available to the international community. And it warned Khartoum that the U.N., through its Security Council, will take actions and measures if Sudan fails to comply." Soon after categorizing the Darfur violence as a case of human rights violations, the U.N. Security Council passed Resolution 1590 (March 24, 2005), which "strongly condemned" all human rights violations but "in particular the continuation of violence against civilians and sexual violence against women and girls" and established the United Nations Mission in Sudan (UNMIS), requiring it to "closely and continuously liaise and coordinate at all levels with the African Union Mission in Sudan (AMIS)." Five days later (March 29), the Security Council passed Resolution 1591, which required the government of Sudan to seek "prior approval . . . for the movement of military equipment and supplies into the Darfur region" from "a Committee of the Security Council consisting of all members of the Council." This single provision practically placed Darfur under U.N. trusteeship. Yet another resolution, passed two days later (March 31), number 1593, "determined that the situation in Sudan continues to constitute a threat to international peace and security" and "decided to refer the situation in Darfur since 1 July 2002 to the Prosecutor of the International Criminal Court." It was tantamount to declaring Sudan a failed state.[78]

None of this stopped the continued growth of an international campaign calling for external military intervention in Darfur. The campaign scored its first victory when the U.N. Security Council passed two resolutions in succession: 1706 on August 31, 2006, and 1769 on July 31, 2007.[79] Resolution 1706 called for a new 17,300-troop U.N. peacekeeping force to supplement the poorly funded, ill-equipped, 7,000-troop AU peacekeeping mission in Sudan. But if the problem with the AU force was lack of funding and equipment, it was not clear why Western donors were unwilling to supply these. That their preference was to run down the capacity of the AU force in favor of strengthening the case for a U.N. force suggested that their objective was more than just to upgrade the effectiveness of the force on the ground. That this force would more than likely be the same AU force, only "blue-hatted," suggested worse: that their objective went beyond upgrading the force's effectiveness to taking overall charge of it. It was only a matter of time before some of the African leaders began to fall in line with U.N. strategists. President Idriss Deby of Chad was the first to voice support for the new U.N. peacekeeping force in September 2006. Speaking in Ethiopia the following month, on October 12, President Obasanjo of Nigeria, still chair of the African Union, for the first time began to use the language of "genocide," warning that he would not "stand by, fold our hands and see genocide being developed in Darfur."[80]

Resolution 1769 began by affirming that this "hybrid operation should have a predominantly African character and the troops should, as far as possible, be sourced from African countries." It called on the secretary-general to "immediately begin deployment of the command and control structures and systems necessary to ensure a seamless transfer of authority from AMIS to UNAMID" (the United Nations–African Union Mission in Darfur) and left no doubt about the meaning of "immediately": "as soon as possible and no later than 31 December 2007." At the same time, the resolution emphasized—as do all Security Council resolutions on Darfur, routinely—that "there can be no military solution to the conflict in Darfur" and stressed the importance of the Darfur Peace Agreement as the basis for a "lasting political solution and sustained security in Darfur." It even deplored the fact that "the Agreement has not been fully implemented by the signatories and not signed by all parties to the conflict" and called for an immediate cease-fire, including a stop to the government's aerial bombings. But the contradiction at the heart of Resolution 1769 was clear: It aimed to enforce a cease-fire that did not exist. It set a firm deadline for the transfer of authority to UNAMID but suggested neither a process nor a deadline for reaching a cease-fire or a political agreement between the warring parties. An external force can monitor a cease-fire agreed to by belligerents, but only if such an agreement exists. The collapse of a cease-fire was firm evidence that no such agreement existed. It was, after all, the breakdown of the N'Djamena cease-fire that had reversed the fortunes of AMIS.

Nothing showed that Western powers were eager to secure a political settlement in Darfur. When the Security Council instructed the International Criminal Court (ICC) to investigate the fifty-one alleged perpetrators named by the International Commission of Inquiry on Darfur, the ICC issued warrants against only two, both from the government side in the war. Even though rebels were alleged to have committed "war crimes"—crimes as serious but not as pervasive—none were indicted, and the Security Council said nothing. In fact, when the Security Council was faced with rebel reluctance to negotiate with the government and Russia proposed sanctions against the rebels, the United States and Britain objected, instead calling for a no-fly zone to bar government flights over Darfur.[81]

Abdu Katuntu was chair of the Pan-African Parliament's Select Committee on Darfur between 2004 and 2006, during which time he made six lengthy visits to Darfur, including stays in IDP camps. I met him in Kampala in August of 2007 and asked him why the United Nations could not have given AMIS more resources and made its mandate more robust, instead of "blue-hatting" it. "It would have rendered them irrelevant," he answered, "because the international community would have said the Africans have sorted out their own problem." I have also spoken to U.N. personnel who are puzzled by the organization's focus on only one set of belligerents. "There is something wrong with the U.N. mission," an Afghan security officer in the United Nations' Department of Safety and Security reflected. "Everyone knows that for the U.N., the problem is only the government and the Janjawiid. They are here to disarm them and not the rebel forces. How, then, can you get a political solution between them?"

Trying to keep the peace in the absence of a peace agreement made the African Union "part of the conflict." There is no reason to believe that the fate of the United Nations will be any different. To strengthen the mandate of an external military force in the absence of a political agreement is more likely to deepen the dilemma than to solve it. To seek to impose a cease-fire unilaterally will mean taking on the role of an invading—and not a peacekeeping—force. In that case, Darfur, which is larger than Iraq, will surely require a force of more than the 26,000 currently planned by the United Nations.

The irony was that the transfer from the African Union to U.N. command and authority was taking place at a time when the situation in Darfur was no longer an emergency. As in Burundi and Liberia, in Darfur, too, African forces had been asked to do the difficult work of creating conditions for stability, only to hand over command to the United Nations once that work had been accomplished. Why, one may ask, were the United States and the European Union—key players driving the U.N. Security Council—investing their energies in a military rather than a political solution? Why were they pretending that there was only one side that needed containing—the government—in what was both a civil war and an ongoing cycle of insurgency and counterinsurgency? Why were they publicly blind to the rebels' role in the continuing violence? Why were they silent about the fact that this humanitarian disaster is a consequence of a political conflict that requires a political resolution?

Before we can answer these questions, we need to understand that the U.S. government in particular was both marching in tandem with the leadership of the Save Darfur movement and responding to pressures from Save Darfur's ever-growing mass following. Neither the rap on the knuckles by the GAO nor the dramatic change in the situation in Darfur seemed to dampen the enthusiasm of the Save Darfur advocacy machine. In fact, one is struck by the tenacity with which Save Darfur ads clung to the figure of 400,000 as the level of post–February 2003 mortality in Darfur. To make sense of this, one needs to keep in mind the central political thrust of the Save Darfur movement. The Save Darfur Coalition (SDC) is determined that there is only one way to save Darfur—that is, to occupy it through a military intervention. Its raison d'être is to be sought in the War on Terror.

2

The Politics of the Movement
to Save Darfur

Save Darfur's first major nationwide action in the United States was in 2005, when it persuaded Congress to designate July 15–17 as "a national weekend of prayer and reflection for Darfur."[1] Soon after, it launched a website and "a million voices for Darfur" postcard campaign. The dramatic and sustained decline in mortality beginning in early 2005 had little impact on the Save Darfur Coalition. If anything, SDC intensified its efforts, launching its 2006 "Global Days for Darfur" with an April rally in the East Meadow of New York's Central Park calling for a U.N. intervention in Darfur. Organizers handed out thousands of orange stickers numbered from 1 to 400,000, the last being the number said to have died in the Darfur conflict, and young people were urged to memorize the number they were given, as the identity of the person who had been killed in the ongoing "genocide." Long after the GAO verdict on high-end estimates of mortality in Darfur, as late as the spring of 2007, ads placed in New York buses and subways proclaimed that the latest tally of the dead in Darfur had exceeded 400,000. Both the U.S. government and the United Nations responded to these pressures. If Save Darfur kept calling it "a continuing genocide," U.N. groups continued to pronounce Darfur "the worst humanitarian disaster in the world."

In early 2007, the Save Darfur Coalition mounted a media blitz. *The International Herald Tribune* reported that the SDC's executive director had received "a sudden influx of money from a few anonymous donors" and decided to go on a binge, spending it "in an advertising blitz to push for action." That "high-profile advertising campaign" began with "full-page newspaper ads, television spots and billboards calling for more aggressive action in Darfur, including the imposition of a no-flight zone over the region."[2] A full-page advertisement appeared several times a week in *The New York Times* in early 2007 calling for intervention in Darfur "now." It demanded that the intervening forces be placed under "a chain of command allowing necessary and timely military action without approval from distant political or civilian personnel." That intervention in Darfur should not be subject to "political or civilian" considerations and that the intervening forces should have the right to shoot *to kill* without permission from distant places—these were said to be "humanitarian" demands.[3]

A parallel campaign was mounted in the United Kingdom by Save Darfur along with Britain's Aegis Trust. This is how the expensive ads began: "SLAUGHTER IS HAPPENING IN DARFUR. YOU CAN HELP END IT . . . After three years, 400,000 innocent men, women and children have been killed."[4] This time, a pro-Sudan business group called the European-Sudanese Public Affairs Council (ESPAC) hauled Save Darfur representatives before Britain's advertising monitor. It backed up its complaint with the text of a letter, published in *The Financial Times* in May 2005, from CRED's director, Professor Debarati Guha-Sapir, criticizing the claims of 300,000 to 400,000 deaths in the Coalition for International Justice (CIJ) report as "sensational," alongside GAO findings that studies by CRED were "the most objective and methodologically the strongest." The complaint continued, "the mortality in Darfur in 2006 had decreased below emergency levels and provided copies of The World Health Organization's Weekly Morbidity and Mortality Bulletins as substantiation for that." It also presented comments from Jan Pronk, a U.N. special representative in Sudan, who stated that "the mortality and malnutrition rates had decreased dramatically in 2005." After summing up the complaint, the regulator gave its own judgment: "We told SDC [Save Darfur Coalition] & AC [*sic*: AT] to present the figure as opinion not fact in future."[5]

A second set of responses came from international NGOs in Darfur. A minority of the powerful, usually well-intentioned, INGO commu-

nity in Darfur added its voice to those who saw the presence of the
United Nations, and of the Western powers in particular, as the only
viable solution to the crisis. Refugees International called on the United
Nations to take charge of African peacekeepers, on the grounds that
" 'blue-hatting' a mission . . . has worked in the past in such places as
Burundi and Liberia, where the AU or Economic Community of West
African States, after providing initial stability, handed over a mission to
the UN." In line with demands by the Save Darfur campaign, RI even
called on the U.N. Security Council to establish a no-fly zone over Darfur and on NATO and other forces to assist the African Union Mission
in Sudan (AMIS) in enforcing it.[6]

But most of the groups on the ground were alarmed by the campaign.
Many had already complained that the Save Darfur Coalition did not
spend its $14-million-a-year budget on aid for the long-suffering inhab-
itants of the region. Now they were shocked that it would be so irresponsible as to propose action—such as a no-fly zone—that could
endanger the lives of both aid workers and their IDP aid recipients in
Darfur.[7] In a letter to David Rubenstein, executive director of Save Darfur, Sam Worthington, president and chief executive of InterAction, a
coalition of aid groups with a presence in Darfur, minced no words: "I
am deeply concerned by the inability of Save Darfur to be informed by
the realities on the ground and to understand the consequences of your
proposed actions." He noted that contrary to assertions in its initial ads,
Save Darfur did not represent any of the organizations working in Darfur, and he accused it of "misstating facts." He said its endorsement of
plans that included a no-fly zone and the use of multilateral forces
"could easily result in the deaths of hundreds of thousands of individuals." Another aid group, Action against Hunger, said in a statement that
a forced intervention by United Nations troops without the approval of
the Sudanese government "could have disastrous consequences that risk
triggering a further escalation of violence while jeopardizing the provision of vital humanitarian assistance to millions of people."[8]

This time, the effect on Save Darfur was electric. The executive director was forced to resign, and the executive committee mounted a search
for a replacement. But it soon became clear that the change in leadership
would not involve a change in direction. True to form, the search letter
repeated the Save Darfur mantra, including that "the security, human

rights, and humanitarian situations [in Darfur] have continued to deteriorate," and cited the demand for "the deployment of an effective international peacekeeping force to protect civilians and end the violence" as the first of its "five principal goals."[9] When the search was concluded, the Save Darfur Coalition had a new director. Brought in from the United States Holocaust Memorial Museum, Jerry Fowler had been one of the two founders of SDC in 2004.

Despite the change in leadership, the SDC's policy remained unchanged. Just a few days before Rubenstein was fired, President Bush had imposed economic sanctions on Sudan. Predictably, Rubenstein said it was "too little and too late."[10] When the new leadership took over, it reiterated the call for a no-fly zone over Darfur. In June 2007, Save Darfur expanded its campaign to target China, beginning with a series of expensive full-page ads in *The New York Times* denouncing the "Darfur Genocide" in bold. Though it made no mention of numbers, the full caps said it all: "BEIJING GAMES—DARFUR GENOCIDE—CHINA IS ONLY PUBLICIZING ITS ROLE IN ONE."[11] The anti-China campaign turned on two issues: Darfur and Tibet. The Chinese responded that the Tibet campaign was direct interference in its internal affairs, and that Darfur was an internal affair of Sudan. It held that both points of view were consistent with its general policy framework: noninterference in the internal affairs of foreign countries. China had yet to learn that what scandalizes the democratic world is suppressing protests at home, not killing people abroad. With mortality levels in Darfur below emergency levels, China claimed that the priority in Darfur was a negotiated settlement, and all powers needed to invest their energies to make this outcome possible. In the final analysis, however, the anti-China campaign failed because China was strong enough to uphold its own sovereignty.

For the Save Darfur Coalition, advocacy had turned into a series of advertisements. The campaign was organized by a full-time ad agency. The more advocacy turned into a sales pitch, the less the ads corresponded to the reality on the ground. Yet the mobilization continued with increasing success. Save Darfur seemed to have no reality check, either from its board or from the consumers of its product. Why?

Organizing for Darfur

Save Darfur drew its foot soldiers from the student community across the United States. Its cadres ranged from high school to university students. The effort to organize students developed as an outreach activity from the Holocaust Memorial Museum. Starting with a panel discussion before ninety students at the museum on the evening of September 14, 2004, student action grew in a wavelike manner, eventually leading to the founding of Students Take Action Now: Darfur (STAND). Student action diversified the following year with a student-led divestment campaign, launched from Harvard on April 4, 2005. Twenty-six other universities followed suit. The Sudan Divestment Task Force lobbied state governments to divest their monies from pension funds with a $91-billion investment in companies that do business in Sudan. Meanwhile, Save Darfur funded a full-time staff member to coordinate student activity. By 2007, this yielded not only a national steering committee with a centralized leadership structure but also a network of six hundred STAND chapters on campuses throughout the country.[12]

The great strength of the Save Darfur movement was that it was able to move beyond its core student and faith constituencies. Even if Save Darfur's narrative was stretched thin as the intensity of the civil war in Darfur wound down starting in 2005, the lack of a credible narrative did not adversely affect its ability to draw support from multiple constituencies. Indeed, Save Darfur has been incredibly successful in attracting support among entertainers, the spin doctors of modern culture, and literary giants in the world of culture, almost across the political spectrum. All have been seduced to abandon their political dogmas and bathe in the moral glow of a global humanitarian cause that highlights the plight of some of the most wretched of our fellow humans.

That the campaign corresponded less and less to facts on the ground, getting more and more divorced from reality, seemed to make no difference to its credibility. As this happened, Save Darfur increasingly became a feature—an outstanding one—of the contemporary American political scene, especially the War on Terror, whereby the hallmark of a successful political campaign is its ability to create and sustain a credible political spin. In such a context, who cares about reality? Like the War on Terror, Save Darfur was turning into a massive ad campaign, a set of mega posters, dedicated to spreading and sustaining a lethal illusion.

As the campaign grew, so did the diversity of responses to it and the motives for those responses. The most visible of the responses, a mix of the spontaneous and the theatrical, came from the worlds of sports and the arts. The more spontaneous individual responses suggested that the advocacy campaign was indeed having its intended effect. An example was the declaration by 2006 Winter Olympics gold medal–winning American speed skater Joey Cheek that he would donate his $25,000 prize money to Darfuri refugees.[13] The announcement riveted more than just the sporting world. Never slow to seize an opportunity, Save Darfur recruited Joey Cheek to speak on the crisis before a wide spectrum of audiences. Some actors lent their voice and name, perhaps with good and charitable intentions. Actress Meryl Streep introduced a video on Darfur with the words "Don't be distracted. Don't be away. Don't be overwhelmed. Don't be too busy. Don't delay. . . . Darfur can't wait."[14] Angelina Jolie and Brad Pitt announced a $1 million donation to three charities working in Sudan. "What is most upsetting," said Jolie, "is how long it is taking the international community to answer this crisis." A brand-new nonprofit group, the Not on Our Watch foundation, followed with a stellar list of board members on its letterhead: Don Cheadle, George Clooney, Matt Damon, Brad Pitt, and *Ocean's Thirteen* producer Jerry Weintraub.[15]

If some gestures were spontaneous, others were no doubt calculated, even premeditated. Sometimes, those used to being in the limelight moved swiftly to seize the limelight when it shone elsewhere. One such instance occurred during the highly publicized trip by Oscar-winning actor George Clooney and his father, Nick, when they traveled to Darfur—as they made it clear to the media—at their own expense. When Oprah Winfrey invited them to her talk show to screen footage from their trip, son and father obligingly produced images of Darfuri child refugees shouting "Hi, Oprah! Oprah!"[16] Invited by the U.S. government, George Clooney addressed the U.N. Security Council in September 2006: "I am here to represent the voices of the people who cannot speak for themselves. . . . In the time we are here today, more women and children will die violently in the Darfur region than in Iraq, Afghanistan, Palestine, Israel or Lebanon." Having touched all bases, he proceeded:

> Now, my job is to come here today and beg you on behalf of the millions of people who will die—and make no mistake, they will die—for you to take real and effective measures to put an end to this. Of course it's complex, but when you see entire villages raped and killed, wells poisoned and then filled with bodies of its villagers, then all complexities disappear and it comes down to simply right and wrong. It's not getting better. It's getting much, much worse. . . . So after September 30th, you won't need the U.N. You will simply need men with shovels and bleached white linen and headstones. In many ways it's unfair, but it is nevertheless true, that this genocide is on your watch. How you deal with it will be your legacy, your Rwanda, your Cambodia, your Auschwitz.[17]

John Prendergast, considered by many a neocon in the Democratic Party, also coauthor with Don Cheadle of *Not on Our Watch: The Mission to End Genocide in Darfur and Beyond,* was delighted: "Clooney is smarter than any politician I have dealt with on this issue."[18]

Mia Farrow, a UNICEF goodwill ambassador who visited Darfur in 2004 and again in 2006, took the lead in branding the Beijing Olympics as "genocide Olympics." In a letter sent to Chinese president Hu Jintao, Steven Spielberg hinted that he might resign his position as one of the artistic advisers to the Beijing Olympics if the Chinese government did not change its policy on Sudan: "There is no question in my mind that the government of Sudan is engaged in a policy which is best described as a genocide. I have only recently come to understand fully the extent of China's involvement in the region and its strategic and supportive relationship with the Sudanese government. I share the concern of many around the world who believe that China should be a clear advocate for United Nations action to bring the genocide in Darfur to an end."[19] Indeed, Spielberg carried out his threat and resigned in the full glare of publicity in February 2008.

Steven Spielberg and Mia Farrow, like George Clooney, seemed unaware that, according to U.N. staffers on the ground, the death rate in Darfur had by 2006 fallen lower than the level normally considered an emergency. Similarly, they seemed blissfully ignorant of the fact that part of the dynamics driving the contention between the United States and China in the region was that both were knee-deep in oil, the United States on the Chad side of the border and China on the Sudan side. The Saharan belt in Africa was now also an oil belt—some say even a uranium belt—and the United States proceeded to tighten that belt with all the public relations savvy it could muster, branding the state violence of its adversaries as "genocide" and that of its allies as a necessary part of the "War on Terror." In 2007, both Darfur and Chad became part of a new U.S. Pan Sahel Initiative on counterterrorism.

Another constituency, that of Nobel and near Nobel Prize–winning writers in Europe, entered the fray in March 2007. This development was the fruit of a coordinated two-pronged initiative by Tony Blair and Bob Geldof, last witnessed at Live 8 and the Gleneagles summit of 2005. The initiative took the form of two letters, one from Tony Blair to fellow European leaders asking them to back U.N. sanctions against Sudan, and the other from Bob Geldof to leading cultural figures of Europe: Umberto Eco, Dario Fo, Günter Grass, Jürgen Habermas, Václav Havel, Seamus Heaney, Bernard-Henri Lévy, Harold Pinter, Franca Rama, and Tom Stoppard. Together, they demanded of the European leaders that they act instantly in the name of Europe: "In the name of that common culture and those shared values, we call upon the 27 leaders to impose immediately the most stringent sanctions upon the leaders of the Sudanese regime. Forbid them our shores, our health services and our luxury goods. Freeze their assets in our banks and move immediately to involve other concerned countries." In the next breath, they raised the stakes as high as possible, claiming that the violence in Darfur represented the destruction of an entire civilization, presumably that of Africa: "We must not once again betray our European civilization by watching and waiting while another civilization in Africa is destroyed. Let this action be our gift to ourselves and our proof of ourselves. When it is done, then let us celebrate together with pride." If their language was bold, the proposed actions were timid: no more than denying the Sudanese leadership European tourist visas, European health services, and European luxury goods, besides freezing their assets in European banks—anything but the military intervention demanded by Save Darfur. But Bob Geldof's ambitions were as large as any harbored by the leaders of Save Darfur. According to *The Observer*, Geldof, who had personally phoned each celebrity on the list, said that he "wanted an initiative to put Darfur on the same continuum as 'Auschwitz and Srebrenica' " and that "it" could be stopped in no time: "But now people are being whipped and raped at will. We should not let that happen. It could be stopped in a three-week period, but it isn't."[20]

Should we understand this as an act of repentence—and displacement—given that when Srebrenica happened, was about to happen, most of the big names of European culture were silent? How could writers and artists of the moral and intellectual caliber of a Harold Pinter or a Seamus Heaney be convinced that the violence in Darfur was aimed at the elimination of an entire civilization? It was a feat of imagination that required, at the least, a combination of two things: on the one hand, a worthy conviction that even the most wretched and the most distant of humans be considered as part of one's moral universe but, on the other, a questionable political sense that the lack of precise knowledge of a far-distant place need not be reason enough to keep one from taking urgent action. It is this latter fact, the lack of concrete knowledge of the history and politics of Darfur, of which Save Darfur decided to take full advantage by packaging the violence in Darfur in terms that would suit its own agenda.

Stereotyping Religion

If we are to draw lessons from the Save Darfur Coalition's remarkable success, we must begin with an understanding of how the organization packaged Darfur and the means it used to deliver this package to the intended audiences. If you visit the Save Darfur Coalition website, you will find a record of atrocities—rapes, burnings, killings—some with graphic illustrations, maps, and satellite imagery, almost none of it telling you when it happened. There is no discussion of history or politics: no context, no analysis of causes of political violence or possible consequences of a military intervention. What you see and what you get is a full-blown pornography of violence, an assault of images without context. This is the "CNN effect," the war as the camera sees it. *This* is the spin. This pornography is meant to drive a wedge between your political and moral senses, to numb the former and appeal to the latter—to the need to bear witness. This, it says, is our generation's Rwanda; the last generation, Bill Clinton's, messed it up, but not on our watch.

The central thrust of the Save Darfur campaign is that Darfur is a moral and not a political issue. To drive a wedge between morality and politics, Save Darfur worked through religious bodies and presented itself primarily as an interreligious coalition. It offered Americans the possibility of uniting around a moral cause—Darfur—regardless of political allegiance or ideological inclination. Where else could political figures as divided as Al Sharpton and Elie Wiesel speak from the same platform but one dedicated to saving Darfur—as on April 30, 2006, at Washington's National Mall? Both spoke as Americans—saviors—without having to cite any other tradition in common. The Reverend Al Sharpton evoked the civil rights struggle: "This has been a long struggle, but now, when we see you here today, on the same ground that Martin Luther King came, on the same grounds that civil rights and civil liberties came, we know when America comes together, we can stop anything in the world. History will write that we came together in the first decade of the twenty-first century and stopped genocide in Sudan."[21] For his part, Elie Wiesel evoked humanity: "We are here today because if we do nothing, Al Qaeda and the world's number one holocaust denier, the infamous ruler of Iran, Ahmadinejad, will send terrorists there. . . . Darfur today is the world's capital of human suffering. Not to offer our help, not to urge our government to intervene in every manner possible is to condemn us on grounds of inhumanity. Darfur deserves to live. We are the only hope."[22]

A form of religious stereotyping emerged in 2006, when the SDC began to organize a series of public rallies, the first in April and the second in September, to mobilize mass support behind an interreligious call for military intervention in Sudan. The SDC prepared several sets of "action packets" for the April 2006 rally. The packets were identified according to religious affiliation: initially as Christian Faith, Jewish, Interfaith, and General Faith. After the April 2006 rally, with some noticeable unease, Muslims were added to a "civilized" campaign: a "Muslim Faith Action Packet" was added. The faith packets conveyed a clear division of responsibility among faiths. The Christian faith packets were the most explicit: They spoke of "divine empowerment" and "the burden to save." The "Christian Sample Prayer" asked God to forgive their failure to believe that "you have empowered us to protect our brothers and sisters."[23] The Jewish faith packets emphasized "the special moral responsibility of Jews as 'quintessential victims' to identify genocide whenever it occurs."[24] The "Jewish" million postcards material read: "Instead of mourning a genocide, what if we could STOP one? As Jews, we have a particular moral responsibility to speak out and take action against genocide."[25] If Christians were meant to lead and Jews to bear witness, Muslims were asked to fight oppressors in their midst. The text in the Muslim faith packet focused "greatly on training Muslims in how to aid others, deal with conflict, avoid *being* oppressive, and intervene when other Muslims oppress."[26] Clearly, the executive committee of Save Darfur thought of its constituency in terms of a religious hierarchy: If Christians were empowered to save and Jews sensitized to empathize, good Muslims had the potential to check bad Muslims by fighting oppressive tendencies within their own communities.

These "faith packets" have been revised many times over. The main effect has been "to nuance claims about ethnicity."[27] But traces remain, perhaps as testimony to an original sin. Take these examples from material accessed at the Save Darfur site on January 29, 2008. The "Discussion Guide for Christian Congregations" asks: "How will we as a congregation be the keeper of our brothers and sisters in Darfur?" And the "Discussion Guide for Jewish Congregations" asks: "Is it possible to both bear witness to the Holocaust and other events in Jewish history while acting on Darfur? Does one detract from the other?" And then: "Do Jews carry a special responsibility to victims of genocide?" But this is how the "Discussion Guide for Muslim Communities" begins: "The violence in Darfur is inflicted by Muslims on Muslims. Does that change the obligation of Muslim people around the world to intervene?"[28] Clearly, Darfur is a Muslim atrocity to which good Muslims must bear witness.

That Muslims have a special responsibility to fight oppression in their midst is a message often conveyed by *New York Times* op-ed columnist Nicholas Kristof. Kristof chides Muslim and Arab peoples, and the Arab press in particular, for lacking the moral fiber to respond to this Muslim-on-Muslim violence, presumably because the violence is inflicted by Arab Muslims on African Muslims. In one of his early columns (May 29, 2004), Kristof was so outraged by the silence of Muslim leaders that he asked, "Do they care about dead Muslims only when the killers are Israelis or Americans?" Two years later, he asked in an April 23, 2006, column, "And where is the Arab press? Isn't the murder of 300,000 or more Muslims almost as offensive as a Danish cartoon?"[29] Seven months later, Kristof pursued this line on NBC's *Today* show: "The question is, why are Muslims who, in their—in the Quran, who are taught that killing is wrong, it's against Allah, why are they not stepping up, and telling Muslims who are killing other Muslims, to stop?"[30]

The Genocide Debate

The debate over what to call the violence in Darfur turned on two issues: identity and numbers. Genocide is the slaughter of another people. To slaughter one's own kind may be a "crime against humanity," but it is not genocide. To be guilty of genocide, the accused must be guilty of killing a different people or expressing the intent to do so. According to the U.N. Genocide Convention, that difference could be racial, ethnic, or religious. But in the context of twenty-first-century America, it became important to define the difference as *racial*. This is why only after it was determined that perpetrators had targeted victims racially would the question of numbers become important. The scale of the killings would establish an intention to eliminate the victims as a group, absent an explicitly stated intention to do so. It would confirm that this was not just racial strife, with one side doing more killing than the other, but genocide—in which one side was indeed trying to eliminate the other.

Arab Perpetrators and African Victims

The critical work of establishing in the public mind that the violence in Darfur is indeed racial has been the mission of the Save Darfur Coalition. The most powerful mobilization in New York City—where I have lived for the larger part of the year since 1999—was for Darfur, not Iraq. I had expected the reverse, if for no other reason than that most New Yorkers are American citizens and so I thought would feel directly responsible for the violence in occupied Iraq. Indeed, Americans do relate to Iraq as citizens with a special political responsibility and not as humans with a general moral obligation. The average American response to Iraq is far more political than to Darfur. In the American imagination, Iraq is a messy place with messy politics. Americans worry about what their government should do in Iraq. Should it withdraw? What would happen if it did? Would not the Shia, the Sunni, and the Kurds be at one anothers' throats? In contrast, there seems to be nothing messy about Darfur. For Americans, Darfur is a place without history and without politics—simply a place where perpetrators clearly identifiable as "Arabs" confront victims clearly identifiable as "Africans." The point is that those who march and mobilize for Darfur are being asked to do so not as American citizens but as humans. If they were responding to the call of citizenship, then the focus of their action would indeed be the U.S. government's war on Iraq. But Save Darfur has convinced them that they are in fact responding to a higher calling, a human calling. Save Darfur's great political victory has been to thoroughly depoliticize Darfur as an issue.

Perhaps Save Darfur should be credited with an even greater success: depoliticizing Americans, especially those Americans who felt the need to do something in the face of disasters perpetrated by the Bush administration. The Save Darfur Coalition was able to capture and tame a part of this potentially rebellious constituency—especially students—thereby marginalizing and overshadowing those who continued to mobilize around Iraq. This successful displacement was indeed a model campaign, a successful lesson in depoliticization.

Whatever its analytical weaknesses, the depoliticization of violence has given its proponents distinct political advantages. To begin with, they have been able to occupy the moral high ground through a campaign that has presented itself as apolitical but moral, its concern limited only to saving lives. This simplicity has created a huge advantage. Only a campaign targeting an issue where American power was not *directly* implicated could bring together in a unified chorus forces that are otherwise adversaries on most important issues of the day: at one end of the spectrum, the Christian Right and the Zionist lobby; at the other, African American groups born of the civil rights struggle and a mainly school- and university-based peace movement. Among the organizers of the Save Darfur Rally to Stop Genocide in Washington in 2006 were groups as diverse as the American Jewish World Service, the American Society for Muslim Advancement, the National Association of Evangelicals, the U.S. Conference of Catholic Bishops, the U.S. Holocaust Memorial Museum, the American Anti-slavery Group, Amnesty International, Christian Solidarity International, Physicians for Human Rights, and the National Black Church Initiative. Surely, such a wide coalition would splinter if the issue shifted to, say, Iraq.

For a long time, I wondered why there was no mass movement in America around the Iraq war as there once had been around the war in Indochina, when I was a graduate student in the United States. Why was the American response to Iraq so sterile, so devoid of sensitivity, even creativity? I could not but agree when I read Eliot Weinberger's observation in the cultural magazine *OCTOBER 123:*

> As far as I can tell, the Cheney–Bush II era has not produced a single poem, song, novel, or art work that has caught the popular imagination as a condemnation or an epitome of the times. The only enduring image is a product of journalism: the hooded figure in Abu Ghraib photographs. By and large, the artists and writers have been what used to be called "good Germans," making their little sausages while the world around them went insane. There are only a few who have used their skills—or their magazines!—to even attempt to change the way people think. . . . The mass media under Cheney–Bush II (until Katrina introduced a slight hint of skepticism) has been worthy of the Soviet Union in its mindless repetition of what the government wants them to say.[31]

Indeed, I, too, had become a part of this depoliticized audience: For a long time, I was convinced by those who argued that it was the absence of a draft that explained the difference between American responses to Vietnam and Iraq. But the more I observed the growing movement around Darfur, the more I realized I had been asking the wrong question. In speculating on why something did *not* exist—a mass movement around Iraq—I was missing what *did* exist: a mass movement around Darfur. To understand this movement, one needs to appreciate that Iraq makes some Americans feel responsible and guilty, just as it compels other Americans to come to terms with the limits of American power. Darfur, in contrast, is an act not of responsibility but of philanthropy. Unlike Iraq, Darfur is a place for which Americans do not *need* to feel responsible but *choose* to take responsibility. This act of philanthropy is not born of guilt, but of largeness of heart. It reminds me of when I first came to the United States and was struck by the incredible generosity of Americans, by how willingly they gave to charities—but also by their incredible stinginess when it came to paying taxes. Darfur appeals to Americans who hate to pay taxes but love to donate to charities. In Darfur, Americans can feel themselves to be what they know they are not in Iraq: powerful saviors. For Americans tired of Iraq, Darfur is a place of refuge. It is a surrogate shelter. It is a cause about which they can feel good.

Save Darfur is more of a moral than a political issue on the contemporary American political scene. For those who advocate saving it, Darfur is a site where evil confronts good. Like the War on Terror, the Save Darfur Coalition speaks in the language of good and evil: Where there is evil, the response must be moral, not political. Within the parameters of contemporary global politics as articulated through the War on Terror, evil is the great depoliticizer. "Mr. Bush seems proud of his moral clarity," Nicholas Kristof wrote, "his willingness to recognize evil and bluntly describe it as such. Well, Darfur reeks of evil, and we are allowing it to continue."[32] That evil lurks in Darfur and that evil must be eliminated from Darfur is a claim based on two assertions: Only the lesser of these is about the numbers of dead; the more central claim is that perpetrators and victims in Darfur belong to two different racial groups, Arab and African, and that the Arab perpetrator is evil. The Arab is an outsider, a settler. Here is how Save Darfur's "Jewish Faith Action Packet" explained "some facts" to its readers: "Lighter skin northern Sudanese Muslims, dominating the government, have oppressed darker-skinned southern Sudanese Christians and Animists. Then, as the world caught on to that particular problem, the Sudanese government in Khartoum and its violent allies turned their deadly ire on darker skinned Muslims in the western province of Darfur. Millions have been displaced. Tens of thousands have died, with hundreds of thousands at risk of death. The number killed over the years exceeds the tolls of Rwanda, Bosnia and Kosovo combined."[33]

Listen, for example, to Nicholas Kristof's explanation of why the more important issue in Darfur is not the number of deaths but the identity of those being killed. Kristof related this exchange in one of his columns, starting with a question posed to him by a member of a university audience: "When I spoke at Cornell University recently, a woman asked why I always harp on Darfur. It's a fair question. The number of people killed in Darfur so far is modest in global terms: estimates range from 200,000 to more than 500,000. In contrast, four million people have died since 1998 as a result of the fighting in Congo, the most lethal conflict since World War Two." But instead of answering the question, Kristof—now writing his column rather than facing the questioner at Cornell—moved on: "And malaria annually kills one million to three million people—meaning that three years' deaths in Darfur are within the margin of error of the annual global toll from malaria." And from there, he went on to compare the deaths in Darfur to the deaths from malaria rather than from the conflict in Congo: "We have a moral compass within us and its needle is moved not only by human suffering but also by human evil. That's what makes genocide special—not just the number of deaths but the government policy behind them. And that in turn is why stopping genocide should be an even higher priority than saving lives from AIDS or malaria."[34] But that did not explain the relative silence on Congo.

Could the reason be that in the case of Congo, Hema and Lendu militias—many of them no more than child soldiers—were trained by America's allies in the region, Rwanda and Uganda? Is that why the violence in Darfur—but not the violence in Kivu—is called genocide? Is genocide a label to be stuck on your worst enemy, an antithesis of the Nobel Prize, part of a rhetorical arsenal that helps you vilify your adversaries while ensuring impunity for your allies—so that impunity is conferred as a reward upon those who join the War on Terror? Or could the difference lie in the identity of the victim and the perpetrator in each case, so that the difference between Hema and Lendu in Kivu is said to be ethnic but that between Arab and African in Sudan is said to be racial, as Gérard Prunier recently argued, explaining why the violence in Darfur is a greater evil than that in eastern Congo?[35]

In Kristof's words, the point is not so much "human suffering" as "human evil." Unlike Kivu, Darfur can be neatly integrated into the War on Terror, for Darfur gives the Warriors on Terror a valuable asset with

which to demonize an enemy: a "genocide" perpetrated by Arabs. More
precisely, because the crimes in Darfur were perpetrated mainly by
"Arabs," they could be demonized as genocide. The more thoroughly
Darfur was integrated into the War on Terror, the more the depoliticized
violence in Darfur acquired a racialized description: a "genocide" perpetrated by "Arabs" upon "Africans." Racial difference purportedly constituted the motivating force behind mass killings.[36]

The depoliticization of Darfur has turned Darfur into a privileged
point for disseminating a certain kind of politics. The clearest indication
of this is the fact that the refrain that runs through the Save Darfur campaign in the United States is that of race. When Save Darfur advocates
describe the nature of the evil in Darfur, it is unfailingly in the language of
race: "The Darfur killings do look very much like genocide," *The Washington Post* wrote, describing the "physical destruction" of "a group defined
by its black skin." Kristof wrote several columns about a group of refugee
women whose families were "all killed because of the color of their skin,
part of an officially sanctioned drive by Sudan's Arab government to
purge the western Sudanese countryside of black-skinned non-Arabs."
The language described the victims as "black-skinned non-Arabs" and
the perpetrators as "Arabs"—presumably light-skinned. Darfur was
Rwanda, only ten years later. As Nat Hentoff of *The Village Voice* wrote,
"Of course this is genocide. It is also pure evil. Mr. Bush is not afraid of that
word. Let him, right now—unlike Bill Clinton turning away from
Rwanda—save lives in Darfur."[37]

Save Darfur has been reluctant to abandon the description of the violence in Darfur as perpetrated by "Arab Janjawiid" against "African
farmers." Even its 2007 search letter inviting applications for a new executive director latched onto a racialized description of the civil war from
February 2003, when "the rebels ... primarily from the African Fur,
Zaghawa and Massaliet tribes" were pounced upon by the government-
armed "Arab Janjawiid militia." The "unity statement" on its website,
however, speaks of "allied militia" (*not* Arab militia), targeting "ethnic
groups" (*not* African tribes).[38]

The depiction of the perpetrators as "Arab" is a clue to the motivation
of some of the leading elements in the Save Darfur movement. If they
shun history and politics, in what, we may ask, is their understanding of
political violence in Darfur grounded? The short answer is: analogy. At
least three different analogies bathe Darfur in meaning: the Holocaust,

Rwanda, and southern Sudan. For the Christian Right and secular Zionist groups in particular, Darfur is the site of a contemporary holocaust with the "Arabs" cast in the role of contemporary Nazis. This connection explains one way in which Darfur has been integrated into the contemporary War on Terror. The connection becomes clearer when we look at Save Darfur's advocacy work in South Africa.

In April 2007, part of the Save Darfur network in South Africa organized a Darfur exhibition at the Holocaust Centre on Hatfield Street in Cape Town. The exhibition's centerpiece was the following quote: "We have a dream . . . to kill all the Africans." The quote was attributed to a member of the Janjawiid militia before a village raid in Darfur in 2006. A researcher with the Policy Development and Research Project of the Centre for Conflict Resolution, University of Cape Town, reflected on the exhibition in an op-ed in the *Cape Times:* "The subversion of the rallying cry of leading American civil rights campaigner, the late Martin Luther King Jr., would make even the most apathetic visitor uncomfortable." He continued: "Much of the exhibition was meant to remind the South African Jewish community of the devastation of the Holocaust; it brought to the fore my self-identification as a black African and, consequently, my own possible prejudices against the constructed 'Arab perpetrator.' " The author goes on to note that "the polarization of the once-hybrid identities of the peoples of Darfur is a complex and often misunderstood process" and concludes: "Yet the media packaging of the Sudanese crisis sends the message that there can be no peace when Arabs and Africans live within the same borders."[39]

Turning the Holocaust into a paradigm through which to understand Darfur is problematic. Besides the fact that this paradigm turns the protagonists in the Darfur war into two races, one intent on eliminating the other, it suggests an ongoing—even transhistorical—confrontation between evil and innocence, one in which the two never trade places. To be sure, it is a paradigm in which there is no place for an ongoing civil war, nor for a counterinsurgency facing an insurgency. These problems are evident in the way Darfur has been covered by large sections of the media in the United States.

The Rwandan genocide is the second historic event that is the source of moral indignation for many leading lights in the Save Darfur campaign.

After all, the seeds of the campaign lie in the tenth-anniversary commemoration of Rwanda. Darfur is today a metaphor for senseless violence in politics, as indeed Rwanda was a decade before. The "Unity Statement and Call to Action," issued by the organizations that came together at the founding meeting of the Save Darfur Coalition, on July 14, 2004, spoke of the violence in Darfur as unleashed by an "Arab militia" against "African tribal farmers," evoking the Rwanda genocide: "The emergency in Sudan's western region of Darfur presents the starkest challenge to the world since the Rwanda genocide in 1994. A government-backed Arab militia known as *Janjawiid* has been engaging in campaigns to displace and wipe out communities of African tribal farmers."[40]

Most writing on the Rwandan genocide in the United States was also done by journalists. In *We Wish to Inform You That Tomorrow We Will Be Killed with Our Families,* the most widely read book on the Rwandan genocide, Philip Gourevitch envisaged Rwanda as a replay of the Holocaust, with the Hutu cast as perpetrators and the Tutsi as victims. Again, the encounter between the two seemed to take place outside any context, as part of an eternal clash between evil and innocence. This kind of journalism gives us a simple moral world, where a group of perpetrators faces a group of victims, but where neither history nor motivation is thinkable because the confrontation occurs outside history and context. Even when newspapers highlight violence as a social phenomenon, they fail to understand the forces that shape the perpetrators' actions. Often, they look for a clear and uncomplicated moral that describes the victim as untainted and the perpetrator as simply evil. Where yesterday's victims are today's perpetrators, where victims have turned perpetrators—as they did in Rwanda—this attempt to find an African replay of the Holocaust not only fails but also has perverse consequences.

This kind of journalism inevitably sketches what I have called a pornography of violence. It seems fascinated by and fixated on the gory details, describing the worst of the atrocities in gruesome detail and chronicling the rise in their number. The implication is that the perpetrators' motivation lies in biology ("race") and, if not that, certainly in "culture." This voyeuristic approach accompanies a moralistic discourse whose effect is both to obscure the politics of the violence and to position readers as virtuous, and not just concerned, observers. The result is the reduction of a complex political context to a morality tale unfolding in a world populated by villains and victims who never trade places and so can always and easily be told apart. It is a world where atrocities mount geometrically, the perpetrators are so evil and the victims so helpless that the only possibility of relief is a rescue mission from the outside, preferably in the form of a military intervention. Many of the journalists who write about Darfur have Rwanda very much in the back of their minds. In December 2004, Nicholas Kristof recalled the lessons of Rwanda: "Early in his presidency, Mr. Bush read a report about Bill Clinton's paralysis during the Rwandan genocide and scrawled in the margin: 'Not on my watch.' But in fact the same thing is happening on his watch, and I find that heartbreaking and baffling."[41]

The Save Darfur campaign has drawn a single lesson from Rwanda: The problem was the U.S. failure to intervene and stop the genocide. At the U.S. Senate Foreign Relations Committee hearings on Sudan, Senator Bill Nelson asked Secretary of State Colin Powell, "What are the lessons learned in the Rwanda genocide?" Powell answered unhesitatingly, "That you have to get engaged early." Rwanda is the guilt that America must expiate, and to do so, it must be ready to intervene, for good and against evil, globally. That lesson is at the heart of Samantha Power's book *"A Problem from Hell": America and the Age of Genocide.* But it is the wrong lesson. The Rwandan genocide was born of a civil war, which intensified when the settlement to contain it broke down. The settlement, reached at the Arusha Conference, collapsed because neither the Hutu Power adherents nor the Tutsi-dominated Rwandan Patriotic Front (RPF) had any interest in observing the power-sharing arrangement at the core of the settlement—the former because it was excluded from the settlement and the latter because it was unwilling to share power in any meaningful way.

What the humanitarian intervention lobby fails to see is that there were two Western interventions in Rwanda, both self-serving. The open intervention was by France: Operation Turquoise created a sanctuary for both ordinary Tutsi fleeing from the killings and the political leadership of the genocide. The United States, too, did intervene in Rwanda, but through a proxy. That proxy was the RPF, backed up by entire units from the Uganda Army. A green light was given to the RPF, whose commanding officer, Paul Kagame, had recently returned from training in the United States. Not surprisingly, rebel movements in Darfur hope for a replay of that kind of support. Instead of using its resources and influence to bring about a lasting political solution to the civil war in Rwanda, the United States signaled to one of the parties that it could pursue victory with impunity. This unilateralism was part of what led to the disaster, and that is the real lesson of Rwanda. Applied to Darfur and Sudan, it is sobering. It means recognizing that Darfur is not another Rwanda, at least not yet. Fostering hopes of an external military intervention among those in the insurgency who aspire to victory and reinforcing the fears of those in the counterinsurgency who see it as a prelude to defeat are precisely the ways to turn Darfur into a Rwanda. Strengthening those on both sides who advocate a political settlement to the civil war is the only realistic approach for ending the violence.

A third tendency in the Save Darfur Coalition views Darfur through the lens of southern Sudan. This includes many of the African American and Christian groups, which are sometimes one and the same. They had come together previously, through advocacy and support for the rebel cause in southern Sudan, and have a strong tendency to regard their relation to the Darfur conflict as an extension of that earlier solidarity work in southern Sudan.[42] This is also true of many of the African groups active in Darfur solidarity, such as the Kampala-based Darfur Consortium, which was launched at a conference in South Africa in 2005. Simply put, the campaign saw Darfur as just another version of southern Sudan, where perpetrators were Arabs and victims were Africans or blacks, with the antagonism between the two rooted in a history of precolonial slavery and defined in deeply racialized terms. But the analogy with the north-south conflict is extremely misleading, for six reasons:

First, the historical backdrop is different. Whereas slavery in southern Sudan was an Arab institution that developed in the context of the Funj Sultanate, slavery in Darfur was not. As I show in chapter 3, slavery in Dar Fur developed in the context of the expansion of the Dar Fur Sultanate (starting in 1650). It was primarily a Fur institution in which the Baggara (cattle) tribes of southern Dar Fur were involved as junior partners, but not the Abbala (camel) tribes of northern Darfur, those who would provide fodder in the Janjawiid-led counterinsurgency in 2003–04.

Second, as I will show in chapter 4, there is a world of difference in the historical makeup and political orientation of the Arab tribes of riverine Sudan with their privileged identification with power, starting with the Funj Sultanate, and that of the Arab tribes of Dar Fur whose relationship to power and whose social position has been marginal from the time of the Sultanate of Dar Fur.

Third, whereas the conflict in southern Sudan developed as an insurgency against the central government, the conflict in Darfur began as a civil war between settled ("non-Arab") and nomadic ("Arab") tribes in 1987–89. During this internal conflict one side accused the other of waging "genocide" against it, whereas the other side claimed to be the target of a violent "native" assertion to clear the land of settlers. In fact, the language used by the representative of the settled tribes during the reconciliation conference in El Fasher in 1989 did not just refer to "genocide" but to a "Holocaust."

Fourth, whereas Western powers got implicated in southern Sudan only during the course of the conflict, we shall see in chapter 7 that they were directly implicated in the militarization of the 1987–89 civil war in Darfur from its very beginning.

Fifth, the Janjawiid originated during this civil war, long before the insurgency and counterinsurgency of 2003–04. The Janjawiid are a nomadic phenomenon, not an "Arab" one. Born of destitution and political strife, this phenomenon runs through the entire span of the Sahel, from Darfur to Chad and the Central African Republic and beyond. Rather than a single cohesive force, the Janjawiid are groups of outlaw-type bands. These lawless nomads emerged from the crisis of nomadism against the backdrop of a colonial power hostile to nomadism and a protracted drought that devastated the region in the course of four decades. The alliance between the Janjawiid and the government in Khartoum was specific to the counterinsurgency of 2003–04, but Save Darfur turned it into a permanent feature of its narrative, that "the genocide is continuing" in Darfur.

Finally, there is no linear connection between the counterinsurgency in southern Sudan and that in Darfur. The counterinsurgency in southern Sudan was in fact organized under the Turabi wing of the Islamist government that came to power in 1989. Not only were many of the Mujahideen (the counterinsurgency) in southern Sudan recruited from the Islamists in Darfur, their political commissar, Khalil Ibrahim, would later organize one of the two rebel movements in Darfur, the Justice and Equality Movement (JEM), and lead it. In a historical sense, JEM—and not the Janjawiid—was a child of those who led and participated in the counterinsurgency in southern Sudan and who were subsequently disappointed by their marginalization in the Islamist alliance in Khartoum.

The Save Darfur Coalition represents a New Age organization that joins the voluntary effort of foot soldiers characteristic of classic cause-driven movements (such as the Vietnam-era antiwar movement) with advertising skills honed by highly paid professional advertising firms, all under the tight supervision of a select and small, politically driven and charged, executive committee. Save Darfur is undoubtedly the most successful organized popular movement in the United States since the movement against the Vietnam War. But whereas the organized opposition to the Vietnam War was clearly antiwar, the same cannot be said of Save Darfur. In the words of John Prendergast: "Human rights should no longer be traded off against endless peace processes that never quite come to fruition."[43] This mass student and evangelical movement does not seek to end the civil war in Darfur; rather, it calls for a military intervention in the civil war without bothering to address the likely consequences of that intervention. "Out of Iraq and into Darfur," says a common Save Darfur slogan. "Boots on the ground," says another. At best, Save Darfur was a romance driven by a feel-good search for instant remedies. At worst, it was a media-savvy political campaign designed to portray "Arabs" as race-intoxicated exterminators of "Africans."

The political dimension of Save Darfur is best understood in the context of the War on Terror. Because the crimes in Darfur are said to have been committed by "Arabs"—who have already been successfully demonized by the War on Terror—it has been easy to demonize these crimes as "genocide." This conclusion has been reached with scant respect for either historical and contemporary context or the motivation shaped by it. The result has been a host of gross generalizations, as I will show in the chapters that follow. To begin with, it is assumed that Arab tribes of Sudan originate from Arab settlers who came from the

Middle East, but in fact the Arabs of Sudan are as native to Sudan as most of its inhabitants. It is further assumed that Arab tribes in Darfur and in riverine Sudan are products of a single history of "Arabs" and "Arabization," when they are not. It is also assumed that the conflict in Darfur is between "Arab" and "non-Arab" (or "black," now "African") tribes, whereas in fact it is in the main a conflict between tribes with homelands (*dar*) and those without. This conflict has unfolded over two axes: Whereas the conflict along the north-south axis pits northern ("Arab") landless tribes against southern ("non-Arab" or "black") land-rich tribes, the conflict along the south-south axis was between land-poor and land-rich tribes, both sides being southern and "Arab." It is the work of the Save Darfur activists to have obscured the conflict along the south-south axis, and to have identified the conflict in Darfur exclusively with the north-south axis, thereby presenting it as a racial conflict between "Arabs" and "blacks" and masking the land question that has been key to the conflict. The fact is that the conflict in Darfur is a product of two related, if different, developments: the first internal, the second external; the former a civil war focused on the question of land and sparked by a four-decades-long drought and desertification, and the latter a scorched earth government response to a rebellion by one side in the civil war.

The Arabization of the violence in Darfur—of the Janjawiid in particular, and the counterinsurgency in general—derives less from the history of Darfur than from the logic of the War on Terror. The harsh truth is that the War on Terror has provided the coordinates, the language, the images, and the sentiment for interpreting Darfur. In doing so, the War on Terror has displaced the history and politics of Darfur while providing the context to interpret and illuminate ongoing developments in Darfur. The more such an interpretation takes root, the more Darfur becomes not just an illustration of the grand narrative of the War on Terror but also a part of its justification.

It is the purpose of part two of the book to restore the historical and contemporary context of Darfur. Only then will it be possible, in part three, to explain the dynamic that fuels the conflict and the motivation that drives it.

PART II

Darfur in Context

3

Writing Race into History

SUDAN DERIVES its name from medieval Arab writers, who used two names, one general and the other more specific, to refer to the lands to the south of Egypt. They referred to the three Christian kingdoms (Nobatia, Makuria, and Alodia) to the south of Aswan as *Bilad al-Nuba* and their inhabitants as *al-Nuba*. More generally, they called all territories south of the Sahara, stretching from the Red Sea to the Atlantic, *Bilad al-Sudan*, meaning "the land of the blacks." This general, color-coded designation—*Bilad al-Sudan*—had powerful antecedents in both the Old Testament and the ancient Egyptian naming of the world. Ancient Egyptians divided their world into four parts: the land of the Libyans (*Thehemnu*) to the west, the land of the Asians (*Aomu*) to the east, the land of the Blacks (*Tenehasu*) to the south, and the land of the Men (Egypt itself). The biblical tradition traces the blackness of Negroes to the story of Ham's being cursed by his father. The account in Genesis, chapter 9, tells of Ham's contempt for his father, Noah, when he saw him lying naked in a drunken stupor. While Noah's other sons, Shem and Japheth, covered their father's nakedness, averting their eyes from his shame, Ham did not. Noah is said to have blessed the descendants of Shem and Japheth but cursed those of Ham. The claim that Ham's descendants were cursed to be black does not appear in Genesis but in the oral traditions of the Jews as recorded in the sixth-century Babylonian Talmud.[1] The Greeks—and following them, the Romans—called all lands to the south of Egypt Ethiopia, from *Ethiops* ("burned face"), a Greek word for dark-complexioned peoples. They referred to the king of Meroë (located in northern Sudan) as the "king of the Ethiopians." The name Ethiopia was extended to the neighboring kingdom of Axum (and thereby to the land we now know as Ethiopia) in A.D. 350, when Axum captured and destroyed the city of Meroë and annexed large parts of it.[2]

Though widespread, this color-coded designation did not go unchallenged. The best-known critique came from Ibn Khaldūn. Writing in *Muqaddimah* (*Introduction to History*), Ibn Khaldūn rejected the Old Testament explanation of why some people are dark-skinned, offering an alternative explanation that the darker complexion is simply due to the heat of the sun in the regions they inhabit. He went on to observe the "naturalness" with which those in the north designate those to the south by their color as "black":

> The inhabitants of the north are not called by their color, because the people who established the conventional meanings of words were themselves white. Thus, whiteness was something usual and common to them, and they did not see anything sufficiently remarkable in it to cause them to use it as a specific term.[3]

Riverine Sudan has had a longer and more continuous history of uninterrupted internal development than the other two great civilizations in this region, Egypt and Iraq. It was not occupied by a foreign power until 1821, when Ottoman and British forces based in Egypt invaded Sudan. When Turco-Egyptian forces captured the land to the south of Egypt in 1821, they officially named the country the Soudan, or "the land of the blacks." The spelling changed from "the Soudan" to "the Sudan," and the article—*the*—was officially dropped in 1975—in English, but remained very much alive in Arabic, as in Jumhuriyyat al-Sudan.[4]

The contemporary history of Sudan—at least its dominant version—was written in the colonial period. It reflected a racist paradigm common to imperial histories written in Western societies in the early nineteenth century: distinguishing the West sharply from the non-West, explaining progress in Western society as more or less the result of endogenous change but assuming that pathbreaking change in the non-Western world was the result of external influences leading to internal ruptures. This assumption appeared at its most extreme in the writing of African history.[5]

Most nineteenth-century narratives of African history come from Europeans writing in the shadow of the transatlantic slave trade, a time when the Negro was not only identified as a separate race but also vilified as subhuman. The tendency was to write the history of Africa as one of external stimuli breaking an internal inertia. Any evidence of progress in Negro Africa was presumed to be the outcome of an external initiative. Colonial historians explained the history of state formation in West Africa as the result of influences from non-Negroid Berber peoples in North Africa. Similarly, when John Speke and his cohort of missionary-explorers came upon organized political society in the lands of the African Great Lakes, they assumed it must have been built by a non-Negroid people coming, naturally, from somewhere up north. With the rediscovery of Egypt following Napoleon's expedition, or the discovery of a civilized land of a dark people, the biblical story went through yet another transformation: The children of Ham were recast in the role of civilizers of Negroes.

An example of this kind of history can be read from the pen of a historian of Nubia, Professor William Y. Adams,[6] who wrote that Sudanese history is characterized by Egyptian/Mediterranean dynamism and African stagnation. He claimed that civilization arose in Sudan as a result of an external/Egyptian impact, but the Africanization of this impact led to its stagnation and ultimate decline.[7] Some locate this dynamism in the pharaohnic period, others in Arab Egypt. This common orientation stems from a larger Orientalist perspective. In the context of Sudan, its history of several millennia is seen as a sucession of separate periods, each identified with a different external influence: Egyptianization in the pharaohnic period, Christianization with Byzantine power, Arabization in the Islamic period, and Westernization with nineteenth-century colonization. Each such process is said to have been spearheaded by an invading or migrating group that supposedly displaced the previously dominant culture with its own. It is as if the country were akin to a satellite fired into space by a series of missiles, each losing steam in time and being replaced with another.

The point is not that ancient Egypt, Byzantine Christianity, Islamic urbanity, or, for that matter, Western modernity did not significantly influence Sudan or other lands. The point, rather, is to place this influence in the context of a larger historical flow by asking questions such as, What internal forces or conditions made the society in question receptive to these external influences at specific historical periods? From this point of view, the classic problem facing the historian is that of continuity and change. The challenge is less of choosing between the two than of deciding where to place the primary emphasis at different points in the narrative and, ultimately, how to articulate the relationship between change and continuity over the course of time. Migration-centric histories assumed that receiving societies were internally static and that all meaningful change was external. Since the external civilizing influence from the north was presumed to be that of a non-Negro group, called Hamites, this assumption came to be known as the Hamitic hypothesis.

Arabization—The Civilizing Hypothesis

The British official mind of the nineteenth century regarded the African world as made up of races, primarily Negro natives and non-Negro settlers, the former the cause of their own backwardness and the latter a possible solution for this malady. When it comes to Sudan, this mind-set is clearly evident in the young Winston Churchill's late-nineteenth-century journalistic report on the country, titled *The River War: An Account of the Reconquest of the Sudan*:

> The Soudanese are of many tribes, but two main races can be clearly distinguished: the aboriginal natives, and the Arab settlers. The indigenous inhabitants of the country were negroes as black as coal. Strong, virile and simple-minded savages, they lived as we may imagine prehistoric men— hunting, fighting, marrying and dying, with no ideas beyond the gratification of their physical desires, and no fears save those engendered by ghost, witchcraft, the worship of ancestors, and other forms of superstition common among peoples of low development. . . . The smallness of their intelligence excused the degradation of their habits. . . .

Although the negroes are the more numerous, the Arabs exceed in power. The bravery of the aboriginals is outweighed by the intelligence of the invaders and their superior force of character. . . . The aboriginals absorbed the invaders they could not repel. The stronger race imposed its customs and language on the negroes. The vigor of their blood sensibly altered the facial appearance of the Soudanese. For more than a thousand years the influence of Mohammedanism, which appears to possess a strange fascination for negroid races, has been permeating the Soudan, and, although ignorance and natural obstacles impede the progress of new ideas, the whole of the black race is gradually adopting the new religion and developing Arab characteristics. . . .

The qualities of mongrels are rarely admirable, and the mixture of the Arab and negro types has produced a debased and cruel breed, more shocking because they are more intelligent than the primitive savages. . . . Thus the situation in the Soudan for several centuries may be summed up as follows: The dominant race of Arab invaders was unceasingly spreading its blood, religion, customs and language among the black aboriginal population, and at the same time it harried and enslaved them.[8]

In the Churchillian view, race is not culture. Rather, it is biology. Each race has specific qualities, which is why the mixing of races leads to a mixing of qualities: "the qualities of mongrels."

Written almost three decades later, in 1922, Harold A. MacMichael's two-volume *A History of the Arabs in the Sudan* followed the Churchillian script in its broad contours. MacMichael wrote of three "main ethnic elements in Darfur": the Negro, the Hamitic, and the Arab. He said the Negro "is the most ancient" but has been pushed to the south, "partly due to the continuous pressure exerted by the Arabs in north Africa upon the Berber races, compelling them to move southwards and encroach upon the lands of the darker races, a process which began at least as early as the seventh century A.D. and affected every state from the Atlantic to the Nile in a greater or less degree."[9]

MacMichael elaborated this hypothesis into a theory of migration in his two-volume treatise: Part one of the first volume focused on the native tribes of northern Sudan "before the time of the Islamic invasions" and part two on the Arab migrations into Sudan. MacMichael began his enterprise innocently enough, by inviting and gathering genealogical claims from various Arab groups in northern Sudan. He then proceeded to frame these genealogies with an elaborate theory of migrations. If he was skeptical of the factual validity of genealogical claims made by his Arab informants, he showed none of the same skepticism toward his own somewhat speculative elaboration of a theory of Arab migration and Islamic invasions of northern Sudan.[10] It remains for us to identify the viewpoint from which MacMichael made sense of his migration-centered history of northern Sudan. MacMichael's own racist presumptions are obvious at various points in his narrative.[11]

As early as 1907, when he was deputy inspector of Kordofan, Harold MacMichael wrote a manuscript titled "Notes on the History of Kordofan before the Egyptian Conquest."[12] This thirty-page document illustrates the method that MacMichael employed—in particular, his fondness for the settler-native narrative as key to understanding historical change. He began by identifying the "original" inhabitants of the place and then chronicled "the first foreign people" who arrived. The idea was to begin with the presumed core of the onion and then layer it with successive sets of immigrants. Though titled "Notes on the History of Kordofan," this manuscript goes on to describe the founding of the sultanate in Darfur. Having identified the Dago as "the first foreign people" in Kordofan, he describes their most outstanding characteristics as "heathen and black with a strain of Arab blood." The Dago, says MacMichael, came "probably about the 11th or 12th century A.D." but "probably did not settle in Kordofan to the extent to which they did in Darfur, where they seem to have lived side by side with the original FUR for some centuries and to have in time become the ruling power." Having claimed the Dago as the founders of the sultanate in Darfur, MacMichael goes on to describe the next group of state builders: "Probably about the XIV century, a race of Arabs called the TUNGUR began immigrating into DARFUR." The Tungur, he writes, "were of more advanced civilization than the DAGO or the Fur" and "gradually gained greater power and influence and intermarried with the DAGO ruling family finally displacing them entirely, and themselves seizing the reins of government." But "in time however they began to lose their individu-

ality of race and to coalesce with the old Fur inhabitants of the country."
As if to explain their redemption, MacMichael turns to the founder of
the Keira dynasty, Sultan Süleyman, telling us that "Suleiman's mother is
said to have been an Arab, and he himself took on an Arab wife."[13]

According to MacMichael, the Funj Sultanate was established in a
similar manner: "The real FUNG were probably a purely negroid race,
who mingled with the Arab immigrants from the East for centuries until
gradually they became more than half Arabs than slaves but retained
their old appellation of FUNG." He says there persists "considerable
confusion . . . with regard to the question of who these FUNG are," and
that is because "two peoples are spoken of under this name." One are
"the original pure FUNG," and the other are "the mixture of these true
FUNG with Arabs formed [in] 1493 or thereabout." This was, of course,
around the time the Funj Sultanate was founded. The reason for the
confusion, writes MacMichael, seemed to be that the Arabs "intermarried with and subdued these black FUNG and gradually themselves got
darker in colour and called themselves 'FUNG.' " In MacMichael's nar-
ration, the history of Dar Fur and Funj becomes an account of successive "wise strangers" who founded states and dynasties.[14]

Genealogies as Claim to Origin

The Jewish adventurer David Reubeni visited Sudan in the latter part of
1522 and early 1523.[15] Reubeni spent ten months as a guest of the sultan
of the Funj at Lamul on the Blue Nile, an eight-day journey from Sinnar,
the seat of government. The Funj were cattle keepers, and the king had a
large number of servants and slaves. Reubeni posed as a descendant of
the Prophet and was greatly honored by the king, who also claimed a
similar pedigree. According to Reubeni, the king was in the habit of
addressing him like this: "What is it you desire of me, my lord, son of our
Prophet . . . ?" To which Reubeni would answer: "I love you and I give
you my blessing . . . and the blessings of the Prophet Muhammad . . .
and in another year I hope you shall come to us in the city of Mecca, the
place of the forgiveness of sins."[16] Both the king and the adventurer
claimed descent from the Prophet, and this conversation at least reas-
sured both regarding their common claim.

The Funj sultans claimed an Umayyad origin; its earliest mention

occurs in a book of genealogies, the original of which was possibly written in the sixteenth century A.D. Indeed, the Funj king, Badi III, issued a
royal decree announcing that he and his people "descended from the
Arabs, and indeed from the Ummayyads."[17] But by the time the Funj got
around to choosing a suitable Arab ancestry, the field was crowded; several claims had already been made by others, who naturally guarded
them as one would precious family jewels. In the words of Yusuf Fadl
Hasan, Sudan's premier nationalist historian: "The noble 'Abbasi pedigree was already adopted and jealously guarded by the Ja'aliyyin. The
Juhayna were the traditional ancestors of the 'Abdallab, whom the Funj
had reduced to a secondary status. In order to outdo these two groups,
the Funj, with the help of the genealogists, may well have chosen the
Umayyad ancestry."[18] The desire to be linked to the house of the Prophet
made sense as a strategy of statecraft at a time and in a context in which
such a lineage was sure to secure respectability, prestige, honor, and
most of all membership in a network of power. This is why genealogical
claims were more than just a record of one's ancestral history: They
indicated a combination of preference and power, both the choice of a
preferred family history and the power to get others to acknowledge that
preference.

Genealogies were often compiled by learned offspring of wealthy families, in one case, instructed to be of use—more or less as the wealthy are
prone to tell their progeny in contemporary America, "Do something.
Be of use!" One of the earliest genealogies MacMichael recorded
(genealogy AB in MacMichael) had, for example, been compiled in 1853
by Ahmed b. Isma'il al-Azhari of the Bidariyya tribe, who had been
a student at Al Azhar University between 1830 and 1840. Ahmed al-
Azhari was instructed by the head of the Ismailiyya order, to which his
family belonged, to compile the genealogical order of their ancestors,
back to al-Abbās (the uncle of the Prophet) and Adnan, said to be the
original ancestor of all Arabs. Here is al-Azhari's explanation of how he
came to write the manuscript:

> The Imam of the age, the Leader of the Way, the restorer of
> lawful and true knowledge, the master of his time, my lord

and father, el Wali Isma'il, by whose agency God granted me to taste the sweetness of the Faith, ordered me to make a genealogical record showing every one of the ancestors from whom were variously descended those that were yet alive, and to point out all the seed of our ancestor el feki Bishára el Gharbáwi and to carry back their pedigrees to him, and his pedigree also to el Malik Násir son of Saláh son of Musa el Kebir, who was known as Masu and in whose person are united all the branches of GA'AL EL DUFÁR now existing, and [he bade me] to mention also how this ancestor was descended from Serrár son of Kerdam, the ancestor of all the GA'ALIYYUN and to carry back his pedigree to el Sayyid el 'Abbās the uncle of the Prophet, to whom be the blessings of God and salutation, and through el 'Abbās to 'Adnān, and so to arrange all in verse that thereby all our family and suchlike might attain the uttermost of their desire.

On completion, said al-Azhari, "I named the work 'The Complete Compilation of our pedigree to el Sayyid el 'Abbās,' and put it into verse, adding extracts quoted on the authority of the Imáms whose names are familiar to all men of education."[19]

Genealogies were typically compiled by heads of tribes or groups, from the time of the early Funj period in the sixteenth century, and were then adopted by their members or by new entrants to the group. They were later elaborated into generational pyramids and set in formal verse for memorization. Take, for example, the line of descent claimed by the Mahdi, Muhammad Ahmad. Though born of a humble family of boatbuilders, the Mahdi claimed to be Ashraf, a direct descendant of the Prophet, a claim he elaborated through a generational ladder: Muhammad Ahmad, son of Abdallah, son of Fahl, Abd-al-Wali, Abdallah, Muhammad, Haj Sharif, Ali, Ahmed, Ali, Hasb al-Nabi, Sabr, Nasr, son of Abd-al-Karim, Hussain, Awn-Allah, Nejm al-Din, Osman, Musa, Abu al-Abbas, Yunis, Osman, Yaqub, Abd al-Gadir, Hassan al-Askari, Ulwan, Abd-al-Baqi, Sakhra, Yaqub, son of Hasan al-Sibt, son of al-Imam Ali, himself the son of the Prophet's paternal uncle.[20]

MacMichael was openly skeptical of the empirical claims made by the genealogists. In a 1928 lecture to the Royal Asiatic Society, he spoke of the "tendency to fake a genealogy" and cited El Hamdani to the effect that "it was not uncommon for the Arabs to take advantage of coincidences of nomenclature to claim kinship with well-known tribes with whom they had no tangible connection at all."[21] Here is what he had to say about the most elaborate genealogical constructions, such as that of the Asháb, which covers forty generations:

> in the case of a typical *feki* or sheikh of good family one may generally accept the first five or six generations from the present as stated accurately, and the next eight or nine as less so. Then follow seven or eight successive ancestors whose names rest more firmly on the accepted authority of contemporary *nisbah* compiled during that Augustan age of the Sudan, the period of the early FUNG kingdom.
>
> Beyond these are the weakest links in the chain, some fourteen or fifteen names probably due in part to the inventiveness of the genealogists of the FUNG period and their anxiety to connect their own generation with that of the immediate descendants of the Companions of the Prophet.[22]

Unlike riverine genealogies in the Nile Valley, which tend to have much greater historical depth, from forty generations in the instance above to twenty-eight in the case of the Juhayna, Baggara genealogies in Darfur and Kordofan tend to be relatively shallow. Ian Cunnison gives an example, that of the Humr.[23] The tribal genealogy of the Humr is ten or eleven generations deep and easily divides into two periods: five or six for the immediately remembered ancestors and the next five or six linking the Humr to a prestigious ancestor. Often, the result is to link strangers as close kin.[24] In a context in which individuals, as well as small and large lineages, have constantly created brotherhood with others and grafted themselves onto a common genealogical tree, and been received as kin in nearly all respects, genealogies must be more or less infinitely adaptable. Claims of kinship, in this instance, rest less on evidence of filial affiliation in the distant past than on political affiliation in the present.

The genealogical practice of the Baggara of Darfur (and more generally of northern Sudanese Arabs) reflects a common African tradition: to reckon backward in time to connect the name of the tribal ancestor to that of God or some miraculous event at the beginning of time, the world, or society. The people of Bornu in northern Nigeria claim that they came from the Yemen, and the Yoruba of western Nigeria are said to have stories of eastern origin.[25]

His skepticism notwithstanding, the insertion of genealogies in the larger migration narrative was the work of Harold A. MacMichael, whose two-volume text *A History of the Arabs in the Sudan* gave quasi-official sanction to a hitherto semifolk genealogical record.[26] MacMichael grouped the "Arabs" of Sudan into four branches of descent, two major and two minor.[27] The two major genealogies trace descent from the Prophet Muhammad's paternal uncle al-'Abbās (*the 'Abbasi line*) and from Juhayna and, ultimately, 'Adnan, considered forefather of the northern Arabians (*the Juhayni*). The two minor genealogies are *the Sharifi* (claiming direct descent from the Prophet through one of his grandsons, Hasan or Huseyn) and *the Mashaykhi* (descended from the first caliph, Abu Bakr al-Sadiq). They are virtually restricted to small though prestigious clans of religious dignitaries.

As the historian Neil McHugh points out, the two predominant genealogies—the Ja'ali (Abbasi) and the Juhayni—neatly encompass two very different groups of "Arabs," one sedentary, the other nomadic.[28] The sedentary groups are found on the right bank of the Nile in the north and between the Blue and the White Nile in the Gezira in central Sudan. They cultivate fertile lands and live in mud-built villages. Their political association is defined more by territory than by kin. The nomadic Arabs comprise the great nomadic and seminomadic tribes of the west, the Baggara of Darfur and the Kababish of Kordofan, who are said to vest authority in kin-based sheikhs and not village elders as do sedentary Arabs of the Nile. An intermediate group lives on the left bank of the Nile, between the Nile and the west (Kordofan, Darfur). It practices a seminomadic life, cultivating and grazing in the interior during the rains and returning to the river in the dry season to water their flocks and to cultivate.[29] These neat socioeconomic differences tend, in turn, to be reflected in different dialects of colloquial Arabic spoken throughout the northern part of Sudan.[30]

Despite his reservations about the historical accuracy of the genealogical record—and marked differences in modes of living and expression among different tribes of "Arabs"—MacMichael boldly went on to affirm migration as the core experience in the history of Sudanese Arabs. In doing so, the colonial administrator-archivist affirmed the official paradigm that the history of Sudan before colonialism involved an interaction between settler and native races, with Arab settlers dominating—and civilizing—non-Arab natives. Given the close affinity between genealogical constructions and migration histories, there is every reason to extend the now universal skepticism regarding the empirical validity of genealogies to the historical claim of mass migration.

MacMichael's studies on tribal genealogies greatly contributed to the prevailing notion of the stability of tribal and racial structures through the centuries. It also laid the foundation for the notion that Arab migrations were central to the development of Sudan—a notion that must be seen as the Sudanese version of the Hamitic hypothesis. MacMichael gave a succinct account of his argument in his 1928 Burton Memorial Lecture to the Royal Asiatic Society, titled "The Coming of the Arabs to the Sudan." According to him, there were three reasons that propelled Arabs to move southward from Egypt: first, "the lure of pasturage" in Sudan; second, an unfavorable political environment in Egypt from 868 to 1517, a period during which "a series of despotic Turks, Berbers, and Mamluks held the reins of government"; and, third, an open passage into Sudan after Mamluks overran Nubia in 1276.[31] This was an account of motives and possibilities. But it left untouched the empirical question of whether a mass migration did indeed take place.[32] To this we shall return later.

Nationalist History

The model that MacMichael sketched over a period of several decades and through multiple publications became so influential that its assumptions came to inform even the most important contribution to nationalist writing of the history of Sudan, that by Yusuf Fadl Hasan. To understand the thrust of Sudanese history for over a millennium, Yusuf Fadl turned to migration as the core experience, as had MacMichael before him:

> The creation of a culturally Arabized stock in the Sudan was
> the direct result of the penetration of large numbers of Arab

tribesmen over a long period of time. And the process of
Arabization and Islamization had probably gone hand in
hand . . . until the end of the 9th/15th c. Both developments
were almost entirely accomplished by tribal migrations.
Consequently, the inhabitants of the Sudan became Arabized
and assimilated into the Arab tribal systems.[33] [N.B. the
method of dating uses both the Islamic and Christian calen-
dars. Thus, "9th/15th c." is the ninth century after the *Hijra*
and the fifteenth century after Christ.]

Not surprisingly, Yusuf Fadl Hasan's account of the "Arabization" of
Egypt, and then of Sudan, begins not with the ancient pharaohs of
Egypt and the kings of Meroë in an equally ancient Sudan but with the
Arab victory over the Byzantine forces in Syria and then Egypt in the
seventh century. It is notable for several reasons. Together, these cast
doubt on his central thesis: that mass migration explains Arabization.[34]
The first notable fact about this account is that the Arabic language
spread in Egypt despite the decline of Arab power. Yusuf Fadl tells us
that the "Arab kingdom" ended with the overthrow of the Umayyad
dynasty in A.D. 750.[35] Since the new rulers, the Abbāsids, had been supported by a coalition of discontented Arabs and Khorasanis (Persians),
they began to recruit a new army from both. The Arab warrior caste was
gradually stripped of all its privileges. On the morrow of assuming
power, Caliph al-Muʿtasim dispatched an order to his governors in
Egypt to stop paying salaries to all Arabs and to strike their names from
the register of pensions. Arab fighters were replaced by Turkish (Mamluk) and Nubian slaves who became the mainstay of the caliph's army in
Egypt. What explains the spread of Arab culture in Egypt at a time when
the Arabs' power was rapidly eroding? The answer does not lie in mass
Arab immigration but in Arabic's becoming the official language of a
non-Arab power. Almost from the outset in Egypt, Arabic culture was
disassociated from Arab as an ethnic identity: The spread of Arabic culture was welcomed by successive powers because it accompanied the
spread of literacy, which turned out to be critical for the process of state
formation and market expansion. In this period, and up to the colonial
period, "Arab" and "Egypt" were different phenomena.[36]

The second notable fact about Yusuf Fadl's account is that there was
never a successful Arab invasion of Sudan. In 652, a large force from

Egypt "equipped with heavy cavalry and artillery in the form of man-
gonels invaded the northern Nubian kingdom of Makuria and a memo-
rable battle was fought before the walls of her capital at Old Dongola."
The Nubians won this battle decisively. For most of the next six centuries, they were able to dictate their own terms in their relations with
Egypt. This arrangement was commonly known as *baqt,* an institution
of diplomatic trade whereby "royal emissaries conveyed valuable presents abroad at intervals, and foreign recipients who desired to keep the
goodwill of the donor were expected to reciprocate them." Was the *baqt*
a reciprocal agreement between two parties to a diplomatic truce, or was
it a form of tribute paid by Nubia to Egypt? There is no agreement
among historians, but given the kind of settlement that did follow on a
Nubian defeat six centuries later, the terms of the *baqt* make it seem
more like a truce than a defeat.[37]

The successful invasion of Sudan was by a dynasty of Mamluk (Turkish) slaves, not Arabs. The rise of a Mamluk slave dynasty was the end
result of a process that began with a phasing out of Arab soldiers from
the army and their replacement by slave soldiers, at first Sudani, later
Mamluk. The Sudani presence in the Egyptian army escalated dramatically during the Fātimid dynasty, which conquered Egypt with the help
of Berber tribes in A.D. 969. Sudani troops became an essential part of
the Fātimid state during the long reign of al-Mustanṣir (1035–94),
whose Sudani mother is said to have recruited large numbers of her
countrymen and relied on them to check the Mamluks in particular. But
when the Fātimid dynasty gave way to the Ayyūbid, this predominance
ended. Dissatisfied with this development, the influential black eunuch
in the Fātimid court, Mu'taman al-Khilafa, attempted to contact the
Crusaders (in 1168) and lead a rebellion. When found out, he was killed.
Nearly fifty thousand Sudani troops rose up in open rebellion. As a
result, the official demand for Sudani slaves declined sharply.

The Mamluk presence in the Egyptian state reached its zenith in the
Ayyūbid period. As internal differences among various factions fed
interdynastic struggles, the resulting instability provided Egyptian
Mamluks with opportunities to take power. A considerable number of
Mamluks did not even speak Arabic. Arabs resisted Mamluk power and
refused to pay the tax (*kharaj*). Following their defeat by the governor of
Aswan in 1378–79, no less than two hundred Arab tribesmen were sold

as slaves. The Mamluk repression of Arabs was followed by a relentless antinomad policy, which forced more and more Arab nomads to immigrate to Sudan in search of greener pastures. The Mamluk state followed runaway Arabs into Nubia and Beja, breaking existing treaties and mounting an invasion in A.D. 1276.[38] The object of the Mamluk invasion was to prevent Arabs from taking refuge among the Nubians and the Beja of northern Sudan. The victorious Mamluks put their own nominee, Shakanda, on the Nubian throne. Shakanda pledged to remain loyal to the sultan of Egypt, to pay one-half of the revenues of Nubia and a stock of animals (three giraffes; five she-leopards; a hundred swift camels, fawn in color; and four hundred choice oxen) every year, and even to cede the northern quarter of Nubia, al-Maris. In addition, Shakanda pledged not to allow any Arab nomad, young or old, to remain in the country.

When the victors arrived in Cairo on June 2, 1276, ten thousand captives from the war, men and women, were sold in the markets of Cairo at three *dhirams* a head. The point is that, unlike the Mamluks who pursued them, the Arabs entered Sudan as refugees, not as invaders.[39] Did these nomadic refugees marry into and then overthrow the Nubian dynasty in the thirteenth century, as famously claimed by Ibn Khaldūn, who has become the single source on whom rests the supposition of an Arab conquest of Nubia?[40] Harold MacMichael, Yusuf Fadl Hasan, and the British historian P. M. Holt all relied exclusively on Ibn Khaldūn's authority.[41] But all ignore that the thrust of Ibn Khaldūn's remarks is deduced from his general theory about the *destructive* power of nomads in the history of civilization; he thus highlights the impact of the Juhayna in Nubia as purely destructive. If we are to follow the logic of his argument, the result would not be conquest but disintegration. Of the Bedouins, says Ibn Khaldūn, "their rule was inevitably lacking in statesmanship, because of their essential defect, which denied the subordination of one man to another." As a consequence, "they have been divided to this day and there is no trace of central authority in their part of the country. They remain nomads, following the rainfall like the Bedouins." "The Bedouins," concludes Ibn Khaldūn, "are a savage nation, fully accustomed to savagery and the things that cause it. Savagery has become their character and nature. They enjoy it, because it means freedom from authority and no subservience to leadership. Such a natural disposition is the negation and anti-thesis of civilization."[42] While Ibn Khaldūn's interjection serves to reinforce his overall polemic against nomads as destroyers of civilization, it still leaves key questions unanswered: If these Bedouins did indeed give up their nomadic existence and take to a settled life, in the process overcoming "their essential defect" and building a state, when and how did they do it?

The fact is that Yusuf Fadl Hasan provides sufficient evidence to show that "Arabization" did not unfold as a linear tendency in Sudan. His own account shows that the tendency in the land of the Nubians and the Beja was not Arabization but de-Arabization. When the Fātimid traveler Ibn Sulaym al-Aswani visited the area around 975, he found that immigrant Arabs had intermixed with the natives to such a degree that many of them had forgotten the Arabic language.[43] Arabs who settled among Nubians became de-Arabized in both their way of life and their language: They not only learned farming techniques from Nubian farmers but also acquired the Nubian language. The Beja, too, absorbed "small bands of Arab immigrants who settled amongst them and in time adopted the Bejawi language and customs," at the same time incorporating Arabic words into the Bejawi language.[44] When it comes to the process of acculturation, it would seem that the consequences of the Arab migration were not particularly different from those of other migrations.

The history of migration into Darfur involves three groups: Arab nomads, West African peasants, and slaves from the south. None were directly associated with the exercise of power. In all instances, migration led to acculturation. West African immigrants first came to Darfur as pilgrims, as early as the eleventh century. Though the route through Darfur was the longer way to get to Mecca, it was a clear favorite. The "Forty-Day Route" was shorter and safer because it would take them through the Libyan desert and away from highway brigands. But it was also more expensive, for the pilgrims had to start out with "adequate funds to buy camels and provisions for crossing the desert." Most pilgrims were "excessively poor" and had little choice but "to depend on charity or work their way slowly on manual labor," so they opted for the longer route through Dar Fur to Sawakin. But their poverty also meant that they were never certain of completing the trip, which is why some never made it to Mecca and others settled down in Darfur on their way back.[45]

The first significant West African immigration into Dar Fur is said to have been during the reign of Sultan Ahmad Bukr, toward the end of the seventeenth century. MacMichael wrote that the Fellata migrants—which is how Fulani immigrants from West Africa were known in Sudan—were divided between a minority who were sedentary and a majority who were cattle-owning nomads who intermarried freely with the Baggara Arabs.[46] The flow of West African pilgrims expanded with the *Hijra* (the great migration), which followed the death of Sheikh Usman dan Fodio in northern Nigeria in the early nineteenth century. In fact, it is said to have grown so "out of proportion" in the late 1830s that it gave "the Sokoto rulers a lot of worry." Yet another significant exodus followed in the late nineteenth century in the aftermath of British colonization. When the British army killed Caliph Attahiru I at the Battle of Burmi in 1903, his large following relocated to Sudan and settled in the Gezira in a village they named Mai Wurno, after Attahiru's fifth son. Following conquest, the British themselves exiled Fulani groups from Nigeria—the Fellata—and settled them around Tullus.[47]

The largest group of West African immigrants arguably came into Darfur, and Sudan, in the colonial period—most of them running away from oppressive practices such as forced labor in nearby French colonies. In 1922, for example, French AOF (Afrique Occidentale Française) authorities asked their counterparts in Sudan and the Eritrean port of Massawa to halt the flow of undocumented pilgrims across the border, but both the British and the Italian authorities refused outright. Clearly, one man's loss was another's gain. From the time it was constructed in 1925, the irrigation project at Gezira became a magnetic attraction for families fleeing military and labor recruitment. The numbers of West Africans—some from the AOF, others from northern Nigeria—who settled in western Sudan was estimated at a low of 250,000 in the 1950s and "well over 1,000,000" in the mid-1970s.[48] R. S. O'Fahey estimated in 1980 that "today they probably number some 30 per cent of the population of the province," referring to Darfur.[49]

A third group of migrants entering Darfur consisted of slaves from the south. Although these captives came as forced migrants from diverse places, their experience of capture and resettlement far from home eventually marked them with a single identity: They were known as the Fartit. If the historian's gaze has focused mainly on the migration from the Nile Valley, and has had little to say about the impact of West African migration to Darfur over the centuries,[50] it has hardly reflected on the ways in which forced migration of southern peoples has affected Darfuri society. In part, this may be because many of yesterday's slaves are among today's Fur, just as many of the West African immigrants are among today's Arabs. The transformation of "Fartit" into "Fur" was a function of the state-forming process; of slave-raiding; of forcible resettlement; and in this particular instance, of forced Islamization and conquest—as we shall see.[51] This process afflicted two groups of Fartit, one enslaved in the Funj Sultanate and the other in the Sultanate of Dar Fur. The difference was that whereas most former slaves in Funj became Arabs, former slaves in Dar Fur mostly became Fur.

If "Arabization" means the spread of the Arabic language and an associated culture, all available evidence indicates that the experience of Sudan is no different from that of Egypt. Where Arabic was not a language of the state, as among the Nubians and the Beja, the result was de-Arabization rather than Arabization. The spread of Arabic was linked more to its status as a language of official administration, law, commerce, and religion than to the actual weight of Arab immigrants. Without a direct association with power, there would have been no Arabization. The only thing to keep in mind is that that power did not have to be an Arab power. If the spread of Arabic in Egypt was the work of the Mamluk state, in Sudan it was the work of two indigenous sultanates: Funj and Dar Fur.

In Yusuf Fadl Hasan's account, the burden is carried not by the link to power but to immigrants, even to a handful, as is clear from his account of the "wise stranger" thesis:[52] "It is significant to note that as soon as the process of Arabization and Islamization was completed in Upper Nubia some Ja'alis migrated further to the west. On their arrival they inevitably married into the still pagan local population; around them Islamized dynasties sprang up." Here, the "wise stranger," who "migrates from an ancient centre of civilization, where the two processes of Arabization and Islamization have gone far, to a less civilized region where the two processes have hardly begun," is clearly the central figure in explaining radical social and political change.

The conventional history of Sudan is written as the history of migration, the movement of influential individuals ("wise men"), and gifted groups ("Arabs") as well as the spread of extraordinary ideas and practices ("Arabization").[53] One need not question the extraordinary character of these individuals and groups or cultural practices and ideas to point out that such accounts never ask why the societies they encountered were receptive to these new ideas and practices at particular points in time. They explain change more as a miracle than as a moment in an ongoing historical process. The "wise stranger" is invariably an outsider, said to have married into a leading insider family. As one who is supposed to have initiated the process of "Arabization," his role is akin to that of a miracle worker, for he is identified as the founder of the state. To this extent, focus on the "wise stranger" tends to substitute for an analysis of the actual process of state formation.[54] This is why it is not at all surprising that we should find an alternative account to the miraculous role of the "wise stranger" in histories that treat state formation as the political consequence of a larger social and economic history.

The Funj: An Alternate History of African Arabs

If we are to make sense of the contemporary politics around Darfur, it is crucial to grasp the main contours of the history of Funj, especially for one reason: the Save Darfur movement and the intelligentsia that has gravitated around it assumes that Arabs are settlers in Sudan. They also assume that there is a single history of Arabs and "Arabization" in Sudan. The history of Funj is key to unraveling both these myths that seem to have taken on the status of widely held prejudice. To do this, we shall distinguish between genealogies (claimed by Arab tribes) and histories of these tribes. We will also distinguish between different kinds of "Arabs": in particular, between Arab as an identity associated with administrative power (as in the Sultanate of Funj) and Arab as an identity disassociated from administrative power (as in the Sultanate of Dar Fur).

The critics of colonial history came from later archaeologists, historians, and historically inclined anthropologists. The rupture between the two schools of thought was generational at times but inevitably political: The critics were deeply influenced by the growing anticolonial and antiimperial movement, both within Africa and in the West. If the early archaeologists associated periods of decline with Negro influence from the south and progressive change with Hamitic influence from the north, later archaeologists concluded otherwise. The foremost authority on Nubia, William Y. Adams, who had earlier subscribed to migration theory, noted that it fit "so neatly with the racist outlook of the late nineteenth century that migration theory became one of the unacknowledged tenets of the first archaeologists and prehistorians, and its legacy is with us still." Regarding his research on Nubian archaeological history, he observed:

> Changes which were once thought to be abrupt and even revolutionary in nature can now be seen as gradual and natural developments, more probably the result of cultural diffusion or local evolution than of any great movement of peoples. In addition the re-examination of earlier Nubian skeletal collections, as well as a great deal of new materials, has shown that the supposed racial differences between successive Nubian populations are largely mythical. There is no longer today any satisfactory reason for believing that the modern Nubians are a different people from the Nubians of antiquity or of any intervening period. On the contrary, I think everything points to their being the same people. That their numbers have been swelled by immigration, warlike as well as peaceful, from the north as well as the south, goes without saying. That the intruders have occasionally and sometimes drastically upset the orderly processes of social and cultural development is likewise apparent. Yet the threads of cultural continuity from age to age are there for all to see. They provide the underlying warp for a tapestry of Nubian history extending from prehistoric times to the present.[55]

The critics have been in the minority, but their influence is growing. They emphasize dynamism rather than stagnation, and the primacy of internal development over external influences, in understanding change.

Writing in 1971, Bryan G. Haycock[56] noted that recent excavations in Zimbabwe absolutely refute all claims of African stagnation and then suggested that Sudanese civilizations—such as Kerma, Napata, Meroë, and Christian Nubia—should also be understood as results of local concentrations of power, and not a direct result of external stimuli.[57]

The history of the Funj has been key to the ongoing debate on "Arabization." The two viewpoints have made for a sharp—but illuminating—debate on how to understand the history of Nubia. The majority believe that there was a marked discontinuity between the history of Christian Nubia on the one hand and that of Muslim Funj on the other, the former Christian and Mediterranean but the latter Arabic and Islamic in identity. The model of discontinuity (or stagnation) sees the Funj as the product of a period of progressive Arabization and Islamization in the Sudan, a development made possible by *mass* Arab migration and settlement in the Sudan. It thus sees the Funj Sultanate as both Arabic and Islamic from the outset, over time the product of an external racial impulse combined with internal cultural assimilation.

This debate opened with a contribution by William Adams, who had first agreed with Hasan when he wrote of Arabs coming "wave after wave" into Nubia, in the process absorbing most of the scattered inhabitants, but was now admitting to "second thoughts": "When historical annals speak of the movements and conquest of Arab 'tribes,' we can never be sure whether mass migrations or only small redistributions of populations are involved."[58] Adams went on to question the significance of migration theory as an explanatory device. On the basis of a study of ancient and medieval Nubia, he concluded that cultural continuities across different historical periods so outweighed discontinuities that they must be the work of a single people.[59] Whatever the demographic weight of Arab migration from Upper Egypt into the Nubian hinterland, Adams discounted its historical importance arguing that "there was so little cultural and economic change from the late Christian period that the Christian and Islamic eras can be regarded as a single phase in Nubia's cultural development."[60]

Adams's stress on continuity in Sudanese Nubian history was carried forward by Jay Spaulding, who pointed out the absence of empirical evidence suggesting *mass* Arab immigration into Sudan; he thus questioned both the demographic validity and the historical significance of the Arab migration hypothesis. "Evidence regarding the impact of Arab penetration south of Dongola is scanty," so Spaulding wrote in his 1971 doctoral dissertation on the Abdallab provinces of northern Sinnar.[61] His studies of the Funj Sultanate of Sinnar (1504–1821) have been unprecedented in their scope and depth, making him the most prominent exponent of the alternative school of history. Spaulding argued that the sultanate inherited many of its institutional arrangements from earlier Christian monarchies and was, in effect, a "Nubian Renaissance," though its religion was Islam and it flourished well after the alleged advent of the Arabs.[62]

I have already pointed out that the relationship between migration and cultural change is not direct; rather, it is mediated by power. The importance of Spaulding's work is that it takes the argument beyond the question of immigration by integrating it into a larger political history. The Sultanate of Funj arose in the aftermath of tumultuous changes in the fourteenth and fifteenth centuries, following the arrival of two groups: Arabs from the north and Nilotic groups (Shilluk, Nuer, and Dinka) from the south. At the opening of the sixteenth century, two power structures were established in the Sudanese Nile Valley: One was the kingdom of Abdallab in the north, just below the Nile confluence, and the other was the kingdom of Funj in the middle Gezira to the south. Traditional expansion of the tributary states brought the Funj and the Abdallab into open confrontation, and a clash ensued. The confrontation took place near Arbaji in the northern Gezira. The event was mentioned by the traveler James Bruce in his 1773 account. The Abdallab were defeated, and the Funj dominated all the territory that we know as riverine northern Sudan: bounded by Egypt on the north, Abyssinia on the east, Upper Nile on the south, and the edges of Kordofan on the west.[63]

Spaulding begins with a depiction of historical Sinnar (the capital of Funj), founded in the early sixteenth century after the defeat of the Abdallab. Sinnar, says Spaulding, was at its founding a typical Sudanic state, inhabited by two hereditary classes—the nobility and commoners—and a population of slaves whose ranks and roles in society were diverse. He locates the major change in the history of Sinnar not at its founding in 1504, nor when the old matrilineal dynasty was overthrown in 1718, but in 1762, when the warlords (Hamaj) took power: "The old matrilineal Funj dynasty was overthrown as early as 1718, but the decisive coup was the seizure of power in 1762 in which the warlords—by that date often known as the *Hamaj*—definitively tamed the sultans and imposed one of their own as regent." The main focus of Spaulding's book is from 1718 to 1762, a period during which the forces that took power in 1762 gathered strength. Spaulding identifies the transition with the development of a commercial capitalism, and the political shifts with the agency of a new middle class within Sinnar. The middle class was "new" not in the sense that its members were immigrants but in the sense that they "appropriated the surplus" through "new" relations "unknown or unacceptable to ancient custom" and were in turn receptive to new market-friendly ideas critical of "custom." Together, these new relations were "characteristic of commercial capitalism."

The "new middle class" comprised two groups in the main: merchants and holy men. Many of the merchants were multilingual. Sinnar opened "to the outside world between 1650 and 1750," and this "increased the exposure of Nubian Muslims to the cultures of neighboring lands." By the late seventeenth or early eighteenth century, there were traders from Dongola who spoke Italian, Turkish, and Arabic. The new towns were the towns of merchants, not nobles: "If one distinguishes a true 'town' from the administrative capital of a nobleman by the presence of permanent inhabitants—conspicuously merchants— who were not members of the court community, then in 1700 there were probably only two towns (Arbaji and Sinnar) in the Funj kingdom. By the same criterion, at the Turkish conquest the number of towns had multiplied to a figure in excess of 20." The "new towns" also included foreign merchants: "The cosmopolitan community of foreigners in the capital included men from Egypt, Ethiopia, Dar Fur, Libya, Morocco, West Africa, the Hijaz, the Yemen, India, Syria, Palestine, Turkey, Armenia, Greece, Yugoslavia, Italy, France, Germany and Portugal." The king, too, was a merchant. It was said that the sultan had a monopoly over the production of gold, received one-half of all slaves captured by the *salatiya* (royal slave hunt), and claimed probably half of all ivory exports: "The sultan (together with the court officials who carried out his will) was generally agreed to be the greatest merchant in Sinnar."[64]

The second group to inhabit the "new towns" consisted of the Islamic holy men. The conflict between the "new men" and the old powers characterized by the king and nobles developed around which rules would apply in the solution of new disputes. Whereas the traditional powers stood for the supremacy of custom, the new men championed the rule of religious law (Sharia). More than custom, Sharia stood for the enforcement of contracts and the growth of commerce. The *fuqara* (holy men) expanded their jurisdiction, in both a geographic and a juridical sense, claiming to address questions that had previously been settled out of court, an initiative in which they had full support from merchants.

The "new men" of the eighteenth century—"a heterogeneous collection of neo-Alodian noblemen, warlords, slave soldiers, merchants and holy men"—were led to the cause of the Hamaj by Muhammad Abu Likaylik, the first regent who tamed the king in the service of the new middle class. The story of Abu Likaylik is of particular interest because he is said to be the "wise stranger" responsible for initiating social and political development in Sinnar. A fuller consideration of the story allows us to deflate the significance of the "wise stranger" without denying his presence.

There are three different legends regarding the identity of this particular "wise stranger." The *first* is the legend current among the descendants of Muhammad Abu Likaylik, who claim that his mother, Umm Najwar, was a daughter of the makk of Jebel Dali in the province of al-Qarbin. The year was 1716. As the most beautiful virgin of the land, she was chosen as a human sacrifice to appease the wrath of the Powers at a time when they were punishing the people with drought. Supposed to be cast into the waters, she was ransomed at the last moment by a passing northern nobleman of distinguished Arab descent. He later returned her—no longer a virgin—to her father's care and then departed for the north. When their son reached the age of circumcision, Umm Najwar gave him the inscribed sword left behind for him by his father and sent him to join his father's people. The boy is said to have gone through many trials and adventures before he could reach his kinsfolk in the north. There he was reared by an uncle, for his father had passed away. The *second* tradition, also sympathetic to Abu Likaylik, was formulated in later years by staunch supporters of the Hamaj cause, such as the Jamu'iya, after they had overthrown the royal house. This version hoped to emphasize Abu Likaylik's Arab ancestry and obscure his maternal links to the Funj petty nobility and thereby excuse his southern origin. According to this tradition, his mother was merely a southern slave girl in the harem of one or another of the northern makks. The *third* tradition is openly hostile to the Hamaj. Preserved by the heirs of the Funj royal house after they were overthrown by the Hamaj, it strips away much of the romance and all of the claims of distinguished Arab ancestry from the story of Abu Likaylik's origins. This tradition portrays Abu Likaylik and his sister, Umm Najwar, as ordinary hostages sent to Sinnar in typical Funj fashion by their father, the makk of Jebel Dali. After examining all three traditions, Jay Spaulding concludes that "Abu Likaylik was probably from the ranks of the lower nobility of southern Sinnar, was sent to the Sultan's court as a hostage in customary fashion, and was raised up as a soldier in the corps of *qawawid* [palace corps]."[65]

The transition ended in 1762 when the new men took power and imposed a regent in place of the old king. The new king was considered fallible: "A dramatic and therefore conspicuous feature of the state ideology of Sinnar held that a Funj ruler, be he the Sultan himself or a petty lordling, should be judged periodically and executed if found wanting." A whole set of changes followed: A national magistracy was established, and a *faqih* (a scholar of Islamic jurisprudence) was appointed as *wazir* (minister); the royal court was opened to holy men; and *fuqara* were appointed as village tax collectors. Together, these constituted "attempts to integrate the religiously oriented elements of the new middle class into the structure of government." Spaulding points to "legal documents and letters produced by or for Islamic holy men of the Heroic Age, who presided over the formation of a series of increasingly numerous and autonomous religious communities."[66]

Commercial capitalism was accompanied by the spread of slavery in domestic, societal, and foreign commercial relations.[67] The more the slave trade grew in importance, the more the procurement of slaves became the prime objective of southern noblemen and the more they spread a reign of terror throughout the southern territories: "To secure the labor of their subjects, the southern noblemen imposed a condition which may be called 'institutionalized insecurity.'"[68] This had drastic consequences for both the individual and the group. When it came to the individual, "any deviant or unproductive southern subject could be enslaved." At the same time, "groups of subjects who attempted to evade submission to Sinnar by seeking refuge in the hidden corners of a vast and thinly populated region were hunted down and raided by the cavalry of the nobility until each band was persuaded to seek the protection of the lord."[69] The only way subjects could escape the reign of terror was to seek the protection of a nobleman, which meant providing a regular levy of slaves. The overall effect was to further turn the southern Funj into a reserve for procuring slaves and raw materials.

The new middle class saw itself as the harbinger of a new commercial civilization. Its self-identity was Arab. If the Funj dynasty claimed an Arab ancestry, the new middle class of Funj claimed an Arab identity. The "Arab slavery" that ravaged southern Funj over the eighteenth and nineteenth centuries was the doing not of Arab slavers who came from outside Sudan but of a native merchant class. It was a native slavery that reached its greatest intensity during the Turkiyya when Turco-Egyptian and European slave traders joined local traders from riverine Sudan in financing slave expeditions. During the centralized kingdom, the slave trade was a royal monopoly; in the relations between the sultan and the nobility, the sultan had the power to appoint or depose a nobleman. But when "the central government gradually disintegrated" toward the late eighteenth century and the sultanate fragmented, there was a shrinking of political horizons: "Thus the modern Arab tribes of the northern Sudan were born."[70] This is how Spaulding sums up the growth of the "new middle class" in Sinnar:

> The new middle class claimed Arab identity, practiced patri-
> lineal descent, employed coin currencies, and bound itself in
> its dealings by the standards of Islamic law; it elicited alms,
> purchased slaves, monopolized exchange relationships, and
> imposed perpetual indebtedness upon its free subjects; it
> imposed its own legal and ideological concepts upon the
> government, demanded exemption from all obligations to
> the state, and took up a variety of duties hitherto exercised by
> the state or the nobility, such as the administration of justice
> and the collection of taxes. . . . If this middle class was "for-
> eign" to the older structure of Sinnar, it consisted neverthe-
> less of native-born Sudanese.[71]

This historical narrative clarifies one noteworthy fact: "Arab" signified the cultural self-identity of the new middle class. To be sure, there were immigrant "Arabs," many of whom intermarried and became Sudanese over generations.[72] As a group, however, the Arabs of the Nile Valley in the northern Sudan are native Arabs. Using today's political vocabulary, they are *African* Arabs.

Other Histories

The process of Arabization in the Funj Sultanate was not analogous to that in the Sultanate of Dar Fur. Whereas it is true that both Sultanates were highly "Arabized" as states, there was a world of difference in the historical formation and political location of "Arab" tribes in Funj and Dar Fur.

In the riverine Sudan, Arab was an identity of power. But not all Arabs wielded power or were even identified with power. Arabs came from different historical experiences, as varied as former slave-owning merchants and former slaves. A minority had immigrant origins, but the vast majority was native in origin. To appreciate these differences, we need to understand Arab as an identity born more of local assertions than of global migrations. Such a perspective would allow for multiple histories of Arab identity formation, each leading to a specific local outcome. We shall consider several examples of how "Arab" came to be the identity of groups outside of power in northern Sudan. With the collapse of the Funj kingdom, the downtrodden, particularly those in southern Funj, mapped different futures for themselves: Some laid claim to being Arab; others identified themselves in more local and autochthonous terms. In the Sultanate of Dar Fur, however, it is Fur that developed as the identity of power and Arab that became a marginal and insurgent identity.

The southern Funj is the hilly area between the Blue and the White Nile that functioned as a reservoir for the Funj Sultanate, one that its nobility regularly raided, whether for slaves or for raw materials. After the fall of the Funj Sultanate, the peoples of the southern Funj negotiated multiple transitions to a post-Funj future by claiming different lines of descent.

Wendy James, a professor of anthropology at Oxford University in England, has argued that the best way to understand different paths to identity formation in the southern Funj is to see them as outcomes of recent political transitions rather than the cumulative product of family genealogies.[73] The important point is that identity is not simply a matter of choice, but also of recognition. While this is not the place to elaborate on the process that frames the tension between choice and recognition, it will be useful to point at some outcomes. Some became Funj, inspired by the larger fact that the "Funj" empire was spoken of with great pride in the whole Blue Nile region, as being the first indigenous Sudanese state. Among these newborn Funj are former refugees of Jebel Gule, a population that is losing its traditional language as its members become Funj. Others became Arab. They did so by claiming a range of affinities, from female links and adoption to former slave-master relationship and coresidence. This, for example, is how the Berti, vassals of yesterday, are becoming "Arab" ("Ja'ali" or "Dunqulawi"). Becoming Funj and becoming Arab in this way are different ways of negotiating with power, yet others express a determination to resist the claims of power by holding on to an ancestral identity. This claim is accompanied by one for political and cultural autonomy.

Among this third group are the Ingessana, some 35,000, and some 10,000 Uduk speakers.[74] The Ingessana have been the target of external incursions and raids over a long period, from border kings and from the Anglo-Egyptian government, which time and again tried to pacify and administer them but had great difficulty in doing so. An example of this ongoing resistance was recorded by a British colonial official in the *Kurmuk Monthly Report* for November 1939, under the heading "Public Security": "Two Ingessana magicians who were terrifying the inhabitants of their hill by turning into pigs or hyaenas at night and who told the A.D.C. [assistant district commissioner] that they saw from time to time an eagle in the sky sitting on an egg which would break to indicate the millennium when the government would be turned out of the Ingessana Hills, have been removed for short terms of imprisonment."[75] The point about the Ingessana was that, in contrast to many other peoples of the region, their traditional organization was never shattered during nineteenth-century disturbances. This traditional organization included a double hierarchy of authority, with the dual leadership of hereditary war leader and priest as two parallel chains of authority. It is to these hierarchies that the Ingessana turned in difficult times, and it is through these hierarchies that they asserted their claim to an older native identity.

The peoples of the southern Funj were the historical victims of Funj power. After the fall of the sultanate, they chose either to engage with identities of power—becoming Funj or Arab—or to maintain their independence of both defiantly. James's conclusion that their choices were shaped more by political history than by filial ancestry is reinforced by parallel developments in Darfur. The people living on the southern peripheries of the Sultanate of Dar Fur, those who were historically raided by slavers and branded Fartit, went through similar transitions after the fall of the sultanate: at one extreme becoming Fur, taking on the identity of local power, and, at the other, distancing themselves from this identity.

If "Arab" became identified with power in riverine Sudan, the opposite was the case in Darfur. Whereas Arabs of the Nile Valley are sedentary groups, those of Darfur are nomadic: In southern Darfur, they are cattle nomads (the Baggara), and in northern Darfur, they are camel nomads (the Abbala).[76] The political life of nomads is defined by an ambivalent relationship to political power. While they have no desire to pay the tribute that sultans ask of them, nomads are nonetheless dependent on merchants and settled peoples for some essential goods. W. G. Browne, the first European to leave behind a written record of his visit to Dar Fur (1793–96), pointed out that when nomads feel strong and united, they simply refuse to pay tribute. Alternately, when the sultans feel strong, they send in troops and seize as booty whatever they can lay hands on. So, Browne argued, the nomads may properly be seen as "tributaries rather than subjects of the sultan."[77]

Did the cattle nomads of the south, the Baggara, migrate from elsewhere, and, if so, from where? Our knowledge of Baggara history is limited to a few centuries at most. In the absence of firm historical knowledge, scholars have resorted to one of two hypotheses: The conventional hypothesis is focused on migration, speculating that the Baggara were nomads who split off from the Arab invasion of Egypt and migrated either up the Nile or through Tunisia. On the basis of a very incomplete understanding of the past, we can affirm at least one observation: The history of the cattle and the camel nomads needs to be understood on its own terms and not as part of a general history of "the Arabs of Sudan," one that risks lumping together the history of settled and nomadic peoples, those in power and those marginal to it, in a single indistinguishable flow. There are several histories of migration in this region. One is that of West Africans who have migrated to Darfur and of whom many have "become Arab." The second-in-command of the Mahdi, Abdallah Ta'aishi, came from such a migrant family. A second is a history of slaves from the south: Many became Fur, but some became Baggara. Another migration is that of armed parties rather than of entire groups. Such, for example, was the nature of Arab migration to Kordofan. As Ian Cunnison puts it, "We do not know how the Baggara reached their present belt."[78] As Jay Spaulding puts it, given our present state of knowledge, it may be best to look for the history of the Baggara where the Baggara are and not elsewhere.[79]

Who Is an Arab?

I spent my first evening in Darfur at a World Health Organization guesthouse in El Fasher, the capital of North Darfur. Ignoring warnings from fellow occupants of the guesthouse to stay indoors since the sun was setting, my graduate student assistant and I strolled outside in the street and struck up a conversation with the guard of the guesthouse. Very soon, a small group gathered, including the guard, a shopkeeper, and a neighbor. One of them was Arab, the other Fur, and the third Tama. Inevitably, the conversation focused on Darfur. Soon, we were discussing who was an Arab. Two viewpoints were evident: One said that whoever spoke Arabic as a mother tongue was Arab. Another disagreed: Many more than just Arabs spoke Arabic as a mother tongue; this person argued that Arabs were descended from immigrants. The latter was a perspective I had come to recognize as common among many post-2003 writers associated with the Save Darfur movement, who tend to assume that Arabs are settlers in Sudan. Ex–U.S. marine Brian Steidle, for example, describes the conflict in Darfur as one between "Arabs from the Middle East who had migrated in" and "the African world," and argues that the "government who is predominantly Arab chose their

Arab allies over black Africans."[80] That evening in El Fasher, the debate could not be resolved. But it posed a question that cuts through most scholarship on Sudan: Who is an Arab?

The discussion is best understood as cohering around two debates. The first focuses on the significance of genealogies. One side claims this is an objective question, one of truth or falsehood. The other argues that the real issue is subjective: Why are genealogical claims important for those who make them? The first point of view has been forcefully argued by Ian Cunnison in his writings on the Baggara of Darfur and Kordofan. Construction of genealogies may vary from the relatively shallow, such as the Humr claim of being a mere ten or eleven generations from the family of the Prophet, to the more sophisticated claims of the Juhayna of the Nile Valley of being as many as twenty-eight or more generations away. But they are all equally false. Indeed, the Arabs of Sudan are not the only literate group with a myth linking them to the Holy Land in a single bloodline. Ethiopia has its own variant in the Solomonic myth. And the practice, point out Cunnison and others, is familiar in all Sudanic states. In the end, Cunnison claims that all genealogies need to be dismissed as bogus "ideology": "So a genealogy linking Baggara tribes reduces to this: it is an ideology . . . historically a genealogy is, purely and simply, a falsification of the record."[81]

The folklorist Abdullahi Ali Ibrahim disagrees. The real issue, he points out, is not whether the claims of the genealogists are literally true but why they make these claims in the first place. By way of example, he points to Michael Herzfeld's discussion of how Greek folklorists and scholars of the nineteenth century constructed their Hellenic identity to establish a link with classical Greece: "Of course, there are factual errors aplenty in these sources, and one is sometimes tempted to mutter about poor standards or even fraud. But imputations of bad faith lead nowhere—especially when our aim is to discover why our 'informants' thought as they did rather than to assume the answer in advance."[82] This issue was the subject of an extended discussion in anthropology beginning in the early 1920s and focused on variations of the same question: Are recollections of the past—whether concerning myth (Branislaw Malinowski) or lineage claims (E. E. Evans-Pritchard) or other origin-based claims (Paul Bohannan)—confused memories or are they claims on the present?[83]

There is also a third point of view on this. "The Kababish," remarks the anthropologist Talal Asad, "didn't have genealogies going all the way back to Arabia. Could it be a function of who asks the question and how? The Kababish never said, 'We are Arabs and therefore from Arabia.' Who makes these claims and in what context? The Kababish actually never claimed to come from anywhere else."[84]

But with reference to those who do make such a claim, Ibrahim is of course right that we must take "a people's self-concept" seriously, for it illuminates the basis of their understanding, organization, and mobilization. But it still leaves us with the task of understanding the context in which this "self-concept" originates and of which it makes sense. I will return to this question after a brief look at the second debate that has raged around the question, Who is an Arab?

The standard understanding of the meaning of *Arab* in Sudan is derived from the process known as "Arabization," by which is meant acculturation through migration and contact. This viewpoint argues that Arab identity is neither ethnic nor racial but cultural. This is how Yusuf Fadl Hasan puts it: "The slow Arab penetration which commenced in the early decades of Islam in the form of frontier clashes reached a climax in the 8th–9th/14th–15th c., when the Arab tribes overran most of the country. By the tenth/sixteenth c. a culturally Arabized stock emerged as a result of at least two centuries of close contact between the Arabs and the inhabitants of the Sudan. Regardless of a few exceptions, the term Arab was progressively being emptied of nearly all its ethnic significance."[85] From this point of view, Arab is a cultural identity. Whoever speaks Arabic and partakes in "Arab" cultural practices is an Arab—regardless of ethnic origin.

The opposite perspective is provided by the Darfuri anthropologist Sharif Harir, who has pointed out that "Arabism as a cultural acquisition is something common with many groups in the Sudan that are not racially Arabs." He notes that the Sudan People's Liberation Army (SPLA) accepted *Uruba* (Arabic for "Arabism") and Islam as part and parcel of Sudan's reality. "This aspect of our reality is immutable" is how an official SPLA publication put it in 1989.[86] Sharif Harir is right in one respect: that Arab culture, including the language, pervades Sudanese culture, Arab and non-Arab. In Darfur, for example, there are non-Arab tribes that almost universally speak Arabic besides their own mother tongue. Among these are the numerous and well-known Massalit and the Zaghawa, a large nomadic tribe in northwestern Darfur.[87] But they neither identify themselves as "Arabs" nor are identified as such by others. Then there are other tribes, also non-Arab, who speak Arabic as their mother tongue. The Tunjur, traditionally supposed to have supplanted the Daju as the ruling group in Darfur, speak only Arabic—except for those who intermarried with the Fur of Furnung and now prefer to speak Fur.[88] The Qimr, who live between the Zaghawa to the north and the Massalit to the south, on the western borders of Darfur, claim Arabic origin, and they, too, speak only Arabic.[89] The Berti, whose original language is said to have ceased to exist more than two hundred years ago, also speak only Arabic.[90] And there are more—such as the Birgid, the Beigo, the Borgo, and the Mima—who speak Arabic as their native tongue. But none see themselves as Arab, nor are they seen as such by others. A common culture—*Uruba*—may be a necessary condition for being an Arab, but it is clearly not a sufficient condition for it.

What, then, is that sufficient condition for being an Arab? Harir is wrong to think that this condition is racial. It is, rather, political. Those who claim to be Arab claim a genealogy leading back to Arab ancestors.[91] This is why there is little point in wasting energy over whether a particular genealogy is true or false—for the simple reason that genealogy is less a historical claim about migration and more a contemporary acknowledgment of common political association. Genealogy highlights the contours of a contemporary political community but not really its past. Its starting point is not the dead but the living, not ancestors but the present generation. It thus claims a common past for those linked together in the present. This is why it is important that a common genealogy be a publicly known and acknowledged fact.[92] The real problem with MacMichael—and, following him, Yusuf Fadl Hasan—was that he assumed a direct connection between genealogy and history, particularly the history of migration.

Marking boundaries of contemporary political associations, genealogies tend to work backward from the present rather than to mirror the past. They should be seen as part of a larger, nationalist corpus. All nationalisms imagine their past from the vantage point of the present. This imagination may be invented, but the invention is not wholly arbitrary. It bears a relationship to prior events, even if it interprets them selectively. The terms of that selection and interpretation reflect priorities rooted in the present rather than the past.[93] Nonassociation can result in Arab identity's being denied to those who were once "Arab," and association inevitably comes with an identity tag. Just as this identity can be shed by those who were once "Arab," it can be embraced by those who were once "non-Arab." To be an Arab is thus to be a member of any one of contemporary political communities called "Arab." Arab is, above all, a political identity—one that is tribal, not racial. To be an Arab is to be a member of an Arab tribe.

Our discussion up to this point suggests that the Arab identity was more a mark of assertion than of imposition. The assertion was made from multiple vantage points: that of the nobility of the Funj and Dar Fur Sultanates, the new middle class of Funj, the tribute-paying peoples in the southern Funj, and the Baggara in Darfur and Kordofan. Arab was the identity of power in riverine Sudan, but not in Dar Fur. There is no single history of "Arabization." Nor is there one overarching history of Arabs in Sudan, a single history woven around the common experience of migration; the histories of Arab groups are multiple histories in which migration has at best played a marginal role.

The history of communities gives us the view from below. It confirms that there is not a single history of Arabs in Sudan but multiple histories. At the broadest level, the people of Sudan, including the Arabs, distinguish between riverine and western Arabs. Riverine Arabs are settled peoples with territorial, village-based organizations; the Arabs of Darfur and Kordofan are nomadic, and their identity is based more on group affiliation than on territory. Many riverine Arabs tend to look upon the nomadic tribes as uncivilized country bumpkins rather than as members of a common community.

All this is true, but it is only one side of the story. The other side is the official attempt—from above—to compress these varied assertions into one single identity—a uniform Arab identity—by legal and administrative fiat, complemented by history writing. We will examine this in the context of the colonial state's response to the Mahdiyya in chapter 5.

4

Sudan and the Sultanate of Dar Fur

ONE MAJOR ASSUMPTION, regarding the relationship between community and state, informs the contemporary understanding of Darfur and the region to which it belongs: The history of the state is said to be driven by migrations and invasions, but the community is presumed to have remained pristine, traditional, and tribal all along. In this paradigm, the community is said to be the location of the native race, and migrations and invasions are said to be the source of settler races. How credible, one may ask, is this contrast between an ever-dynamic state and a never-changing community?

Part of this larger history is the history of slavery. The institution of slavery, including the slave trade, is presumed to have been an external import, like the state. What was the relationship between the history of state formation and the history of the slave trade? Who drove the slave trade, and who were its victims? Was the slave trade in Sudan—the "Arab slave trade," as it is often called—an institution imposed from the outside, or was it a product of local developments? To answer these questions, we need to rethink the recent past of the Sudanic states in the region, of which the Sultanate of Dar Fur was one example.

Sudanic States

History is important because it permeates memory and animates it, shaping the assumptions that we take for granted as we act in the present.

In this chapter, through an overview of the history of property, Islam, and slavery, I shall examine the twin assumptions that community has no history and that it has forever been tribal, and that slavery and the slave trade were predominantly an external imposition of settler races.

The political history of contemporary Sudan begins with the establishment of two polities: the kingdom of Funj, with its capital at Sinnar, and the Sultanate of Dar Fur, with its capital at El Fasher, the former established in 1504 and the latter in 1650. Institutionally, both polities shared many features with other kingdoms, such as neighboring Wadai in what is today Chad; Kanem and Borno across the Sahelian African savanna, which stretches from the Red Sea in the east to the Senegal River in the west; and states such as Buganda and Bunyoro-Kitara to the south. Contemporary historians refer to these polities as Sudanic states.

The Sudanic state was organized around the institution of "sacral kingship."[1] Ritually elevated to great sacred prominence, the king was in practice constrained in the exercise of absolute power. He was required to practice a ritual seclusion upon his accession; his feet never touched the ground, and he was never seen eating. But in real life, the king was never left alone: He always gave audiences via intermediaries; when he sneezed or coughed, all present sneezed or coughed. The divine king could not die a natural death. When he became seriously ill or just old, his end was hastened by poison or ritual suffocation. In practice, there was nothing absolute about the powers exercised by the king: More often than not, these powers were exercised jointly. In the military domain, the king was joined to the person of his military chief, the *kamni,* so much so that the *kamni* was executed if the sultan died in battle. In day-to-day life, the king's power was constrained by the importance of royal women, known as *mayram,* a word that appears to have been borrowed from Bornu. Of particular importance was the role of the sultan's eldest sister, *Iya Basi* (Fur) and that of his senior wife, *Iya Kuring* (Fur). In the Sudanic states, the sacral nature of power extended beyond the king to important royal women. In Buganda, writes Tor Irstam, the royal title, *kabaka,* could rightfully be borne by the king, the queen (who was the half sister of the king, born of the same father), and the king's mother. All were the objects of worship by their subjects. All had their own staff of chiefs and servants, owned large tracts of land all over the country, and had power over the lives of their subjects. Each lived on his or her own hill, separated by a stream of water, for it was said that "two kings could not live on the same hill." The queen was to visit the king every day; if unable to do so, she was required to inform him of the reason for her absence through a messenger. The queen, like the king's mother, might have as many lovers as she liked, but she was forbidden on pain of death to give birth to a child.[2]

There was a clear disjunction between the image of power and its institutional organization. Ideologically, the king was godlike, sacred, but institutionally, the king's power was checked by a host of other officials. Particularly astonishing to European visitors to Sinnar was the office of the *sid al-qom*, "whose right and duty it was to execute a reigning monarch when condemned by his court." A member of the royal family and one of the highest-ranking officers of the court, the *sid al-qom* was not allowed to attend deliberations of the court. As James Bruce attested, the *sid al-qom* had "no vote in deposing" the king. And the king, in turn, bore no ill feeling toward him, for "the king knew that he had no hand in the wrong that might be done to him, or in any way advanced his death."[3]

The Sudanic state ruled over a two-class agrarian society of nobles and commoners. The ruling nobility lived off the agricultural surplus it squeezed out of commoners. Though this elite controlled some slaves, their numbers were limited and they never supplanted free commoners as producers. The Sudanic state was a decentralized polity in which the exchange system was highly regulated and foreign trade in particular was a closely guarded royal monopoly. A defining characteristic of the Sudanic state was the absence of towns outside of the capital dominated by the court complex.[4] Power was wielded by officials who held their positions at the king's pleasure. Roland Oliver and J. D. Fage say that "as it grew and evolved, the successful 'Sudanic' state tended to become something near to a bureaucracy."[5]

The sacral kingdom declined with the increasing centralization of the state. Three institutions in particular supported the growth of royal power. The first was the development of an estate system in which individual estates were granted by the king, thereby eroding clan control over land. The second was the development of a royal army recruited from slaves, which gave the king independence from chiefs and supremacy over them. The third was the institutionalization of Islam as a court ideology: Islam provided a justification for royal power against the claims of clan-based chiefs. Centralization of the state did not just mean the consolidation of arbitrary royal power. Rather, it led to the rise of a new elite around the king. Organized around and through the centralized state, this elite successfully countered the power of the old chieftains.

Contemporary historians rely on written accounts from three outside visitors in putting together a history of the sultanate of Dar Fur: the Englishman William Browne (1793–96), the North African Muhammed al-Tunisi (1803–11), and the German Gustav Nachtigal (1874). Browne came to Dar Fur on a caravan from Egypt in 1793, lived there for three years, and returned by caravan in 1796. Muhammed Umar Sulayman al-Tunisi came to Dar Fur with his father from Mecca via the Sultanate of Funj. He spent eight years at the court and left us a comprehensive account of it. Nachtigal, a German scholarly traveler, arrived in Dar Fur in 1874 and also left a detailed account of his stay at the court.[6] The conventionally accepted history of Darfur begins with three successive dynasties: the Daju, the Tunjur, and the Keira Fur. Each of these powers arose from a different historical location: the Daju empire from the south; the Tunjur from the northern half; and the Keira from the central mountain massif, the Jebel Marra. All three dynasties were centralized, slave-based autocracies,[7] and legend has it that all three owed their emergence to immigrants. The dynasties succeeded each other without large-scale bloodshed, and the role of Islam grew from one dynasty to the next. Appearing as a court religion during the Tunjur empire, Islam gained even greater importance in Keira times.[8]

The development of the Dar Fur Sultanate is identified with the reign of three kings. The first was Sulayman Solongdungo (circa 1650–1680), the historical founder of the Keira dynasty. Two themes dominated the century that followed his rule: war with neighbors and bitter internal conflicts. The latter went beyond in-house royal squabbles and were mainly driven by ongoing tensions between the sultan and his chiefs, a direct consequence of the process of centralization of royal power in the sultanate. The second most influential ruler of Dar Fur was Muhammad Tayrab (1752–53 to 1785–86), its seventh sultan, who is credited with creating a strong royal army. By the end of his rule, Muhammad Tayrab had conquered the Funj province of Kordofan and extended the Fur Sultanate to the Nile, thereby opening Dar Fur to the expanding international commerce of the seventeenth and eighteenth centuries. The empire now stretched from the borders of the Sultanate of Wadai (on roughly the present Chad/Sudan frontier) to the White Nile. The third major royal influence in shaping the Keira Sultanate was Abd al-Rahman, who completed the centralization of royal power when he founded a permanent capital at El Fasher in 1792. There, he set up a colony for foreign merchants. The new capital was outside the heartland of the Fur. Its establishment followed the conclusion of a bitter civil war, which set Fur against Zaghawa, and in which the latter emerged victorious.[9] The establishment of the capital at El Fasher demonstrated that the sultanate was finally autonomous of the powers of Fur clan chiefs.

The Keira Sultanate expanded in multiple ways. *Spatially,* it expanded outward from the mountains—the Jebel Marra—to the savanna. *Ethnically,* the kingdom reached beyond the Fur to incorporate numerous chiefdoms in both the southwest and southeast.[10] The sultans resorted to interethnic marriages as a deliberate strategy to build state alliances and pave the way for state expansion by military force.[11] With the permanent move to El Fasher in 1791–92, in the words of one historian, "The Sultan took in effect the Fur state away from the Fur."[12] At the same time, the sultanate incorporated smaller and sedentary tribal groups— as well as immigrants from West Africa—into its inner circles. The Fur became a minority in the population; by 1874, the Keira sultan ruled over a population of subjects who were two-thirds non-Fur.[13] But the distinction between Fur and non-Fur blurred as the demands of the sultans fell upon all impartially. *Socially,* the expansion was from peasant to pastoralist groups. A key strategy pursued by Fur sultans was the incorporation of nomadic populations into the sedentary political economy regulated by the state. The pastoralist population provided the hoofed mobility necessary for the maintenance and expansion of the trans-Saharan trade. But swift mobility was also key to the pastoralist impulse for autonomy. As we shall see, relations between the sultanate and pastoralists remained tension-ridden, with pastoralist populations defining the outer limits of the sultanate's power.

The Keira Sultanate remained very much a pro-peasant state with a core sedentary population. The sultanate provided for its public security and related to nomadic and seminomadic peoples through a twin policy that involved cajoling and coercing leaders and their populations.[14] The sultanate's ultimate sanction against nomads was heavy cavalry, wearing chain mail and riding imported horses that were much larger than the local breeds. The nomads could not stand up against them; here the camel nomads of the north (the Abbala) were more vulnerable than the horse-riding cattle nomads of the south, the Baggara, "who were always a problem for the sultans, since they could withdraw ever further south in the western Bahr al-Ghazal."[15]

So long as it had not developed centralized institutions, the sultanate was no more than a glorified chieftainship. To become a sultanate, it needed to recruit, reproduce, and expand an elite that would rival those of neighboring chiefs. To sustain such an elite would require creating an appropriate property system and recruiting an army from neighboring localities to outmaneuver local militias. Finally, to cultivate and maintain the cohesion of the elite and the loyalty of the army and the population it ruled, the court would need a rival system of beliefs, one capable of evoking a translocal and transtribal solidarity.

Land: Tribe and State

The conventional understanding of historical Dar Fur is not very different from that of much of precolonial Africa: that it was a collection of tribal homelands (dars). A historical understanding of the sultanate leads us to question this conventional portrayal of the land system. Not only was land in the Dar Fur Sultanate held under different arrangements, from tribal and communal to individual, with a range of forms in between, but the trend was away from communal and in favor of different kinds of individual holdings.

The Keira sultans emerged from a society organized as so many chieftaincies. To build a sultanate, they first had to contain, then tame, and eventually subdue these same chieftaincies. Without that, the sultanate would have been just another chieftaincy, albeit one more powerful than its neighbors. For the sultanate to grow into a kingdom, political power would have to build its own institutions, involving at least an army and an officialdom, anchored in a property system that would provide countervailing forms of landed property alongside existing communal ones, and a belief system other than kinship to justify and hold together the new complex of institutions. As they built a centralized state (sultanate), at first separate from the localized power of clan chiefs and then opposed to it, the Keira sultans introduced changes that first relativized the notion of land as tribal property and then broke with it.

The break came as the sultans began to grant rights over land and people to their own followers and officials. These rights were embodied in written charters, *wathiqa al-tamlik,* which were given not only to local leaders and clan chiefs but also—and increasingly—to a newly recruited state elite that was drawn from different ethnic groups. The result was the development of a grid of estates, first and foremost in the "agriculturally or strategically favored regions" that "increasingly submerged the older chiefly order." R. S. O'Fahey estimates that "the charters and the rights promulgated" in the estate system "had probably come into use already by 1700, not long after the emergence of the sultanate from the mountains." In the three-volume history he wrote at the start of the twentieth century, Naum Shuqayr traced the beginning of the system of landed estates to Sultan Musa Ibn Suleiman, the second ruler of the Keira dynasty (1680–1700). Sultan Musa introduced a new system of granting land titles called *hakura* in Arabic (plural: *hawakir*). The grant of a *hakura* was a formal legal act; the land granted was demarcated. In some regions, such as Zalingei, that demarcation was effected with drystone walls.[16]

The *hawakir* were of two types, the first an administrative *hakura* and the second a more personal *hakura* of privilege, the former known as *hakura* and the latter as *hakurat al-jah* (literally, honorable standing).[17]

The two types of grants were distinguished by scale and the extent of privilege over the land and its occupants. The administrative *hakura* was usually given to clan leaders and allowed limited taxation over extensive tracts of land on which entire communities dwelled. The holder was granted immunity from taxation and from other exactions of the state so that the right to tax a particular community was transferred from the sultan to the grantee. By awarding a grant of administrative rights to his nobles, the sultan hoped to maintain control over outlying areas through those men. But the grant had limited juridical implications since the holder of the administrative estate had neither exclusive rights to the estate nor exclusive legal jurisdiction over tenants. When granted to clan leaders, the administrative *hakura* effectively confirmed communal ownership of land for a given group of people. In this case, the sultan ensured the loyalty of the group's leader in return for officially confirming his position. Since not all land was granted as administrative estates, it meant that the older system of communal tenure continued to exist side by side with the *hakura* system in various places around Dar Fur, with kin groups considering the land they occupied as synonymous with an administrative *hakura*.[18]

In contrast, the *hakura* of privilege was more exclusive. It gave the holder all rights to collect taxes and religious dues. The *hakura* of privilege was granted to the new men (and some women)—religious leaders, merchants, members of the royal clan, army leaders, state officials— around whom the institutions of the sultanate were built. The privileges conferred by this *hakura* had only one guarantor: the power of the sultanate. A royal charter bestowing land as alms upon an immigrant holy man contained the following warning to any who might dare transgress the privilege conferred by the charter: "He who splashes him with cold water, I will splash him with warm blood."[19] The *hakura* of privilege greatly increased during the nineteenth century, both as a way of making land grants to the holy men (*fuqara*) being invited into the sultanate by its rulers and as a way of providing "an income to the hordes of hangers-on, petty *maliks* and courtiers with antique titles, royal sons and daughters clustered around the later Keira court." As the system expanded, key officials of the state came to hold multiple *hawakir,* so that a great *malik* might have as many as twenty or thirty scattered around the country. Besides being a way of accommodating newcomers, it was also a way of ensuring a regular income to both members of the royal house and important state officials—since there was no regular payment of salary. At the same time, it was given as a reward to individuals for services. On all counts, this new type of *hakura* broke radically from the older form of kin-based property in land. Whatever the objective in granting it, the *hakura* of privilege provided an effective way of opening up virgin land and encouraging new settlement in a land with a scarcity of inhabitants, at a time when there was a premium on density of population in a polity.[20]

The recipients of the *hawakir* were many, but the most important fell into three categories. The first were high-ranking officials and army commanders for whom a *hakura* provided an opportunity to collect taxes and dues, *ushur,* from farmers. The second were prominent religious men who came from West Africa and were wooed with grants of land and exemption from taxes for themselves and their followers. The third were important clan leaders. That they were all granted estates as a means of obtaining their support played an important role in shaping tenure arrangements. Land grants to clan chiefs were one of two types: Whereas the administrative *hakura* officially acknowledged their already existing control over communal property, the grant of *hakura* of privilege to these same chiefs had the effect of establishing individual forms of tenure.[21]

The *hakura* of privilege also led to a variety of forms of management, from the familiar to the radically different. If kin group leaders continued with a form of communal tenure, nobles usually installed slaves as their stewards, and the *fuqara* of the court preferred to employ relatives. Not all estate holders were absentees; most *fuqara* were not appointed to the court and so lived on their estates, just as royal women often came to live on the land they were granted. In fact, it is the holy men who took the lead in settling large sections of the sultanate and who strongly influenced the social pattern of subsequent settlements. As we shall see, an enduring result of the grants to the rural *fuqara* was the growth of religious communities throughout the sultanate. Within these, the *fuqara* exercised formal and informal influence as teachers; mediators in local conflicts; and writers of magical texts, or *hijabat.*[22]

A growing distinction developed between two key recipients of the *hakura* of privilege: holy men and state nobles. The *fuqara* seldom lost their land, but nobles were more vulnerable since their estates were an integral part of the political spoils system, which is why land and people evidently changed hands regularly among nobles. Not only did estates revert to the sultan when the grant lapsed, but the abandonment of an estate also led to its loss. Given the distinction between how the state related to religious and political nobles, the holy men turned out to be the main beneficiaries of the *hakura* system in the long run.

The estate system was never the major source of income for the political class. So long as Dar Fur was thinly populated, those dissatisfied with their lot could easily move away; this single fact proved an effective check on those who wanted to maximize the exploitation of farmers.

Both farmers and nomads probably gained protection from the patron-client ties of the estate system, and especially from the partial immunity gained by settling on the land of an influential *faqih*. The most enduring legacy of the system was undoubtedly the protection and security it provided for the *fuqara*.

In the Sultanate of Dar Fur, the estate system was marked by a progressive detribalization of both the land system and the system of governance. Though this development could be traced in other Sudanic states that ranged across the sub-Saharan belt, from the Niger River to the Red Sea, the available information suggests that the process of detribalization was far more advanced in Dar Fur.[23] In other Sudanic states land grants still carried traces of kin-based ownership of land and ties of dependence, unlike Dar Fur. Two differences in particular suggest this conclusion. In Borno, for example, the Shehu granted two types of land rights to the big lord (*cima kura*). The estate could be either territorial or ethnic. Whereas the territorial estate comprised a contiguous piece of land, the ethnic estate was a grant of rights over a group defined by birth irrespective of where they lived. The *cima kura* lived at court and administered his estates, which could number twenty or more, through his *cima gana,* or "junior lords." The latter were the critical link between the *cima kura* and the local communities under their lineage chiefs. Only the territorial estate obtained in Dar Fur. As in Borno, titled officials could possess estates throughout the sultanate and administer them through stewards called *wakil* or *kursi* (literally, "chair") in Arabic or *sagal* in Fur and collect revenue through them. But there is no conclusive evidence to suggest the existence of ethnic estates in Dar Fur. Corresponding to this is another related fact of governance: Unlike in Borno, local chiefs in Dar Fur were drastically subordinated to estate holders and their stewards.[24]

The development of the *hakura* system shows some parallels with the feudal system. Title holders put in place a steward/manager called *sid-al-fas* ("master of the ax") who managed the estate by allocating pieces of land for settlement or cultivation and was in return able to exact customary dues (*ushur*) equal to one-tenth of the farm yield from those who cultivated their land. The dues from land were shared by various officials in the administrative hierarchy. Jay Spaulding and Lidwein Kapteijns have shown that customary dues were exacted from producers on the land in two different ways: rent or tribute. Whereas rent left the individual producer with ownership rights, tribute bound the producer to the land and, through it, socially to the master, hand and foot.[25]

More individualistic forms of property seem to have developed out of this feudal-type arrangement. The concession of property rights (*milk*) is comprehensively described in several charters as "[rights of] cultivation, causing to be cultivated, sale, demolition, building, alms and purchase." Thus, under the long seventy-two-year reign of Muhammad al-Fadl and his son, the most common form of grant became the topographically defined estate given as a "gift" or "donation," *hiba* or *sadaqa,* which conceded both *milk,* or property rights, and immunity from taxation. These later land charters used the expression *iqta al-tamlik*—that is, concession of property rights—which makes the *hakura* of privilege similar to a freehold.[26]

Islam and State Centralization

As it rapidly expanded and centralized, the Sultanate of Dar Fur—like other Sudanic states—sought ideological inspiration in the great tradition of Islam, which offered multiple resources. Immediately, the *ummah*—Islamic community—provided an effective counter to kin-based clan solidarity. In the longer run, however, Islam not only counteracted the ideology of kinship but also reproduced it in different forms in the course of welding together a supratribal order. If the former was part of its promise, the latter was part of its lived reality. In subsequent centuries, the tension between the promise and the reality would weave through Islamic movements, posing questions to which there were no easy doctrinal answers, thereby providing the impulse to drive them forward.[27]

In the seventeenth and eighteenth centuries, when the Sultanate of Dar Fur centralized, the spread of Islam was closely associated with Arabic culture, which provided a crucial resource for both state formation and market expansion. Written Arabic provided an administrative language for communication among functionaries of the centralizing state, regardless of the distance separating them. Islam also offered membership in a wider regional community and, with it, the possibility of co-opting traders and teachers from the wider Muslim world.[28] As the

official religion of the centralized court, Islam gave meaning and significance to the process of state centralization and a set of associated
changes in the wider society: the evolution of the estate system, the creation of new administrative forms, the integration into wider trading
networks, and the restatement of the ruler's position in quasi-Islamic
terms.[29]

Islamic influences in Sudan were felt through three major channels:
along the Nile, across the Sahara, and across the Red Sea. Though they
opened up as early as the seventh century, these routes were of a highly
irregular nature for almost a millennium, being associated with the itin-
erant presence of immigrant pilgrims, traders, and nomads. It is the
arrival of a new group beginning in the sixteenth century that marked
the starting point of an organized and doctrinal Islamic influence. This
group was the *fuqara,* Islamic holy men well grounded in the doctrine of
the new religion and in Sufi mysticism. Rather than from the east or
along the Nile, they came mainly from West and North Africa.[30]

Islam spread along with two institutions: the Quranic school and the
mosque.[31] Traditional Quranic schools, or *khalawi* (singular: *khalwa,*
meaning a "solitary den"), spread throughout the Sudanic belt, stretching from the Horn of Africa in the east to Mali and Senegal at the western coast of the continent. It was customary for parents to send their
children to centers of Islamic learning, where in many cases they spent
much of their childhood and returned to their families only after learning the entire Quran by heart. During such a period, the student was
known as a *muhajir,* or one who "migrates" for religious knowledge.
Even today, Darfuris are commonly known for their dedicated recitation
of the Quran. Dar Fur provided the ceremonial woven cloth that draped
the holy stone, the Kaaba, at the center of the annual pilgrimage in
Mecca. For purposes of more advanced learning, Darfuris used to travel
to centers in Egypt and North Africa, such as Al Azhar, the famed
Islamic mosque and university in Cairo. In the nineteenth century, a
special student hostel, known as Rewaq Dar Fur (or Dar Fur Vestibules),
was built at Al Azhar to accommodate students from Dar Fur pursuing
advanced degrees in Islamic studies, Arabic, and the like. The *rewaq* survived into the twentieth century, although by 1925 there were reportedly
only four students in attendance. Other destinations included univer-
sity-style mosques in Tunis, such as al Zaitouna and al Qayrawan.[32]

The community of Muslims in both central and western Sudan, from the Funj to Kordofan to Dar Fur, came to be organized in Sufi *tariqas* (brotherhoods). The origin of Sufi orders lies in initiatives taken by migrant religious men who were able to use land rights (*hawakir*) granted them by the sultans to support a specialized following and to nurture educational institutions through which they reproduced as well as refined the knowledge that became the basis for a special class of Islamic teachers called *fuqara*.[33] Most of these institutions later developed into Sufi orders. These hierarchically organized Islamic brotherhoods refrained from seeking temporal authority but at the same time reinforced the legitimacy of the existing authority. Though the brotherhoods didn't enter the "palace," they wielded considerable temporal authority over their members (ideally said to be "like corpses in the hands of their washers") through practices such as mediation (*suluh*). The result was a quasi-secular development of two parallel institutions: on the one hand, the sultanate, a centralized political authority with a quasi-religious character, and, on the other, centralized and formalized religious institutions, the Sufi brotherhoods, which were both autonomous of this authority and dependent on it for the allocation and protection of exclusive rights of access to land and exemption from state-enforced dues.[34] Urban settlements were first authorized for foreign merchants, but soon after pressure mounted for similar concessions for locals. It is said that the inhabitants of one of the new towns in early-nineteenth-century Dar Fur marched behind a holy man, waging an eleven-year-long insurrection calling on the last Keira monarch to grant them autonomy.[35]

Three Sufi orders in particular became popular over western and central Sudan, from Dar Fur to Kordofan and the Funj. These were the Qadiriyya, the Khatmiyya, and the Tijaniyya. Each was introduced from the outside, but none was an imposition. Whereas the Sufi orders were established long ago, there developed influential circles (singular: *zawiya,* plural: *zaweaya*) around particular sheikhs.[36]

These migrant religious scholars were also reformers. They combined Islamic learning with Sufi mysticism. Their emphasis was more on miracles (Arabic: *karama*), magic, and hereditary spiritual charisma (Arabic: *baraka*) than on the law and its institutions.[37] A Sufi was said to possess *baraka,* blessing or goodness believed to emanate from a holy man, and he was believed to act as an intermediary between man and God.[38] In the range of practices that define lived Islam, mystical practices in Sufi Islam constituted one extreme in a range whose other end was defined by the rational and legal discourse of Islamic jurists and scholars known as the *ulama*. Though some authors have tended to portray rationalism and mysticism as opposite poles in the development of Islam, the two are often found intermingled in the teaching of some of the most important Muslim thinkers, such as Abu Hamid al-Ghazali of Iran and Mohammed Abdu of Egypt. My purpose is not to counterpose Islamic mysticism to nonmystical forms of Islamic thought but to emphasize the significance of egalitarian versus hierarchical institutional practices. The *ulama* and the Sufi *tariqas* differed less in modes of thought than in institutional practices. In Sudan, it is the Sufis who would define local Islam and the *ulama* who would come to be allied with foreign powers, whether during the Turkiyya or during the Anglo-Egyptian condominium.

The Sufi holy men did not come into a social and spiritual vacuum. The *fuqara* were very much like the spirit mediums or diviners who continue to operate in such parts of the Nilotic Sudan, as the southern Gezira near the Ethiopian frontier or the Nuba hills of Kordofan. They resembled the spirit mediums both in the functions they fulfilled and in the styles of ritual and the symbols they employed.[39] This said, the difference between the two lay in the fact that, unlike spirit mediums or diviners, the traditional brotherhood of Sufi *tariqas,* or religious orders, knew no kin limits, geographical boundaries, or political frontiers. Their followers often journeyed for weeks in order to visit their sheikhs. Hence, religious orders were of immense value in promoting a sense of fraternity and integration among the peoples of the Sudanic belt, so much so that it was widely believed that "to be a Muslim meant to have a spiritual guide or mentor, a shaykh."[40] In other words, to be a Muslim was to belong to a Sufi order.

Though Islam spread throughout northern Sudan, in both the Sultanate of Dar Fur and the kingdom of Funj, there is a difference in the source of the Islamic influence in each case. In both sultanates, the holy men (*fuqara*) came from Muslim lands beyond their borders, but in the case of the Funj kingdom, they came mainly from Egypt, up the Nile, or from Iraq, whereas in the Sultanate of Dar Fur, they came mainly from West and North Africa. The spread of Islam in the Funj kingdom is amply documented in a Sudanese text of 1805, the *Tabaqat,* which provided a collection of biographies of holy men. According to the *Tabaqat,* the sultans of Funj invited noted Islamic scholars from Egypt and Baghdad upon assuming power: So renowned sheikhs came to the Funj from the sixteenth century onward.[41] The introduction of Islam in Kordofan took place in roughly the same historical period and was influenced more by the Funj kingdom than by the Fur Sultanate.[42] Although individual *fuqara* from the Funj kingdom contributed to the progress of Islamic culture in Dar Fur, the region came under the cultural sway of the central Sudan and the Maghreb. A key center of influence—commercial, cultural, and political—over all of central Sudan (central Sahel) was the empire of Kanem/Bornu, which had formally been an Islamic state since the eleventh century.[43] In time, however, Dar Fur became the meeting ground of several different African Islamic traditions, not only from the northern Sudan and from West Africa but also from Egypt via the "Forty-Day Route." A not surprising result of this history was that the clans of holy saints (*fuqara*) in Dar Fur were all foreign.[44]

The difference in the routes by which Islam came to the Funj Sultanate and to Dar Fur is clear from the form of Arabic adopted by each: While those in the Funj Sultanate adopted the standard Arabic calligraphy, those in Dar Fur followed the Andalusian or Saharan handwriting, which was current all over the Maghreb. Similarly, the dominant Sufi orders in Dar Fur—notably the Tijaniyya—came from West Africa, though they were North African in origin.[45] Whereas the study of the *faki* families and their origins in Darfur has been neglected, in comparison with that in Nilotic Sudan, a broad understanding of the *fuqara* influx suggests a distinction between two periods: before and after the nineteenth century. According to R. S. O'Fahey, West African influence "played the greater part" until the end of the eighteenth century, after which the dominant influence shaping Islam in Dar Fur was from the east, drawing it closer to the Funj.[46]

It was Sultan 'Abd al-Rahman al-Rashid (1787–1801) who invited more and more of the *awlad al-balad* ("people of the Nile Valley"), both merchants and religious men, to immigrate to the new capital at El

Fasher.[47] Previous sultans had encouraged the spread of Islamic ideas and institutions throughout Dar Fur: For example, Ahmad Bukr (circa 1682–1722) built mosques and schools, and Sultan Muhammad Tayrab (circa 1756–1787) procured scholarly books from Egypt and Tunisia. But it was 'Abd al-Rahman al-Rashid who encouraged religious teachers from other countries to settle in Dar Fur. Among these was Muhammed Umar Sulayman al-Tunisi, the Tunisian Arab who had already spent some time in the Funj kingdom on his way back from Mecca and was later followed by his own son Muhammad, whose account of Dar Fur is one of several important sources for its history.[48]

Slavery, Foreign Trade, and State Centralization

The development of slavery from the ancient to the capitalist periods is marked by one great distinction: a radical change in the source of demand for slaves. In contrast to the capitalist period, when demand came to be driven by rapidly growing sugar and cotton plantations supplying an expanding world market, the demand for slaves in the ancient period was mainly state-driven. The royal house needed to be independent of land-based interests, whether they were feudal lords or clan-based chiefs. To build up an independent army and officialdom, it was necessary to have a source of human power that was independent of local clans and tribes. Loyalty was at a premium, and loyalty was seen as a function of lack of attachments. For a source of loyal soldiers and officials, the court turned either to mercenaries or, more likely, to slaves. Forcibly separated from their home societies, slaves could be moved at will, whether from one location to another or up and down the occupational ladder, to a position prestigious or degrading. The castrated slave, the eunuch—the most extreme example of this lack of attachment—was prized as a highly desirable agent by those in positions of power and authority. This is why royal slaves were often castrated and why the most ambitious of the slaves sometimes underwent castration, hoping to pursue ambition. Since it was condemned in Muslim law, castration could not be carried out in the Sultanates of Dar Fur and Funj. For that reason, it was mostly performed by Christian priests, outside the boundaries of the Muslim world—usually in Ethiopia.[49]

    In the empires of the precapitalist world, unlike on the plantations of the capitalist world, it was not unusual for some talented slaves to rise up within the state hierarchy and be among the most powerful of state officials. The title-holding hierarchy of the expanding and centralizing state, in Egypt as in many other ancient states, including Dar Fur and Funj, included persons of both slave and free origin. To gain a full understanding of the rise and fall of slavery and the slave trade in the Sultanate of Dar Fur, it is necessary to take a brief look at the role of Sudanese slaves in the formation of the Egyptian state.

Slavery and Egypt: Most of our information on the slave trade that fed Egypt comes from a comprehensive manual written by Ibn Butlan, a Christian physician in Cairo who in the eleventh century wrote a treatise on the qualities, uses, and methods of sale of various slaves, drawing mainly on his own vast experience and on information he gathered from slave-brokers.[50] Two categories of slaves were in great demand and were acquired in large numbers: The first were Turks recruited as soldiers or Mamluks; the second were the Sudanese slaves from the south, commonly known as *al-Nuba*. The demand for slaves came from several sources. The first was a domestic demand for household servants in the homes of the wealthy; there was also a market-driven demand from enclaves of production that relied on large-scale organized labor, such as that for the salt-works of Basra, where thousands were employed in reclaiming the soil and extracting salt.[51] But the greatest demand for slaves, both the Mamluks from Turkey and the al-Nuba from Sudan, was as troops. As early as the ninth century, Ahmad b. Tulun, the governor of Egypt (868–84), was said to have recruited 7,000 freeborn fighters (possibly Arabs), 24,000 Turkish slaves, and 40,000 Sudanese slaves for his army. The ratio among these figures is more important than the actual numbers. Each group had its cantonment, and that of the Sudani was called the Nubian camp.[52]

The attraction of slave soldiers was particularly great for dynasties seeking an alternative to free Arab recruits tied down by particular loyalties. This is how the founder of the Ikhshidid dynasty (323–58/935–69) recruited a large army of Sudani slaves. Among his personal bodyguards was a Nubian eunuch, Kufur, who soon distinguished himself as a trustworthy and capable administrator. Kufur became the virtual ruler of Egypt after the death of his master in A.D. 946. For nineteen years, he conducted the affairs of Egypt and defended the country with some success. During this time, he recruited many troops from his own countrymen, the al-Nuba. In time, the Mamluks and the Sudani came to power rival dynasties: The Fātimids turned to the Sudani slaves for recruits, and their rivals to Mamluks.

With the extinction of the Fātimid state and the rise of Mamluk power in Egypt, the demand for Sudani slaves died away. But the demand for slave soldiers continued to grow in both the Funj (1504–1821) and Fur Sultanates (1650–1874), where they constituted the core of the armies. With the decline of Mamluk power, the demand for Sudani slaves rose again in Egypt. Even as late as the nineteenth century, it was Muhammad Ali's desire to acquire black slaves from Dar Fur and Funj—and turn them into soldiers—that is said to have been the driving force behind his conquest of the Sudan in 1821. Indeed, prior to the conquest, in A.D. 1819–20, Muhammad Ali Pasha declared a state monopoly of all Sudani imports, including slaves, ivory, and gum, and took control of Wakkalat al-Jallaba, the slave trade guild that handled the sale of slaves in Cairo. Although he abandoned his original plan for a slave army, Sudani slaves continued to constitute a sizable portion of the Egyptian army throughout the nineteenth century, with some participating in a French military expedition against Mexico in 1863.[53]

The Egyptian markets were fed by three major caravan routes. The first two fanned out of Dar Fur and Sinnar, and the third came from Bornu/Wadai via Fezzan, Tunis, and Tripoli. A regular trade caravan proceeded from Sinnar, twice a year, through Qarri in the north to the capital of the Abdallab chiefs to Upper Egypt.[54] A large number of slaves sent from Sinnar were originally imported from Dar Fur. It is estimated that the value of slaves imported from the two regions into Egypt constituted about 40 percent of all imports from al-Nuba.[55] By the beginning of the nineteenth century, Dar Fur was Egypt's largest African trading partner.[56]

When it comes to estimating the number of slaves brought to Egypt from Dar Fur, historians rely on various European reports toward the end of the eighteenth century. According to a French writer who accompanied Napoléon Bonaparte's expedition to Egypt, the annual import of slaves was around three thousand. The caravan that took William Browne to Egypt in 1796 was said to have carried roughly five thousand slaves. A second French scholar, Girard, basing his estimates on the year

1799, stated that five thousand to six thousand slaves were imported every year from Dar Fur. Yet a third French scholar, Lapanous, estimated the number of slaves in the caravan led by the son of the Fur sultan in 1800 at twelve thousand.[57] Even if we regard the specific numbers as not too reliable, the trend is worth noting: Rising estimates most likely testify to an increase in the volume of the trade toward the beginning of the nineteenth century. For it is in the latter part of the eighteenth century that the Nile and the eastern part of Africa became fully integrated into a market-driven slave circuit.

Three major trade routes linked Dar Fur with the outside world. The first was the famous "Forty-Day Route," the *Darb al-Arba'in,* which had long been a difficult desert path to Asyūt in Upper Egypt. The sultans built a caravan route along it at the same time they created an authorized settlement for foreign merchants from the north in the permanent capital at El Fasher.[58] This route began at Kobbei (25 miles north of El Fasher) in Dar Fur, passed through Jebel Meidob, crossed the Libyan desert through Bir Natrum, and went on to Asyūt. The journey traversed nearly 1,100 miles of desert in all and involved a forty-day march. This route mainly carried slaves and ivory from Chad and Dar Fur to Egypt and had been active for more than a thousand years. The great attraction of the Darb al-Arba'in was its security: Unlike the alternative routes along the Nile, it passed through uninhabitable desert for most of its length; the discomfort notwithstanding, this single fact made it virtually immune from attacks from camel nomads along the way.[59]

The second great trade route that went through Dar Fur was the west-to-east *pilgrimage route.* It connected the western Bilad al-Sudan to Mecca and Medina and had probably been in use since around the eleventh century, which is when Arab sources first begin to speak of royal pilgrimages and annual pilgrimage caravans from West Africa. Starting in West Africa, this route went through Bornu, Wadai, Dar Fur, and Sinnar to the Red Sea ports and then to the Hejaz.[60] As late as the nineteenth century, it was presumed that people setting out on pilgrimages from West Africa were unlikely to return and were reportedly mourned as if they had died.[61] The third and probably the least significant was a northwesterly trade route to Tripoli and Tunisia via Fezzan.[62]

Throughout this period, the sultans actively traded on their own behalf through royal merchants, who operated with ambassadorial status. One of these was Al-Hajj Muhammad b. Musa, who led the great caravan that was said to have arrived in Egypt with twelve thousand slaves in late 1798, not long after the French occupation.[63] We do not have precise figures on the ratio between slaves exported and those retained inside Dar Fur, but R. S. O'Fahey estimates that "it is possible that the latter considerably exceeded the former"; indeed, "the numerous casual references to domestic slaves in the sources appear to confirm that slavery was widespread and had deep social roots."[64] This suggests that the export of slaves was an extension of their internal use—and not the other way around. Put simply, both slavery and the slave trade most likely began as *internal* institutions. It is Muhammad Tayrab who had created a slave army in an attempt to lessen his dependence on clan chiefs and title holders. Tayrab also had several slave eunuchs as advisers. Among these was the famous Muhammad Kurra, who held the title of Abu Sheikh Dali and who, from about 1770–71 to 1803–4, was considered the most powerful man in Dar Fur, after the sultan.

Slaves proved a great asset for sultans who wanted to tame pastoralist subjects at the periphery or ambitious chiefs at the center.[65] The challenge of rule led the sultans to create new institutions of control. The key institution was that of the *magdume:* a commissioner who represented the sultan in person, was supplied with external marks of royal dignity during his period of office, and exercised supreme authority.[66] The title of *magdume* as a new official who functioned outside the old titled hierarchy first appeared around 1800. Initially created to rule over nomads and seminomads, the institution of the *magdume* became universal as its appointment spread to sedentary subjects. The more sultans tried to centralize rule, the more they preferred to appoint commissioners over local areas rather than acknowledge local clan leaders and thereby rule through them.

Originally, these provincial administrative offices were held on a hereditary basis; later, the sultans began appointing officials on the basis of personal loyalty, starting from among the inner members of the court. Such an officer was called a *magdume* and the province itself, a *magdumate.* Checking the ambition of successful *magdumes* remained an ever-present necessity.[67] From this arose the practice of choosing recruits for these offices from among royal slaves. The rationale for this was obvious: A *magdume* with such a background would have very little support were he to attempt secession or try to weaken central authority by any other means. Indeed, some of the best known of the *magdumes* were from the slave population, such as Abdallah Runga, a Dinka slave who for a time administered Dar al-Gharb.[68]

The office of the *magdume* had the same significance for governance that the institution of *hakura* had for landed property. Both eroded the strength and significance of communal forms of power and property. It is with the creation of *magdumes* and the subsequent centralization of the state that the "customary" claims of a territorially based clan leadership began to break down.[69] The provinces were divided into *shartayas,* each under an appointed *shartay,* and each consisting of a number of *dimlijiyyas* (singular *dimlij*), or chieftaincies. Every village had its headman; wherever there was a literate *faqih,* he would deal with all written matters. Even at the level of the *shartaya,* "administrative divisions were not based on the ethnic identity of inhabitants."[70] Kin-based chiefs were increasingly subordinated to a class of title holders recruited from slaves and freemen who derived their position from the sultan as the lord and master of the land.

Slavery was the pivot around which state power centralized. Whether as military commanders or as administrators, slaves provided sultans with a counterweight to check the aspirations of a kin-based or territorial nobility. In the absence of a mercantile or clerical class, developing an administration to control an increasingly centralized state would have been difficult without slaves. Within the court, slaves functioned as soldiers, administrators, concubines, domestics, guards, and attendants. They were organized in a complex hierarchy of groups and titles that paralleled and overlapped with the free hierarchy. The apex of the slave hierarchy consisted more often than not of eunuchs, of which there were said to be more than a thousand! Some had been castrated as a punishment for crime, others because of illness, and yet others had done it to themselves out of ambition. Ambition undoubtedly motivated the greatest slave in Dar Fur's history, Muhammad Kurra, ex officio governor of eastern Dar Fur under Muhammad Tayrab.[71] In a context in which castration was a means to upward mobility, the eunuch was a public servant precluded from building a family dynasty.

The great period of the Dar Fur–Egyptian trade, 1750 to 1850, coincided with the emergence of a centralizing sultanate in Dar Fur, and slavery was key to its expansion and centralization. Slaves could be found in a hierarchy of positions, parallel to those in the society at large. First, slaves were a part of the bureaucratic and military elite and acted as concubines to noblemen. As recruits for the royal army, they comprised small bands of heavily armed cavalries used to collect taxes, put down intertribal disputes, and awe peasants. A second category of royal slaves were war captives who were settled around the capital as its defenders; they served the sultan both as producers of wealth and as defenders of his power against ambitious territorial nobles.

In Sinnar, for which more specific information is available, the earliest of the slave garrisons were founded in the mid-seventeenth century and numbered 14,000. Slaves also provided a labor force for royal estates, but they were a small proportion compared to free commoners working on the land: In Sinnar, they numbered 4,500, or 4 percent of the population at the time of colonial conquest in 1821. Finally, they were the sultanate's major item of export; the export of slaves enabled the sultan to pay for imported luxury goods. Whereas the internal trade in Dar Fur was mainly in food and such items as cotton, hoes, and copper sold in large rings weighing ten or twelve pounds, the external long-distance caravan trade dealt mainly in slaves, camels, ostrich feathers, gum, cotton, and gold. When it came to foreign trade, the king was the country's chief merchant. The slave trade was a quintessential royal monopoly.[72]

That slaves could be found in a range of social positions, mirroring the hierarchy in nonslave society, did not prevent them from being socially degraded. Documents of the era suggest that slaves were sometimes legally classified along with livestock, even referred to as "talking animals," given peculiar individual names ("sea of lust" for a woman, "increase in wealth" or "patience is a blessing" for a man); their corpses were sometimes exposed to scavenging animals or just thrown in the river. There is also evidence to suggest that, unlike in other Islamic societies, northern Sudanese owners commonly sold slaves born in their households.[73]

In sum, then, precapitalist slavery in the Sultanates of Funj and Dar Fur was not the benign institution its apologists sometimes portrayed it as, with slaves integrated into families as kin. Surely, the point of peculiar slave names was both to identify slave offspring and to keep them in their place. At the same time, this degradation needs to be placed in a larger context, for the slave status reflected a quasi integration at all levels of society, from the tiny elite at the top to the serflike status of many commoners below. This quasi integration suggests the most important difference from the totally debased chattel slavery that developed on plantations in the Americas. After all, neither Dar Fur nor Funj was a free society. Neither claimed that to be human was to be free. Different groups, from commoners to nobles, lived in different degrees of social dependence. To be a slave in this context could not have been as debasing as to be one in a post-Renaissance society that claimed freedom as the hallmark of the human and thus universally degraded the not-free as nonhuman.

Slavery in northern Sudan—in both the Sultanate of Funj and that of Dar Fur—was not introduced from the outside. All evidence points to slavery's developing as a local institution, alongside the development of centralized power in the two sultanates. Despite the expression *Arab slavery* in Sudan, we must be aware that the entry of non-Sudanese—both Europeans and Arabs—into the slave trade really followed the advent of Turco-Egyptian rule in the early nineteenth century.

By the beginning of the nineteenth century, an elite had coalesced in Dar Fur, drawing its members from three new elements: *fuqara,* merchants, and slaves.[74] Slaves were without exception captured from tribes to the south that lived outside Dar Fur. The *fuqara* were mainly of West African origin, and the traders came disproportionately from the lands around the Nile. As a number of *khabirs,* or large-scale merchants, became intimately connected with the court, the ruling Keira dynasty recognized this fact in the customary way—that is, by intermarriage. Early-nineteenth-century Dar Fur was a cosmopolitan society with its elite drawn increasingly from immigrants. But it was not a settler elite superimposed on a native society.

The growing power of elite royal slaves mitigated the succession crisis among the Keira. The question of succession had traditionally fueled an ongoing conflict between the reigning sultan and the rest of the Keira clan. The great change in succession politics came with the establishment of El Fasher as the concentration of political power led to a rapid transfer of decision making from territorial potentates and warlords to informal coteries of slaves, *fuqara,* and merchants around the sultan.

The importance of slaves increased in the nineteenth century; indeed, it appears as if royal slaves tended to function as kingmakers after 1803. Following the accession of Muhammad al-Fadl (1803–38), the politics of succession were never again decided on the battlefield; the eunuch Muhammad Kurra, who had put Muhammad al-Fadl on the throne, was the first and greatest in a line of slave officials who dominated the court until the end of the sultanate. The politics of the court could be said to rotate around two parties, the old and the new, the former being old, established territorial chiefs and the latter slave administrators and other "new men." At the center of the old party were "free or genuine Fur," as Gustav Nachtigal called them,[75] whereas the new forces tended to coalesce around slave confidants and adventurers. That the succession issue was no longer resolved by conflict but with the blessing of the slave hierarchy testified to the power of slaves. Peaceful transition became possible because slaves, who could not personally ascend to the throne, were strong enough to give assent to those aspiring to the throne.

Slavery and Violence: By the beginning of the nineteenth century, Dar Fur had ceased to be a regular war-making state; foreign expeditions were a thing of the past. Indeed, between 1800 and 1874, Dar Fur mounted only one such expedition: against Wadai in 1837. Throughout the nineteenth century, war became a matter of raiding for slaves. It turned into a form of savagery with little military content, a glorified name for targeting unarmed civilians.[76] Systems of slave acquisition, one from Funj and the other from Dar Fur, are briefly described below. Together, they give us an idea of the various ways in which slaves were acquired—from regular taxation to the slave hunt, whether sanctioned by the state or undertaken by individual entrepreneurs.

In the Sultanate of Funj, slaves were acquired in two ways, both leading to extreme forms of violence. The first was through the system of taxation. Though levied in gold, tax could also be paid in nonagricultural equivalents, particularly slaves. The effect was to generate slave raids between communities in the south. But the individuals enslaved through this method were usually those most vulnerable: women and children. It was the government's desire for young men who could be deployed as soldiers that led to the official slave raid as the second method for capturing slaves. Whereas women and children were moved northward from south Kordofan, sold in return for iron or other local goods, and then incorporated into local communities as dependent members of households, the young men captured in official slave raids, the *salatiya*, were forcibly integrated into regiments or forcibly exported to northern lands. The slave hunt was organized each year by a court official, the *muqqadam al salatiya*. Of the slaves captured, half belonged to the sultan. Some were incorporated into the army, the bureaucracy, and the harem. The rest were sold abroad. These raids kept up the supply of slaves, who over the course of time came to compose the major force in the army, the state bureaucracy, and enclaves of large-scale organized labor such as mining. In addition to those acquired as tax payment or abducted as captives, enslavement was also meted out as a form of punishment to those who transgressed social taboos: Thus, children born of illegitimate unions or subjects who failed to pay tribute were enslaved.[77]

R. S. O'Fahey has described slaves as the Dar Fur Sultanate's "staple export" and the slave raid as "a mobile Sudanic state." The slave trade activated all distinctions key to political life in Dar Fur: between the centralized state and the decentralized political order to the south, between Muslim subjects of the sultanate and its non-Muslim prey, and between Fur and Fartit.

The *Fartit* was a generic term for southern tribes whose members could be enslaved: Runga, Kara, Yulu, Kresh, Binga, Banda, Feroge, Shatt, and a number of smaller tribes around the copper-mining area of Hufrat al-Nahas, "the effective southern limit of the Sultanate." The sultan granted the right to raid in Fartit country to those who applied with a suitable present. The granting of the right involved a procedure as formalized "as the granting of estates." To the recipient, the sultan "issued a letter of marque together with a spear of the salatiya type (a long broad-bladed lance particularly used by the Baggara)." Though there was a class of professional slavers—one Ahmad Tiktik had led twenty such expeditions—nobles and others also regularly got involved. The expedition "was a carefully organized commercial operation, in which violent capture played only a limited part." Once the expedition's leader had gathered his followers, he negotiated with the merchants for suitable credit. The credit system involved merchants supplying the expedition with goods in exchange for captured slaves; all transactions were confirmed in writing. The number of slaves a trader received for a fixed amount of goods depended on whether he took delivery of slaves near the point of capture or waited for their arrival. The payment at point of capture could be twice as much as after the journey. Traders often covered the risk of some slaves dying along the journey by a system of differential credit.[78]

The expedition usually prepared to set out after the June–July rains to ensure pasture for their horses. The sultan is said to have granted permission to between sixty and seventy expeditions every year, but O'Fahey thinks this may be a bit of an exaggeration. The permission specified the route to follow and the tribe to raid. The expedition was organized as a prototype of the sultanate, since it would function outside the boundaries and authority of the state. The leader assumed the attributes and powers of the sultan and gave his close companions titles associated with the court; in turn, they acted out their assigned roles toward him. A raid could last three months or more. All slaves given as presents by tribal chiefs or captured without resistance became the property of the leader. Those captured through any kind of struggle were distributed at intervals in a "levy" held in a thorn enclosure erected for the purpose. If the leader died, all slaves went to the real sultan in Dar Fur, so the "courtiers" had reason to keep their "sultan" alive. The leader kept between a third and half of the capture, depending on his rank and investment. The merchants accompanying the expedition were paid after each "levy." Slaves brought north were classified as carefully as other valuable merchandise such as ivory or ostrich feathers, with an elaborate terminology devised for the classifications. Besides the royally sanctioned expeditions that hunted slaves in droves, there were also opportunistic hunters, usually nomads, who looked to capture a stray individual and use him or her to herd or to farm and produce food as insurance against periodic scarcity.[79]

The relations between hunter and prey tended to stabilize over time, with particular tribes agreeing to pay a fixed number of slaves as tribute every year, "so that from the perspective of notables, slave-raiding was a form of tax-farming." Though each expedition moved the frontiers of the sultanate farther south, the limit of this southward progression was set by the ability of horses to penetrate the terrain, leaving slave traders to turn to hand-to-hand combat without any added advantage. That limit was breached only in the mid-nineteenth century when rifle-using trading companies from outside Sudan replaced local horse-mounted expeditions.

The primary acquisition of slaves was carried out by local merchants or chiefs who fought one another and then exchanged their captives for products acquired through long-distance trade. Abu Salih, an Armenian thirteenth-century writer, states that slaves and cattle were bartered for manufactured goods near Upper Maqs, where the Lord of the Mountain was said to reside. Whereas exported slaves came mainly, but not exclusively, from southern tribes, slave raiders were from three groups: the Fur trading parties sent by the sultan southward to hunt for slaves, the Baggara tribes of southern Dar Fur, and the Fulani immigrants. Their captives were then sold to slave traders. The historical traditions of several of the tribes that now live in the western Bahr al-Ghazal contain accounts of migrations from southern Dar Fur as a result of slave-raiding by the Fur and Baggara.[80]

This is where the violent nature of both the Sultanate of Dar Fur and the kingdom of Funj was most apparent. The state reproduced itself by dispatching its armies to the south, obtaining slaves and other forms of plunder, and exporting them northward to Egypt and the Mediterranean. At the heart of this political regime were slave soldiers, traders, and royal power.[81] In the final analysis, extreme violence was part of the history of Darfur for more than three centuries, and this history cannot be tagged as either "Arab" or "non-Arab," for no such distinction divided slaves from their captors. The real division was between subjects of the sultan, who could not be enslaved, and those who lived in tributaries to the south, who could be. It was, in the main, the history of state formation, at first indigenous and then colonial, and it also came to mark movements that resisted state oppression.

It was the collapse of the royal monopoly over the slave trade that led to the collapse of the sultanate, which came when the demand for slaves skyrocketed in the late eighteenth century with the incorporation of the region into the larger slave plantation economy. The horse-riding slavers of Dar Fur were suddenly faced with a new and superior force, the rifle-based trading companies that advanced by way of a network of armed camps in the region. In the end, they were faced with the ruthless ability of a local agent of the trading companies, al-Zubayr Rahma al-Mansur, whose strength was based on control over communications. When al-Zubayr moved north in 1874 to conquer the sultanate, he brought with him some seven thousand of his *bazinqirs,* or slave troops; broke the Baggara and, through them, the tenuous Keira hold on southern Dar Fur and the northern Bahr al-Ghazal; and ultimately destroyed successive armies sent south by Sultan Ibrahim Qarad.[82] Thus came to an end, after two and half centuries, the independent Sultanate of Dar Fur.

The Mahdiyya

A half century before the fall of the Sultanate of Dar Fur came the collapse of the kingdom of Funj. A Turco-Egyptian force occupied large sections of northern Sudan at the end of the second decade of the nineteenth century, thereby colonizing it for the first time in its known history. The immediate consequence of the occupation was to end the independence of the kingdom of Funj and to strip the Sultanate of Dar Fur of the entire territory of Kordofan.

More recent assessments suggest that the impact of the *Turkiyya*—as the Sudanese call the period of Turco-Egyptian rule—was not as uniformly grim as was painted by rival imperial powers.[83] The downside of the Turkiyya came from the fact that, even though the slave trade was abolished, the demand for slaves was rising steeply, both locally and regionally. Turkish tax collectors demanded payment in coin or slaves; the effect was to drive land into the market and accelerate its private ownership.[84] Northern Sudanese, Turco-Egyptian, and European traders moved the frontiers of slavery farther south. For the first time in known history, the northern and southern portions of contemporary Sudan were forced to interact within a single polity. The Turkiyya established the boundaries of what would become the contemporary state of Sudan—with the notable exception of Kordofan and Beja country. The Turkiyya also accelerated the process of urbanization and detribalization. The city of Khartoum was established during the Turkiyya. By the time of British colonization at the end of the nineteenth century, the twin cities of Khartoum and Omdurman stood in sharp contrast, the former a colonial implant, the latter a product of native modernity. Omdurman had become a cosmopolitan city. A former British governor of the provinces of Berber and Halfa in the Sudan contrasted the "European" city of Khartoum and the "African" city of Omdurman in the early 1900s:

> Omdurman was as African as Khartoum was European. . . . Nowhere except perhaps in Mecca is so large a number of different races congregated in so small a space as in Omdurman. Indians, Armenians, Turks, Greeks, Syrians, Persians and strangers from the Middle East; Europeans from many countries; Fallata and other pilgrims from the West Coast of Africa; fuzzy-wuzzies, Arabs, Nilotics, Nubas, Negroes, Burberines, and all the medley of races and tribesmen that compose the modern Sudan are to be seen in the crowded streets.[85]

Here was a multilingual, multiethnic *mela*.

With its emphasis on state building, the Turkiyya initiated a brutal system of exploitative taxation. The brutality either destroyed or subordinated the old ruling elites, leaving the *fuqara* (holy men) and their *tariqas* (religious brotherhoods) as the only surviving institutions to which the Sudanese could turn at a time of dire need. This development terminated in a revolt led by a holy man, born Muhammad Ahmad but known to history as al-Mahdī, the leader of the popular messianic revolt against the Turkiyya. The idea of a *jihad,* a religiously inspired militant struggle against foreign oppression, led by a *Mahdi,* or messiah, was more of an import from West Africa than a local idea. It had come in the wake of West African migrants, who for centuries had been moving into western Sudan, particularly Dar Fur, at first as part of the trail of pilgrims heading east to Mecca, later as followers of the *fuqara* attracted to Dar Fur by its sultans. Talk of the imminent coming of the Mahdi was rife in West Africa toward the end of the nineteenth century and had spread eastward along the pilgrim route. A fresh wave of West African immigrants into Dar Fur followed popular speculation that the promised Mahdi would appear in the eastern part of Sudan with the close of the Islamic millennium.[86]

The brutality of the Turkiyya sparked a widespread resistance over northern and western Sudan. Among those claiming to be the promised

messiah was Muhammad Ahmad ibn Abd Allah, whose parents had
come to central Sudan from the area of Dongola in the north. In 1881,
Muhammad Ahmad ibn Abd Allah sent letters from the island of Aba in
the White Nile claiming to be the "expected Mahdi." Spurned by riverine
sophisticates, the Mahdi turned to western Sudan for support. In Kordofan, he met a mendicant of West African ancestry, Abdullahi Mohamed
Torshien, known as al-Ta'aishi because his family had settled among the
Ta'aisha Arabs of Dar Fur. Together, they migrated westward to the
heartland of Dar Fur and Kordofan, determined to liberate the land
from foreign usurpers, both Muslims and non-Muslims, and thereby
restore justice. The Mahdi's rallying cry was simple: For justice to
exist, Islam must be purified. Islam provided the ideology that rallied
the multiplicity of ethnic groups and the glue to bind a transethnic
movement.[87]

The resistance evoked radically different responses, immediately from
the population at large and in time from historians. These responses
focused on contradictory aspects of the movement, highlighting its
combination of reactionary social practices and progressive political
objectives. As a political enterprise, the Mahdiyya was at once emancipa-
tory and repressive. On the positive side, the Mahdiyya forged a broad
alliance of peoples across the entire span of northern Sudan; indeed, it
was the first time in history that the peoples of the west (Darfur and
Kordofan) and those of the Nile had come together to form a single
political movement. More than any other social movement, it is the
Mahdiyya that forged the basis of a common northern Sudanese political identity. If not for the Mahdiyya, we would speak of western Sudan
and the Nile as two separate political entities, much the same way as we
do of north and south Sudan.

To appreciate the significance of the Mahdi's achievement, one needs
to put the Mahdiyya in the context of anticolonial revolts in late-
nineteenth- and early-twentieth-century Africa. The problem that confronted resistance to empire in that period was that of unity, how to
weld together a transethnic movement to confront the transnational
forces of the empire. Writing of the leaders of the Shona revolt in
Rhodesia, Terence Ranger noted that "the greatest political problem of
pre-colonial Africa" was "the problem of scale." John Iliffe confirmed the
observation when he wrote of the organization of the Maji Maji rebel-

lion in Tanganyika in similar terms, that "it was necessary to enlarge the scale, both of resistance and of religious allegiance." According to Iliffe, "The central figure in such an enlargement was the prophet, proclaiming a new religious order to supersede the old, a new loyalty to transcend old loyalties of tribe and kinship." In German-controlled Tanganyika, just as in many an anticolonial movement in early-twentieth-century East and Central Africa, the prophet offered holy water (*maji*) both as a bond between those who accepted it and as immunity against the white man's firepower. The *maji* united peoples with no known prior unity in a common rebellion. German observers were terrified by the Maji Maji, for they glimpsed in it signs of an effective political transformation.[88]

Islam provided the ideological glue for a similar, even greater, transnational revival in nineteenth-century Saharan Africa. Not one but two great Islamic reform movements promised to sweep away foreign despotic rule from the region and, with it, the corrupted form of Islam patronized by colonial rulers. Both movements were led by a charismatic reformer: al-Sanusi (Sayyid Muhammad ibn Ali al-Sanusi al-Khattabi al-Idrisi al-Hasani) in Libya and al-Mahdī (Muhammad Ahmad ibn Abd Allah) in Sudan.[89]

The Mahdiyya was arguably the most impressive of the late-nineteenth- and early-twentieth-century anti-imperialist movements, for it united disparate peoples on a scale far wider than any movement the empire had confronted in the region. When the Mahdi's forces completed a countrywide uprising against British and Turco-Egyptian forces in Sudan, and capped their victory with the killing of General Charles G. Gordon, the British governor-general of the country, on January 26, 1885, shock waves reverberated across England, Europe, Turkey, and other centers of power in the nineteenth-century world. The London *Times* of February 6, 1885, noted: "The shock caused by the news of the fall of Khartoum has no parallel in the experience of the present generation." A British government publication, *The Daily News,* agreed: "Seldom in the memory of living man has news been received of such a disaster in England."[90] Fourteen years later, the young Winston Churchill paid his own grudging tribute to the Mahdi:

> There are many Christians who reverence the faith of Islam
> and yet regard the Mahdi merely as a commonplace religious

imposter whom force of circumstances elevated to notoriety. In a certain sense, this may be true. But I know not how a genuine may be distinguished from a spurious Prophet, except by the measure of his success. The triumphs of the Mahdi were in his lifetime far greater than those of the founder of the Mohammedan faith; and the chief difference between orthodox Mohammedanism and Mahdism was that the original impulse was opposed only by decaying systems of government and society and the recent movement only came in contact with civilization and the machinery of science. Recognizing this, I do not share the popular opinion, and I believe that if in future years prosperity should come to the peoples of the Upper Nile, and learning and happiness follow in its train, then the first Arab historian who shall investigate the early annals of that new nation will not forget, foremost among the heroes of his race, to write the name of Mohammed Ahmed.[91]

But this anti-imperialist movement also unleashed a brutal violence against those who chose to remain outside its ranks, whether they opposed it or remained indifferent to it. The brutality of the violence evoked comparisons with the slave raids that had for centuries bloodied the southern frontiers of the Sultanates of Funj and Dar Fur. It attested to the legacy of political violence in the regional history of these polities. The same violence unleashed by pre-Mahdiyya states over the centuries in the course of organized slave raids now propelled a messianic anti-imperialist movement. The Mahdi built a transethnic movement but also divided it in new ways, both by suppressing all other expressions of Islam in the north and by invigorating the slave trade in the south. This violence also came to characterize internal relations within the Mahdiyya, as with forced population transfers from western Sudan to Omdurman in the Nile Valley.

In western Sudan, in particular in Dar Fur, the Mahdiyya swept through both Arab and non-Arab groups, the former led by the Baggara of the south and the latter by the Fur of Jebel Marra, for both wanted to be rid of the hated Turkiyya and the Ja'ali merchants from the Nile who had followed the Turkiyya. A large portion of the Mahdist armies derived from the Baggara of Dar Fur. The Baggara constituted most of the Ansar, the followers of the Mahdi who, on November 5, 1883, annihilated ten thousand Egyptian troops in the famous battle at Shaykan. The Mahdi's second-in-command, Abdallah Khalifa, in fact came from Ta'aishi West African immigrants.

The first phase of the Mahdist movement was that of revolt, from 1882 to 1885, when the hated Anglo-Turkish enemy was defeated. Mahdist forces entered and took Khartoum in January 1885. The Mahdi died of disease on the morrow of victory, and for most of its existence, the Mahdist state in Omdurman was ruled by the Khalifa and his Ta'aishi kinsmen. The Mahdist state lasted from 1885 to 1898. Ever since, the western provinces of Sudan, Darfur and Kordofan, have been the fortresses of Mahdism and of the Ansar, the Sufi brotherhood that came out of it.[92] The Ansar are not an ordinary Sufi brotherhood. The Mahdi was a "post-Sufi" who claimed that the time of the Sufi orders had come to an end (in the messianic sense) and that there was now only one order, the order of Muhammad, which he represented. The Ansar combined this explicitly anti-Sufi position alongside Sufi accoutrements (the organizational structure, litanies, et cetera.).[93] Not only was the Mahdiyya a Darfuri enterprise in important respects, but the Baggara and other nomadic tribes, not significant before the Mahdiyya, loomed as a powerful presence in Darfur after the Mahdiyya.[94]

The greatest social effect of the Mahdiyya was its all-around assault on chiefly power: If popular response to the call for jihad challenged chiefly power from below, the highly centralized Mahdist state broke it from above. The Mahdiyya deeply disrupted tribal life in Sudan. The Khalifa's rule was extremely centralized and autocratic, and he saw any power wielded by tribal sheikhs as a threat to his own supreme authority. For thirteen years, the main axiom of the Khalifa's policy was to break the power of any tribal sheikh who might possibly oppose his authority. The Mahdiya was extremely hostile to tribal organization along political or administrative lines. Any attempt at tribal autonomy was ruthlessly suppressed. When the Khalifa found that the Kababish "were not sufficiently submissive," he gave instructions to Ibrahim Adlan, one of his generals, to confiscate everything they had. Their leadership suppressed, and money and flocks confiscated, the Kababish quickly submitted, practically ceasing to exist as a people. The Beja chiefs in eastern Sudan fared no better. None were spared, not even the chiefs of the Baggara Arabs in the south of Darfur.[95]

Following the death of the Mahdi, there emerged a schism in the Mahdist leadership, between those from the Nile and those from the western provinces of Darfur and Kordofan. To strengthen his hand, the Khalifa responded with a policy of forced migration of the Baggara from their homeland in Darfur to Omdurman. It was a call that the Baggara chiefs were reluctant to heed, despite threats and promises designed to get them to do so. By 1888, however, the great migrations of the Baggara started under the threat of destruction and dispersion by the military power of the Khalifa. By the early months of 1889, their first contingents reached Omdurman. In subsequent years, the Khalifa demanded a constant supply of men for his army, most of all to conduct campaigns against the Abyssinians, the Italians, and the Egyptians. These were recruited from all tribes, with severe punishment for those who refused to serve. There was widespread movement among groups and much dislocation. This policy, which turned nomads into a standing army, coincided with the devastating famine and epidemic of 1889–90. These two periods—the Turkiyya and the Mahdiyya—came to be known as *umm kwakiyya,* "years of misery, burning, and banditry."[96] It is estimated that nearly a third of the population of northern Sudan perished as a result of political violence and famine and disease during the eighteen years of the Mahdiyya.

Against this background, relations between the Mahdiyya and its main base of support in Darfur, the Baggara and the Fur, took a downturn. From 1885 to 1888, there was a series of revolts against Mahdist rule in Darfur, first by the Rizeigat Baggara, the cattle nomads of the south, and then by the Fur. There was also opposition to the Mahdists led by a *faqi* (holy man) from Dar Tama on the western frontier.

It is in this context, of famine and ferment and death and disease, that British forces led by General H. H. Kitchener entered Sudan. Kitchener's objective was twofold. The immediate goal was destruction of the Mahdist state, which stood in the way of European colonial expansion, as did Bunyoro-Kitara and Buganda in eastern Africa and the Sokoto caliphate in the west. No less apparent was a second objective, belied by the haste with which Kitchener rushed to meet the French mission that, led by Captain Jean-Baptiste Marchand, was heading up the Congo and the Nile through the Bahr al-Ghazal. For the British, it was imperative that the victory against the Mahdiyya in the middle Nile be joined to an accommodation that would keep the French out of the upper Nile. Nearly two decades later, in 1913, Harold MacMichael, then in the Sudan Political Service, reminisced in a speech before the Royal Empire Society: "By 1896 Belgians and French were advancing. . . . The chief danger came from the French who by the time of Omdurman had reached Fashoda. Kitchener had at once to hurry south, meet them, and point out that their action constituted 'a direct violation of the rights of Egypt and Great Britain.' It was only after a period of very acute tension that the French withdrew and renounced their claims in the Nile Valley."[97] The meeting between the two commanders took place at Fashoda, a place of little significance but subsequently etched in the annals of interimperialist rivalries that propelled the late-nineteenth-century scramble for Africa.[98]

Kitchener was credited with a dual accomplishment: defeating the Mahdist state and keeping the French out of the upper Nile. But Kitchener's real moment of triumph was not at Fashoda but at Omdurman, to which he returned from Fashoda. The famed British sense of justice had left him. Consumed by vengeance, he desecrated the tomb of the Mahdi, ordering the remains to be dug up from the bowels of the earth, the head severed from the body, and the body thrown into the Nile so it would never be recovered. Kitchener kept the head as a trophy, fashioning it into an inkpot for his writing table. It was testimony that, in death as in life, the Mahdi held Kitchener's gaze.

Given the duration and depth of its impact on society, the Mahdiyya must be regarded as a revolutionary movement. When revolution came to Darfur, it was not Spartacist but Sufi. The soldier-slaves in Darfur were always armed, and they constituted the bulk of the sultan's army. Slavery was a counterweight to tribal identity and a building block of state formation. But the armed slaves of Darfur did not provide its revolutionaries. Churchill understood this better than any colonial official. It is Sufism that heralded an egalitarian rebellion against authority. The center of that revolution was Darfur, from which it spread to Kordofan and then the north. Even the Dinka of the south thought the spirit of the deity Deng had caught the Mahdi. And then came the counterrevolution, led and organized by the British. The center of the counterrevolution was also Darfur. And the core of the counterrevolutionary agenda was to reorganize state and society—by *retribalizing* them. The Sultanate of Dar Fur had worked to create a kind of detribalization through a combination of influences ranging across the land (*hakura*), the administration (*magdume*), and belief (Islam) systems. The colonial order would proceed to reverse these developments with all the resources it could muster.

5

A Colonial Map of Race and Tribe:
Making Settlers and Natives

WRITINGS ON COLONIALISM in Africa have tended to emphasize the economic side of the process, pointing out that the object of colonialism was to reorganize production in the colonies to serve the empire's needs. Surveying the colonial landscape on the eve of independence, the Guyanese political economist Clive Thomas commented: "We do not produce what we consume, and do not consume what we produce." From this perspective, the prime example of colonial policy in Sudan was the creation of the Gezira project to produce long-staple cotton in the fertile lands between the Blue and the White Nile in order to meet the needs of the British textile industry at a time when it was faced with "a cotton famine." Though perceptive, this literature often downplayed the political impact of modern empires.[1]

The political objective was to reorganize colonized populations around narrower identities. Sometimes, this involved a benign acknowledgment of existing identities, but at other times, it involved a wholesale reidentification of peoples. Never entirely arbitrary, the reidentification often involved exalting older, narrower identities as historically legitimate. At the heart of the political objective was a compact with fading elites: propping them up as "traditional" in return for recognition of colonial tutelage as "legitimate."

If the Romans were by and large content to tap a minority as citizens and rule the rest as they found them, the British were not.[2] More than anything else, British colonial governance was about identity formation. The technology of colonial rule revolved around three very modern techniques: gathering census data, writing histories, and making laws. This way, colonial power endeavored to shape the totality of colonial time: the present (census), the past (history), and the future (law). The colonial political objective involved more than just redefining the relationship between colonial power and the colonial subject; it involved reshaping the very self-consciousness of the colonized, how they thought of themselves, their self-identity. The Romans took their subjects' self-consciousness as a given; they played politics as a game of set pieces. In contrast, British indirect rule—which set the gold standard for modern empires—reshaped the self-identity of the colonized through forms of law and administration. It can be said of the British empire that it took the old Roman strategy of "divide and rule" a step further: "re-identify and rule."

Modern colonialism usually began with a comprehensive assessment of the prize that had been won. When possible, a variety of surveys were carried out—geological, ecological, economic, and so on—to assess the colony's potential and decide how best to tap it. The most important survey involved the census. The key to mapping the human population was deciding on the categories around which census data would be gathered. Once the categories had been agreed upon, the practice was to give them a time-honored credibility—naturalize them, as social scientists say—by also making them the starting point for the production of the past (through writing history) and the making of the future (through the force of laws). In Sudan, British colonial administrators mapped the local population through two master categories: race and tribe.

One administrator more than any other played a crucial role in the production of knowledge about Sudan. Harold MacMichael spent a total of thirty years—from 1905 to 1934—in the Sudan Political Service. Starting out in Kordofan (1905–12) and Blue Nile (1912–13), he moved on to being a senior inspector in Khartoum (1913–16), from where he was attached as a political officer, first to the Red Sea Patrol (1915) and then to the Darfur Expeditionary Force (1916) in El Fasher. He went on to become the subgovernor of Darfur (1917–18) and ultimately assistant civil secretary (1919–25) and civil secretary (1925–34) of the Sudan government in Khartoum. After his retirement in 1934, Sir Harold went on to join the Foreign Service, becoming the governor and commander in chief of Tanganyika (1934–38) and then high commissioner and commander in chief, Palestine, and high commissioner, Transjordan (1938–44), among other high-level posts. MacMichael's importance in the colonial undertaking in Sudan cannot be overstated: He devised the categories that became central both to the collection of census data and to the writing of history.

Organizing Census Data

In 1922, Harold MacMichael wrote the founding text for the colonial history of Sudan, the two-volume *History of the Arabs in the Sudan.* Seven years later, he distributed a paper titled "Tribes of the Sudan."[3] Meant "to provide a frame for the purpose of the Population Census," it announced that the census would focus on gathering "tribal information" in order to understand "tribal differences." MacMichael went on to propose that the census be carried out around three main classifications: "It is the intention that the Census enumeration should be done by tribes. . . . Each tribe has three coding numbers; the first relating to 'race,' the second to the 'group' and the third to the tribe within the group."[4]

The profoundly political nature of the census is clear from the method used to gather the data. The collection of census data began with the category *tribe:* Every person was asked to identify his or her "tribe," and the answer was recorded as given, with no questions asked. What happened next, though, was beyond the reach of the person interviewed: The census authority classified the tribe within two other categories: "groups of tribes" and "races."[5]

Groups of tribes are language-based cultural groups (what anthropologists call "ethnic groups"). While being crafted from this raw material, the tribe is an administrative division officially demarcated for purposes of colonial governance. When the census was first organized, the section on "background and method" spoke of 450 "tribes," but when it was finally conducted in 1954–55, the census recorded "about 570 tribes in Sudan," classified into 57 "groups of tribes." As the number of administrative divisions increased, so did the number of tribes. To ask the resident of a place his or her tribe was to ask the name of his or her "native authority."

This is why "tribe" has a double meaning: cultural and administrative. It is crafted from the actual cultural raw material found by the colonial state, but it is limited to the administrative units established by the colonial state. Tribe was the group identity that the colonial state recognized in law and administered in practice: It is the tribe that had representation in the colonial state, and it is as a tribe that the population could legitimately organize to make demands upon the colonial state. The tribe informed both colonial policy and how the colonized responded to it. The real difference in how the colonial state and the colonial scholar each classified the population lay in the following: If the anthropologist was preoccupied with considerations of knowledge, seeking to distinguish among different cultural communities, the colonial state sought to discover in this knowledge a suitable basis for administration and governance. For the colonial state, then, *tribe* was as much an administrative category as a cultural identity.

Whereas the census could shape group reality and its perception, it could not just freeze it. Changes continued under the radar, in spite of the census, sometimes subverting it. Identity remained fluid, especially at the individual level. As the social anthropologist Gunnar Haaland discovered during his research in Darfur, "Fur" could become "Arab," and "Arab" could become "Fur." Haaland began his research with the assumption that ethnic identities were fixed and permanent, so that a person's ethnic identity determined his or her occupational "specialization":[6] "My first impression during fieldwork was that the Fur, Masalit and Daju were identified with grain cultivation and sedentary village life," whereas "the Fulani and Baggara ideologies show preferences for pastoralism." But then he came across "cattle camps whose members came from Fur, Masalit and Daju villages." Fieldwork showed that many transit processes were at work: Not only were some peasants becoming nomads ("nomadisation"), but some nomads were also becoming cultivators ("peasantisation"). Furthermore, the transitions were not just occupational; they were also ethnic. Not only could Fur become Zaghawa (non-Arab) or Baggara (Arab), but a Zaghawa or Baggara person could also become Fur.

This process is evident in a few examples from Haaland's research in

Dar Furnung. The first is that of a Fur who becomes a Zaghawa nomad. When a Fur farmer invests in cattle, Haaland points out, his herd may grow to the point where its needs outweigh the needs of his crops and determine his decisions. At this point, "it might be preferable for a herd-owner to leave his village and move in the Zaghawa [that is, nomadic] area the whole year." A move from one group to another is politically risky, requiring the Fur farmer to establish relations with "groups that he can trust for support." One way to do this would be to marry a Zaghawa girl: "The occurrence of such marriage is widely recognized; thus the population just north of Dar Furnung is called Fur a-Merita by the Fur and Kora-Berri by the Zaghawa, both terms meaning Fur-Zaghawa, and referring to inter-marriage and to the mixed origin of the population there." But this mixed transitional group is already identified as Zaghawa in ethnic terms, for the behavior of its members is judged and sanctioned according to the standards of Zaghawa culture. It is "political circumstances," says Haaland, that "induce them to change ethnic identity by inclusion in a Zaghawa local community."

Fur also do become Baggara (Arab). In the lower wadi area, where Fur rub shoulders with Baggara Arabs, "grain cultivation and cattle husbandry can hardly be combined," for "the change from one subsistence activity to the other is . . . drastic." In these circumstances, "the [Fur] nomadic novice joins some other nomadised Fur in a camp community. The style of life associated with cultivation is categorized as Fur, the pastoral way of life as Baggara. A Fur is thus categorized by others as Baggari the day he leaves the village and migrates with his cattle." At the same time, "his performance in various roles is evaluated with reference to the standards of Baggara culture." Take the example of milking: "Among the Fur, milking is codified as female work and it is considered shameful (*ora*) for men to perform this task. In the camps of the lower wadis, however, both men and women milk, as do the Baggara." The final act in becoming "Baggara," as we have already seen, is for the former Fur to acquire an authentic Baggara genealogy, thus becoming "Arab."

There is nothing unique about the fluidity of ethnic relations in Darfur. One is reminded of relations between Hutu cultivators and Tutsi pastoralists in precolonial Rwanda.[7] The rare Hutu who accumulated cows could go through a process involving intermarriage, its end result being that he and his family would acquire a Tutsi status. There was a formal name for this transition: *kwihutura,* meaning "shedding Hutuness." Conversely, an impoverished Tutsi, one without cattle, would go through an opposite process, *gukupira,* taking on a Hutu identity. Both social processes occurred over generations. Though their statistical significance was nominal, their social, political, and ideological significance could not be overstated. Whereas the transition between occupational and ethnic categories affected a tiny minority, the impact on the vast majority who remained Fur or Zaghawa or Baggara was that their culture absorbed numerous elements of what had previously been considered a different culture.

The census authorities also determined the "race" of each tribe. Crucially, they decided that "Arab" and "Negroid" were two "races," even if they spoke the same language. "Race," unlike "tribe," had less of a cultural and more of a political meaning. It is worth noting that "Arab" defined as a language group was almost twice as large as "Arab" defined as a racial group. This could only be because a person's race was distinguished from his or her language group. For example, the ninth report of the 1953 census recorded that Arabic was the "language spoken at home" by 51.4 percent of the Sudanese population and 54.6 percent of the population of Darfur. But when it came to race, the census recorded only 38.9 percent of the Sudanese population, and 28.2 percent of the Darfuri population, as "Arabs." Conversely, it noted that "Darfurian" was the "language spoken at home" by 41.7 percent of the population in Darfur and "West African" by 2.5 percent—that is, a total of 44.2 percent of the population of Darfur. Yet when it came to recording population by "race," the census classified 65.3 percent of the Darfuri population (57.1 percent "tribes of Darfur" and 8.2 percent French Equatorial tribes and Nigerian tribes) as a "race" it called "Other Negroid 'Westerners' " (a designation changed to "Westerners" in the ninth report).

Race was wholly a political construction for political purposes. It was the master category that distinguished between native and settler, the former considered indigenous and the latter foreign. The marker of a settler race was that it was not tied to locality: As we have seen, Arab tribes of Darfur were counted as "Arabs," not as "Westerners." In contrast, all non-Arab residents of Darfur (including "French Equatorials" and "Nigerians") were counted as "Other Negroid 'Westerners.' " If Arab was the single settler "race," the census listed four native "races": two Negro "races," then the Hamitic and the Nilotic "races." It is worth noting that unlike the Arab race, which was defined in the singular, the two Negro races were distinguished by locality: Thus, "Negros" were defined as a race separate from "Other Negroid 'Westerners.' "[8]

By the ninth report of the census, the authorities decided to replace the term *race* with the term *people*. A revealing explanatory note followed: "As explained in the supplement to interim reports, 'race' does not mean more than group of 'tribal groups' and it has no relation to the definition of 'race' as understood by anthropologists. However, owing to a number of objections after the term appeared in the interim reports, it was replaced by 'people.' This term appeared in the final report tables."[9] There was no explanation of what *race* or *people* was supposed to mean, of what objections had been raised to the use of the term *race*, nor why these were considered weighty enough to alter this terminology midcensus. One can only speculate about these matters given that the publication of the census was timed to coincide with the independence of Sudan in 1956. Even if the language was changed, the damage was done—namely, the distinction between settlers and natives, written into official practices, from administration to law to history-writing.

Neither the categories employed in the census nor the classification of the population was benign. As we shall see, the census had teeth: "Native" tribes would be treated preferentially, and nonnative tribes would be discriminated against. The main preference was with regard to questions of access to land and participation in governance, both of which were said to be defined on a "customary" basis—so that only members of a tribe said to be native to a place would have the customary right to a tribal homeland (*dar*) and to participate in native (local) administration. If the ambition of the law was to give a future to the categories embedded in the census, that of history-writing was to make these categories come alive in flesh-and-blood terms. Through a combined project—stretching from lawmaking to history-writing—the colonial power would pass off modern discrimination between tribes as a "customary" practice.

The census summed up the counterrevolutionary effort. To begin with, it split the social base of the Mahdiyya into settlers and natives. It

then turned land rights and participation in local governance into a prerogative of native tribes in each locality, turning tribe from a benign
administrative identity into a basis for discriminating against one group
of colonized and in favor of another. Thus, the census developed teeth.

Colonialism: Retribalizing Darfur

British administrative policy in the colony of Sudan was shaped by one
supreme objective: to remove every trace of Mahdist influence from the
country by attacking the very basis of its transethnic mobilization. For
the first time in the history of Sudan, the Mahdiyya had created a state
that joined riverine Sudan with the west—lands that had hitherto been
organized as two separate sultanates, Funj and Dar Fur. The state created
by the Mahdiyya (1885–98) had zealously continued the centralizing
political plan of the past few centuries, which had begun with the Keira
and Funj Sultanates. It is against this historical background that British
colonialism championed a sharp reversal in policy, one of retribalization, heralding "tribe" as the authentic political identity of Africans as
opposed to all other wider translocal identities. The first step in this
strategy was the formal restoration of the kingdom of Dar Fur, except
this time as a Fur sultanate.

When the Mahdiyya fell in 1898, the objective of the new Anglo-
Egyptian power was to excise the cancer of Mahdism—which it saw as a
transethnic malady—from Sudanese society by restoring chiefly power
and tribal identity. This overall perspective guided British colonial policy in Darfur, from the 1898 restoration of the sultanate as an ostensibly
sovereign state but in reality a British dependency to its formal incorporation into Anglo-Egyptian Sudan in 1916.[10] If Ali Dinar revived the
power of the Fur, it was as clients of the new British masters on the
Nile.[11] Even though the name of the state was the same as that of the historic sultanate, Dar Fur, the restored kingdom led by Ali Dinar was an
ethnic—Fur—affair, in contrast to the transethnic Keira Sultanate.

Ali Dinar defined his mission as one of restoring both the external
independence of Darfur and its internal balance against a background
of Mahdist mobilization, which had come to lean on the mobility of
nomadic groups to replenish its military might, in the process both
changing the balance between settled groups and nomads in favor of the

latter and undercutting the authority of tribal leaders. When Ali Dinar was restored to kingship in 1898, he noted that the cattle nomads of the south had tried to use the rule of the Mahdiyya to get even with settled Fur peasants, and so he drove the nomads back from settled areas.[12]

After Britain assumed direct control over Darfur, broke up native society into different ethnicities, and "tribalized" each ethnicity by bringing it under the absolute authority of one or more British-sanctioned "native authorities," it finally balanced the whole by playing one off against the others. The policy went by the names "native admin-istration" and "indirect rule." The policy debate within the colonial administration and among its policy makers focused on how best to realize these objectives in a changing context. Several factors shaped the course of the debate: the inclinations and attributes of those who led the colonial administration over the course of time; an ongoing discussion of colonial policy with Egypt, formally a partner in the colonial enter-prise following the 1899 Condominium Agreement regarding Sudan; and the fear of nationalist rebellion shared by both. This fear more than any other dictated the imperatives of colonial policy and defined the boundaries within which the policy debate unfolded. This is why a deci-sive change in policy was more a reaction to native responses to colonial power than an effect of shifting idiosyncrasies of policy makers.[13] Below, I shall try to explain key shifts in colonial policy by relating them to changing native responses.

There were three stages in the evolution of colonial policy. In the first stage, the ruling power was a *military autocracy* whose immediate aim was to establish British power in the new colony. The second phase saw the establishment of *civilian indirect rule,* regarded as necessary to con-solidating colonial power in the face of native resistance. The third phase was that of *colonial reform,* born of the recognition that native resistance could not be extinguished by force but would have to be co-opted through strategy.

The establishment of a military autocracy followed the conquest of Sudan under H. H. Kitchener. The period of pacification coincided with the governor-generalship of General Reginald Wingate, from 1899 to 1916. Politically and administratively, this was a period in which martial law was exercised through direct control from the center. Economically, the period was identified with bold initiatives that led to the building of an economic and administrative infrastructure, from establishing experimental long-staple cotton plantations to constructing a health and education infrastructure (including Gordon College, which, despite its name, was only a primary school for several years after its founding). The British administrative autocrat who directed these changes combined the roles of judge, administrator, chief surveyor, inspector of education, chief of police, and military ruler all in one. In the words of the Sudanese scholar Abd al-Rahim, this was "an autocracy on military lines, for civil purposes."[14]

The military autocracy faced a crisis because of political resistance. The target of British political policy was the nascent political forces organized around Sufi orders, in particular the Ansar, born of the Mahdiyya. Driven by the realization that only the *tariqas* had the potential to unite town with country, and one ethnic group with another, and thereby to challenge colonial rule through a widespread popular mobilization, the British sought to distinguish between "good" and "bad" *tariqas,* so as to wean the former and isolate the latter. The starting point of this policy was the recognition that whereas the Mahdiyya had rallied support in the west and center of northern Sudan, the north had followed the Khatmiyya *tariqa* to acquiesce in continued Ottoman rule. With the defeat of the Mahdists in 1898, the British turned to woo the "quietist" Khatmiyya brotherhood and to build the orthodox *ulama* as a counterweight to Sufi orders.[15] So in 1900, Lord Cromer arranged for a decoration to be awarded to Sheikh Mirghani, whom he described as "head of the leading religious sect in the Soudan [who] possesses great political influence." The *ulama,* in contrast, were very much created by the *Turkiyya* and the British, who set up colleges for the training of *ulama* (learned scholars of Islamic law). The object was to create a Sunni orthodoxy to counter Sufi orders. Since the *ulama,* unlike the Sufi heads of brotherhoods, made no claim to *baraka* and had no central organization, the government set up a Board of Ulama in the Omdurman mosque with the express purpose of advising it on religious affairs.[16] When they decided to send a Sudanese delegation to England to congratulate the king on winning the First World War, the authorities put together an even broader alliance comprising three (rather than two) conservative forces: the three *sayeds* (an honorific title that is also a claim to being a descendant of the Prophet) at the head of the three most important Sufi *tariqas*, three representatives of the *ulama*, and four tribal leaders who had fought for the British against the Mahdi.[17]

Soon the British had reason to doubt whether the alliance would be able to ensure stability for the colonial order. A succession of local revolts broke out when self-styled "Nebi Eisas" (Prophet Jesus) appeared and proclaimed that Prophet Jesus would descend from heaven in the aftermath of the defeat of the Mahdi and lead the Ansar faithful against the anti-Christ, with whom the British were identified, and so usher in the Muslim millennium. Such outbreaks occurred in a wide range of locations, from Kordofan (1902) to Sinnar Province (1904), Berber Province (1910), and the Nuba mountains (1915).[18] The British were even concerned whether the policy of playing off different *tariqas* against one another would work in the long run. If the Mahdists had been staunch opponents of Anglo-Egyptian rule, the Khatmiyya brotherhood had strong pro-Egyptian sympathies. With the upsurge of national agitation in Egypt, first in 1918 and then in 1924, these sympathies took on an anticolonial coloring. When nationalist sentiment found its way into the army and emerged into the open with the 1924 White Flag Rebellion, there was great concern among colonial policy makers.

Early nationalist activities in the 1920s took the form of a secret organization called Society for the Sudanese Union, the aim of which was "the liberation of the Sudan from British imperialism," a liberation that was to be achieved "with the support of Egypt."[19] The members of the union were mainly government officials and students in higher levels of education. Gordon College, for example, had 205 Sudanese students in 1906. Of these, 138 were designated as "Arabs" and 67 as "Black," all were settled in the north, and most were receptive to nationalist agitation.[20] Another group of nationalists acted in the open under the leadership of a young Sudanese officer, Ali Abdel Lateef, who was a Dinka from the south and whose White Flag League was a transethnic movement looking for inspiration to the Egyptian national movement with which it hoped to unite in a struggle for the independence of the Nile Valley. They sent telegrams to Egyptian authorities supporting their claims against England and staged anti-British demonstrations in leading

Sudanese towns. The agitation reached a high point in August 1924, when military cadets paraded through the streets of Khartoum openly expressing nationalistic demands. The league affixed posters to houses and walls in different towns, all condemning British domination. The assassination of the governor-general, Sir Lee Stack, in November in Cairo brought matters to a head. The British responded in crisis mode with an ultimatum, unilaterally evacuating all Egyptian troops and personnel from the Sudan by December 4, 1924, with a single stroke hoping to remove all Egyptian influence from the upper Nile.[21]

The rebellion signaled to the British that they could no longer rely on educated Sudanese, no matter what *tariqa* they belonged to, for they seemed all too susceptible to nationalist influences percolating in from Egypt. In fact, the search for a new set of allies to strengthen the colonial enterprise had been on for some time. Among the earliest papers on the subject was one by Harold MacMichael, who had already been awarded a DSO (distinguished service order) for his work as political and intelligence officer attached to the expeditionary force in Darfur during World War I.[22] MacMichael circulated his views to his colleagues in an unpublished paper titled "Indirect Rule for Pagan Communities,"[23] undated but issued sometime in the 1910s. In it, he came straight to the point by citing Sir Percy Girouard's views from *Report on East Africa for 1909–1910*: "If we allow the tribal authority to be ignored or broken, it will mean that we, who numerically form a small minority in the country, shall be obliged to deal with a rabble, with thousands of persons in a savage or semi-savage state, all acting on their own impulses, and making themselves a danger to society generally. There could only be one end to such a policy, and that would be eventual conflict with the rebels." He then went on to cite another colonial authority, C. L. Temple, late lieutenant governor of the northern provinces of Nigeria, confirming that the only way to avoid such a catastrophe was to set up "the government of natives through their own institutions."[24]

MacMichael had no illusion about the disadvantages of propping up chiefly power: in particular, abuse of power and "predilection for tyranny." But this must be endured for the sake of order, for "the native prefers to submit to a few abuses at the hands of his own Chief than to be pestered with rules and regulations and view-points of alien origin."

He warned against "the white man" who would be tempted "to aim at himself becoming de facto chief of a native tribe," for "he would *ipso facto* lose his racial prestige—if not his racial qualities—for 'familiarity breeds contempt' as much in one part of the world as in another, and vulgarization must always impair value."[25]

Nobody doubted that the colonial enterprise would not work without native allies. The real question involved the nature of these allies. And that is the debate that unfolded in the first phase of colonial rule: Which natives should be the key allies of the colonial administration, bureaucrats or chiefs?[26] There were two schools of thought, one led by R. Davies, who had visited northern Nigeria to study its system of administration, and the other by MacMichael, who was by September 1924 the assistant civil secretary. Davies advocated Nigeria-style indirect rule. He defined this in a memo submitted to the governors at the request of the governor-general in 1925 as "the utilization by the ruling power of existing, or after resuscitating them, of pre-existing native administrative institutions and their development on the lines suited to the genius of the people." He said tribal authorities would prove a "valuable bulwark against outbreaks of fanaticism."[27] This approach would also save money. He admitted it would not be cost free: efficiency would suffer and "graft" would proliferate. So far there was no disagreement with MacMichael. The debate surfaced when it came to discussing the most appropriate indirect rule authorities: Should they be religious or secular?

Davies wanted the existing centralized system of *kadis* courts, composed of graduates administering custom, to be replaced by religious courts composed of the local *faki,* or "holyman."* MacMichael recommended further developing judicial powers of native authorities. MacMichael's reasons for preferring secular to religious courts were

---

* We need to distinguish between three different kinds of religious persons. First, there is the *faqir* (plural *fuqara*), literally, "the poor one" and more poetically "he who is in spiritual need," which can refer to Sufi sheikhs as a humble recognition. In more contemporary times, it has come to refer to the followers of these sheikhs and not really the sheikhs themselves. Second, there is the *faqih* (plural *fuqaha*) a term that refers to a scholar of Islamic jurisprudence (*fiqh*). And, finally, there is the *faki* (plural also *fuqara*) that is a Sudanese word that refers to many varieties of "holy men," including Sufi sheikhs. Today, though, it seems to refer to only those without a clear Sufi genealogy. (Source: Noah Salomon, personal communication.)

entirely political: "The religious leaders in this country will always . . . carry much weight, and I think it is essential to develop the power of the secular chiefs as such, by way of counterweight to them." Fearing a possible combination of religious neo-Mahdism and graduates under a single banner, "Sudan for the Sudanese," the administration hastened to dismantle Sudanese elements in the bureaucracy in order to devolve powers upon tribal authorities. Already, Darfur had provided a lesson: Faced with a series of neo-Mahdist uprisings from 1914 to 1920, the British had looked for reliable allies who would collaborate against the rebels and found these among tribal leaders, particularly of the Massalit, Rizeigat, and Birgid.[28]

The second decade of the century came to a close with widespread agreement in the Colonial Office in London that collaboration with and rule through native chiefs was the way to stability and order. The new policy was given a name: indirect rule. The call for a general shift from direct to indirect rule was issued in the report of the colonial secretary—the "Milner Report" of 1920—which suggested that given the "vast extent and varied character of its inhabitants, the administration of [its] different parts should be left as far as possible in the hands of the native authorities wherever they exist under British supervision." But what of places where tribal organization no longer existed? The governor-general of Sudan's "Annual Report for 1921" acknowledged the problem, conceding that tribal organization had "ceased to exist," but added that "it may still be possible to recreate it."[29] Sir Lee Stack, the governor-general in 1923, assured one and all that "hardly a community in the northern Sudan existed where the old tribal organization has so decayed as to leave no foundation for the reestablishment of tribal authority and tribal justice."[30]

But the matter was far from settled. The call to shift autocratic powers from on-the-ground British officials to tribal chiefs (albeit under the watchful guidance of British officials) elicited a lively debate among British officials, not simply on the merits of the shift but also on whether retribalization was a feasible goal. Many a critic wondered whether power could be transferred to dormant tribal chiefs. The critique first came from those with fresh eyes and without restrictive ties to the hierarchy in the colony. Take, for example, this observation from the director of education, Sir James Currie, who visited Sudan in 1926. Drawing attention to the part played by both the Turkiyya and the Mahdiyya in breaking down tribal barriers and unifying the country, Sir James quipped about "young administrators diligently searching for lost tribes and vanished chiefs, and trying to resurrect a social system that had passed away forever."[31] Contrast this with the comments of governors-general who took it upon themselves not only to oversee the reintroduction of tribal government among natives but also to silence any doubts as to whether the policy might be feasible, let alone advisable. Sir John Maffey wrote in the "Annual Report for 1926," his first on assuming the office of governor-general, that "the Sudan may be regarded as still in its 'golden age,' " an era in which "tribal organization, tribal sanctions and old traditions still survive, though their validity varies from province to province."[32]

The second phase of British rule was marked by a shift of native policy to indirect rule. The shift is identified with the administration of a new governor-general, Sir John Maffey, from 1927 to 1933. The "Governor-General's Minute" of January 1, 1927, boldly set out the new policy, in both its rationale and its substance.[33] Warning that "old traditions may pass away with astonishing rapidity," he suggested the administration "fortify them while the memories of Mahdism and Omdurman are still vivid and while tribal sanctions are still a living force." To those who may think "such anxiety on my part . . . far-fetched," he cited the Indian experience: "But I have watched an old generation give place to a new in India and I have seen how easily vague political unrest swept over even backward peoples simply because we had allowed the old forms to crumble away. Yet the native states in India remain safe and secure in the hands of hereditary rulers, loyal to the King Emperor, showing what we might have done if we had followed a different course. We failed to put up a shield between the agitator and the bureaucracy." Counseling that "nothing stands still and in Khartoum we are already in touch with the outposts of new political forces," he warned British administrative officers accustomed to "function[ing] as 'Father of the People' " that "this cannot last": "The bureaucracy must yield either to an autocratic or to a democratic movement and the dice are loaded in favor of the latter." And so he concluded without hesitation: "If we desire the former [that is, autocracy], the British officer must realize that it is his duty to lay down the role of Father of the People. He must entrust it to the natural leaders of the people whom he must support and influence as occasion requires." He explained that the policy of indirect rule would have the advantage of splitting the country into so many units, each safely quarantined from political agitators: "In this manner the country will be parceled out into nicely balanced compartments, protective glands against the septic germs which will inevitably be passed on from the Khartoum of the future. Failing this armour we shall be involved in a losing fight throughout the length and breadth of the land. The possibility may be remote but the course of events in other parts of the world show that it is never too early to put one's house in order." Sir John made it clear that the policy had high-level approval—from the secretary of the colonies, Alfred Milner—and that it would have to be implemented without delay for political reasons: "Before old traditions die we ought to get on with extension and expansion in every direction, thereby sterilizing and localizing the political germs which must spread from the lower Nile into Khartoum."

The change was set in motion with a number of legal ordinances that gave combined administrative and judicial powers to officials in the native authority. Beginning with nomadic sheikhs, these ordinances were extended to sheikhs in the villages.[34] The 1927 Powers of Shaykhs Ordinance built on the 1922 Nomad Shaykhs Ordinance, giving the governor-general the sole right to set up sheikhs as native judges.[35] As they became the focus of collaboration, native chiefs were allocated a bundle of powers that were previously the preserve of British administrators. The only qualification was that native officials use this clenched fist under the watchful eye of British advisers. Governor Bence Pembroke claimed in 1927 that Darfur was the most suitable place in which to implement the model of indirect rule established by Frederick Lugard in Nigeria.[36]

That same year, Sir John Maffey's 1927 "Minute" had closed with two "constructive" recommendations: He warned the administration to make "no fetish of efficiency" and to "be prepared to grant a worthy scale of remuneration to the Chiefships we foster, great and small, in order to give them dignity and status." In other words, be tolerant of inefficiency and graft if you want to continue to rule. Two years later, Harold MacMichael dutifully drove home that same point: "It can hardly be doubted that there will be a great deal of favouritism, bias and corruption when Native Administration has become normal routine." A little tyranny and a little corruption were surely a small price to pay for the stability of the colonial order.[37]

Darfur became the heartland of indirect rule. The new framework of tribal governance and administration was set within a broader agenda that sought to separate the north from the south, and the center from the west. The 1920s ushered in a combination of three kinds of legislation. Together, these made for a racial and ethnic mosaic rather than the more fluid social and political space that one would expect to be the product of a market economy. First, the set of native administration ordinances turned ethnicity from a cultural into a political identity by making it a principle for the administrative organization of native authorities. Second, the Closed Districts Ordinance cut off riverine northern Sudan from the south and to some extent from Darfur. Third, the southern policy—in tandem with indirect rule—set about building a mosaic of politically self-contained tribes in the south.[38] These changes would come to have a devastating effect on the colony.

Some unintended effects of indirect rule began to surface with social and economic change. New social groups, ranging from wage workers in plantations (such as the ambitiously irrigated Gezira cotton project between the White and the Blue Nile in central Sudan) and those in the newly constructed factories in urban areas to merchants and government functionaries who were products of colonial schools and colleges, began to appear. Unable to find a place within the scheme of indirect rule administration, these new social groups agitated for further change. Their small numbers were more than offset by their capacity to understand the world on their own terms and organize accordingly. Sooner or later, they would provide a new leadership vying to take control of the colony's future. The 1937 De La Warr Commission to the Sudan warned that the continued pursuit of "indirect rule" would lead to "a danger of the bifurcation of the Sudan, at this early stage of its growth, into Native Administrations in the countryside and the relatively small but influential groups of *effendia* [a class of supervisors] in the towns and the government departments."[39]

The warning became reality the very next year, 1938, when many among the educated class organized as the Graduates General Congress (also known as the Graduate Congress) and demanded reform.[40] Perhaps the most articulate voice was that of Muhammad Ahmed Mahjub, whose public lectures at the Graduates Club in Omdurman were published as articles in *al-Fajr,* the principal Sudanese journal of the 1930s, where he concluded that "Sudanese nationalism must be firmly based on Islam, Arabic culture and African soil and traditions and that it should be open to, and freely interact with, international currents of thought." A national culture, he concluded, "would have close friendly relations with the neighboring Egyptian culture but would be independent of it; it would retain its own distinct character but learn from the culture and thought of all other nations both ancient and modern."[41]

The next shift in colonial native policy was informed by the need to address the rift between town and country, socially reflected in relations between educated classes and tribal leaders. If the rift was to be healed in favor of stabilizing colonial rule, the next phase of reform would need to open up political and administrative space for the incorporation of educated classes into the colonial system, but without ceding leadership to them.[42]

This needed reform of the system of indirect rule is identified with the governor-generalship of George Stewart Symes (1933–40), who was regarded as a colonial modernizer. By providing space for the educated stratum in the native administration system, the reform sought to broaden the alliance to include those with an interest in checking the spread of militant nationalism. In the words of G.M.A. Bakheit, who would later become President Gaafar al-Nimeiry's minister of local government: "The educated urban classes and the tribal chiefs . . . were to be united in a common front against ultra-nationalism represented in the traditional sector by the Mahdists and in the modern sector by the pro-Egyptian elements and forces dominated by Egyptian culture." The onset of the reform was signaled by a change in the name of the governmental machinery that ruled over natives, from *native administration* to *local government.* In theory, this was meant to signify a shift in the basis of administration from tribe to territory. In reality, however, the change turned out to be cosmetic. According to Bakheit: "Local Government was in reality not the grave of Native Administration but the waiting room in which she finished her make-up and reappeared more lively and fascinating."[43] In Darfur, however, even the cosmetic effect was limited, for the simple reason that those incorporated into the administrative machinery as representatives of the educated strata did not come from Darfur; they were by and large imported from the riverine north.[44]

The reform of indirect rule began with legislative changes that defined and narrowed the powers of native authorities. The Chiefs' Court Ordinance of 1931 and the Native Courts Ordinance of 1932 restricted the powers of native agencies to judicial fields and the collection of taxes. Subsequent legislation, such as the Local Government Ordinances of 1937 for the rural areas, townships, and municipalities and associated 1938 regulations, indicated that the Sudan government envisaged the future role of native administration as part of local government.[45] The reform process was capped by the passage of the Local Government Ordinance in 1951. According to this new arrangement, tribal leaders were to assume an honorary role in the newly established local councils, which would take over the financial and executive powers previously held by tribal leaders.[46] The reform reduced the powers of tribal leaders in favor of urban authorities in the local councils where they had been brought together, but it in no way detracted from their power over the peasants.

These reforms were discussed in official and semiofficial gatherings where it was emphasized that when it came to local government reforms, Sudan must be upheld as a model for British colonies in Africa to follow. For these reasons, Sudan's experience is eloquent testimony to the effects of indirect rule.

The colonial period had manifold impacts on Darfur. Two are of particular importance in understanding the crisis that engulfed Darfur beginning in the late 1980s. The first was its marginalization in relation to the country as a whole; the second was its internal retribalization.

Marginalization

The marginalization of Darfur was the result of multiple facets of colonial policy, both political and economic. The policy of indirect rule reorganized Darfur's internal administration along ethnic lines. An ethnic group (or a part of it) that became an administrative unit was defined as a "tribe," and its leaders were hailed as "tribal leaders" whose duty it was to maintain "tribal order" in return for small privileges. All together, the administrative hierarchy of this ethnic group was called its "native authority." Key to its police function was keeping an eye on millenarian preachers and discontented graduates. In Darfur, in particular, the government used the 1922 Closed Districts Ordinance to target both wandering preachers and West African immigrants.[47]

To ensure tribal order, the British accorded practically unlimited administrative powers to native authorities, while restricting judicial ones. But even limits on judicial powers were waived for pragmatic reasons when necessary, as with the *nazir* of the Kababish, Ali el Tom, in neighboring Kordofan. In his case, officials agreed to avoid any formal definition of powers, since "this would set limits on his punitive powers."[48] Not only was the Kababish *nazir* given "the largest powers of sentencing possible," his court was also not required to do "the kind of detailed record-keeping which was required of others." The administrators involved made it clear that they were "evidently acting with the approval of their superiors." Few doubted that Ali el Tom's *hukm* (power) derived from his "power to judge." Yet this *hukm* was neither "traditional" nor subject to the rule of law.[49] It exemplified the nature of colonial tradition, which was as modern as colonial rule of law—without being a part of it.

The overall objective was to marginalize areas that had been central to driving the Mahdiyya. Through its economic policy, the colonial state concentrated development efforts in a triangular area that lay between Khartoum and the valley of the Nile in the north and the stretch of land between the Blue and the White Nile (bordering central Kordofan and the southern parts of Kassala Province) in the south. Together, these came to be known as the three *K*s—Kosti, Kassala, and Khartoum.* These same areas benefited most from the spread of education and health services in the colonial period.[50] As the heart of the Mahdiyya, Darfur was turned into a backwater ruled by a few colonial officials. After being in a position to shape political development in northern Sudan for several centuries, Darfur was reduced to a labor reserve. Its young men regularly left this backwater and journeyed eastward to find work in the cotton projects in the Gezira, the area between the White

---

* Although Kassala is not in the land between the Blue and White Nile rivers or Khartoum and the Nile Valley.

and the Blue Nile, later also to Libya in the north, or they joined the colonial army and police. An exporter of slaves during the sultanate, Darfur turned into an exporter of cheap labor in the colonial period—except that, unlike the slaves who came as captives from across the borders, labor migrants were all Darfuri.[51]

The colonial administration's social policy was a consequence of this overall orientation. Philip Ingelson, the governor of Darfur in 1934–41, summed up the strategic thrust of educational policy in the province as follows: "We have been able to limit education to the sons of chiefs and native administration personnel and can confidently look forward to keeping the ruling classes at the top of the education tree for many years to come."[52] The allocation of scarce resources such as education was not based on merit: Sons of prominent families got preferential treatment. As late as 1939, officials considered it "undesirable" to base selection on examination; whenever there were too many applicants for seats available, the children of "people who mattered were moved up the list."[53]

With the state refusing to expand the system of state-run secular schools, it was left to religious schools (the *khalawi*) to respond to the popular demand for basic education. As the number of primary schools remained static—10 in the early part of the 1920s, 11 in 1928, and 10 again in 1929—the numbers of the *khalawi* rose from 161 with 5,444 students in 1925 to 768 with 28,699 students in 1930, leveling off at 605 schools with 22,400 students in 1936.[54] But even in *khalawi*, openings continued to be scarce. The authorities saw virtue in scarcity, for it allowed them to limit enrollment, even in the lowliest *khalawi*, to sons of notables. In the words of an English official, W. F. Crawford, "The advantage of dealing with the sons of the sheikh alone is that they run no risk of being swamped in class by the sharp-witted sons of merchants."[55]

An elite-focused educational policy had a devastating impact on a region where the urban elite was increasingly drawn from outside the province. By 1944, there were only two primary schools in the whole province of Darfur, one in Nyala and the other in El Fasher. By 1956, the year of independence, this situation had improved, but only marginally. The number of primary schools had risen to twenty, and two middle schools had been built, one in El Fasher by a self-help effort and the other in Nyala by the government for a population of 1,329,000.[56]

There were some positive changes after independence. A railway was built to Nyala in 1959. Cash crops such as mangoes and oranges began to be grown in the fertile region around Zalingei in the southwest for export to markets farther east.[57] Yet none of these changed Darfur's marginal position in the country as a whole. Darfur was the poorest of all northern provinces in 1967–68 and remained so in 1982–83.[58] According to figures compiled by the International Labour Organization, Darfur had the lowest average household income of all provinces in the northern part of Sudan in 1967–68.[59] In 1999–2000, the people of West Darfur were among the poorest in northern Sudan (comparable data for the south is not available), with poverty rates of above 51 percent of the population; poverty rates in North and South Darfur were not far behind, estimated at 50 percent and 41 percent, respectively.[60] And yet federal transfers to the three states from 2000 to 2005 were not only the least for all states in Sudan, but they had also been declining for the years for which figures are available.[61] The marginalization was across-the-board, economic and social. Access to public health services in Darfur was far below Sudan's average.[62] Sudanese universities were said to have graduated more than nine thousand students from Darfur since 1996, but fewer than six hundred of these were said to be formally employed a decade later.[63] The colonial legacy of marginalization was continued during a half century of independence.

Retribalization

Retribalization in Darfur was an all-encompassing project. To begin with, the province was administratively demarcated into so many tribal homelands. Everywhere, land rights were vested in communities, such as tribe, section, or village.[64] In each tribal area, authorities distinguished between "native" and "settler" tribes. The law associated rights with tribal identity, claiming that this was a "traditional" or "customary" practice. The result was to introduce a system of discrimination along tribal lines. Once "custom" was officially sanctioned and enforced as "tribal," the official system distinguished between residents who were members of the "indigenous" tribe and those who were not. The "native" tribe was entitled to two "customary" rights: the ownership of land and appointment to key posts in the tribal administration. By defining both the right to access land

and the right to participate in local governance as the preserve of those who belonged to the "native" tribe, the indirect rule system turned tribe into a master identity in the native administration. The result was a system that officially discriminated between native and nonnative (settler) tribes. No matter how many generations they had lived in an area, members of a tribe said to have immigrated into the area were considered settlers and were disenfranchised.

When it came to giving newcomers to a village access to land, officialdom distinguished between outsiders who belonged to the tribe and those who did not. Members of these groups were treated differently. Allocation of farmland for individual households within the community was the responsibility of the *sheikh* (village headman). To allocate land to fellow tribesmen—migrants from villages within the tribal area—the sheikh had to consult the *omda* (subdistrict chief). But to allocate land to newcomers from outside the tribal *dar,* the sheikh was required to consult the higher level of the native administration (the *malik, shartay, nazir,* or *magdume*). Furthermore, tribal strangers were required to give a portion of their annual produce as a "gift" to the local chief.[65]

The most disenfranchised in this arrangement were pastoralist groups whose very mode of life was based on seasonal movement. The nomads divided between two types: camel nomads (Abbala) in the north and cattle nomads (Baggara) in the south. Cattle nomads might combine cattle grazing in the vicinity with semipermanent agricultural settlements, while camel nomads were totally mobile, with no fixed settlement. Camel nomads everywhere had a transient relationship to land. Their lack of settlements (villages) meant that they had no *dar,* or tribal homeland, anywhere. Immigrants everywhere and indigenous nowhere, they lacked any basis of a claim to rights in this retribalized system.[66] A tribally sanctioned limit on movement tended to erode the very basis of a pastoral mode of living.

But even when it came to the cattle nomads of the south, the colonial system went on to create *dars* for some pastoral tribes but not for others. *Dars* were created for the largest tribes among the Baggara at the outset of colonial rule and for the Beni Hussein in the 1940s.[67] Whereas the Baggara tribes were simply too large to be alienated, the Beni Hussein were rewarded for joining a pro-British coalition during the Mahdiyya.

.   .   .

The immediate aim of the "traditional" system—constructed by the colonial power through a combination of broad legislation and detailed administration—was to return Darfur to the presultanate period. But the long-term effect of this counterrevolution was to purge Darfuri society of the most dynamic part of its history by reconstituting the province as an administrative mosaic of tribal polities. We can see this at four levels. Ironically, the first basic change made a mockery of the claim that colonialism had revived and resuscitated tradition: For the very revival of "traditional" authority shifted the source of the leader's power away from his relationship to the kin group to his relationship to the colonial power, thereby corrupting the very principle of tribal identity.

Second, the very definition of *dar* changed from one that had been both multifaceted and nuanced to one that was narrow and restrictive. Hitherto *dar* had meant "home" in a variety of senses: a location, an administrative unit, the specific territory of an ethnic group, the whole sultanate, or simply a part of it. It is only with colonial rule that the definition of *dar* became identified with a single place: "an ethnic territory in which the dominant group had legal jurisdiction."[68] Tribal homelands were named after the tribe—for example, Dar Zaghawa. This development assigned two new functions to land: Land became both the asset of a tribe and the exclusive marker of the tribe's political identity. It is in this sense that tribe became the master identity.

Third, the system of *dars* institutionalized a regime of inequality favoring supposedly original residents at the expense of all others, who were considered immigrants. The more invidious effect of tribal governance was to turn tribal identity into the basis of official discrimination. The inevitable consequence of a program to re-create an ethnic administration to rule over a multiethnic society was to cast both law and rights in ethnic terms and thus introduce ethnic discrimination in each administrative unit. Everywhere, the "traditional" or "customary" system was driven by two features: (1) *a land policy* whereby both ownership of land and access to it were regulated on a tribal basis and (2) *a governance policy* whereby the right of participation in community affairs—particularly administration—was tied to tribal identity. Superimposing a grid of ethnically defined *dars* on a multiethnic population was a recipe for an explosive ethnic confrontation between two kinds of residents in every *dar:* those with and those without political and land rights.[69] The rest was only a matter of time.

Finally, the system drove a wedge between two kinds of tribes: at first glance between the more settled tribes and tribes for whom mobility was crucial to their mode of life. More fundamentally, however, the dividing line separated tribes with a *dar* from those without one. It is this division that would explode in the Darfur crisis that began in the mid-1980s.

The word *tribe* has had many meanings. In the anthropology of the Arab world, it has been used to distinguish nomads (Bedouins) from settled peoples on the basis that territory is the principle of governance among settled peoples but that governance among nomadic tribes is based on kinship. Existing works on colonialism have shown that the incorporation of nomadic groups into state-administered polities has changed this radically; more specifically, the introduction of indirect rule subordinated kinship to the administrative power of appointed leaders whose clan came to be linked to colonial power.[70] This gave rise to yet another—corrupted—meaning of *tribe* among nomadic populations. The organization of the tribe as an administrative unit often subverted the kin-based principle of tribal governance and replaced it with administration through a narrow elite.[71] Suffice it to point out here that Arab tribes must be thought of as an administrative *consequence* of British indirect rule rather than just a holdover from the precolonial era.

Anthropologists have often used *tribe* and *ethnic group* synonymously, in both cases to denote groups that are culturally identifiable, such as through language. The final meaning of *tribe* came from its usage by colonial power under indirect rule. Whether colonial rulers invented tribes or acknowledged existing ethnic groups as tribes, the meaning of *tribe* under colonial indirect rule was that of an administrative unit. When I speak of *tribe* in this book, I will do so in the sense in which colonial power employed the term: as meaning an administratively produced political identity.

.   .   .

Whereas the British wanted to administer the colonized population as so many tribes, they also wanted to group these tribes into so many races. Identifying the population in terms of "native" and "settler" races provided a justification for discriminating between "native" and "settler" tribes. At the provincial level, a first plan to divide the population into two federations—"Arab" and "Zurga" (black)—was submitted by the governor in the 1920s. In 1926, the governor even suggested that tribal groups living in the territory of another tribe be governed on a racial basis—as Arab or Zurga—and not on the basis of location.[72] The 1927 ordinance urged smaller tribal units "to coalesce or to attach themselves to larger tribes."[73] Over the next decade, the governor continued efforts to create two grand tribal confederations—Arab and Zurga—one "bringing all the tribal groups commonly known as the Baggara, who were presumably of Arab descent" and the other "non-Arabized groups locally known as the Zurga."[74]

But "Arabs" and "Zurga" did not really exist outside the census, since all were organized as multiple tribes, not as discrete races. We shall see that the first expression of a popular consciousness of a separate Arab identity in Darfur did not surface until 1987–89. Even when "census Arabs" and "census Negroes" (Zurga) did spring to life—decades after their invention in the census—their mobilization was still tribal. This continued to be true during all three phases of the conflict in Darfur: whether in 1987–89, in the mid-1990s, or after 2002–3. Unlike Rwanda in the 1990s, political violence in Darfur never took on a racialized dimension.

6

Building Nation and State
in Independent Sudan

THE DEBATE ON SOCIOECONOMIC CHANGE in independent Sudan was framed by a contest between tradition and modernity. "Tradition" was defended by forces that organized around the identity of tribe and religion: in particular, chiefs in the native authority system and religious leaders in the Sufi *tariqas*, both of whom provided urban politicians with a rural base. Sudan's national movement, led by an elite of the educated class, had no choice but to straddle the divide between tradition and modernity, for its success depended on the mass movement of religious sects.[1] Two sectarian parties dominated the national movement. On one side was the Democratic Unionist Party (DUP), closely associated with the Mirghani family and the Khatmiyya *tariqa*. The other side was led by the Umma Party, organically linked to the Ansar *tariqa* and the family of the Mahdi.

The split in the northern political class began at the time of the Mahdiyya. British power had leaned on the quietist Khatmiyya order to mobilize against the Ansar. In the 1940s, the two orders pioneered two different political strategies, whereas the Khatmiyya called for a union of Sudan and Egypt to preserve the "unity of the Nile Valley," the Ansar stood for complete independence under the slogan "Sudan for the Sudanese." In addition to these forces, urban traders (the *Jallaba*, named after their full-length dress) who had come to constitute countrywide networks also developed as a distinct political force during the colonial period. Even though the Graduate Congress had been established in 1938 as a nonsectarian organization, most graduates soon became members of one of the two sectarian movements. Whereas the main support for the Unionists came from riverine and eastern Sudan, also the place of origin of most of the *Jallaba,* the primary base of the Ansar was western Sudan, including Darfur.

The defense of "modernity" typically came from urban-based social classes and groups, in particular those who belonged to the ranks of the intelligentsia, the army, and the merchant class. Modern intellectuals were both secular and religious in orientation: The former were mainly linked to the Communist Party and the latter to an amalgam of Islamist groups from which later emerged the "fundamentalist" National Islamic Front and its much smaller "antifundamentalist" rival, the Republican Brothers. Ambitious members of the intelligentsia saw themselves as representing "modern" enclaves in a sea of "tradition." They could not conceive of coming to power with the support of the majority. In their eyes, "democracy" was less a modern or revolutionary movement than the means by which traditionalists stayed in power. When they thought of breaking with "tradition," they could think of doing so only by a violent overthrow of the existing power, a fact that inevitably led them to seek allies in the army. This was true of both secular and religious intellectuals, those who belonged to the Communist Party and those who formed the National Islamic Front. In contrast, the camp of "tradition," dominated by sectarian parties that drew their main support from historical links with rival Sufi *tariqas,* was confident of winning the battle for democracy.

It is this rivalry between the defenders of "tradition" and the champions of "modernity"—and not the electoral contest between the two mass parties, the NUP and Umma—that drove the seesaw of Sudanese politics between civilian parliamentary politics and a series of military-led coups d'état. The civilian parliamentary governments were inevitably led by one of the two main sectarian parties, NUP or Umma, championing "tradition," whereas military factions were invariably allied with one or another group of modernist intellectuals.

Sectarian politics in the north was sharply regionalized. If Dar Fur voted Umma (Ansar), the east and the north invariably voted NUP (Khatmiyya). The first democratic parliament, elected in 1953, was led by the NUP. The NUP had forty-six seats, Umma twenty-three, and the south twenty-two. In December 1955, the two religious leaders and their parties agreed on the formation of a postindependence coalition government.[2] The second democratic period (1964–69) was led by the Umma Party, and the third (1986–89) was again an Umma Party–led alliance of the two. In contrast, the military regimes were defended by "modernist" intellectuals, the non-Communist secularists in 1958, the Communists in 1969, and the religious radicals in 1989, promising "modernity" in one form or another.

The clash between "modern" reforms and "traditional" institutions is key to understanding the conflict in Darfur. The two systems are built on different and opposing foundations—the "traditional" system on community-based rights and responsibilities, and the "modern" system on the power of the state and the rights of individuals. If "tradition" is said to sanction tribal rights of "natives," "modernity" is said to be the basis of individual rights of "citizens." As such, they are said to represent different ways of organizing society and governing the behavior of its members.[3]

Despite the decades-long contention between "traditional" and "modern" forms of power, both shared certain assumptions. Both the "traditionalists" and the "modernists" bought Britain's version of Sudan's history. Both identified historical change with "modernity" and believed that "tradition" was inimical to change. From this standpoint, modernity stood for change, particularly revolutionary change, and tradition was marked as a force for conservation. Both believed that the colonial system had conserved tradition, and that this had indeed been the essence of British indirect rule. Postcolonial politics chose the modern over the traditional. The problem with this political vision was that it locked both sides into a cul-de-sac: Since only a minority of the population participated in the modern sector, modernists had no way to think of change except as an imposition from above; at the same time, traditionalists tended to regard all change as a threat to tradition. It is this assumption that explains why "modernists" in Sudan were inevitably antidemocratic, why they assumed that the vast majority of people—those living in the traditional sector—would oppose modernity and change. And this led to yet another assumption: that the institutions of modernity would not be the product of internal developments in Sudan—no matter how fructified by external influence—but would have to be imported from elsewhere. Like "Arabization," "modernization," too, would be an import. As long as Sudan's intellectuals were locked in a worldview that counterposed "tradition" to "modernity," there was little possibility of their finding a way out of this political impasse.

Even if they viewed democracy with suspicion, more as a break with their ambitions than a vehicle for them, the "modernizing" minority had no choice but to look for a vehicle to mobilize that same majority. That vehicle was the nation. But the nation-building project raised another question: If the end of colonialism would lead to the independence of the nation, who constituted the nation? This is how the battle between "tradition" and "modernity" became joined to that over the nation. We can see the political history of Sudan since independence as a series of attempts to define and constitute a viable nation. There have been four such nation-building projects to date: The first saw the nation as Arab, the second as Muslim, the third as secular and territorial (that is, Sudanese), and the fourth as African. The contention among them has been the driving force of politics in Sudan in the postindependence period. Each nation-building project was carried forward by a leadership that sought to mobilize and draw strength from a set of social movements. Each national movement had its own internal debates. It is within this larger social and intellectual context that different tendencies vied for supremacy. But as important as the debate among these projects was the debate within them. For in each camp, those who called for an exclusive definition of the nation fought it out against those who held more inclusive notions. We shall in each case distinguish between inclusive and exclusive definitions of the nation—Arab, Sudanic, Islamist, or African—and the contention between them at different stages in the development of each nation-building project. I shall elaborate each of these in turn in the rest of this chapter.

Arabism

Nation building in the Sudan began as an anticolonial social movement, as it did in most African countries. The consequence of colonial policy was to create many Sudans within a single state. The deepest rift of all was between north and south. This outcome evolved over time. In the first stage, Britain followed a policy of joint development of the south and the north. Fearful of Mahdist sentiment among northerners, British power staffed the colonial army with troops recruited from the south.

The decision to separate the north from the south was triggered by the onset of the Egyptian anti-British revolution of 1919. In 1924, the governor-general of Sudan was assassinated by Egyptian nationalists in Cairo. When Britain withdrew Egyptian troops from Sudan in retaliation, Sudanese troops—southerners included—demonstrated in solidarity and refused to obey British officers. The revolt was put down mercilessly, and southern troops were withdrawn from the Sudanese army. A strategic decision was made to separate the development of the south from the north so the south might henceforth develop as a "self-contained racial unit."

Henceforth, the south was run by British administrators, each in charge of an area.[4] This personal rule was augmented by a complement of missionary societies, each of which was assigned and given free rein over this same area, which it ran as a religious fief. Christian missionaries were given exclusive charge of educational and social policy. English replaced Arabic as the official language. Socially, all references to Arabic culture were discouraged, whether with regard to names, language, or clothing. Sunday replaced Friday as the official day of rest; Islamic proselytization was banned, and Christian proselytization was encouraged. The government pursued a policy of ethnic cleansing: northern traders were weeded out of the south and Christian traders—Greek and Syrian—brought in. Collaboration between pastoralist and agricultural groups, whether over grazing lands or water rights, was discouraged. From then on, the elite in the north would be Muslim and in the south Christian.

A single piece of legislation, the Closed Districts Ordinance of 1922, criminalized movement between the south and the north, while the 1922 Passport and Permits Ordinance declared the south "a closed district." All emigration from the south to the north was declared illegal, subject to jail or a fine, and a pass was needed for movement of persons into and out of the south. In short, north and south were run as two different countries meant to have two different and contrasting destinies. The overall objective was eventually to link the south to a settler-dominated federation of East African territories.

Britain's southern policy evolved in the context of its overall policy of retribalization in the Sudan. Retribalization, in turn, was pegged to a policy of racialization, one whose strategic objective was to categorize the population of the Sudan into different races, Arab and non-Arab, and to the extent possible quarantine the former from the latter. Both the problem and the solution were articulated with abundant clarity by that master strategist of indirect rule, Harold MacMichael, in a 1928 memo on a key problem of administration in the south: "The problem is whether to encourage the spread of Arabic in the South as a lingua franca and medium between the governing class and the governed, or to resist it on political grounds." The memo provided a detailed rationale for why a policy that spread Arabic in the south would be "basically unsound":

> . . . The spread of Arabic among the negroes of the South means the spread of Arab thought, Arab culture, Arab religion. . . . The path . . . would carry those that took it into grave dangers. The most serious of these is the automatic extension of the zone in which Islamic fanaticism is endemic to an equally large and far more populous area where at present it is not so. One may vary the metaphor by saying that to encourage the spread of Arabic in the South would be to sprinkle gunpowder in the neighborhood of a powder magazine, or to sow weeds because they grow more quickly than corn.[5]

MacMichael's real fear was of an alliance between two groups that he defined as "Arab" and "black," the former Muslim and the latter not: "The simpler type of black, for his part, regards the Arab as a cultivated aristocrat, and, more especially when detached from his tribal environment, is apt to succumb to a form of snobbery and ape Arab fashions. He finds that he is not admitted into the circle of the elect so long as he remains uncircumcised and he adopts Islam as a potent form of ju-ju well worth acquiring." He acknowledged that there were pragmatic "advantages to be gained by encouraging Arabic in the South." It would make the "task of administration . . . easier . . . For a year or two—even for several years—it might be so in as far as we should have the hearty cooperation of the Arab trader, the Moslem divine and the detribalized riff-raff of the South." Politically, however, "the policy would be a very short-sighted one, for the day of reckoning would come sooner or later, and we should then find that our troubles were of our own brewing." So he urged the administration that "surely it is wiser and better and safer to take the longer view," whereby "a series of self-contained racial units will be developed with structure and organization based on the solid rock of indigenous traditions and beliefs, the daily life of the family and the individual will be regulated by customs which are natural to them, the sense of tribal pride and independence will grow, and in the process a solid barrier will be created against the insidious political intrigue which must in the ordinary course of events increasingly beset our path in the North."[6]

All hues of nationalists in northern Sudan saw Britain's "southern policy" as an attempt to thwart the development of the Sudanese nation and were united in opposition to it. For Britain, however, a separate southern policy was part of a larger project, which included linking Sudan to Egypt in a comprehensive effort to contain the development of nationalist consciousness and organization. But the project fell apart with the resurgence of Egyptian nationalism in the period that followed World War II. It was now clear that the link with Egypt was more likely to fuel than to contain the growth of nationalism in Sudan. It was this realization that made Britain reverse the course of its southern policy in the 1940s. By acceding to the nationalist demand that the south be integrated into Sudan, Britain hoped to wean Sudanese nationalism away from an Egyptian orientation.

The termination of the southern policy was a great victory for northern Sudanese nationalists. Yet the end of the southern policy did not mean an end to its effects. By the late forties, when the southern policy was reversed in favor of integration with northern parts of the country, major structural inequalities were already visible. A cumulative outcome of this process was the development of two parallel elites in the country: a missionary-educated Christian elite in the south and a riverine Muslim elite in the north. Whereas the latter inherited the colonial state upon independence, the former felt so cut off from access to the state that it took recourse to armed struggle.[7]

Northern writers would speak of the southern policy as a colonial aberration that had created a Christian and non-Arab elite in the south.[8]

But the fact was that the southern policy was simply the flip side of Britain's northern policy, which had coddled a tribal and sectarian (Muslim) elite in the north, the former installed in the local system of native authorities and the latter led by the three *sayeds* at the head of different Sufi brotherhoods—al-Mahdi, al-Mirghani, and al-Hindi—who together defined the tempo of national politics. Together, the two policies had nurtured two wings of the nationalist movement in the country. If northern nationalists saw themselves as Arab, then southern nationalists saw their common feature as being not-Arab. To this extent, both were products of colonial policy. Whereas the southern elite saw itself in parochial terms, as non-Arab and southern, the northern elite saw itself as Arab and national (that is, Sudanese).

Arab and African nationalism were also rooted in global trends, though in each case the influence matured at a different time. Arab nationalism reached its high point in northern Sudan in the 1950s, in the aftermath of the Free Officer-led overthrow of the Egyptian monarchy, and the subsequent upsurge of Arab nationalism. The "Arab" political identity in riverine Sudan developed in three phases: if the Funj royalty claimed an Arab descent in the sixteenth century and the middle class of merchants and holy men embraced an Arab identity in the late eighteenth century, it is only in the course of anticolonial agitation in the post–Second World War period that Arab identity can be said to have become the hallmark of a popular political consciousness. An African political consciousness would dawn in the south much later, beginning in the 1980s.

From a southern point of view, nationalism turned out to be a fig leaf for the domination of the riverine Arab elite from the north. This became clear as two key safeguards in the transitional process—the Sudanization Committee, meant to create a national civil service, and the Constitutional Committee, meant to create a national political framework—were subverted by this very elite. The Sudanization Committee of Six was appointed by the governor in 1946. It comprised three British officials and three Sudanese picked from the colonial civil service. It resolved that "three factors were necessary to the make-up of a good official; firstly, character and background; secondly, academic qualifications; and thirdly, acquired experience."[9] The committee was preoccupied with Sudanization, not with the equity of representation among different groups of the Sudanese. Its work was carried forward by another committee, the Committee of Five—one British, one Egyptian, and three northern Sudanese—constituted in 1953. With no room for correcting historical imbalances, all senior posts were allocated to those with experience, who inevitably came from the north. Only six of eight hundred vacated posts went to southerners. The Constitutional Committee was appointed by the National Assembly, and only three of its forty-six members were southerners. All three called for federalism. But the committee refused even to discuss the question of federalism, with the result that its three southern members boycotted the committee's work. The work of both committees showed that the northern riverine elite was unwilling to make any concession to southern demands for political and cultural autonomy. Marginalized in both committees, the southern political class withdrew from the process.[10]

The withdrawal of the southern elite led to the first major political schism in the coalition government created at independence. The Umma Party, with its main base of support in the western part of the country, joined the southern parties at a conference in Juba in October 1954. The Juba Conference called for a federal status for the south. The Democratic Unionist Party, with its main base in the riverine north, resolved to oppose a federal project in the name of keeping the country united. With the southern political class paralyzed in the postindependence period, the response came from southern units in the army. Their mutiny at Torit in 1955 turned into a revolt and ushered in the first phase of the southern armed struggle.

The government's declaration that the only appropriate response to an armed revolt in the south would be armed repression from the north paved the way for a military coup pledged to pursue "Arabization" with maximum vigor. The 1958 coup brought General Ibrahim Abboud to power. The response of the DUP government, and the 1958 junta that followed it, was a top-down nation-building project: Arabization. The junta declared that there must be "a single language and a single religion for a single country." At the most elementary level, state-enforced Arabization simply turned Britain's southern policy of 1922–47 upside down. Arabic became the official language in government offices and schools, and Friday replaced Sunday as the official public holiday. All religious gatherings outside churches were banned in 1961, and all foreign missionaries were expelled in 1962. State funds were advanced to build mosques and Islamic religious schools, and chiefs were pressured to convert to Islam.[11]

The effect of state-sponsored "Arabization" was not only to reinforce a self-consciously Arab power at the center but also to broaden the resistance that began in the south to other marginal areas in northern Sudan, particularly the east and the west. When civil organizations in the capital launched street action against the 1958 junta, Darfur joined the national cause enthusiastically. The agitation was finally successful in 1964, when the military junta invited the population to demonstrate in the streets in favor of national unity and the war in the south. The civilian population did pour into the streets of Khartoum and Omdurman by the tens of thousands, but when they unfurled their banners, their target was the junta in Khartoum, not the insurgency in the south. Following the fatal shooting of a university student attending a public meeting to discuss the war in the south, violent clashes broke out at the funeral between thirty thousand demonstrators and police. A variety of civil organizations—the Sudan Workers Trade Union Federation (SWTUF); the professional associations of lawyers, medical doctors, and engineers; and the University of Khartoum Students Union—came together under the banner of the "Professionals' Front" and declared a general strike that paralyzed Khartoum. This coalition opposed "not only the military dictatorship but also the fractious and self-interested traditional forces [of the sectarian parties]; accordingly, demonstrators chanted 'la zaima lil qudama' ['no leadership for the antiquated']."[12] Signed by the Professionals' Front, the charter of the October Movement called for a return to democratic rule and presented a united opposition to the government's policies of Arabization and Islamization in southern Sudan. When soldiers refused to fire at demonstrators, the junta tottered. Its overthrow came to be known as the October Revolution. After rioting had continued for several days, General Abboud dissolved the Supreme Council of the Armed Forces and dismissed the cabinet.[13] It was the first time the educated class and the young graduates outside sectarian and traditional political parties had found an opportunity to participate in the national political process—and it would not be the last.

.   .   .

Led by the students, the opposition to state-sponsored "Arabization" was strong in the provinces. Darfuri students held a conference at El Fasher in 1956, with the object of promoting development and progress in the province.[14] The student initiative followed in the wake of a long history of activism around this question. As early as 1938, Dr. Adam Ahdam had founded an organization called Black Block, with the stated aim of representing non-Arab Sudanese in Anglo-Egyptian Sudan.[15] The successor to the Black Block in the postindependence period was the Darfur Development Front (DDF), formed in 1964 on the heels of similar regional initiatives, such as the Beja Congress in the east and the General Union of the Nuba Mountains southwest of the Gezira.[16] The initiative to establish the DDF came from the educated class. The committee was headed by Ahmed Diraige, who was later to become governor of North Darfur. Other representatives in this group included Dr. Ali al-Haj, Professor Abdul Rahman Dosa, and Dr. Mohammed Adam Showa, all prominent Darfuris. All except Dr. Ali al-Haj were members of the Umma Party.[17]

The status quo in Darfur was supported by both traditional sectarian parties. The Umma Party had strong support among both the Fur and the Baggara of Darfur. Grandsons (literally, male heirs) of Darfur's pre-twentieth-century rulers had risen to positions of power within the Umma Party.[18] If the Umma Party treated Darfur as its traditional reservoir, a kind of closed region, the NUP was content with its support among riverine traders—the *Jallaba*—in the region and did little to upset this arrangement.[19] The DDF began by questioning the conventional practice of bringing Khartoum politicians to work in Darfur—where they were known as "exported members"—regardless of whether they knew anything about the circumstances of the people they purported to represent. The Umma Party, for instance, used to send such outsiders as Ziyada Arbab and Abdalla Khalil to stand for elections in areas that they had never seen before but still won because they had the support of the imam. The local people voted for a candidate they did not know because of the imam's backing.[20] The DDF went on to mediate several intertribal disputes in Darfur; success in this endeavor made its claim to the region's leadership sound viable.[21]

The DDF soon linked up with two clandestine groups that had been at
the center of organizing discontent in the province between independence and the October Revolution in 1964. The first group was named
al-Lahib al-ahmar, "The Red Flame." Its main activity was to distribute
leaflets threatening action against the *Jallaba* in the main trading centers
of Darfur. But it was the second group that the government took more
seriously, mainly because it recruited from rank-and-file members of
the army. Organized in 1963, this underground clandestine group called
itself Sooni, after the name of a place just below Jebel Marra. By pledging to fight the *Jallaba* for the benefit of Darfuris, Sooni had also
claimed the mantle of Darfuri nationalism.[22]

Sooni was a secret organization, and there are many stories about
how it began. The first traces Sooni's origins to early efforts to organize
western Sudanese communities in Khartoum, Gezira, and Kassala
Provinces; laborers in the Khartoum industrial area; and even among
Chad rebels waging war against their government. Sooni members held
riverine merchants responsible for the problem of backwardness in Darfur and were said to be behind many unauthorized threats demanding
that these merchants evacuate the region. These threats led the Ministry
of Interior, the Provincial Authority, and the security forces to accuse
the organization of wanting to separate Darfur from Sudan. It is in this
context that there developed an organic link between riverine traders
and security forces that continues to this day.[23] A second account held
that Sooni developed as a result of influence and guidance from the
southern rebels, who pointed out the irony of the fact that although the
west was as marginalized as the south, the center used the west to fight
the south. For their part, the southern rebels advised the Darfuri to form
a secret organization rather than wage an armed struggle given the cultural links between Darfur and Khartoum.[24] According to a third version, Sooni was a leftist organization formed by some educated youth
from western Sudan who had been members of the Communist Party–
influenced Sudanese Youth Union. As evidence, they pointed to this
organization's slogans, such as socialism, nationalization and confisca-
tion, dissolution of native administration, and popular democracy
without political parties.[25]

It is more than likely that all these influences contributed to forming Sooni and shaping its activities. It is as a result of the work of these two underground organizations, Sooni and The Red Flame, that an internal debate began among the now growing body of educated Darfuris on the merits of having an aboveground organization that would wage an open and legal battle for a legitimate goal: to advance the interests of Darfur within Sudan. This discussion led to the launching of the Darfur Development Front (DDF) in Khartoum in 1964. From Sooni to the DDF, there developed a tendency in Darfur to see itself as the home of "native" tribes. Many of those I interviewed claimed that this tendency had been strongly influenced by Anyanya I and II—the early rebels—in southern Sudan and in turn shaped Quraish I, purporting to be a coalition of "Arab" tribes.

There is also a debate about the political impact of the DDF. Sharif Harir says the DDF expressed its ideology "in a demagogic manner," one that conceived Darfur's problem as "a struggle between the poor majority who are originally from inside the province and the privileged minority who consist mainly of the riverine merchants and the corrupt bureaucrats." Many connected the spread of the DDF message with the growing number of incidents violating law and order in Nyala, Zalingei, Geneina, and Kutum. This speculation was reinforced when some of those tried for breach of peace were found to be members of both the DDF and Sooni.[26] The Ministry of Interior and security forces in Darfur accused Sooni of being the military branch of the DDF, a plausible hypothesis given that Westerners were conscripted in the army. A contrary viewpoint stresses the differences between the DDF and other regional organizations that were launched around the same time, such as the Beja Congress (BC) and the General Union of the Nuba Mountains (GUNM). Whereas these were organized on a distinctly narrow ethnic base, the DDF was founded on a wider multiethnic base, for its ambition was to unite the entire region.

The Umma Party both wooed the DDF leadership and tried to isolate it. During the 1968 elections, leading factions within the ruling Umma Party, in particular those identified with Sadiq al-Mahdi, alternately appealed to sedentary peoples by blaming the region's underdevelopment on Arabs and to the Baggara seminomads by calling on them to support their fellow Nile Arabs. At the same time, both sectarian politi-

cal parties waged a propaganda war against the DDF. Unionist supporters, many of them riverine merchants, accused the DDF of mobilizing
the people along ethnic and demagogic lines. As pressure mounted from
established parties, the DDF's leadership found it increasingly difficult
to maintain its autonomy. Following a lecture by Ahmed Ibrahim
Diraige, the first chairman of the DDF, the parties filed a complaint with
the resident judge accusing Diraige of several crimes. Soon after, the
accused joined the Umma Party and became a minister in the government, following which the case was suspended by the attorney general.[27]
This is how Darfur got its first and only member in the Cabinet of
Ministers—Ahmed Diraige—in 1968. It would be another thirty years
before a Darfuri would become a member of another leading state body,
in this case the five-person Supreme National Council.[28]

If the DDF leadership gained by joining the Umma Party, the gains
were limited to individuals. Ahmed Ibrahim Diraige became a minister
in the government and then emerged as a leader of the Umma parliamentary opposition in 1968. But there was also a price to pay. Organiza-
tionally swallowed by the Umma Party, the DDF was unable to keep its
popular base intact. When revived in 1986 as an autonomous organization, the DDF could no longer claim to be fully representative of all sections of the Darfuri population. As Sharif Harir observed, the reborn
DDF "came to be viewed by the majority of Darfurians as representing
not a regional base but the Fur."[29]

Nimeiry and Sudanism (1969–83)

We have seen that when the junta invited public demonstrations of support in 1964 for its southern policy, the public demonstrated—but
against the war and the junta. The 1964 October Revolution brought
down the Abboud military regime. There followed a caretaker regime
that excluded the two sectarian parties and whose expressed agenda was
to "solve the Southern problem." A Roundtable Conference of all northern and southern parties (and exiles) was called for March 18–25, 1965.
When the conference failed, the coalition of leftist parties fell, the traditional parties returned to power, and the war resumed. The second
parliamentary regime was, like the first, dominated by the sectarian
political parties. The parliamentary regime was overthrown by a second
military coup, led by Gaafar al-Nimeiry.

The Nimeiry regime provided a Sudanese version of militant nationalism in postcolonial Africa. Uncompromisingly modernist, the regime was determined to chart a course free of the sectarian parties. Its belabored efforts to achieve this end took the regime through three different alliances: the first with the Communist Party, the second with the southern rebel movement, and the third with the Islamists. It was a journey that spanned the entire political spectrum. To many observers, the passage from one alliance to another seemed to make for a bewildering—and opportunistic—set of twists and turns. Yet there was a consistency to these shifts. Its chosen allies had one thing in common: All championed a modernist agenda, and all were pledged to fight the legacy of sectarian politics in Sudan's modern history. By the time the regime was overthrown in 1983, it had exhausted the entire list of organized political forces with a modernist agenda.

The Nimeiry regime has two achievements to its credit: the Addis Ababa Agreement of 1972, which ended the first phase of the war in the south, and the only attempt to date to effect a fundamental reform of the local government system inherited from colonial times. Through these reforms, the regime tried to lay the basis for a modern state and citizenship rights. Neither reform, however, proved sustainable in the long run. To understand this, one has to grasp the political dynamics behind the deepening crisis of a military regime that tried to build popular reforms on a political foundation of autocracy.

The moment it came to power, the Nimeiry regime faced organized opposition from sectarian parties. The coup leadership responded by banning all existing political organizations and creating a single state party. The list of banned organizations included the Umma Party and the DDF, which had become a part of it. Henceforth, the only way for a political group to organize was to wage factional struggles within the ruling party, the Sudan Socialist Union. Throughout 1969 and the spring of 1970, Nimeiry's principal opposition came from the Ansar brotherhood and the Umma Party, with their political and military strongholds in Kordofan and Darfur. When Sadiq al-Mahdi was placed under house arrest, the mantle of leadership passed on to the grandson of the Mahdi, Imam al-Hadi. The new imam publicly denounced Nimeiry and openly defied his officers by retiring to Aba Island, 150 miles south of Khartoum, where the Mahdiyya had originated almost a century earlier. Here the imam surrounded himself with thousands of the faithful, many heavily armed to defend the Ansar's mission. It was more than just a symbolic pledge to rejuvenate the struggle that had been the Mahdiyya. On March 27, 1970, Nimeiry confronted the Ansar, and in a fierce engagement, the Sudanese Army of the Free Officers, presumably representing the modern and progressive future against a traditional and conservative past, killed the imam and twelve thousand of his Ansar followers. Sadiq fled into exile.[30]

In this opening phase, the Nimeiry regime was allied with the Communist Party. The party saw the alliance with nationalist officers as more of a tactical than a strategic measure, not so much a way to implement a set of reforms as an opportunity to build its presence within the state and tighten its grip on the levers of power. The sad fact was that every self-avowed modernist political force in contemporary Sudan—from the Communist Party to its mirror image on the political right, the National Islamic Front—was locked into this kind of top-down putschist power-grabbing strategy. For the Communist Party, the dilemma was a direct result of its analysis of Sudanese society and the avenues of action open to it. The party analyzed Sudanese society through a binary of the modern (identified with the technically advanced sectors of the economy, such as industry, education, communication, and the state apparatus itself) and the traditional (identified with technologically backward sectors—agriculture, pastoralism, and crafts—all bonded by religious and ethnic sentiment). Such an analysis inevitably resulted in a dilemma: Since the modern sector constituted a minority and the traditional sector a majority, the party could not hope to come to power with the support of the majority. Its only chance was to usurp power through a conspiracy, which is why it spent so much effort hatching one and looking for ways to execute it by building up alliances within the army.

With the coup of 1969, the party seemed to have its first opportunity to translate this program of action from theory to practice. But since the instigators of the coup were not Communist officers under the party's discipline but nationalist officers with whom the party was allied, 1969 represented only the first step in the party's political strategy. The second step would be to overthrow nationalist officers and take direct control. This step was indeed taken when Communist army officers led by Major Hashim al-Ata staged a coup d'état on July 19, 1971. They briefly captured Nimeiry, but he escaped and went on to rally his supporters and stage a comeback with the support of Egyptian troops on Sudan's northern frontier and the dramatic intervention of Muammar al-Qaddafi of Libya. With army officers spearheading the coup, the two principal civilian Communist leaders who had been away in London flew to Khartoum to participate in the formation of the revolutionary government. It was in this context that Colonel Qaddafi ordered his Mirage fighters to intercept the BOAC (British Overseas Airways Corporation) plane carrying them, forcing it to land at Benghazi airport. It was a flagrant act of air piracy, but it worked. As the coup collapsed, its two Communist leaders were arrested and sent to Sudan, where they were promptly executed.[31]

The end of the alliance with the Communist Party both freed the regime of its ideological straitjacket and opened the way to realizing its most important political victory on the domestic front: negotiating an end to the war in the south. While both the Communist Party and the nationalist officers had agreed that the civil war would end only through peaceful means, they disagreed on the key to reform in the south. The Communist Party's program for the south called for "development," not "democracy." From the party's point of view, the south needed preferential access to resources so it could "develop," but in return it would have to accede to a national program implemented by a national leadership. Autonomy would be the price the south would have to pay for development. When the leadership of the southern rebel movement refused to accept this quid pro quo, the party saw no option but to continue with armed repression. But once the Communist Party was out of power, a new coalition of nationalist non-Communist officers coalesced around Nimeiry and began to explore a different array of political reforms, including regionalization. It was the military's willingness to agree to regional autonomy that cleared the way for the 1972 Addis Ababa Agreement, thereby settling the southern problem.

The irony was that while the agreement moved toward reforming the structure of power in the south, it did not set in motion a similar process in the north. The post–Addis Ababa regime was Janus-faced: It combined reform in the south with repression in the north. In time, the regime gained popularity in the south as it lost support in the north. The process resulted in a curious anomaly whereby the regime increasingly depended on the armed power of southern rebels to maintain its hold over Khartoum, so much so that there came a time when Nimeiry's presidential guard was drawn from the south. In contrast, popular opinion in the north, in both the riverine center and areas to the west and east, seethed with discontent.

The gains of the Addis Ababa Agreement were summed up in the Regional Autonomy Act of 1972. In 1980, the May regime—identified by the month during which it took power—decided to extend this act to all the other regions of Sudan. The implementation of the act led to the appointment of a governor for Darfur, but the regime's appointment of a non-Darfuri as governor triggered popular opposition demanding that a Darfuri be appointed instead. The Darfuris referred to this revolt as the intifada ("upheaval"). The intifada led to clashes with police and casualties among demonstrators. Soon, the central government gave in and appointed Ahmed Diraige, the original chairman of the DDF, to the post. He was the first Darfuri to govern the province since independence—a milestone that Sharif Harir said marked the end of internal colonialism.[32]

But success also had an unintended consequence: It unleashed internal political competition in Darfur and opened the gates to a fuller ethnicization of politics in the region. As long as the region's administration was controlled by members of the riverine group, the movement against outside control and for internal autonomy could appeal to all Darfuris and indeed claim to represent them all, thereby keeping a lid on internal competition among tribes. But the granting of internal autonomy in 1981 began to erode the region's unity.[33] There were already signs of an impending division during the intifada. On one side were those who participated in the upheaval through demonstrations, and on the other side were those who tried to sabotage the upheaval whenever possible. When a smaller group of inhabitants of El Fasher staged a nighttime demonstration against the commissioner of North Darfur, the majority labeled them "dogs of the night" (kilab el Leil). A "dog," in this case, was any person who opposed the call that Darfur be governed by an ethnic Darfuri.[34]

The events before and after the 1981 intifada divided the Darfuri public, especially in urban areas, into two opposing groups. The tension between them was historically fed by an ongoing competition for natural resources (mainly pasture and water) coupled with raiding for livestock—against the background of colonial retribalization of land and administration in Darfur. But it was now exacerbated by the devolution of power. In the past, such conflicts were relatively easily settled by government-supported tribal reconciliation conferences, for the government was an external force whose main interest was in maintaining law and order. The original DDF had also proved a successful arbiter of differences. Mainly because its ambition was to unite all ethnic groups in Darfur, it was able to intervene in ethnic conflicts as a supraethnic force and settle them through mediation. Whether from the outside or from within, the mediating authority could have a chance of success only if both parties to a conflict regarded it as nonpartisan.

This condition ceased to exist in 1981, and the new regional authority—not considered bipartisan by any side—was born in the midst of tensions among ethnic groups, exacerbated, as we shall see, by an ongoing ecological crisis. As soon as the regional cabinet was formed and began to function, two opposing political alliances crystallized and cut through the cabinet and the population it claimed to represent. One side was identified with an alliance of all nomadic groups (the Zaghawa and the Arab nomads) and the doctrinaire Muslim Brothers. On the other side were the major sedentary groups, mainly the Fur and the Tunjur, alongside elements of urban Darfuri elites. The former group was led by Mahmoud Jamma (then deputy governor of the region, himself an ethnic Zaghawa) and the latter by Ahmed Diraige (then governor, an ethnic Fur).

These alignments provided the building blocks for the alliances that contested the 1986 election, one where the Islamists defeated the FRD (Front for the Resistance of Darfur), which included many former DDF stalwarts. The Islamist victory was the result of two factors. First, Islamists had the support of Darfuri graduates who had shifted from the "Arabist" to the "Islamist" camp following the October Revolution. Strongly supported by the graduate constituency, the National Islamic Front (NIF) won two geographical and four graduate seats. The FRD, in contrast, did not win a single seat. Second, the FRD's dismal performance attested to the fact that many in the population had not forgotten that the DDF had formed a coalition government with the sectarian Umma Party after the 1965 elections and that many of its members had occupied leading positions in the Umma Party. Popular support for the Islamists expressed popular opposition to sectarian parties. Islamist support clearly went beyond the boundaries of ethnic Zaghawa and the Arab tribes: Many Darfuris thought the NIF capable of creating a transethnic movement, indeed duplicating the DDF's achievement before 1965.[35]

If provincial autonomy was the first in the two-pronged reform of the local government system, the second was a reform of laws that defined landholding and the system of local governance. Throughout the colonial period and for more than a decade after independence, all rural land had de facto been held as tribal land. On April 6, 1970, the Registered Land Act declared all unregistered land the property of the government of Sudan. Its legal consequence was to turn tribal into state property. Initially, the act introduced an ambiguity in the legal status of land because many families did not formally own the land they cultivated. This ambiguity was removed in 1984 with the passage of the Civil Transactions Act (CTA), which confirmed recognized occupation (use) rights alongside ownership (exchange) rights. With this revision, the state achieved a dual objective: declaring most land (99 percent) as state-owned and at the same time recognizing the rights of actual cultivators and users of this land.[36]

The reform of local governance was the purpose of the People's Local Government Act of 1971, which abolished the native authority system and in its place created a series of twenty-two rural councils. This attempt to reform the colonial state failed in the long run mainly because it lacked a viable democratic orientation. Like all modernists, the Nimeiry regime saw electoral democracy as a means of reproducing the hold of sectarian religiously based parties, an arrangement it replaced with the rule of a single party. The 1971 act had two important consequences. The first was an inflated bureaucracy, staffed by insensitive officials from the Nile and directed by the single political party, the Sudan Socialist Union. This single-party bureaucracy began by intruding upon the historic independence of villagers and nomads in the west. The 1971 act also undid the 1951 ordinance by which the departing colonial power had introduced separation of powers into the native authority system. By arguing that the reform had separated decision making from implementation and thereby paralyzed decision making as a process, the act fused rule-making and rule-enforcing (legislative and executive) powers in the hands of the new single-party bureaucracy.[37] By replacing the power of chiefs with that of bureaucrats, the very act that claimed to end the decentralized despotism of colonial administration laid the institutional basis for a centralized despotism.

Many think that the internal dynamic set in motion by the post-1981 devolution of regional power was responsible for the intensification of internal conflicts within Darfur, particularly the Arab-Fur conflicts of 1987–89 and the Arab-Massalit conflict of 1996–99. Their argument is that the appointment of a Fur governor politicized the civil service and led to Fur dominance in the new regional government. From the viewpoint of many an Arab tribe, this could spell a return to Fur dominance of Darfur during the days of Ali Dinar.[38]

It is not surprising that abolishing the tribal ownership of land should have brought to life all dormant interethnic land disputes. For that reason, others have held the post-1971 reforms responsible for accelerating ethnic conflict in the province.[39] To draw such a conclusion, however, would be to forget that every reform, no matter its overall consequence, has a destabilizing effect. We need to evaluate the May 1969 regime not simply in light of its actual results but also in light of its strategic perspective, its promise and ambitions, even if it did not always succeed in fulfilling them. On this count, the May political regime appears different from all its predecessors. It was the source of many new political ideas that penetrated even remote parts of the country. The first among these was the regime's opposition to the involvement of chiefs and chieflike sectarian notables in politics. This alone began to undermine the sacrosanct authority of those who had hitherto been canonized as "traditional" leaders. Land reform was a second important factor. According to the new regime's policy, land belonged to the state; individuals or groups could no longer claim exclusive rights to land, only rights that were explicitly protected by law and registration. Alongside these was a third change, perhaps the most important: the liquidation of native authorities as a major agency for maintaining law and order in the rural areas.[40] If successfully implemented, these reforms would have provided the basis for a transition from tribe to nation as the effective political community, laying the basis for a common Sudanese citizenship.

Those who blamed the Nimeiry reforms for growing ethnic conflict in Darfur were not entirely in the wrong. Their mistake, however, was to trace this outcome to the introduction of reform rather than to the failure to sustain it. The colonial order had a dual impact in the countryside, both negative and positive. On the positive side, chiefly authority ensured order at a reasonably low cost, especially in areas where basic changes in economic and social structures had yet to be introduced. The chiefs' powers rested upon customary sanctions by which they could keep the balance among different interests and ensure harmony among tribespeople. But these same customary powers—a colonial euphemism for lack of accountability—also made for the colonial order's negative side, ensuring continued stagnation in rural areas. The challenge was to distinguish between two different needs in the countryside so as to balance them: on the one hand, to maintain law and order and, on the other, to galvanize forces capable of ushering development into the region.

Though they failed, the Nimeiry reforms placed an important question on the agenda: how to change indirect rule. The argument for replacing native chiefs with a modern bureaucracy rested on the need to combine the maintenance of law and order with creative administrative duties that normally come under the rubric of "development." If the state's role in the countryside is limited to maintaining law and order, then there is little doubt that this role can be performed both more efficiently and more cost-effectively by chiefs. But if the point of state intervention is to break the cycle of stagnation that has gripped Darfur over the past several decades, then the case for a modern bureaucracy to replace chiefly rule will be that much stronger. For those convinced that chiefly rule must give way to administration by a modern bureaucracy, the reform also raised a second question, one having to do with accountability at all levels: Should accountability be bureaucratic or democratic or something else? We shall return to this question after a discussion of the contemporary crisis in Darfur.

Gaafar al-Nimeiry's regime (1969–85) came to an end after sixteen years of oppressive rule, in the midst of large-scale protests over food shortages and price increases. Once again, the masses in the "modern sector"—lawyers, medical doctors, teachers, and engineers—led by the Professionals' Front, were joined by student-coordinated demonstrations and a national strike. On April 6, 1985, the commander in chief of the armed forces, General Abdul Rehman Swar al-Dahab, took over as head of the Transitional Military Council and dismissed the president. In the weeks that followed, a genuine popular mobilization shook off remnants of Nimeiry's security state. Within a month, nearly forty new political parties had been formed, a renewed trade union movement had emerged, and state-controlled papers were forced to fire managers and journalists alike. Large party meetings of five thousand to twenty thousand people were held daily, in which new and old parties alike presented and explained their programs. Soon after, a civilian government was appointed, largely containing technocrats recruited from professional associations. As with the overthrow of the Abboud regime in 1964, those in the "modern sector" had successfully mobilized to dislodge a dictatorship but were unable to provide the leadership to replace it with a national government that would provide the country with a new paradigm for the period ahead. Yet again, popular protests failed to crystallize into popular reforms.[41]

Islamism

There was more than just a passing resemblance between the Bashir-led Islamist coup of 1989 and the earlier Communist-led coup. The resemblance flowed from a shared orientation. Both the Communist Party and the National Islamic Front were modernist to a fault. Both thought in universal terms and believed themselves to be free of parochial alignments, whether of locality or ethnicity or sect. Their organizational efforts focused on the modern sector; both competed to mobilize the same urban constituencies: educated youth and women, graduates and professionals (doctors, lawyers, teachers, professors, engineers), and salaried and wage workers. They combined open agitation with clandestine cadre-based organization. Most important, neither believed it could come to power through a democratic struggle; both prepared actively for clandestine and conspiratorial politics. With that in mind, both organized within the army. Like the Nimeiry–Communist Party coup of 1969, the NIF-backed 1989 coup of Brigadier Omar Hasan

Ahmad al-Bashir also portrayed itself in revolutionary terms, as a "revolution of national salvation," used emergency laws to dissolve political parties and trade unions, and ruled by decrees issued by the Revolutionary Command Council (RCC).[42]

The NIF had a strong base among students. Its cells in Khartoum University were dominated by students from Darfur. Following the introduction of regional government in 1983, these students had returned to Darfur on instructions from the party leadership and held prominent positions in the regional government. Among Darfuris with a conspicuous presence in the NIF were people such as the late Daud Yahya Bolad, Faroug Mohamed Adam, Idris Abdulmawla, and Abdul Jabar Adam. When fifteen army officers of the Revolutionary Command Council led by Brigadier al-Bashir overthrew the civilian government of Sadiq al-Mahdi on June 30, 1989, they reorganized the army, civil service, and police force and filled positions with members of the NIF. In addition, a parallel armed organization called the Popular Defense Forces was established.[43] The NIF-orchestrated military coup of 1989 also created the first opportunity since independence for many of Darfur's educated political elite to enter national politics. They did so as part of a faction—the Turabi faction—within the NIF.[44] If the first few Darfuris to enter national political leadership had done so under the patronage of the Umma Party in 1968, the second round of Darfuris did so under the wing of the NIF in the early nineties.

When fresh elections were held in 1986, the year after Nimeiry was overthrown in a coup, Islamists won 54 seats in the 301-seat parliament. By emerging as the third largest bloc, ahead of the Communist Party and its allies, it could claim to represent the modern sector of society. Twenty-eight of these seats were based on the revival of the so-called Graduates Constituency. It was the first time an ideological political movement had succeeded in finding such a prominent place alongside mass-based sectarian parties. With an Umma-DUP coalition government, the National Islamist Front became the official opposition in parliament.

Hassan al-Turabi, the head of the NIF, provided a double critique, theoretical and practical, of the traditional parties and their sectarian religious orientation.[45] He reminded his audience of the deeply historical nature of Islam and its law and asked them to use reason to reform the law (Sharia) in line with the movement of history: "Muslims have failed to absorb and understand their history. They are not able to renew their movement because they do not understand the ever-changing movement of history. They have assumed that human thought, or the body of achievement of Islamic *ijtihad,* is not connected in any way to time and place. They have stripped the application of *shari'ah* from its practical and realistic aspects, and turned it into abstract concepts existing outside the time-space framework." Asked whether Muslim groups that claim "a monopoly of sacred truth" would not "impose their ideas and beliefs on others by force" if they were to come to power, he responded that the use of reason to interpret religious truths in light of time and place (*ijtihad*) was a right of every Muslim and not just of specialists: "I respect the Sufi tradition but I do not pay allegiance to a sheikh. I also respect the *mujtahideen* [interpreters of *fiqh,* jurisprudence] but do not believe that they have a monopoly on *ijtihad;* . . . I believe that *ijtihad* is open to every Muslim, no matter how ignorant or illiterate he or she might be." On the question of knowledge, he argued, there can be no absolute authority: "Knowledge is a common commodity and people attain various degrees of it, and can exercise *ijtihad* at various levels." Which is why there could be neither an official church nor a canonized truth: "I am not in favor of sitting somewhere and issuing a fatwa and forcing people to accept it. Nor am I by any means a believer in a church that monopolizes the truth and separates man from God. I regret to say that the Muslims have been affected by the Western malaise, and they have developed pseudo-churches where '*ulama* and sheikhs pontificate and issue sacred edicts."

All this translated into a warning against sectarian Islam, for it had confused the general principles of the religion with values and practices prevalent in specific places at particular times. This is why Islam in Iran could come packaged in "Iranian chauvinism" and in Pakistan bundled with a legacy of the Indian caste system: "I fear that it [*Jama'at-e-Islami* of Pakistan] might have been influenced by some of the traditions of the Indian culture. That culture is based on a caste system dividing society into Brahmins, middle caste, and the deprived classes that carry no weight in society at all. The Jama'at at times looks as if it has this division within its own structure. . . . Women are totally separated from men, which of course has nothing to do with Islam, and a religion that is for men only is a deformed religion." Closer to home, Turabi warned of the need to distinguish Islamic principles from their particular cultural wrapping, Arabism.

Many have emphasized Turabi's opportunism in practical politics but failed to recognize that it was not his practical opportunism but his theoretical perspective that set Turabi apart from other politicians. It is what he said, not what he did, that galvanized non-Arab Islamists and explains his long-term impact on Sudanese politics. Turabi's seismic impact derived from the distinction he made between the universalism of Islamic principles and the parochialism of Arabic cultural practices, and the need to free the former from the latter. Islamism presented itself as a worthy successor to Arabism precisely because it could claim that unlike Arabs, who were a minority in Sudan, Muslims were in the majority—and the making of a Sudanese nation would have to be a majority project if it was going to be successful. It is the NIF's insistence on distinguishing between Arabism and Islamism that explained why non-Arab Darfuri Islamists poured into the NIF's ranks at an early stage. Finally, it is the collapse of this distinction by the Islamists in power that explains both the split among Islamists and the retreat of Darfuri Islamists to a separate organization. Critics would later deride NIF's claim to be upholding a universal Islam, one not historically contingent as tantamount to championing an Islam from nowhere, whereas in reality it too was an unmistakably sectarian (for example, "Arabist") tendency.

If Communists and allied officers tried to change the very structure of local government, Islamists took the broad structure for granted and attempted to carry out reforms within these parameters. The point of these reforms was to give "justice" to the "*dar*less" tribes—because they had historically gotten a raw deal. This, at least, was the rationale behind the local government reforms of 1991 and 1995. When the reforms are looked at from this point of view, we can understand both the official expectations that drove the reforms and why the results were at such cross-purposes with these expectations.

The Islamist regime began by appointing a military governor for

Darfur in August 1991. This was the infamous Colonel Al-Tayib Ibrahim Muhammad Kheir of the Revolutionary Command Council. He was known as Al-Sikha, "the iron bar," a reference to an actual iron bar he carried and applied with enthusiasm during street riots in Khartoum.[46] The reform began in February 1994, when the minister of federal affairs, Ali al-Haj, split Darfur into three separate states, North, West, and South, with their respective capitals at El Fasher, Geneina, and Nyala. Supporters of the reform explained it as a skillful way of balancing a Fur majority in one state with non-Fur majorities in other states, but opponents decried it as an equally skillful way of dividing the Fur, Darfur's largest ethnic group, into so many minorities spread over different states. A second reform took land from some of the settled tribes with officially designated *dars* and created *dars* for hitherto "*dar*less" tribes. The process began when the government of West Darfur issued a decree in March 1995 dividing the traditional homeland of the Massalit into thirteen emirates, nine of which were allocated to previously "*dar*less" Arab groups. The result was a fragmentation of the territory hitherto demarcated as Dar Massalit. With the creation of a new native administration, the authority of the Massalit sultan was also reduced. Furthermore, Dar Erenga and Dar Jebel in Kulbus Province became two different administrative entities outside Dar Massalit Sultanate.[47] If the division of Darfur into three separate states alienated the Fur, the granting of land to "*dar*less" tribes alienated the Massalit. When the Massalit protested, the regime's response was to replace the civilian governor with a military one. The new governor immediately took to imprisoning and torturing prominent leaders of the protest.[48] This was the background of raging conflicts between the Massalit and the Arab tribes in the late 1990s.

When they began in 1995, these conflicts were still local, fought around local power, tribal territory, and access to natural resources. The central government made things worse by a patently partisan reform that did not claim to be changing the system as a whole and yet seemed to tilt in favor of the region's Arab tribes at the expense of the Massalit and the Fur. As the existing system of administration came undone, traditional mechanisms of conflict resolution also began to come apart. Three separate reconciliation conferences—one in 1995 and two in August and November of 1996—came to naught. The more the government became a party to a hitherto local conflict, the more the conflict spiraled into an officially recognized state of emergency as different ethnic groups established, trained, and armed militia groups. They began by remobilizing traditional village militia structures, *warnang* among the Fur and *ornang* among the Massalit, both historically used to organize hunting parties, communal work in the fields, and feasts.[49] The Massalit drifted into a guerrilla war until January 1999, when government troops, helicopters, and Arab militias crushed the Massalit insurgents, killing more than 2,000 and displacing 100,000, of whom 40,000 were said to have fled to Chad.[50] When interviewed in 2004, Massalit peasants recalled the period from 1995 to 1999 as one of devastating losses.[51] If the Nimeiry regime combined the rule-making and rule-enforcing powers of local authorities, the Islamists not only revived colonial-style native authorities but also militarized them by broadening their duties to include preparation of youth for counterinsurgency (dubbed jihad), touted as part of the duty of an official who it was said must lead his people in both prayer and war.[52] The broader impact of the escalating conflict in Darfur was to split the Islamist leadership in Khartoum.

The split in the Islamist elite occurred at two levels: national and provincial. Whereas the national crisis split the ruling party, the provincial crisis ignited rebellion in Darfur. The first indicator that all was not well within the Islamist political camp came before the 1989 al-Bashir coup: Two parliamentarians, both from Darfur, resigned from the NIF block during the 1986–89 democratic period, underscoring the fact that the division between settled and nomadic factions within Darfur had national implications. The Fur-dominated DDF had earlier evolved into a pro-cultivator lobby, claiming that the "national salvation" government was tilting too much in favor of nomads. This prompted a leading Fur member of the NIF, Daud Yahya Bolad, to sever his relationship with the government and join the Sudan People's Liberation Army / Movement (SPLA/M). One of the leaders of the Bolad incursion, Abdal Aziz Adam Al-Hilo, came from the Massalit revolt against the central government. The government responded by mobilizing recent immigrants from Chad. These militia, which came to be known as the Janjawiid, began to operate in the lands of both the Fur in Jebel Marra and the Massalit to the west.[53] Caught, Bolad was executed by his fellow brothers in the National Islamic Front.

The second split divided the National Islamic Front into two ethnically polarized groups: the Quraish as the symbol for Arab tribes and *The Black Book* as the symbol for non-Arab—increasingly called African—tribes. The leadership split between al-Bashir and Turabi ultimately took an organizational form in 1999, with al-Bashir heading the ruling National Congress Party (NCP) and Hassan al-Turabi heading the opposing Popular National Congress (PNC).[54] For many, Turabi symbolized the interests of Darfur in contrast to the NCP and riverine Arabs. The Turabi faction's claim to stand for the people of Darfur was based on the presence of a prominent Darfuri in its ranks: Dr. Khalil Ibrahim, who had been the minister of health before the al-Bashir–Turabi split—even more significant, a leader of the brutal counterinsurgency in the south—and would subsequently become the leader of one of the two main rebel movements, the Justice and Equality Movement (JEM). Subsequently, Turabi's Popular National Congress took the line that the ruling party—which had won only three seats in Darfur in the 1986 elections—was excluding people from Darfur and other peripheral regions from senior posts. Even after he left for Europe to do groundwork for JEM, Khalil Ibrahim sided with the PNC in 2002.[55]

The Black Book was full of information illustrating the extremely narrow base from which Sudan's governing class had all along been drawn, beginning with the first independence government in 1954. Table after table showed that with only 5.4 percent of the nation's population, the northern region was home to the bulk of Sudan's political elite: 79.5 percent of those holding central government positions in 1986, 59.4 percent of ministers and 66.7 percent of representatives in the Revolutionary Command Council in 1989, 83.3 percent of those in the presidential palace, 60.1 percent of holders of federal cabinet posts, 56.2 percent of governors, 51.1 percent of commissioners, and 47.5 percent of all state ministers in 2000—not to mention 67 percent of all Sudanese attorneys general and 76 percent of all representatives in the National Council for Distribution of Resources.[56] The narrow clique that has ruled Sudan since its independence comes mainly from three ethnic groups; the Shaigiya (ex-president Sir El-Khatim El-Khalifa, cur-

rent vice president Ali Osman Mohamed Taha), the Jallayeen (President
Omar Hasan al-Bashir), and the Dangala (ex-president Nimeiry, ex-
president Sadiq al-Mahdi, and ex–vice president Al-Zubayr Mohamed
Salih Alzibair).[57] This group gained an awareness of sharing a common
interest as early as 1976: When a Kordofan army officer—someone not
from their ranks—nearly succeeded in organizing a coup against the
Nimeiry regime, the clique responded by forming an organization
called KASH (Kayan al Shamal, or the Northern Entity), otherwise
known as Al Thalooth (the Tripartite Coalition), which has ruled Sudan
since independence.

In March 2004, the government arrested ten middle-ranking officers,
all from Darfur and neighboring Kordofan, on suspicion of plotting a
coup. Days later, it detained Turabi, along with six top PNC political
figures, accusing them of inciting regionalism and tribalism in Darfur.[58]
It was testimony of how deeply the split in the ruling Islamist group was
beginning to affect Darfur.

Africanism

When the Sudanese political class coalesced around an "Arabization"
project on the morrow of independence, it built on deep-seated
assumptions that had driven intellectual pursuits throughout the colonial period. The key assumption was that civilization in Sudan had been
mainly an exogenous affair, narrowly a product of "Arab" immigration
and intermarriage and broadly an outcome of "Arabization" of the
indigenous population of Sudan. Even if there had never been an "Arab"
invasion of Sudan, and even if all studies confirmed that the spread of
Arabic in Sudan had been more of a consensual than a coercive project,
postindependence "Arabization" literally took the form of a state-driven
cultural and institutional invasion of "non-Arab" Sudan, in particular
the south.

There were two kinds of responses to Arabism as a state-imposed
national project. The first was Islamist and the second Africanist. Both
claimed that the Arabist project was caught in a dilemma of its own
making: Since "Arabs" were a minority in Sudan, the Arabist project
would have to be imposed on the non-Arab majority. Both claimed to
stand for a majority project. Instead of a state imposition on the major-

ity in society, such a project would do the opposite: refashion the state in the image of the majority.

Neither side, however, was in a mood to think through the contradictions of the majority position. There were at least two. The first and more obvious question concerned rights of a minority in a democracy. How could a state designed in the image of the majority still claim the legitimate right to govern all the people of Sudan—especially if it turned its majority status into a permanent one, using it to lock the minority out of power, also permanently? The second was a more complex question, one that concerned the definition of the majority. As the very contention between Islamist and Africanist projects showed, there was no single, self-evident, and permanent majority in society that could be arrived at through a simple arithmetic calculation. Because people had multiple identities—religious, linguistic, regional, and so on—there would be not one majority but several overlapping majorities. In this case, the overlapping ground was occupied by African Muslims, who belonged simultaneously to two majorities, African (which, in this context, meant non-Arab) and Muslim. Their particular political identification would determine which identity would translate into a political majority at a given point in time. Finally, the nature of a majority project, Islamist or Africanist, was not at all self-evident. As the Islamist period demonstrated clearly, there were rival notions of Islamism, presenting alternatives that were inclusive or exclusive, with radically different consequences for democratic politics. Similar questions would arise when it came to the debate on how state and society in Sudan should be reorganized in line with Africanist conceptions.

Africanism in Sudan had deep intellectual and political roots in all parts of the country. A recent history of artistic and political expression in Sudan traces the Africanist assertion to debates inside the first literary society formed by young graduates in northern Sudan.[59] This was the Sudanese Union Society, formed in 1920 "to strengthen the nationalist consciousness of Sudanese, partly through literary activities and partly through directly disseminating views critical of the Condominium government." It is a split in the Union Society that led to the formation of the first explicitly political organization, the White Flag League of 1923.

That split was an outgrowth of a debate as to which dedication would be the most appropriate for a collection of religious poems: "to a noble Arabic nation" or "to a noble Sudanese nation." The division came to reflect an ongoing ideological chasm in Sudanese politics between two sides, one championing Arabic nationalism and "the Unity of the Nile Valley" and the other a Sudanese nationalism calling for "Sudan for the Sudanese."

Sudanism and Africanism became the terms of two different critiques of Arabism in the artistic and literary world, the first more focused on the cultural diversity of Sudanese society than the second. Both currents found expression in northern Sudan in the 1960s, and both presaged later political currents. Quite often, these currents drew inspiration from the historical example of Sinnar, the capital of Funj Sultanate. The visual artist Zein al-Abdin coined the term *Sudanawiyya* ("Sudanism"). According to Mohamed Abusabib, it "defines the cultural basis of a pioneering and influential trend in modern Sudanese visual art" and refers to "artists who derive inspiration from local heritages with the aim of creating an 'authentic Sudanese' art." As Zein al-Abdin put it: "This is our destiny of Africanism or of Africanized Arabism. Sudanawiyya exists in our consciousness as an unclear area that we have not yet explored." The poet al-Nur Osman Bubakar coined the metaphor "jungle and desert" in the early 1960s. He referred to northern Sudan as the land of Nubia and "jungle and desert" as symbolizing its heritage, a reconciliation very much in the manner of the historical kingdoms of Funj and Abdallab. Another poet, Abd al-Hai, described in his masterpiece *al-Awda ila Sinnar* (The Return to Sinnar) the epic moment "when a new identity emerges out of the fusion of Arabic-Islamic and indigenous elements." That moment, the rise of Sinnar, is said to bring together a multiple heritage—from the south (the jungle), from Arabic and Islamic Sufism (the desert), and from Nubia—and creating "a new tongue, history and homeland" for the author and for the rest of the Sudanese. In the 1970s, Nuba intellectuals began to speak of Nuba as an "African" area, marginalized under the rule of an "Arabist" central government.

The political roots of Africanism lay in the struggles of southern peoples. As independence approached, members of parliament and the educated class from the south called for a form of government that would give them the right to choose their own state system; most

demanded a federal form.[60] No sooner had Sudan become an independent state than an armed insurgency began raging in the south. That
insurgency has been like an undertow shaping the history of independent Sudan, either directly by its own impact or indirectly by inspiring
movements in peripheral regions. The southern insurgency went
through three different phases: The 1955 insurrection was followed by
an armed struggle that unfolded in two phases, the first from 1963 to
1972 and the second from 1983 to 2003. Two major political shifts
occurred during these periods.

The first shift was in the method of struggle, from the insurrection of
1955 in Torit to a protracted guerrilla struggle from 1963 to 1972. The
second was a shift in perspective. Both the 1955 insurrection and the
guerrilla struggle that began in 1963 looked for a specifically southern
solution to a problem both defined as southern in manifestation. A radical change in perspective came after 1983 with the formation of the
Sudan People's Liberation Army (SPLA). Unlike its predecessors, the
SPLA refused to be confined within the borders of southern Sudan. It
demonstrated an ability to mobilize beyond sacrosanct ethnic boundaries, first beyond its supposedly Nilotic heartland to eastern Equatoria,
and then beyond the old north-south border to the Nuba Mountains in
Southern Kordofan and the southern Blue Nile.[61] The SPLA presence in
the southern Blue Nile Province was first heard of in late 1985, when
armed SPLA units began passing through it as they moved between
Ethiopia and the White Nile.[62] The SPLA issued an all-Sudan demand
calling for the reorganization of the Sudanese state and society around
the recognition that Sudan was an African country. The key question
was: Who is an African?

John Garang explored this question in his statement to the Koka Dam
conference, a preliminary dialogue held on March 20, 1986, between the
SPLM/SPLA and the northern Sudan–based opposition coalition, the
National Alliance for National Salvation: "I present to this historic conference that our major problem is that the Sudan has been looking for
its soul, for its true identity. Failing to find it (because they do not look
inside the Sudan, they look outside), some take refuge in Arabism, and
failing in this, they find refuge in Islam as a uniting factor. Others get
frustrated as they failed to discover how they can become Arabs when
their creator thought otherwise. And they take refuge in separation."[63]

Next he distinguished between Arabism as a political project and Arabic culture:

> We are a product of historical development. Arabic (though I am poor in it—I should learn it fast) must be the national language in a new Sudan, and therefore we must learn it. Arabic cannot be said to be the language of the Arabs. No, it is the language of the Sudan. English is the language of the Americans, but that country is America, not England. Spanish is the language of Argentina, Bolivia, Cuba and they are those countries, not Spain. Therefore I take Arabic on scientific grounds as the language of the Sudan and I must learn it. So, next time, I will address you in Arabic if Daniel Kodi, my Arabic teacher, does his job well, and if I am a good student. . . . We are serious about the formation of a new Sudan, a new civilization that will contribute to the Arab world and to the African world and to the human civilization. Civilization is nobody's property. Cross-fertilization of civilization has happened historically and we are not going to separate whose civilization this and this is, it may be inseparable.[64]

Sudan's problem was that of political power, not cultural diversity: "I believe that the central question, the basic problem of the Sudan is that since independence in 1956, the various regimes that have come and gone in Khartoum . . . have failed to provide a commonality, a paradigm, a basis for the Sudan as a state; that is, there has been no conscious evolution of that common Sudanese identity and destiny to which we all pay undivided allegiance, irrespective of our backgrounds, irrespective of our tribes, irrespective of race, irrespective of religious belief."[65] And the way to solve this problem is to address the question of how power is organized: "The method which we have chosen in order to achieve the objective of a united Sudan, is to struggle to restructure power in the center so that questions as to what does John Garang want do not arise, so that questions as to what does the South want do not arise. . . . I totally disagree with this concept of sharing power, for it is not something in a 'siniya' (food tray). I use the words restructuring of political power in Khartoum rather than power sharing because the latter brings to mind immediately the question, who is sharing power with whom? And the answer is usually North and South, Arabs and Africans, Christians and Muslims. It has the connotation of the old paradigm."[66]

John Garang died prematurely, only a few weeks after he assumed the position of first vice president in Sudan. The very day of his arrival suggested that even if the guerrilla struggle had ended, its impact on civilian politics was just beginning. The million-plus crowd that gathered to welcome him cut across all conventional political divisions: north-south, Muslim-Christian, Arab–non-Arab. It had the hint of something new.

It may be that with Garang, as with Turabi, what he said had a much greater effect than what he did. The effect of what both men said could be read in the actions of those who took their words seriously. This much is clear from developments in Darfur, particularly the mushrooming of two rebel movements, the SLA and the JEM, one inspired by the African secularism of John Garang and the other by the African Islamism of Hassan al-Turabi.

7

The Cold War and Its Aftermath

ARMED CHADIAN GROUPS have been involved in all major wars in Darfur since the mid-1980s. The 1987–89 Arab-Fur war was begun by Acheikh Ibn Omer and the CDR (Conseil Démocratique Révolution-naire, or Revolutionary Democratic Council). The Arab-Massalit wars included large numbers of Chadian Arabs, and the Janjawiid-rebel wars that started in 2001 have also included armed groups of Chadian origin on a large scale, again on both sides. These wars have been propelled by increased militarization and fought with growing ferocity. To under-stand the reasons for increased Chadian involvement in Darfur and its heightened desperation, one has to look both at the Sahelian region and beyond it.

Within the Sahel, the ferocity of these wars derives from the crisis of nomadic peoples, who are homeless, fighting for survival and land. When asked by the head of Sudan's Refugee Commission when he will return home, a Chadian refugee replied, "Where ever there is land and rain will be my homeland."[1] The Chadian flight across the Darfur bor-der is in response to a double crisis: ecological *and* political. The ecolog-ical crisis is regional, and the political crisis is national. To understand the stepped-up militarization of these conflicts, one needs to focus on the ways in which the region was pulled into the Cold War during the presidency of Ronald Reagan.

The Ecological Crisis

The Sahel is a narrow transitional band that extends across the breadth of Africa, from Senegal in the west to Sudan in the east, sandwiched between the arid Sahara to the north and the humid savanna to the south. Before the great drought of the past few decades, the Sahelian climate was shaped by eight to eleven dry months per year, and its landscape was marked by baobab and acacia trees, with sparse grass cover. Over the past half century, however, this landscape has been subjected to desertification and soil erosion caused by natural climate change as well as overgrazing and farming. As a result, the countries of the Sahel zone suffered devastating droughts and famine starting in the early 1970s. The most severe drought occurred in 1980–84 and was accompanied by widespread displacement and localized famine.[2]

In 2007, the United Nations Environment Programme (UNEP) published a comprehensive analysis on the depth of the ecological crisis in different parts of this region. Although the study is specific to Sudan, its analysis of trends in Darfur is equally applicable to the Sahelian part of Chad. In Darfur, a third of the forest cover was lost between 1973 and 2006.[3] Ever since 1917, which is when precipitation records began being collected, the ten-year moving rainfall average for El Fasher in North Darfur has declined from three hundred millimeters per annum to approximately two hundred millimeters. The UNEP study goes on to point out that this kind of "scale and duration of the reduction in rainfall . . . is sufficient to have changed the natural environment, irrespective of human influence." The result was "a southward shift in desert climate of approximately 100 kilometers over 40 years."[4] This scale of historical climate change "is almost unprecedented: the reduction in rainfall has turned millions of hectares of already marginal semi-desert grazing land into desert." The shift is "manifest first and foremost in the widespread death of trees during drought events, which are not followed by recovery." The main impact of climate change has been to steadily turn the northern part of the Sahel belt into desert, a development that has forced pastoralist societies "to move south to find pasture."[5]

The great Sahelian drought of the twentieth century reached its depths in Wadai and Darfur in 1966; the rains did not return to normal for another two decades.[6] It is estimated that by 1973, 70 percent of the cattle in Chad had been slaughtered or had perished. The militant cattle nomads, the Baggara of Wadai, Darfur, and Kordofan, were impoverished and angry. Deprived of food, thousands of Baggara and Toubou nomads from Chad fled into Darfur. Tens of thousands of the inhabitants of the Sahel, particularly in Wadai in Chad, began to move eastward to the Nile in search of water and work, looking for anything that would help them survive. The more hardy sons of the Gourane, the Zaghawa, and the Bedeiyat reverted to that traditional occupation of hard times, banditry. During the decades of drought in the Sahel, there was little security throughout the borderlands between Chad and Sudan for merchants or pilgrims or even the unwary soldier. The Cold War hardened attitudes on both sides and introduced the widespread devastation of modern warfare, which in turn contributed to undermining the flexibility of traditional means designed to solve conflicts between farmers and herders. "War," asserts one writer, "is the principal cause of famine, not drought, whether in the fifth, the fifteenth or the twentieth century."[7] But what is the cause of war?

The Political Crisis

Even though Chad had been a French colony, it did not look especially unfamiliar to someone who knew Sudan. Like the British in Sudan, the French, too, had cultivated a privileged group set apart from the rest of the country in regional, religious, linguistic, and ethnic terms. Since the French considered the northern part of Chad useless (*Tchad inutile*), the Francophone elite was not surprisingly southern. It was also army-based and Christian, and was led by an army officer, François Tombalbaye, who assumed the presidency of the country at independence. If the south was Christian, the north was Muslim and nomadic, both Arab and non-Arab. The Muslim population was barred from both the army and the civil service, and generally excluded from participation in the state. The most deprived of the Muslims, the lowest of the low, were the Arab nomads. As in Darfur, the Arabs of Chad were socially and economically underprivileged Bedouins. Many grievances raised in the context of southern Sudan were valid in the context of Chad, except that the aggrieved of Chad were Muslims and Arabs rather than non-Arab Christians and animists.

Less than a year after independence in June 1960, Chad became a dictatorship dominated by a French-educated southern elite whose members rarely traveled north of the capital, Fort-Lamy (renamed N'Djamena). The dictatorship became a formal and legal reality in January 1962, when all political parties except for the ruling party—Parti Progressiste Tchadien (PPT) of President Tombalbaye—were dissolved and prohibited. Riots broke out in the capital city in 1963, marking the onset of decades of civil war. Close observers of Chad noted that the main surprise was not that the civil war broke out in the first place but that it had not erupted earlier.

The 1963 riots were followed by the Toubou Rebellion of 1965 in the BET (the Borkou-Ennedi-Tibesti Province), the northern third of Chad. The rebellion was triggered by the new government, whose merciless exaction compounded the effects of a relentless drought. An investigative team sent to the area by the United States embassy found that, in every prefecture they visited, nomads were forced to pay tax for both themselves and their animals, thereby ending up paying five or six times the taxes they should have. Selectively imposed only on Arab nomads, these exactions decimated their herds. Resentment against discriminatory treatment by the independent government came to a boil on November 1, 1965, when Tombalbaye's minister of the interior paid a government "goodwill" visit to Mangalme, a small town located three hundred miles east of Fort-Lamy. There was widespread rioting, and the government's armed response left more than five hundred demonstrators dead.[8]

There were other parallels between the nature of power in Chad and that in Khartoum. At about the same time the regime in Khartoum launched a program of "Arabization," the government in Chad began its own program of "Africanization." Modeled on a set of government decrees issued by President Mobutu Sese Seko of Zaire, the Africanization program claimed to return the Chadian people to their "authentic" condition. For its duration, the program demanded absolute obedience to President Tombalbaye. The new party's Mobutu-style "authenticité" campaign was formulated by its new adviser, Dr. Vixamar, a Haitian intellectual and physician. The campaign turned Yondo, a ritual manhood ceremony for young males in the tribes of southern Chad, into a requirement for getting a job with the government, making government employment into a monopoly of southerners initiated into Yondo rites. Lasting several weeks, the ceremony is held every six or seven years at a limited number of sites, where boys gather and women are not allowed, even to witness, and where rituals "transform" boys into adults, reinforcing male bonds and male authority. The effect was to broaden the opposition beyond northerners to southern Christians who considered Yondo a pagan initiation rite. Tombalbaye retaliated by expelling Christian missionaries and demanded that all Chadians abandon missionary-led religions and practices and follow him in the search for a more African "Tchaditude." Like Mobutu, Tombalbaye used the authenticity campaign to purge the party's cells of undesirable elements: He "Africanized" the Parti Progressiste Tchadien in September 1973 and reconstituted it as the Mouvement National pour la Révolution Culturelle et Sociale (MNRCS). The next year, in January 1974, the regime issued new passports and identity cards, giving "authentic" African names to all citizens of Chad.

Opposition to the Tombalbaye regime was focused in the north of the country, from which emerged the first well-known leader of the opposition, Ibrahim Abatcha, who declared himself a Nasserite socialist and publicly pronounced his opposition to the Tombalbaye regime. Ibrahim Abatcha's 1963 pamphlet "Toward a United National Liberation Front" declared war on three enemies: the Tombalbaye regime, Western imperialism, and French neocolonialism. Ibrahim Abatcha was one of the first Chadian dissidents to receive material support from Khartoum and to be given political access to Chadian refugees in Darfur. The radical nationalist language of the opposition was summed up in its motto: "Chad for Chadians." But the motto sounded more like an aspiration than a reality as the opposition narrowed to mainly Chadian Arabs and Sudanese converts from Darfuri tribes that straddled neighboring Chadian provinces. Not surprisingly, the Chad National Liberation Front (FLT) was founded at Nyala in South Darfur on June 22, 1966, with Ibrahim Abatcha as its secretary-general. It subsequently became known by the acronym FROLINAT. Supported by the Sudan government, FROLINAT also received arms from the Egyptians. Sources linked to the U.S. embassy estimated that though FROLINAT had engaged government forces in at least thirty battles during 1967, none had taken place more than fifty miles west of the Chad-Sudan border.[9]

FROLINAT grew by feeding on popular discontent. No one was surprised when FROLINAT rebels appeared in the BET after the 1965 Toubou Rebellion, bearing arms to support the Toubou. If the link with the Toubou provided fuel for FROLINAT to grow, integration within the ranks of a political movement gave the Toubou Rebellion a coherence it had hitherto lacked. Even then, the rebellion flickered all too briefly, like a flame in a storm, as it was put out in a matter of days by fifteen hundred French troops who were dispatched to Fort-Lamy to suppress it.[10]

As the colonial power, France had clearly defined interests in Chad. Historically, its interests had been focused on cotton, grown in the south and traded by metropolitan French commercial interests through a state company, renamed Société Cotonniere du Tchad (COTONTCHAD) and granted a semiautonomous status at independence. The north, considered "useless" during the colonial period, became an object of great interest following reports of possible uranium reserves in the BET and of oil elsewhere. France also had a military stake in Chad. U.S. State Department sources estimated that 10 percent of Chad's one thousand–strong postindependence gendarmerie and military forces were French. Not only did French military advisers command and train the new Chadian national army, but another three thousand French troops were garrisoned in Chad. Even more important, the administration of the BET remained the responsibility of the French military, so much so that even President Tombalbaye's trusted cadres from the south were not permitted into the BET to ensure they would not provoke its nomadic inhabitants.[11] Within two decades of Chad's independence, the French presence was eclipsed by American involvement as the region became a flashpoint in the Cold War. As this happened, the French tried hard to steer a middle course, one autonomous of the Americans and not as openly hostile to Libya. They hoped to reduce Libyan influence in Chad, but without damaging France's interest in continuing to refine Libyan oil at Marseille.[12]

The north-south character of the political conflict that emerged in Chad after independence bore a strong resemblance to the conflict in neighboring Sudan. In both cases, the contours of the conflict were shaped by developments in the colonial period. But over the decade and a half that followed the end of the war in Vietnam, the conflicts grew in scale, fanned by the flames of the Cold War. Two individuals, more than any others, played a key role in stoking local into regional conflicts. One was Colonel Muammar al-Qaddafi, and the other was Ronald Reagan. Although Qaddafi was the first to appear on the scene, Reagan would loom larger. To better understand the impact of the Cold War on the region, one has to look at some of the dynamics of the region itself.

The Cold War

Relations between Darfur and Libya have been forged through lively trade relations over centuries. Libya has been a key destination for Darfuri livestock as well as labor migrants. Before the Darfur insurgency in 2003, livestock production provided a living for some 20 percent of the population in Sudan.[13] During the colonial period and after, Darfuri youth traveled, at first to the Gezira and the towns along the Nile, and then to Libya, looking for gainful employment. Libya, in contrast to Darfur, is a labor-importing society: by 2000, there were estimated to be more than 2.5 million immigrants in Libya. This made for one immigrant for every two Libyans. Among these were an estimated 150,000 to 200,000 Darfuri migrant workers.[14] The close-knit character of this region is evident from the *hawala* system that fueled commercial transactions before the arrival of Western capital in the region, and that is the medium through which migrant remittances are made today. The *hawaldars* (*hawala* agents) are traders who transfer money and goods both within and across borders. Today, *hawaldars* make use of satellite phones to greatly improve communication. The *hawala* system continues to reach as far as Kebkabiya in Darfur, where there are *hawaldar* agents.[15]

The Libyan revolution, which brought Muammar al-Qaddafi to power in 1969, proved a turning point in the history of the region. Qaddafi had embraced the geopolitical concept of three concentric circles—Arab, Islamic, and African—as elaborated in Gamal Abdel Nasser's book *Egypt's Liberation: The Philosophy of the Revolution*. A leader in a hurry,

Qaddafi raced to implement an agenda of unity, proposing a union, first with Egypt and then with Sudan, only to be rebuffed by each. Qaddafi's more immediate impact was at the global level: He not only demanded that the British evacuate the military bases they had taken over from the Italians and Germans but also stipulated March 1970 as the deadline for the evacuation. He similarly demanded the Americans evacuate Wheelus Air Base by a specified deadline. On the second anniversary of the transfer of the base to Libya, Qaddafi announced a number of solidarity measures, including sending "arms, money and volunteers" to Sinn Féin in Northern Ireland, to Muslim freedom fighters in the Philippines, and to African Americans struggling against "American arrogance."[16]

Qaddafi's impact on Chad began a few months after he came to power. Qaddafi began with a double initiative, inviting FROLINAT to open its first permanent base in Tripoli in November 1969 and supporting the Toubou in the BET with light machine guns and mortars. Darfur soon became the base for the training of Chadian militias, formed and trained under FROLINAT command.

More often than not, Qaddafi's attempts to shape regional politics to suit his preferences boomeranged. Such, indeed, was the case in Sudan. When the Libyan-backed Mahdist coup of July 1976 failed, Nimeiry decided to make the enemy of his enemy his friend and thus repair relations with Chad under its new president, Felix Malloum. In September 1977, Nimeiry brought together Malloum and his chief rival, Hissen Habre, at a peace conference in Khartoum. The two formed a new coalition government pledged to take on the FROLINAT rebels and their Libyan sponsor.[17] After several years of factional fighting within the coalition, Hissen Habre emerged victorious in 1982. When he became president of a government dominated by northern Muslims, Hissen Habre also became the centerpiece of the American Cold War strategy during the Reagan era.

If Qaddafi's coming to power in 1969 began Libyan interference in the internal affairs of Chad, Reagan's coming to power in 1981 put Chad firmly in the grip of Cold War politics. The American interest in Chad centered around the Aozou oasis, a part of Chadian territory occupied by Libya since 1973. *The New York Times* had explained that "geological investigations showed that [there] might be an extension of a uranium belt running through Niger and Mali further west." Libya had built a modern road to Bardai and was constructing a second all-weather road from Kufra to Jebel Uwaynat, where the borders of Egypt, Libya, and Sudan meet. The U.S. interest in the road was based on a State Department estimate that Libyan forces could easily use it to move from Jebel Uwaynat into Darfur and El Fasher to the east and Abéché and Wadai in Chad to the south.[18]

Sworn in on January 20, 1981, only two weeks after Qaddafi had announced the union of Chad and Libya, President Reagan began by breaking diplomatic relations with Libya, closing the U.S. embassy in Tripoli, and asking the Libyans to close their embassy in Washington, D.C. On cue, the CIA declared Qaddafi "the most prominent state sponsor of and participant in international terrorism" and thus a clear and present danger to the United States. Reagan openly announced support for Hissen Habre's efforts to launch a guerrilla war to displace the government in Chad. Close on the heels of the American embrace of Hissen Habre came Israeli military advice and the training of intelligence personnel for Habre's forces.[19]

To isolate Qaddafi within the Organization of African Unity (OAU), the United Nations, and the Muslim world, the United States embarked on building another tripartite alliance, of the United States, Egypt, and Sudan. U.S. relations with the Nimeiry regime had warmed up considerably after the failed Communist coup of 1971. In August 1983, the Sudanese army joined the "Bright Star" military exercises being held in the western desert by Egypt and the United States. As the U.S. link with Sudan evolved into a close military and economic alliance, there began a regular and significant flow of arms from the United States to Sudan, including M-40 grenade launchers and Stinger ground-to-air missiles.[20]

Nimeiry's most significant contribution to the alliance was to provide Hissen Habre's forces with a rear base in Darfur. This included both training facilities and the passage of arms. As long as Hissen Habre continued to demonstrate an ability to shape the Chadian National Armed Forces (Forces Armées Nationales Tchadiennes, or FANT) into a reasonably disciplined force, the United States was happy to facilitate an expanded flow of American and Egyptian arms to help him confront the Libyan-assisted forces of the government of Chad. In 1982, FANT forced Goukouni Oueddei, the Libyan-supported president of Chad, out of office. Not only was Darfur the staging ground for the operation, but the Nimeiry government played a leading role in the military operations. Habre's post-1982 government was put together as a coalition of southerners and northern Muslims, all except Arab and Zaghawa nomads of the north. But the coalition grew increasingly weak and wobbly, as nomadic groups—both Arab and Zaghawa—responded to their continued marginalization by taking up arms.

For the moment, though, Hissen Habre's importance as a Cold War asset increased, and the United States supplied him with arms and the French Air Force provided air cover. The latter gave him immunity from Libyan air strikes, and the former increased the firepower of his ragtag army. This combination worked wonders for nearly a decade, with several notable successes. The first was the dramatic strike by Habre's guerrillas against the Libyan air base at Wadi Doum in March 1987. Supplied with U.S. arms and guaranteed French air cover, Habre's men overran the base and captured war matériel estimated to cost half a billion dollars. They took a sizable Libyan force as POWs. "This astonishing victory," write two authors with strong U.S. government connections, "took the West completely by surprise." According to Human Rights Watch, the United States used a clandestine base in Chad to train captured Libyan soldiers and organize them into a Contra-type anti-Qaddafi force. The FANT followed up this dramatic victory with another strike, this time across the frontier into Darfur, where it clashed with Libyans and recruits in the Islamic Legions. Having already promised Habre $32 million in military assistance, the United States celebrated with the promise of another $10 million.[21] Later in the year, on August 8, 1987, FANT again attacked Libyan positions on the Aozou oasis and easily overran them—again with French air cover neutralizing the Libyan Air Force. The State Department hailed Habre for having "done a very effective job of nation-building under very difficult circumstances. There is no parallel in Africa to his ability to co-opt his opposition."[22]

The Reagan administration combined a regional involvement with direct air attacks on Libya. The most flagrant was the bombing of the Libyan presidential palace on April 14, 1986, by twenty-four F-111Fs of the U.S. Air Force's Forty-eighth Tactical Fighter Wing, which had taken

off from the Royal Air Force base at Lakenheath, England. Operation El
Dorado Canyon aimed to assassinate Colonel Qaddafi but ended up
killing his eighteen-month-old daughter Hanna.

Libyan response to growing American involvement in the region was
twofold. Qaddafi immediately moved to strengthen relations with the
Soviet Union. Libya already had an estimated four thousand foreign
military advisers by 1984. Of these, two thousand were from the Soviet
Union. This meant one foreign adviser for every twenty Libyan soldiers.
Qaddafi's second move was to reestablish relations with the Hissen
Habre government, calling for normalization of diplomatic relations
with Chad during OAU anniversary celebrations on May 25, 1988.[23]

At the same time, the Libyans learned from the United States and
shifted from a direct confrontation to a proxy war. They trained one
failed proxy after another: from the so-called Islamic Legions (*al failaq
al Islami*)—an improvised multinational force made up of migrant
workers and the remnants of Chadian opposition groups—to the Arab
Gathering (*Tajamu al Arabi*), which, despite its name, included all
Libyan allies in the region, whether Arab or non-Arab, including some
Zaghawa and other non-Arab Bedouins such as the Toubou, Gourane,
Meidob, and Tuareg.[24]

With France actively providing air support for Hissen Habre's Chadian army, the dynamic of the proxy war began to move to Chad's eastern
border, Darfur. Not only had Libya been humiliated by the ragtag Chadian army comprising a coalition of several guerrilla forces, but the active
involvement of the French Air Force also prevented it from having a second go at the Chadians. Qaddafi looked for a way out of this cul-de-sac.
He turned to nomadic Arab tribes, the only group that had been system-
atically excluded from participation in Chadian power configurations
and were open to Libyan overtures, to arm their militias as so many
proxies through which to open a second front in Chad.

A proxy's success depended on tapping a real grievance. It is the Chad
government's continued repression that had created a valid and sustained grievance among its African Arab population, many of whom
had fled to Libya and Sudan for safety. The first thing to understand is
that this was a historic reversal of the direction of movement at the
Chad-Darfur border. Those who lived on different sides of the Chad-
Sudan border have negotiated and crossed it with ease for a long time

and for a variety of reasons, beginning with the ecological. This movement has customarily been from Darfur to eastern Chad. Mainly because of higher rainfall on the Chadian side, the Abbala camel herders have traditionally moved from Darfur to eastern Chad in search of grass and water. But the decades from the 1960s to the 1990s saw a reverse flow of Chadians across the border. The refugees were both economic and political, civilian and militia. In 1973, as a result of the Chadian civil war and drought, West Darfur hosted more than 200,000 Chadian refugees. Another 94,000 people, mostly Zaghawa and Toubou, were in Sudanese refugee camps by November 1994. The region's population increased from a reported 1.33 million in a 1956 census to an estimated 6.5 million in 2004. This far exceeds any possible rate of natural increase, suggesting that immigration from Chad was probably a major factor in the change.[25] Observers estimated that no less than 10 percent of the Chadian population lived in Darfur by the end of the 1990s.[26]

Chadians in Sudan included both those who entered as individuals and families, and those who migrated as entire groups. Individual migrants rarely retain a Chadian identity. That they come from near the border and have relatives across it makes an identity change comparatively easy: It involves shifting allegiance—and therefore tribal affiliation—from former Chadian administrative leaders to leaders from related Sudanese tribes. This enables migrants to join official paramilitary forces, such as the nomadic security forces and the Popular Defense Forces, which in turn facilitates acquiring Sudanese nationality when necessary. The flip side of this development is that the government in power is tempted to see the growing pool of youth from Chadian-origin tribes as a ready source of easy recruits for militias in times of crisis.

Most Chadian immigrants are Arabs, although some non-Arab tribes have also migrated to Darfur, where they join with Arab tribes out of both fear and self-interest. For those who emigrate as entire groups, it is not as easy to melt into Darfuri society. This is clear from the example of the Salamat federation of tribes, who represent the single largest tribal migration from Chad to Darfur. Salamat migration stretches back many centuries and has continued through the middle years of the twentieth century. The first Salamat *omda,* or subdistrict chief, in Sudan was appointed in 1974. Since then, three Chadian *omdas* have taken office in Wadi Salih, four have been appointed in Nyala-Kubbum, two in Buram, and still more in Geneina. Despite repeated demands from Salamat leaders, they have yet to be awarded either a *nazir* (paramount chief) or their own administration or jurisdiction over land.[27]

In this respect, the case of the Salamat resembles that of the Banyamulenge in eastern Congo, who, having migrated from Rwanda to Kivu just before the close of the nineteenth century, continue to strive for a native authority of their own in the hills of Mulenge in South Kivu.[28] Like the Banyamulenge, who proved a fertile recruiting ground for Rwandan Patriotic Front–allied militias, Chadian refugees in Darfur also became an important source of recruits for different types of militias in training.

The developments that drove militarization on the Chad side were an intensifying drought and political repression. The Chadian influx into Darfur comprised two distinct groups, refugees fleeing the drought and opposition groups seeking shelter from government repression. As the Sahelian drought intensified between 1968 and 1973, the Dar Massalit Rural Council wrote a number of letters to other local government authorities informing them of an influx of migrants into the administrative area from the neighboring areas of Chad and other West African countries.[29] Successive rounds of political conflict and alternating rounds of starvation affected Chad just as they affected northern Darfur in the decade of the 1980s and forced many Chadian groups, both nomadic and sedentary, to take refuge in western Darfur.[30] Even though the sedentary Fur in Wadi Salih usually distinguish *kain-Solonga* (Fur: "our Arabs") from other Arabs—differentiating Sudanese Arab nomads who usually move from north to south Darfur from Arab groups that came east from Chad[31]—the distinction was not always easy to make since the majority of the nomadic population in Chad and Darfur share a kinship. As kinfolk, they have a long history of taking refuge with one another in times of crisis. So when areas immediately south of the Sahara were gripped by drought and starvation in the early 1990s, groups from Chad simply moved in with their kin across the border rather than ask for refugee status.[32] Sudanese police estimated that whereas approximately 100,000 individuals had moved from northern Darfur into areas of western and southern Darfur, the movement from Chad into western Darfur had already exceeded 500,000.[33]

Instability and long-standing wars in Chad affected Sudan because warring factions always sought refuge among ethnic relatives across the border. The tendency for defeated groups was to move eastward with their military equipment and look for secure areas from which to rebuild power. Also, since the 1983–86 drought came in the wake of serious political conflict between the forces of Hissen Habre and Goukouni Oueddei, most Chadian refugees crossing into Darfur were already experienced in the use of arms. Not surprisingly, many turned to armed robbery for survival.[34] Because the Jebel Marra range was difficult terrain for Chadian government forces to negotiate, it provided natural protection for Chadian opposition groups and their livestock. This is why the Jebel Marra became the focal point of the conflict between armed Chadian refugees and sedentary Fur farmers. Faced with a Chadian influx, the Fur "resorted to the mass burning of pasture fields with a view to forcing the Arabs to move to other pasture areas," while "attempt[ing] to withhold access to sources of water and retaliat[ing] in kind when their livestock were stolen by Arabs." Chased across the border by Chadian military and paramilitary forces, and finding their access to the Jebel Marra blocked by the Fur, their backs against the proverbial wall, Chadian Arabs fought back tenaciously. They turned to Arab nomads in Darfur and neighboring Kordofan Province for assistance. It is in this context that they issued the call to form a wider organization called "the Arab Congregation."[35]

The Chadian Arab groups were the source of a new ideology that spoke of the need for Arab tribes—and, by extension, for nomadic tribes—to come together in a single congregation to defend common interests and use new weaponry to confront all enemies. They had acquired both the ideology and the weaponry from the Libyans. The resulting "Arab Gathering" was a Chadian initiative in Darfur that had first appeared in the Quraish manifestos, whose founder, Ahmat Acyl, is hailed as the father of Arab nationalism in Chad.[36] This drive was backed up by an ideology that highlighted the marginalization of Arabs in the region and called for an extension of the Arab belt in Africa.[37] In Chad, the "Arab Gathering" was a call to mobilize Arab nomads who had since independence been excluded from participation in the Chadian state. But when given support by Qaddafi, the "Arab Gathering" made for a contradictory agenda beneath a single banner, bringing together oppressed and privileged Arab groups under an agenda that promised emancipation to the former and resonated with the expansionist ambitions of the latter.[38] While Chadian opposition groups were the main recipients of Libyan weapons, Sudanese nomads, both Arab and non-Arab, also benefited from Libyan largesse.

Darfur as a Rear Base

Today Darfur has become to Chad what eastern Congo (Kivu) is to Rwanda, a place where the opposition of the day seeks refuge and respite, where it trains and waits for a suitable opportunity to make a bid for power. A succession of Chadian opposition leaders has found safe haven in Darfur since 1964 and arms and logistical support from Sudanese governments since 1966. No matter the twists and turns in Libyan and American policy toward Chad and Sudan, no matter the identity of the proxy that each sought to arm, there was one constant: Libyan involvement in Chad and Sudan inevitably came to focus on Darfur. For this, there were several reasons. To begin with, the boundary dividing Chad from Sudan had little meaning for the local population; even among Darfuri groups, few saw Wadai as foreign territory. This view was also shared by many in Wadai, where there were few opportunities for education and where it was customary practice to send promising students from the *khalwa,* the Quranic elementary school, to Darfur and Khartoum and then to Cairo for more advanced academic or theological studies.[39]

A related development of long-term consequence was the forging of a link between a subaltern Arab nationalism in Chad and Arab groups in Darfur, particularly the Mahamid in the north. The Mahamid were the largest section of the Rizeigat Abbala, the camel Arabs, who live in North Darfur and Chad. Militant Arab nationalism in Chadian politics is traced to the leadership of Mohamed al Bagillani and Ahmat Acyl. Under Libyan direction, Ahmat Acyl divided his army into three factions, one of which entered Chad from Darfur in 1976. It is this group that provided the historical link between Ahmat Acyl and Sheikh Hilal Mohamed Abdalla, the chief of the Mahamid in Sudan. In 1986, Sheikh Hilal was incapacitated, and his son Musa took over.[40]

Libyan assistance paved the way for an alliance between the Mahamid and Chadian opposition militias. In 1981, Libyans are said to have provided the Mahamid with thirty boxes of weapons and ammunition, both to be used for their own protection and to be supplied to the Burkan forces. Beginning with the Mahamid, the Libyans went on to arm other tribes in Darfur, including the Arab Rizeigat from the south and non-Arab nomads such as the Gourane, the Zaghawa, and the Bedeiyat elsewhere. Over time, CDR forces began to participate directly in internal Darfuri struggles, going beyond resisting Habre's troops to fighting alongside the Mahamid and other Darfuri Arab tribes in the land wars of Darfur. Chadian Arab forces joined Um Jalul of the Mahamid and the Beni Helba Baggara of Darfur in violent assaults on Jebel Marra in March 1988. Often, when opposition groups went back to Chad (as with Ibn Omer), returning fighters would distribute their weapons to the Mahamid and other local allies before leaving.

It was during this war that the Darfuris first began to hear the word *Janjawiid* to describe Arab militias. *Janjawiid* had been used in the sixties as a pejorative term to describe poor vagrants from nomadic tribes. Nomadic life was hard, and periodic drought made it harder still, prompting banditry and making the borderlands increasingly insecure. Later, sedentary groups began to use the term *Janjawiid* to describe the militia nomads called *fursan,* or "horsemen."[41] As a social phenomenon, the Janjawiid are an expression of the crisis of nomadism across the entire Sahelian belt. The social crisis of youth in different African societies is evident in the flow of teen and even preteen recruits to roving militias from Sierra Leone and Liberia in West Africa to northern Uganda, eastern Congo in the Great Lakes region, and Mozambique in southern Africa. As the interethnic conflict in Darfur turned into a civil war, the Janjawiid came to the fore as a military force.

The arming of nomadic tribes alarmed their sedentary neighbors, who also began to look for ways to arm themselves. There was no shortage of arms in Darfur in the 1980s. Not only was the Chad civil war at its most intense at this time, but so was the global Cold War. The Fur in particular benefited from this opportune moment. The Fur militia was called the Federal Army of Darfur and was founded by a small circle of clandestine *Jakab* ("struggle") fighters. By May 1988, the Fur were said to have six thousand armed militiamen serviced by training centers located in no-man's-land situated in southwestern Darfur, specifically in the part of Western Bahr al-Ghazal on the border with the Central African

Republic. Different sides in the Chadian civil war changed places with a regularity that made it seem like a game of roulette in which players took turns playing power and opposition. If one side (usually the nomadic tribes) was financed and armed by Qaddafi, the other (particularly Hissen Habre) was supported by Reagan's Cold Warriors.

The Reaganites were most active in Darfur during the Nimeiry regime (1971–85), particularly after he broke with the Communist Party in 1971. Their focus was on training the large influx of refugees, about sixteen thousand, who had moved from Chad to Darfur between 1979 and 1982. They were supporters of Hissen Habre and were accommodated in Dar Massalit.[42] When Nimeiry was overthrown on April 5, 1985, the Sudanese Transitional Military Council (TMC) of Swar al-Dahab approached Libya for weapons to fight the SPLA insurgency in the south. As part of the bargain, the TMC stopped giving arms to Habre and closed the western frontier, and Qaddafi ended his military assistance to the SPLA and began to recruit Sudanese cadres for the Islamic Legion. It is said that Libyan agents swept into Khartoum and in six months recruited more than two thousand Sudanese to join the Islamic Legion. When Sadiq al-Mahdi, who had tried to mount an armed opposition to Nimeiry from exile in Libya, returned to power in Khartoum following the TMC-organized elections, Libya's connection with Darfur was fully restored. The influx of arms into Darfur continued.[43]

The consequence was the militarization of Darfur. As Darfur was flooded with Libyan- and American-supplied weaponry, the Kalashnikov became ubiquitous in Darfur. "The Kalash brings cash; without a Kalash you are trash." By 1986, a Kalashnikov assault rifle (AK-47) with accessories sold for less than US$40 in Darfuri markets. The same held true for rocket-propelled grenades and other more destructive weapons.[44] Though short of water, Darfur was awash in guns.

Proxy Wars

When Reagan and Qaddafi decided to extend their war into Darfur through proxies, they were tapping into a colonial tradition. Proxy war in this region has a dual origin. The use of tribal groups to fight government wars began in colonial times. The government of Anglo-Egyptian Sudan provided arms and ammunition to both the Kababish of Kordo-

fan, under the leadership of Sheikh Ali el Tom, and the Rizeigat of Darfur, under the leadership of Said Madibo, to harass and fight the forces
of Ali Dinar, the last sultan of Dar Fur.[45]

This same strategy was adopted by independent governments in
Sudan to pursue their respective counterinsurgency agendas. Governments began by embracing existing militias and incorporating them
into official counterinsurgency forces; later, the initiative extended to
establishing local militias as part of an unfolding counterinsurgency
agenda. The Reagan administration embraced proxy wars with missionary zeal following the U.S. defeat in Vietnam. Once again, the lesson
was eagerly emulated by governments in the region. The best-known
government-sponsored militia was the Murahileen, organized to fight
the counterinsurgency in the south.

The government's militia strategy can be traced to two related events:
the Gardud massacre of 1985, when groups of armed Dinka attacked a
Baggara village in southern Kordofan, and the Baggara retaliation that
followed the massacre. It is in the intervening period between these
massacres that Prime Minister Sadiq al-Mahdi decided to arm his
Baggara supporters on the southern Sudan frontier with automatic
weapons and create an officially sponsored militia, known as the
Murahileen, to join the counterinsurgency against the SPLA. The connection was easy to make since Sadiq's minister of defense was the
influential Ansar and Baggara leader, General Burma Nasr. Officially, the
government encouraged the Murahileen to protect nomadic migratory
routes to the south. Unofficially, it condoned time-honored practices
such as cattle rustling and hostage taking. The effect for the next decade
was to incorporate the Murahileen into the larger counterinsurgency
against the Dinka of the Bahr al-Ghazal and the upper Nile.[46] The notoriety of the Murahileen began to spread in 1987, when two scholarly
human rights activists, Ushari Mahmoud and Suleyman Baldo, documented the massacre in the Darfuri town of El Daien and enslavement
in Bahr al-Ghazal by the Murahileen militia drawn from the Baggara
Rizeigat.[47] Two years later, a report by Amnesty International documented a wide pattern of killings by the Rizeigat and Misiriya
Murahileen and the army in Northern Bahr al-Ghazal.[48] As one would
expect, there were several versions of these events. The government of
the day accused the SPLA/SPLM and condoned the retaliation by the

Baggara; the SPLA/SPLM accused renegade tribesmen of exacting vengeance for earlier cattle raids by the Baggara of El-Gardud.[49]

The government extended the militia strategy from north-south borderlands to the heartland of the south as it made proxy war a key part of its strategy to win the war in the south. The idea was to arm the tribes of Equatoria—in particular, tribal militias from among the southern tribes of Murle, Toposa, and Mandari (Equatorian tribes) and the Nuer—and turn them against civilian populations of the Dinka tribes in Jonglei and Lake Provinces. The Anyanya II forces were also recruited by the government as "friendly forces" to fight the SPLA in and around the Nuer tribal districts in the southern provinces of the upper Nile.[50]

The militia strategy was at the heart of the proxy war that marked the second counterinsurgency, which followed the breakdown of the 1972 Addis Ababa Agreement. The second counterinsurgency deliberately targeted civilian supporters of the insurgency and spread mayhem and terror among them. Its consequence was to decentralize violence; by combining violence with raiding, the strategy directly contributed to eroding discipline among those meting out the violence. The army's anxiety became clear when, in February 1989, the chief of staff wrote to the prime minister expressing fear that the militia strategy would undermine the state.[51]

After the 1989 al-Bashir coup, the Islamist junta decided to elevate tribal militias from a local to a national phenomenon, by knitting them together into a network called Popular Defense Forces (PDF) and putting these under the leadership of trusted Islamist officers in the professional army corps. In 1992–93, the government took the pacification strategy to a new level of atrocity. Taking a cue from British counterinsurgency in Kenya and American practices in Vietnam, it went beyond targeting the civilian population to moving it wholesale to another location. In its assault on the Nuba Mountains in 1992–93, the government defined its objective as not only crushing the rebellion and its civilian supporters but also forcibly relocating the entire Nuba population from their ancestral homelands to "peace camps" where they would take on a new identity.[52] The full force of this legacy, from proxy wars in the south to forced population transfers in the Nuba Mountains, would be unleashed in Darfur in the counterinsurgency that began in 2003.

From Habre to Deby

Part of the cost of the Cold War came to light after it was over, as the United States showed no reluctance to cast away its assets in the region. When Hissen Habre was overthrown in 1990, human rights groups began to document the atrocities committed by his regime and the external links that had made these possible. Human Rights Watch dubbed him "an African Pinochet." Here is what the Human Rights Watch website says of its findings:

> Documents obtained by Human Rights Watch show that the United States provided Habré's DDS (National Security Service or Direction de la Documentation et de la Sécurité) with training, intelligence, and other support despite knowledge of its atrocities. Records discovered in the DDS' meticulous archives describe training programs by American instructors for DDS agents and officials, including a course in the United States that was attended by some of the DDS' most feared torturers. According to the Chadian Truth Commission, the United States also provided the DDS with monthly infusions of cash and financed a regional network of intelligence networks code-named "Mosaic" that Chad used to pursue suspected opponents of Habré's regime even after they fled the country.[53]

His victims first tried to indict Hissen Habre in Senegalese courts. When the courts ruled that Habre could not be tried in Senegal, they turned to Belgium, which had from 1993 to 2003 adopted a universal jurisdiction—meaning that it allowed serious violations of human rights to be tried in its courts, even if there was no direct connection to the country of the alleged perpetrator, the victims, or the location of crimes. After a four-year investigation, a Belgian judge issued an international arrest warrant in September 2005 charging Habre with crimes against humanity, war crimes, and torture committed from 1982 to 1990 during his time in office. The European Parliament, too, demanded that Senegal, where Habre had been living in exile for seventeen years, turn him over to Belgian courts. When a Senegalese court refused to rule on the extradition request, the Senegalese government announced that it had asked the African Union to recommend "competent jurisdiction" for Habre's trial. The African Union asked a Committee of Eminent African Jurists to suggest a course of action. Following its recommendation on July 2, 2006, the African Union called on Senegal to prosecute Hissen Habre "in the name of Africa." Under pressure from the African Union, Senegal decided in July 2006 to place Habre under house arrest and set up its own special war crimes court.

Though Hissen Habre's government had a broader internal base than the Tombalbaye dictatorship, it remained weak because it was opposed by nomadic groups, both Arab and non-Arab (mainly Zaghawa). Hissen Habre had been overthrown by a Zaghawa commander, Idriss Deby. Like Habre, Deby, too, came to power through a military invasion, also launched from bases in Darfur. The difference this time was that Deby had agreed with the regime in Khartoum that both sides would henceforth refrain from interfering in each other's internal affairs. The deal held for twelve years, and for twelve years there was peace at the border. When Darfur rebels began to organize in 2002, Deby's initial response was to keep his hands off of what he considered an internal Sudanese affair. He mediated the first cease-fire agreements in Abéché in September 2003 and N'Djamena in April of the following year, and reportedly cooperated with Sudan in some of its counterinsurgency operations against the rebels. Under pressure from his Zaghawa kinsmen—and especially when faced with an ultimatum that they would not hesitate to overthrow him if necessary—he changed course and began to support Zaghawa-dominated JEM rebels.

Meanwhile, French troops, a key force in Chad's civil wars for the past half century, upped their presence in the region by providing the mainstay of the new NATO European protection force for eastern Chad and northeastern Central African Republic, designated as EUFOR (or European Union Force). The French masked this intervention as an action intended for the protection of human rights. Is the purpose of this force to protect Darfuri refugees in Chad, or is it to provide a military cover to Darfuri rebels as they recruit from and militarize refugee camps in Chad? Is its political objective to defuse the military situation in Chad, or is it to up the ante in Darfur through a cross-border military intervention?[54]

. . .

The fact is that the most intractable internal conflicts in contemporary Africa are driven by regional tensions, which are in turn a by-product of the Cold War that led to a regionalization of proxy wars and internal conflicts in postcolonial Africa. These local tensions can neither be understood nor solved unless we locate them within regional dynamics. This is as true of the conflict in Sudan and Chad as it is of that in the Mano River countries (Liberia, Sierra Leone, Guinea) and the Great Lakes (Congo, Rwanda, Uganda), just as it is true of conflicts in other places, such as those in Afghanistan and Iraq.

PART III

Rethinking the Darfur Crisis

8

Civil War, Rebellion, and Repression

THE CONFLICT IN DARFUR began in the mid-1980s as a civil war. It was known as the Arab-Fur war. For the first time, all Arab tribes came together under a single banner known as "the Arab Gathering," that being the signature to a letter sent to Prime Minister Sadiq al-Mahdi demanding affirmative action for the Arab tribes of Darfur. In the advocacy of Save Darfur groups, "the Arab Gathering" has taken on a monstrous significance, as the main organization whose ideas would inspire the genocide. Nothing could be further from the truth. In fact, the cattle nomads who were the majority of those in the Arab Gathering in 1987–89 were not involved, either on the side of the insurgency or the counterinsurgency, in the fighting that began in 2002–3. It was the Arab camel nomad tribes—the minority in the Arab Gathering—who supplied the foot soldiers for the counterinsurgency, the *janjawiid.* Like the insurgent rebel movements, they, too, bolstered their ranks with Chadian recruits.

The 1987–89 conflict came to an abrupt halt when the elected government in Khartoum was overthrown and the leaders of the Islamist coup cited the previous government's failure to stop the fighting in Darfur as one of several reasons for their action. The 1987–89 Arab-Fur war had persisted in spite of several reconciliation conferences convened to halt it. That it stopped in response to a government declaration to help resolve it was adequate proof that both sides looked to the government for a solution. This simple fact should remind us that the conflict in Darfur began as a civil war to which the government was not a party.

The government became a party to the conflict only *after* 1989, through an initiative that tried to address the basic cause of the conflict. When the government initiative failed, it implicated the government in the conflict, which erupted on a bigger scale, reaching a new level with the Massalit confrontation with Arab tribes in 1995. The conflict flared yet again in 2002–3, when active connections developed between the antigovernment forces in Darfur and the organized opposition at the center. These relations were forged through two separate initiatives—one in which local rebels (SLA) linked up with the southern opposition (the Sudan People's Liberation Army, or SPLA), and the other in which the Islamist opposition at the center (Hassan al-Turabi's Popular Congress Party, or PCP) developed its own rebel movement (JEM). What had begun as a local conflict took on broader dimensions as the government got involved in 1995 and the opposition in 2003. In contrast to the 1987–89 conflict, which was largely a civil war confined to Darfur, the post–2003 conflict turned into an all-Sudan affair—even if it played out only in Darfur.

When the first round of the civil war, between the Fur and the nomadic Arab tribes, came to a close in 1989, Sharif Harir—himself a Zaghawa and a social anthropologist—wrote a penetrating analysis of the conference held to end the conflict.[1] According to Harir, each side saw the other through the lens of a settler-native paradigm, one I have argued was forged in the colonial period. Even more illuminating is the fact that each claimed to be a victim in the conflict.

The Arab tribes claimed to be victims of a Fur-sponsored drive to rid the land of Arabs as settlers. According to them, the problem began in the 1970s when the Fur started to talk about being native to the land, calling on the Arabs to leave. In a land where it had been customary to refer to all groups by their tribal identity—for example, Fur or Rizeigat—the Fur had recently taken to speaking of themselves as "Africans" menaced by "Arabs," building on specifically colonial historiography. Community leaders who had never before called themselves "African" now readily identified as such in conversation with international interlocutors. Thus came into being a newly constructed and highly polarizing political dichotomy: Arab versus African.

The Fur, in turn, saw themselves as victims of a supremacist Arab dialogue, racist in its implications. They cited the letter written by a constellation of nomadic tribes—twenty-seven in all—to the then prime minister Sadiq al-Mahdi. The letter's authors referred to themselves as "the Arab Gathering" and appealed to the prime minister as one of their own, calling for a better deal for Darfur's Arabs. The Fur quoted the language of the letter as proof that the Arabs wanted to eradicate them.[2]

The tenor of the exchange was shrill on both sides. In Harir's words, "The war took on ideological and 'racist' leanings which were heavily laden with tribal bigotry. Arab bands called *Janjawid* (hordes) and *Fursan* (knights) roamed Fur areas, burning villages, killing indiscriminately and appropriating Fur property at will. The Fur also started developing their own groups, the *Malishiyat* (militias) and responded in a similar manner."[3] After continuous fighting over two years (1987–89), both sides came together at a conflict resolution conference at El Fasher, organized by the national and regional governments, from May 29 to July 8, 1989.[4]

This conflict was unlike any other that anyone could remember. Both sides attributed its novel dimensions—the transtribal mobilization, the brutality, the lack of restraint, the unmitigated hostility—to the ideology of racism harbored by the other. The Arabs claimed the Fur had started the whole thing by attempting to extend the "black African belt" (*ifrigia al souda*) or "Negro belt" (*al hizam al Zunji*), aimed at excluding Arabs who, as citizens—and in keeping with the constitution—should have enjoyed equal rights of access to natural productive resources at a time of crisis. The Fur pointed to the coming together of twenty-seven tribes in a single alliance inspired by "the Arab Gathering" demanding an extension of the "Arab belt" (*al hizam al Arabi*).[5]

There is no better depiction of how each side understood the threat the other posed than the presentations their own representatives made to the conference. The secretary of the Fur delegation, a young primary school teacher, delivered the Fur position on May 29, 1989:

> The dirty war that has been imposed upon us began as an economic war but soon it assumed a genocidal course aiming at driving us out of our ancestral land in order to achieve

certain political goals. . . . The aim is a total holocaust and no less than the complete annihilation of the Fur people and all things Fur. . . . How are we supposed to understand the mobilization of 27 Arab tribes, including some from across regional boundaries and others from across international boundaries, against only one tribe? The basic fuel of this war is racism. This conflict is about their attempt at dividing people of Dar Fur region into "Arabs" against "Blacks" (*Zurga*), with superiority attributed to the former. The racial nature of the conflict is clearly revealed by the organizational vessel adopted by them, "The Arab Congregation."[6]

The Arab position, too, was articulated by a young primary school teacher, secretary of the Arab delegation:

Our Arab tribe [note the singular form—Harir's comment] and the Fur co-existed peacefully throughout the known history of Dar Fur. However, the situation was destabilized towards the end of the 70s when the Fur raised a slogan which claimed that Dar Fur is for the Fur, "Dar Fur for Fur." This coincided with the fact that the first regional government of Dar Fur was led by a Fur individual who did not lift a finger to quell this dangerous trend. To further exacerbate the situation, some Fur intellectuals in the Dar Fur Development Front and the Independent Alliance have embraced the "Dar Fur for Fur" slogan. The Arabs were depicted as foreigners who should be evicted from this area of Dar Fur. To give substance to this slogan, Fur "militia" forces were trained under the supervision of the Fur governor of Dar Fur in the period between May 1986 and September 1986. . . . Ours is a legitimate self-defense and we shall continue defending our right of access to water and pasture. However, let us not be in doubt about who began this war: it is the Fur who in their quest to extend the so-called "African belt" (*al hizam al Zunji*) wanted to remove all the Arabs from this soil.[7]

Speaking on the same occasion, the Umma Party–appointed governor of Darfur, Dr. Tigani Sese Ateem, a Fur, pointed out that mass atrocities perpetrated by both sides were historically wholly out of character: "The extraordinary aspect of the Fur/Arabs conflict is not in the manner in which it began but the speed with which it spread from the Jebel Merra areas to engulf communities in Wadi Salih, Zalingei, Kas, Kabkabiya and Nyala rural council areas. The reckless use of fire arms to ruthlessly massacre our peaceful citizens and the macabre mutilations are completely out of character with the people of Dar Fur." He then went on to attribute the mass slaughter to the intervention of external forces: "It is my conviction that this brutal war has been imposed on us by external forces that did not like our democratic way of government."[8]

The story of Darfur for the past two decades has been one of spiraling violence. But violence is not self-explanatory. Casualty and mortality figures—atrocity statistics, as the U.S. government termed them—do not tell their own story. Some say that the violence flared when the colonial period ended: The number of ethnic conflicts requiring formal mediation soared from barely two during the entire four decades of the colonial period (1916–56) to at least one a year after independence.[9] These statistical contrasts may be striking, but they hide both the fact that the real break came in the 1970s (and not with the end of the colonial period in 1956) and the combination of developments that drove the break: the relentless Sahelian drought, the failed attempt by the Nimeiry regime to reform the colonial system of native administration, and the spillover of the Chadian civil war that militarized Darfur.

The Sahelian drought had its worst effect in northern Darfur, from where it pushed people south. Around that same time, the Nimeiry reforms dismantled the colonial system of native administration, creating a vacuum in administrative authority just as those displaced by the expanding desert were rushing to settle in different parts of the south and west. Not surprisingly, one began to hear Fur demands that rights of natives be honored and counterassertions from displaced peoples from the north that what really counted were not the rights of tribes but those of citizens. When bearers of these contradictory rights clashed, they had at their disposal an entire arsenal of modern weapons, brought over from Chad's civil wars, with consequences more devastating than any in the history of local conflicts in the region.

Although militarization was spurred from across the Chad border, it also had internal roots in Sudan. Militarization in Sudan accelerated in the period between the failed Communist coup of 1971 and the mass slaughter of the Ansar by Nimeiry's forces the following year. The Ansar leadership retreated to exile in Libya after 1970. They tried to return to power in 1976 but failed. Many returned to Sudan as part of national reconciliation in 1977, hoping to be absorbed into the army, but were disappointed that they were instead settled in farming projects. Disproportionately drawn from the Baggara tribes, the Ansar had been organized, trained, and armed alongside Qaddafi's Islamic Legion, which drew recruits from across the Sahelian countries. Former Ansar fighters were instrumental in the creation of the first Baggara militias in the mid-1980s. A second group of Ansar returned from Libya in 1986, a year before the Islamic Legion was defeated by the Chad army.[10]

Before the mid-eighties, all conflicts in Darfur had been between neighbors. Even the most intense of them were localized and usually involved only two sides: the Zaghawa and the Mahariya in 1968; the Maaliya and the Rizeigat in 1968; the Rizeigat and the Misiriya from 1972 to 1974; the Beni Helba against the Mahariya from 1975 to 1977; and so on. Conflicts were infrequent and of low intensity, and all were settled through traditional mediation. The 1987–89 Fur-Arab conflict was the first time a united front of tribes confronted the Fur, whose different sections mobilized as one—also for the first time—along the length and breadth of Darfur. The background to 1987–89 involved desertification, administrative failure, and militarization. All these events coalesced around the single issue of land, turning it into a powder keg.

Land Conflicts in Darfur: Background to 1987–89

The unprecedented deterioration of environmental conditions in the northern part of Darfur led to a massive movement of population groups and livestock into the farming belt of South Darfur, the heartland of the Fur and of other groups (Birgid, Berti, Daju) with a long tradition of rain-fed cultivation.

The drought affected the nomadic *and* sedentary populations of northern and central Darfur. Their response to the encroaching desert was to migrate farther south and occupy lands for subsistence and commercial farming. The majority of the early migrants were from Zaghawa and Berti communities. The newcomers concentrated on the central (*qoz*) lands north and east of South Darfur. As the migration moved southward, it targeted the homelands of different Baggara tribes: the Rizeigat, Habania, and Beni Helba. Given that Nimeiry's 1970 decree had abolished native administration in the rural areas but had yet to forge an effective alternative mode of governance, this movement proceeded relatively unhindered. The sedentary tribes from the north occupied both Baggara boreholes (*dwanki*) in South Darfur and surrounding veterinary centers where the Baggara used to concentrate their herds for veterinary services. The effect of the new settlements was to block Baggara animal routes (*Marahil*) and deprive the Baggara of some of their grazing lands. In the three decades that followed 1972, a total of seven veterinary centers were closed and changed into farmlands.[11] In 1986 alone, a total of 384,010 people migrated south from North Darfur.[12] This movement and its consequences were the subject of research conducted for the African Union's Darfur-Darfur Dialogue and Consultation (DDDC) process.

For all populations, nomadic or sedentary, the effect of the ecological crisis filtered through the land and governance system created during the colonial period. The colonial system had two features: It defined rights on the basis of ethnicity rather than citizenship, and it discriminated in favor of settled groups (which it defined as native) as opposed to nomadic groups (which it branded as nonnative strangers or settlers). If settled agriculturalists such as the Fur were accorded a priority claim to a homeland (*dar*), the claim of the seminomadic cattle-herding Arab tribes of the south was limited to the villages they had settled and not the lands they grazed. The worst off were the fully nomadic camel-herding Arab tribes of the north, who were accorded no established claim to a homeland, presumably because they had no settled communities. Based on an exclusive notion of tribal property, the colonial homeland system had no room for multiple and overlapping rights except in a hierarchical sense: Members of a tribe settled in the *dar* of another could access land, not as a right but on sufferance; similarly, they could participate in local administration, but only as subordinates. Rather than a conflict between farmers and herders, the civil war in Darfur developed as a conflict between groups with homeland rights and those with diminished or no homeland rights. As refugees from Chad streamed into Darfur, they threw in their lot with local groups that lacked homeland rights.

On the ground, matters were even more complicated. Generally, the division between tribes with a *dar* and those without was one between sedentary and nomadic tribes, with nomads further divided between cattle nomads with qualified *hakura* (land) rights and camel nomads with none. In reality, however, even cattle nomads in the south were further differentiated: The larger tribes tended to have homelands but not the smaller ones. As the effects of the drought intensified, and one and all started feeling the squeeze when it came to land and water, there developed a generalized demand among the *dar*less tribes: All wanted their own *dar*—their own piece of land, a homeland. This had two kinds of consequences. The *dar*less cattle nomads of the south who continued to live on the same land as before demanded that their erstwhile hosts acknowledge these lands as *their dar,* where they would have both right of access to tribal land and right of governance in their own native authority. In contrast, the displaced *dar*less peoples of the north, particularly the camel nomads, demanded an equal right of access to natural resources as citizens of the land. If the former demanded a *dar* of their own, the latter wanted an end to the exclusive system of tribal *dars* and *dar*-based rights. If the former demanded a reform of the system, the latter wanted a radical overhaul. If the former demand resulted in ethnic tension and conflict among neighboring Arab tribes in the south—all cattle nomads (the Baggara)—the latter demand usually created conflict between the *hakura*less camel nomads (the Abbala) and sedentary "native" tribes of the south. The Darfur-Darfur Dialogue and Consultation research into ethnic conflict in Darfur provided examples of both types of conflict.

Looking at three tribes—the Maaliya, the Fellata, and the Gimir—one can see the different ways in which the conflict has developed in South Darfur between smaller *dar*less tribes and larger tribes with *dars.* Historically a part of the Rizeigat Baggara administration, the Maaliya have struggled hard to acquire their own homeland, where they can have both tribal rights over land and a native administration of their own. The Rizeigat Baggara opposed it on grounds of "tradition"—that the Maaliya had no traditional right to a *hakura.* A bloody conflict began in 1988 and continued intermittently until 2004. The consequence was that the Maaliya, an Arab tribe, allied with the non-Arab Zaghawa start-ing in 2003. The conflict ended only when the Rizeigat Baggara agreed at a reconciliation meeting in Nyala that the Maaliya should have an inde-pendent *nazirate*.[13]

The Fellata are immigrant nomads from West Africa who over the centuries have taken on an Arab identity. The Fellata have no *hakura*. Their claim for tribal lands was rejected by all neighbors and led to bloody conflicts with all: Habania, Fur, Massalit, Gimir, Mararit, Mahadi, and Beni Helba—Arab and non-Arab. Other tribes in South Darfur also continue to struggle for a *dar* of their own. The Tergum, for example, have historically been part of the Fur *magdumate* administra-tion in the south but have long been claiming tribal land rights and a separate native administration where they live. The demand for their own homeland has involved them in a dual conflict: with the Rizeigat Abbala over tribal land rights and with the Fur over the right to a sepa-rate native administration. Three bloody conflicts were reported between the Tergum and the Fur as late as July and August 2007.[14]

Since the eighteenth century, the Gimir had a sultanate with a seat at Kulbus in West Darfur, around the Jebel Moon hills. Given a long his-tory of conflict with the Zaghawa Kabka and Kobi who live in the vicin-ity, the Gimir allied themselves with the Khartoum government and with Arab nomads to counterattack Zaghawa rebels.[15] Because of this alliance, the Gimir, a non-Arab tribe, have come to be identified by their adversaries as an Arab tribe. The Gimir also have a conflict with (Arab) Beni Helba nomads despite their both being on good terms with the central government. The conflict stems from the fact that Gimir farmers have been living in a locality (Idel Fursan) in the Beni Helba homeland; having prospered commercially, they seek to advance beyond having one *omda* and a number of sheikhs in the Beni Helba native administra-tion to having a locality and a native administration of their own. The Beni Helba countered in the conventional language of tradition, that since the Gimir had no tribal lands, they could not ask for a separate native administration—for the right to self-governance can be claimed only by those with a tribal homeland.[16]

The fight for tribal lands and representation takes place at different levels of administration. While the Gimir and others battle for their own *dar* and their own native administration, smaller and weaker tribes fight for representation inside a native administration identified with another tribe.[17]

The second face of the conflict is between camel nomads of the north forced to move down south and southern tribes with *dars*. The impact of the drought on nomadic life was drastic. Until 1970, cattle nomads of the south (the Baggara) and camel nomads of the north (the Abbala) had lived in separate habitats, each with their separate annual cycle of movements. Then, it was a rarity to see camel herders roaming the Baggara homelands in South Darfur. All this changed between 1972 and 1984. The Sahelian cycle of drought hit North Darfur so hard that it ruined the ecological system of the Rizeigat Abbala. They had no alternative but to change their cycle of movements.[18]

To understand the survival strategies of tribes that faced ecological disaster in the Sahel zone in North Darfur, we shall take the examples of two tribes, the Abbala Rizeigat and the Zaghawa, both camel nomads of the north, one Arab and the other not, but both forced to migrate to survive the drought.

As the Abbala migrated to Baggara homelands in South Darfur, they first asked for grazing rights and ended up demanding land rights. The inevitable result was a conflict between erstwhile guests and hosts. One of the earliest conflicts was with the Beni Helba Baggara in 1974. The 1976 agreement to end the conflict included the following conditions: that Rizeigat Abbala should not come to the Beni Helba homeland before January 20 each year nor cut any tree for camel feeding, and that their members should observe the authority of local Beni Helba leaders during their stay in the Beni Helba homeland. An agreement such as this could not be honored in the face of a persistent ecological crisis. The result was that the Baggara and the Abbala continued to be at loggerheads throughout the decade of the 1980s.

The turning point in the conflict was most likely 1980, the year Ahmed Diraige was elected governor of Darfur. It marked the turn to politics in the region. Darfuri Arabs were alarmed at the Fur assertiveness that followed this event. They argued that they would command an absolute majority if only they could unite and draw the Fellata into their constituency. All that was needed was an "Arab alliance." Leaflets and cassette recordings purporting to come from a group calling itself the "Arab Gathering" were distributed anonymously around this time; they proclaimed that the Zurga had ruled Darfur long enough and that it was time for Arabs to have their turn.

The parliamentary period of 1986–89 further contributed to Arab fears of political isolation and social marginalization. The Massalit had taken the political route: They had voted overwhelmingly for the victorious Umma Party and swept the seats reserved for the district. Perhaps as a consequence, the sultan's uncle, Ali Hasan Taj el Din, was elevated to Sudan's five-member collective presidency, the Council of State. Dar Massalit's Arabs stood in stark contrast: Uneducated and outvoted, they "did not have a single representative to speak for them in the National Assembly in Khartoum." There would be no end to their troubles if Massalit leaders consolidated their hold on political power: They could go so far as to "even disenfranchise them altogether by labeling them as foreigners."[19] When Prime Minister Sadiq al-Mahdi chose Tijani Sese Ateem as the second Fur governor of Darfur the following year, 1988, the sense of alarm increased.[20]

The Abbala came to change their strategy in South Darfur in the 1990s. They, too, started to think in terms of building alliances. Locally, they began by supporting *dar*less cattle nomads of the south in their demand for a *hakura* and a native administration: thus their support of the Tergum's demand on the Fur *magdumate* for a full *nazirate* administration, one that would put them on a par with other sections of the Baggara. At the same time, however, they opposed the idea of the Tergum's exercising exclusive rights in the *hakura,* demanding open access to land and water resources in this *nazirate.* The tensions between the two nomadic Arab groups have continued into 2008.[21]

Abbala efforts at alliance building extended from local to central politics. The first big opportunity for alliance building at the center came when the new military regime seized power in 1989. The Abbala offered the regime political allegiance and support in return for a homeland. The strategy worked. In 1995, the commissioner of Nyala granted the Hamdania section of the Abbala the right to the position of an *omda* in registered government land south of Nyala. Though this land was within the Fur *magdumate*, the Fur *magdume* was not consulted. By 2005, seven Rizeigat Abbala *omdas* had been established.[22]

The Zaghawa, too, adopted migration as a deliberate strategy as early as the 1970s. When the farming season totally failed in 1984, many were compelled to sell the roofs of their houses in order to buy food. Entire villages moved to South Darfur. At the same time, as the Zaghawa made their way into the Birgid homeland, an estimated 40 percent of the Birgid moved farther south to Baggara areas. In 1995, the Zaghawa won the national constituency elections against the chief of the Birgid tribe. As Zaghawa migrants began using the vote to convert their numbers into political power, they triggered a conflict with the Birgid over political leadership and land.[23]

The Zaghawa political strategy changed when the Islamists split in the late 1990s. With Hasan al-Turabi's move into the opposition, Zaghawa politicians in Khartoum took the initiative to constitute the Justice and Equality Movement (JEM), their own rebel movement. JEM became the leading fighting force after 2005. By 2005, Zaghawa constituted the majority in almost all Birgid villages in the Sheria locality. Taking a leaf from the Zaghawa, the Birgid also took to armed struggle but paid a heavy price for it. First they allied with the Sudan Liberation Army–dominated armed movement against the Arab nomads. Later, they made an alliance with local Arab elements—such as the Misiriya and Saada—against the Zaghawa. As a result, they faced the wrath of both Zaghawa rebels and the Arab Janjawiid militia. More than six hundred Birgid villages were burned in the Sheria locality alone, their inhabitants becoming IDPs (internally displaced persons) in the different camps in South Darfur.[24]

Ethnic conflict in Darfur developed around two axes: one north-south (between camel nomads [Abbala] of the north and sedentary tribes in the south) and the other south-south (with cattle nomad [Baggara] tribes of the south pitted against one another). In both cases, those with *dars* were pitted against those without. The tendency has been for those with homeland rights to call for native rights alongside regional autonomy and for those without homeland rights to call for citizenship rights while looking to the central government for support. But the international media and the Save Darfur groups have downplayed—

even ignored—the south-south axis of the conflict and played up its north-south axis, thereby racializing it as a conflict between "Arabs" and "Africans."

A Breakdown in the System of Reconciliation: 1987–89, 1991–95

Darfuri society has a tradition of reconciliation. This tradition has been nurtured by a symbiotic relationship between farmers and cattle nomads who depended on access to postharvest pastures and restraint in the use of violence in settling conflicts, for conflict was always at the margins, and its settlement required no more than borderline adjustments. Instead of building on a tradition of conflict, pastoralists and cultivators created ties through a tradition of intermarriage.[25] No side challenged the other's legitimacy or right to exist. How, then, did conflicts between neighbors turn into confrontations between insiders and outsiders?

Part of the answer lies in developments in the marketplace. As the better-off farmers look for ways to prosper, commercialization has disrupted the centuries-old traditions of symbiosis. Farmers who once used to allow pastoralists to feed their livestock on crop residues preferred to harvest and sell crop stalks. The response of resentful pastoralists was to let their animals loose into farms. Similarly, the expansion of farmland blocked some of the migration routes, forcing pastoralists to take longer and more circuitous routes.[26] The Beni Helba of southern Darfur, for example, built extensive protective enclosures, thereby triggering a tribal war of tragic consequences between them and northern Rizeigat camel nomads. The Fur, who also possessed considerable herds, followed suit and began building enclosures as a way to protect pasture. Though the effect of the enclosure movement was gradual and imperceptible at the outset, it gathered momentum during periods of political crisis so its effect over time appeared sudden and seismic.

Another development that adversely affected livestock movement was the spread of armed conflict. When rebel groups such as the SLA took control of an area, they often cut off movement to it; if the area was part of a traditional migratory route, the consequence was to restrict pastoralist access to wet-season grazing reserves. As a result, only three of eleven migratory routes that existed in the 1950s were functioning by early 2007.[27]

Even when pastoralists retaliated by looting livestock from farming populations, the effect was to worsen the crisis of pastoralist tribes by concentrating livestock in their dry-season grazing reserves. The further concentration of livestock in dry areas brought an increased danger of livestock's dying both from lack of water and from water-borne diseases.[28] The more they stripped large sections of society of assets, groups associated with the looting of livestock became their own worst enemies: They could neither access the wet-season grazing reserves nor sell looted animals, for trade routes were no longer safe.[29] As the crisis intensified, settled ethnic groups—the Fur and the Birgid—developed their own collective solutions; more often than not, they tried to exclude migrant groups. In 1982, for example, there was a strong movement among Fur communities, spreading from Kutum in northern Darfur to Kebkabiya and Zalingei in southern and southwestern Darfur, to get rid of immigrant groups. In response, nomadic groups, both Arabs and the Zaghawa, joined in an alliance of convenience.[30] The mutual exclusion from each others' nearby pastures, not to mention the exclusion of those without exclusive pastures, was bound to lead to conflict. But it ignored the central issue driving the conflict: the tribal definition of right of access to productive natural resources.

The high point of the drought ravaged the region and ushered in the great war between tribes with a homeland and those without. This war was fought in two rounds. The first round was between camel pastoralists of the northern semidesert, a constellation of Arab (comprising Mahariya, Mahameed, Eraigat, Etaifata, and Awlad-Rashid) and non-Arab (the Zaghawa) groups against settled Fur farmers around Kebkabiya and the northwestern reaches of Jebel Marra; the second round pitted Fur farming communities of the entire Jebel Marra area against a broad coalition of virtually all Arab and Zaghawa nomads. According to one author, this post-1985 conflict was the result of "a systematic drive by the nomads to occupy land in the central Jebel Marra massif." "Fought primarily over the control of a thriving resource base in the middle of a zone of scarcity," this was "a classical ecological conflict." The 1987–89 conflict between the Fur militia and nomadic fighters was not easy to solve: Two conferences were held, and though agreements were reached, their terms proved difficult to implement.[31]

Each side developed its own defense of the right of access to productive natural resources, and each did this in the language of rights. Settled groups with *hakura* defended their rights as "customary" and "tribal," whereas those with diminished or no homeland (*dar*) rights claimed access to productive natural resources as the right of a "citizen." The clash between rights took the form of ethnic wars. As each side undertook to defend an exclusive right, its defense began to take on an increasingly racist tone. The important thing is to recognize the trajectory along which this conflict unfolded: The more they saw themselves as victims with little control over this rapidly unraveling situation, the more both sides tended to slide into an exclusionist rhetoric that inevitably opened them to outside influences that further racialized and inflamed the discourse. One outcome was the coming together of the most contradictory forces. On one side stood a combination of *dar*less camel nomads of North Darfur and landless Chadian refugees driven into Darfur, now joined with powerful rulers with vast ambitions, at first Colonel Qaddafi in Tripoli under the banner of an "Arab Gathering" and later the new Islamist regime in Khartoum. On the other side were sedentary groups in Darfur drawing support from non-Arab forces in Chad, particularly those led by Hissen Habre and, through them, Western allies such as France, Israel, and the Reagan administration looking for effective proxies in the Cold War.

The polarization of opposing narratives fed on a growing tension on the ground. Attacked by the nomad Arab militia, the Fur developed their own militia. By May 1989, ethnically organized conflict had spread beyond the Fur lands around Jebel Marra all the way to the Chad border. As Libyans distributed arms to the Bedeiyat and Zaghawa refugees just arrived from Chad, the Fur found themselves invariably outgunned. For the first time, nearly all the pastoral tribes of Darfur—Arab and non-Arab—came together under a pan-Arab banner backed by Libya.[32]

The surest indication that the traditional system of resolving conflicts had broken down came when parties to the conflict showed an open disregard for conventions. Contrary to customary practice, Baggara chiefs boycotted the reconciliation conference called for late May 1989 in El Fasher. When this happened, the fighting resumed within days and with uncontrolled ferocity. More than fifty thousand Fur sought refuge in Nyala. In Khartoum, the little-known Sudan Rural Solidarity Group issued a statement calling for Sudanese groups—Abbala, Baggara, Fur, Zaghawa, and Massalit—to end their feuds and for the government to suppress ethnic militias. The Sudanese Supreme State Council deplored the "serious situation in Darfur" and criticized the activity of "several" foreign elements "entangled in this bloody struggle." The *Sudan Times* pointed to Chad as the foreign element in the conflict.[33] On June 30, 1989, a small circle of hitherto unknown Sudanese army officers led by Brigadier Omar Hasan Ahmad al-Bashir overthrew the civilian government of Prime Minister Sadiq al-Mahdi.[34] By then, the war in Darfur had turned into a conflict over land driven by two uncompromising ideologies—one Arab supremacist, the other Fur nativist.[35]

As the conflict continued, the destruction escalated. Conventional restraints in farmer-herder conflicts, in which neighbor fought neighbor with the knowledge that tomorrow they would have to live together, were shed, bit by bit, over time. The violence began to take on a near-total character. Its object was no longer to define the boundary between the self and the other but to question the very existence of the other. The shift was deadly, and it was marked by several developments. The first was the coalescing of allies into a single organic force: As many Arab tribes came together into one entity defined as "Arab," the Fur who lived in scattered communities also jelled into a single ethnic force. As twenty-seven groups coalesced into a confederate alliance they called "Arab," it was the Beni Helba, neighbors to the Dar Dima of the Fur, who emerged as its leaders.[36] In that same way, Fur groups, otherwise scattered, throughout the region managed to mobilize themselves as a single ethnic group.[37] The second development was the discrediting of the central and regional governments—the former as pro-Arab (at least until July 1989) and the latter as pro-Fur (at least until its replacement in early 1988)—as too partisan to be credible arbiters in the conflict. The third was an escalation in the level of brutality unleashed by militias on both sides, confirming, yet again, that civil society at war is more brutal than states at war. "The Arabs using mounted razzias called 'knights' (*fursan,* Arabic), cut the throats of their Fur victims and burned them alive when they survived their machine guns and rocket-propelled grenades. The Fur did likewise whenever they had a chance, using their combatants called 'militias' (*malishiat*). The Arabs violated Fur farms and burned their produce and uprooted orchards. The Fur counterattacked by burning pasture and by denying their enemies access to water sources."[38] The fourth development was the progressive incorporation of the conflict into national, regional, and international domains as each side looked for allies. At the center, "the Arabs were closely allied to the Umma Party and the Fur were allied to the Democratic Unionist Party (DUP) who were coalition partners at the time."[39] Regionally, the Arabs looked to Libya and the Fur to the SPLA and to the Hissen Habre forces in Chad—and, through them, to "the anti-Libyan mosaic" (the United States of America, France, Israel, and Egypt)—for armaments and even ideological inspiration. As the tribal conflict began to have a wider ideological resonance, one side claimed to be fighting for an extension and liberation of the "Arab belt" in Africa; the other called for a similar emancipation of the "African belt."[40]

In their opening statement, the Islamist coup makers of 1989 promised a way out of the crisis as they advanced the government's inept handling of Darfur as a justification for overthrowing it. The effect on both sides was electric: The Fur and the Arabs quickly reconciled their differences. In less than a week, the adversaries had signed a peace protocol.[41] But in another decade and a half, the situation had returned to what it had been before the coup. As the government became a party to the conflict, it lost its handle on it. As a result, the civil conflict became internationalized.

A government faced with land conflicts as in Darfur could choose among only three alternatives. The first was business as usual: The government would direct its efforts toward organizing tribal reconciliation conferences to solve existing disputes and take measures that would prevent further conflicts—measures such as delineating migration routes and keeping them free of obstacles, or agreeing on the dates when nomads could enter or must leave the farming belt, or preventing farmers from cultivating around watering points. The second alternative was to take stock of the entire situation with a view to overhauling it: With no empty lands to allocate to whole tribal groups, the only way to meet such demands was to reform the land and governance system so as to detach land and governance rights from tribal identity. The most ambitious effort to do so was by the Nimeiry government in 1971. The third alternative was to reform the existing system but without challenging its basic provisions. This is the route that the Islamist regime took after 1989.

At first, it seemed that little had changed. The governorship reverted to being a prerogative of riverine Sudanese.[42] When Daud Yahya Bolad, previously the National Islamic Front's (NIF's) man in Darfur, defected to the SPLA and attempted to lead an uprising in Darfur in 1991–92, the government used Arab militias to put down the revolt. The government then made several attempts to address the grievances of *dar*less Arab tribes of Darfur and immigrants from Chad by carving out *dars* for them from lands that settled groups had come to consider their traditional patrimony. This attempt to reform native administration began in March 1995, when the governor of West Darfur issued a decree dividing the traditional homeland of the Massalit into thirteen emirates; nine of these were allocated to *dar*less Arab groups to create Arab emirates. As a consequence, Dar Erenga and Dar Jebel in Kulbus Province became administrative entities outside Dar Massalit Sultanate.[43] Yet another attempt to reform the native authority system—which involved the twin features of tribal land ownership and tribal governance—led to separating the system of land tenure from the administrative and governance system, so as to reform the latter without changing the former. In 1995, the government of West Darfur State appointed some Arab leaders to positions in the native authority system by giving them authority over their people but not over the land. The settled groups with homeland rights objected vehemently.[44]

The government's clumsy attempt to reform the land and governance system in Darfur should not hide the fact that the Arab tribes of Darfur—in particular, the camel nomads—had a genuine and long-standing grievance. While the Fur and other sedentary groups complained that Darfur had been marginalized by the center in Khartoum, the fact was that Darfur's Arab tribes were doubly marginalized, first as Darfuri inside Sudan, and then as Arabs inside Darfur. The most marginalized of the Darfuri Arabs were the *dar*less camel nomads of the north. Following the January 1995 conference on native administration in Khartoum, some Arab tribes from Darfur and Kordofan demanded their own native administrations. They claimed this right on grounds of citizenship and of tangible participation in the national economy. In West Darfur State, *dar*less groups, most nomadic but some sedentary, demanded that local authorities as well as the state *wali* (governor) offer them native administrations.[45]

Top-down reforms triggered a local-level conflict between the Massalit and their Arab neighbors, one that escalated from 1995 to 1999 and culminated in a state of emergency. Whereas the problem of the *dar*less tribes was a real and urgent one demanding consideration, the government's resolution worsened the problem, for it ended up entrenching rather than reforming the system. Its pro-Arab tilt removed the government from the role of a credible arbiter in the eyes of the Massalit, for whom the 1995–99 period turned out to be one of devastating setbacks.[46] Eventually, both sides suffered heavy losses: Hundreds were killed, thousands of families lost livestock and possessions, and at least 100,000 refugees fled to Chad.[47] No authority seemed to be in charge of maintaining order, and no mechanism of conflict resolution seemed to be in place. Several attempts to set in motion the traditional mechanism of reconciliation conferences—once in 1995 and twice in 1996, in August and November—failed. With no end to the conflict in sight, different ethnic groups began to establish, train, and arm militia groups, setting the stage for the latest and most destructive round of violence.[48]

When the conflict resumed after 2003, the violence surged to new heights: Thousands of innocents lost their lives as entire villages were burned and wiped out and property was looted and plundered. This time around, Zaghawa pastoralists were allied with settled Fur and recruited from the Chadian military across the border; on the other side, camel pastoralists of northern Darfur and a few small tribes of cattle nomads in the Jebel Marra area were joined with Chadian nomads.[49] As the conflict grew into a war, tribal mobilization became subsumed under larger identities on both sides, with the insurgency driven by two armed movements (the SLA and the JEM) and the counterinsurgency led by the government, which aided and armed a shadowy bandit militia, the Janjawiid.

Rebel Movements—The Insurgency

The armed struggle that began in Darfur in 2003 was organized around two movements: the Sudan Liberation Army and the Justice and Equality Movement. Of the two, the SLA was the leading movement. On February 26, 2003, some three hundred insurgents calling themselves the Darfur Liberation Front (DLF) seized the town of Gulu, capital of Jebel Marra Province in the state of West Darfur. They were led by Abd al-Wahid Muhammad al-Nur, a young Fur lawyer who had graduated from the University of Khartoum in 1995 and had been a member of the Communist Party and the Sudan People's Liberation Movement (SPLM). Two weeks later, the DLF changed its name to the Sudan Liberation Movement / Sudan Liberation Army (SLM/SLA), its vision no longer embracing just Darfur (the *D* in *DLF*) but the whole of Sudan (the *S* in *SLM*). At the same time, the leadership was expanded with the appointment of a Zaghawa, Minni Arkuwa Minnawi, who was a renowned fighter but lacked political experience or direction, as the secretary-general of the SLM.[50] The Fur had forged an alliance with the Zaghawa as early as 2001. For Abd al-Wahid, this was a test of the politics of inclusion, for the Zaghawa had stayed out of the 1987–89 civil war until their leaders in Khartoum responded to the split in the Islamist regime with an initiative to join the rebellion.

If Abd al-Wahid had a model to follow, it was that of John Garang.[51] Garang had reportedly asked for two assurances before assisting the new organization: first, a change of name to disavow any intention to separate Darfur from Sudan and, second, an assurance that the embryonic SLA would declare itself a political movement and not an anti-Arab militia. Ahmed Abdel Shafi and Babikir, sent by Abd al-Wahid, made clear that the SLA believed in the New Sudan "as a concept." The SLA Manifesto, made public on March 16, 2003, declared: "The Arab tribes and groups are an integral and indivisible component of Darfur's social fabric who have been equally marginalized and deprived of their rights to development and social participation. . . . The real interests of the Arab tribes of Darfur are with the SLM/A and Darfur, not with the various oppressive and transient governments in Khartoum." At the same time, Shafi and Babikir made it abundantly clear that Darfuri rebels could not join the SPLA: "If we declare we are SPLA, the Arabs will not join us. Let us have our own movement first, then we will see." Assured that the SLA was on the right course politically, Garang sent twenty-two SPLA officers to North Darfur in February 2003. Eritrea was a second external source of military supplies for the SLA.

The SLA leaders were both inspired by the earlier example of Daud Bolad and determined not to repeat his mistakes. At his Eritrean base, Abd al-Wahid had joined a group of students to analyze Bolad's defeat in 1991. They concluded that his main weakness stemmed from a top-down approach that relied on traditional leaders ("friends of the strong, enemies of the weak") for support and so failed to organize a popular Darfuri force. This explained why it had been easy for the government to isolate and eliminate Bolad. Unlike Bolad, Abd al-Wahid pledged to mobilize popular Darfuri support across all groups—including Arabs—so as to isolate the government and confront it as the enemy.

The second rebel movement that burst on the scene in 2003 was the Justice and Equality Movement.[52] The JEM began among the "riverized" Darfuris in Khartoum. Its leader was Dr. Khalil Ibrahim, a physician who had held a series of positions in several regional governments (as minister of education in the old Darfur province, state minister of health in North Darfur in the mid-1990s, minister for social affairs in Blue Nile in 1997, and adviser to the governor of South Sudan in Juba in 1998) and then as minister of health in the Islamist government in Khartoum.[53] Khalil Ibrahim's Islamist credentials were impeccable: He had even led the anti-SPLA government militias, first the Murahileen and later the Mujahideen. This single fact should caution those who tend to see the counterinsurgency in Darfur as a linear development from the earlier counterinsurgency in South Sudan. The facts were otherwise: Not only the counterinsurgency, but the insurgency, too, had links with the repression in South Sudan.

The JEM had established secret cells in El Fasher in 1993, Kordofan in 1994, and Khartoum in 1997. This fervently Islamist tendency had hoped to reform the NIF from within. Toward that end, its members formed a committee of twenty-seven in 1997 and then issued a publication that documented the marginalization of Darfuris in the Islamist government.[54] That document, *The Black Book: Imbalance of Power and Wealth in Sudan,* was distributed secretly in Khartoum in May 2000. A second, revised, version of *The Black Book* appeared in 2002. *The Black Book* documented the privileged position of riverine Arabs and the marginalized position of westerners in the Islamist government.[55] Like the SLA, the JEM also represented an alliance of several tribal elites, the Kube of the Zaghawa and the western Meidob. But, unlike the SLA, its coalition also had some Arab members, including from the Misiriya, suggesting that the JEM, unlike the SLA, was an ideologically cohesive formation.[56]

Although nowhere near as important in terms of numbers, a third group merits attention for the caliber of its leadership. This is the Sudan Federal Democratic Alliance (SFDA), led by Ahmed Diraige, previously a member of the Umma Party, a minister of state, and the first elected governor of Darfur in 1980 during the Nimeiry period, and his deputy, Sharif Harir. As soon as the armed struggle began, the SFDA put its political resources at the disposal of the larger SLA. Sharif Harir in particular placed himself in the service of the SLA/SLM negotiating team.[57]

The new rebels received support from a variety of sources. The most important came from those dissatisfied with the negotiated outcome to the civil war in the south. These could be found on both the government and the rebel side. They included the Islamists around Hasan al-Turabi, organized as the PCP in Khartoum, and sections of the SPLA in the south. Both had vowed to continue the struggle on a different terrain, Darfur. The Turabi section of the Islamists had a close link with the JEM through Ali al-Haj, Turabi's deputy, just as the SPLA had close links with the SLA. Both translated association into direct support, which came as a welcome development for the two movements, the SLA and the JEM, which learned from the SPLA that only direct pressure would get Khartoum to make concessions. Not surprisingly, their demands echoed SPLA gains: the appointment of a vice president for Darfur, the establishment of a regional government in Darfur, and the integration of their fighters into the national armed forces.[58]

Yet another important source of support was regional: from Eritrea and Chad, each for its own reasons. The independent state of Eritrea was born in 1993, after an armed struggle against Ethiopia that had lasted for more than three decades. Soon after independence, Eritrea locked horns with Ethiopia. From then on, its foreign policy was shaped by the strategic need to win friends in a neighborhood dominated by two big countries, Ethiopia and Sudan. Small in size and lacking command over a strategic resource, Eritrea took to playing host to opposition movements from neighboring countries and to treating these movements as so many water taps to be turned on and off to suit the requirements of its own foreign policy. To begin with, any dissident from Sudan was assured of dormitory-style accommodations and a passport to facilitate international travel, even if for just a few months; all in all, support was on a short leash. It is in accord with this logic that Eritrea played host to the armed opposition from all over Sudan, and not just from Darfur.

Whereas the SPLA and Eritrea had been important centers of support for the Darfur insurgency ever since it was launched in 2003, this had not always been the case with Chad.[59] Chadian president Idriss Deby's first move when Darfur rebels struck in March 2003 was to convene formal peace talks in August 2003 and cooperate with the African Union to help work out a cease-fire in Darfur the following year. But things changed after an attempted coup in Chad in May 2004, when some of the regime's core supporters—including members from the security apparatus, the Republican Guard, and the inner circle—defected and established an armed opposition in Darfur. The Deby government responded by building links with the Darfuri opposition, particularly the JEM, through which Deby sought to reunify the Zaghawa elements of the Darfur insurgency to protect his own regime. The Chad government's initiative led to a meeting in N'Djamena in January 2006, which resulted in the formation of the Alliance of Revolutionary Forces of Western Sudan, led by the Zaghawa leader of JEM, Khalil Ibrahim. With less of a stake in internal Chadian politics, the SLA was less active in this organization. Military supplies reportedly came from Eritrea. The next time Chad rebels attacked N'Djamena and several border towns, in April 2006, JEM fighters fought alongside Deby's supporters. When the JEM and parts of the SLA did not sign the peace agreement in Abuja on May 5, 2006, Deby reportedly provided them with military support. Once again, Eritrea, Chad—and the SPLA—cooperated to help with the establishment of yet another nonsignatory group, the National Redemption Front, whose leaders were provided facilities in N'Djamena.[60]

The Counterinsurgency

When faced with the insurgency, the Islamist government's initial response was to encourage reconciliation. It invited hundreds of local leaders, representatives of ethnic groups and new elites, to a conference in El Fasher on February 24–25, 2003, to look for solutions to the conflict. It set up four committees along ethnic lines to negotiate with the rebels. The rebels reportedly agreed to talk with the government as long as they were not asked to represent particular ethnic groups, rejecting this as a divide-and-rule tactic.

The rebel claim was credible on paper, but not for those who had followed the course of developments in Darfur over two decades. From the time of Diraige's election in 1980, when Fur ethnic pride built up just as Darfur's Arab tribes suffered disproportionately from drought and misfortune, there had been a parting of the ways between the two. The rift was so wide by 2003 that when the DLF publicly announced itself with the attack on Gulu, it came as a total surprise to Arabs, for "no Arab had been consulted in the formation, or strategy, of such a front." In the words of al Sanosi Musa, a young Mahamid Arab, "Our people asked, 'Who are they going to liberate Darfur from?' The conclusion was they were going to liberate Darfur from the Arabs!"[61] The simple fact is that all armed movements in Darfur were predominantly ethnic. This is why when rebel movements claimed to "liberate" land from Sudanese government forces, those living on the land saw it as in fact an attempt to "occupy" rather than "liberate" the land. And those without a *dar* saw it as a preemptive attempt to deny them one.

In the end, the conference split, with the hard-line military approach winning out on both sides.[62] Another attempt at a peaceful solution was made by two senior officials in the Reformed Umma Party, the minister of education and the governor of Upper Nile State. This time, too, the SLA said it would negotiate as long as the government recognized the political nature of its struggle, stopped calling its members "armed robbers," and disarmed the Janjawiid. But the initiative got bogged down within the Reformed Umma Party.[63] A third attempt was made by the architect of the peace agreement for the south, Vice President Ali Osman Mohamed Taha, who met the exiled Darfuri leader, Ahmed Ibrahim Diraige, in Nairobi in January 2004. Diraige reiterated that Darfur's problems were political and economic and called for a cease-fire. Once again, nothing was achieved. Other attempts were made by the Zaghawa traditional leadership and by the umbrella group the Sudan Peace Forum. All failed. These cumulative failures suggested the absence of a government—and rebel—consensus on whether to opt for a political or a military response to the other.[64] Slowly but surely, the counterinsurgency moved to an overwhelmingly military response.

If the rebels drew their support from mainly non-Arab groups, both sedentary (Fur, Massalit) and nomadic (Zaghawa), the government drew its support mainly from the *dar*less camel nomads of North Darfur, the *dar*less smaller tribes of South and West Darfur, and recent arrivals from Chad. The larger cattle-raising Arab (Baggara) tribes of the south, who constituted the vast majority of Darfur's Arabs, did not take part in the conflict. The difference in the response of the Baggara and the Abbala Arabs was clearly shaped not by their common Arab identity but by the fact that the Abbala had no claim to a tribal homeland (*dar*) whereas the Baggara did.

The Sudan government gradually shifted responsibility for prosecuting the war from the army to the military intelligence. The problem with the army was that it mirrored the pattern of discrimination in Sudanese society, with the officer corps composed predominantly of riverine Arabs and the majority of troops drawn from western Sudan, many of them Darfuris (*awlad al-gharib*). This single fact led to widespread official concern about the loyalty of many of the Darfuri noncommissioned army officers and soldiers. There was the additional fact that the armed forces would also need to be retrained and redeployed to fight this new kind of desert war. After all, the rebels were said to hold the initiative in the early phase of the war: They had won thirty-four of thirty-eight engagements in the middle months of 2003, destroyed a battalion, killed 500, and taken 300 prisoners, all at Kutum in May, and killed another 250 in a second attack on Tine in mid-July. By the end of 2003, the SLA was threatening to extend the war farther east into Kordofan.[65] This is when the government changed its strategy, shifting reliance from the army to a combination of three groups: military intelligence, the air force, and armed nomads (named *Janjawiid* by their victims and adversaries) whom the government had begun directing against the Massalit uprising as early as 1996–99. Once the better-organized Janjawiid were put at the center of the new counterinsurgency strategy, they quickly gained the upper hand.[66]

The term *Janjawiid* had first been used for the nomadic tribal militia—predominantly but not exclusively Arab—fighting in the Fur-Arab war of the late 1980s. Then, it involved two main groups: members of nomadic groups without access to land, and a variety of outlaws, bandits, and common criminals (it was said that some had even been released from prison for the sole purpose of fighting).[67] There were reports of four Janjawiid camps armed and trained by the government: Misteriha in North Darfur, Jebel Adola and Gardud in South Darfur, and Jebel Kargo in West Darfur.[68] But to pinpoint the genesis of the Janjawiid phenomenon, we need to cross the western border of Darfur into Chad and trace the development of armed groups that formed during the civil wars in Chad between 1962 and 1991 and examine how these contributed to the formation of armed militias in Darfur. The Janjawiid originated from these armed militias. If anything, the crisis of nomadism was even deeper in Chad than in Darfur. To get a fuller understanding of the social context that made for a phenomenon such as the Janjawiid, we need to appreciate a wider fact: Janjawiid recruits were mainly teen and preteen unemployed youths, reflecting the deepening crisis of nomadism in the Sahel. The widespread prevalence of teen soldiers in Africa's postindependence wars suggests that this is an outgrowth of a continentwide economic, social, and generational crisis.

Researchers who have focused on the impact of the Chadian civil war on Darfur have noted "that all major conflicts in Darfur over the last 20 years have been associated with the presence of armed Chadian groups and that armed Chadians constitute a significant proportion of the Janjawiid."[69] It is said that when Musa Hilal of the Um Jalul clan developed a strong connection with the Khartoum government, he made "forays into Chad where he recruited some 20,000 Chadians into the Janjawiid in return for a horse, a gun and [the promise of] unlimited loot."[70] Even among progovernment Darfuris, Janjawiid are depicted as "banditry gangs, whose activities are frowned upon, and considered as criminals and outlaws and not under the authority or control of any tribe."[71] As a blanket term, however, *Janjawiid* covers a variety of tribal militias operating in Darfur today, each with its own resources and autonomy of command. Of these, it is the group with the greatest latitude that has been responsible for the greatest number of atrocities.[72]

The counterinsurgency mainly comprised three groups: the Janjawiid, the "additional armed forces," and the Popular Defense Forces (PDF). When the Islamist movement split in 1999 and most Darfuri Islamists went into the opposition, the most powerful Darfuri remaining in the security apparatus was an air force general from the Abbala Rizeigat. On his initiative, a number of Janjawiid militias were put in place as the Popular Defense Forces.[73] It was with the intensification of the rebellion in 2003 that the air force, the Popular Defense Forces, and indeed the military intelligence began to develop links with these militias and to transform them into a semiregular paramilitary force. But the paramilitary force was not limited to the Janjawiid.[74] In fact, it was first organized in parts of North Darfur where the Janjawiid phenomenon did not exist. When the government stepped into these parts and created a regular militia or took already existing militias under its wing, these, too, became part of the Janjawiid phenomenon.[75]

In contrast to the Janjawiid, which is more of an antisocial and outlaw phenomenon, the "additional armed forces" are men mobilized by their own tribe to become military personnel. They are not only trained by government forces but also paid by them and come under their direct control.[76] These groups have fought alongside regular armed forces. Nor are these militias attached exclusively to Arab groups. There are the Gimir, who responded favorably to the government's call to fight the rebellion, claiming to follow the example of two prominent Fur and Zaghawa *omdas* who a decade previously had joined the Murahileen in response to an earlier government call to fight the rebellion in the south and east.[77]

The Popular Defense Forces were a creation of the Islamist regime. Before the coup, Turabi had methodically recruited young officers at the military academy into the NIF; among them was Omar Hasan Ahmad al-Bashir. When the Islamist officers seized power on June 30, 1989, the Revolutionary Command Council passed the Popular Defense Forces Law and founded the PDF as a paramilitary force. The stated object was to protect the June 30 revolution and to suppress the rebellion in the south, but in practice, the PDF was used to establish political control over a variety of key institutions. The establishment of the PDF followed a practice initiated by the government of Sadiq al-Mahdi, who, as prime minister in 1986, had created militias to join the war against the SPLA. Over the years, these militias came to perpetrate the worst atrocities committed against civilian communities in southern Sudan. The Islamist government continued to pursue the militia strategy after 1989, incorporating many of the Murahileen militias into the Popular Defense Forces. Turabi made it explicitly clear that the ideologically armed PDF was to be a replacement for the professional army, for it would be impossible to "Islamize" the Sudanese army as long as it was led by professional "secularized" officers. The creation of an "Islamized" society would require a "large popular defense force." This ambition was reflected in the fact that by 1999 there were reportedly 80,000 regular troops in the Sudanese armed forces, 3,500 NIF commissioned army officers, and 150,000 in the PDF.[78]

Unlike the army, which was made up of volunteers, PDF soldiers were conscripts of a very unpopular draft. In this, they differed even from the Murahileen militia recruited by the Sadiq al-Mahdi government in the mid-eighties. Their training was more ideological than professional, more religious than military. The PDF reflected an attempt to militarize society—in Islamic idiom—through forced conscription. The Murahileen militia of the Rizeigat cattle nomads of South Darfur, formed in 1985 to fight against the SPLA in southern Sudan, did not participate in other internal conflicts until 2004. Even when the government responded to the onset of the rebellion in 2003 by mobilizing the entire native authority system as a military chain of command, creating militia units up to the brigade level, the Rizeigat *nazir,* Saeed Madibu, resisted government efforts to align his tribe along with the Janjawiid. There were two reasons for this. The first was political wisdom: After the practical experience of having participated in the anti-SPLA Murahileen, the Rizeigat leader was determined to keep his people neutral in the Darfur conflict.[79] The second was prudence born of calculated interest: Unlike the camel nomads of the north, the cattle-owning Rizeigat of the south had a stake in the status quo by way of their own *dar.*

Once the counterinsurgency began in 2003, there was a blurring of the lines between the Janjawiid, the "additional armed forces," and the Popular Defense Forces. To begin with, there were reports that many Janjawiid gangs had returned to their own ethnic group in order to join the additional armed forces recruited by the government. The reason was obvious: Unlike the Janjawiid, who had to depend exclusively on looting and robbery for a living, the additional armed forces received regular pay from the government. The Janjawiid who joined the additional armed forces would have the advantage of being able to continue to indulge in banditry to provide supplementary income. All told, the Janjawiid was not an ideological force nor the fighting arm of an ideologically driven movement. If anything, it was a bandit-type formation that changed alliances to suit changing conditions—so much so that Janjawiid leaders would be open to exploring affiliations with rebels in the changed political climate after Abuja.

The government, too, began to adopt irregular practices in its effort to maximize the mobilization for the counterinsurgency. It extended the call for additional armed forces beyond the territory of Darfur to as far away as West Africa. As a result, a large proportion of the additional armed forces began to include foreign elements, so that another type of armed group came into being. Its members were mercenaries, providing protection to whoever would pay the going rate, be these villages—such as the Fur in Wadi Barei[80] and the Tama and Gimir around Kebkabiya[81]—or motortrucks traveling to Omdurman from El Fasher.[82]

The conflict in Darfur began as a civil war (1987–89) between local militias, each with an ethnic identification. None were organized along transtribal, racial lines. The government got pulled into this dynamic following the failed local government reforms of 1995, and the opposition jumped into it in 2002–3. In a context in which ethnic conflict has interfaced with the wider struggle between rebels and the government—insurgency and counterinsurgency—outcomes have tended to vary from one locality to another. Just like the mobilization for the conflict, its outcome, too, has been along tribal lines. Three examples will illustrate the range of outcomes: ethnic cleansing, warlordism, and a standoffish autonomy.

The first example comes from North Darfur, which includes the historic Dar Massalit. The British fashioned Dar Massalit out of two former political units: the historic Gimir Sultanate of the seventeenth century and the Massalit Sultanate established following the Turco-Egyptian conquest of the Fur Sultanate in 1874—which the British later conquered with Egyptian forces in 1922. The British governed the sultanate as a set of tribal administrative systems run by British-appointed rulers, even if with most un-British titles: sheikhs, *maliks,* and *fursha.* Into this supposedly traditional arrangement, they inserted the Arab groups, each under its own *omda,* subordinate and responsible to the sultan of the Massalit. Since the colonial period, the Berti, the majority tribe in North Darfur, managed to increase administrative areas under its tribal

administration from three to twenty-three. Since this endeavor was
at the expense of neighboring tribes, such as the Zaghawa and the
Zayyadiyya, it led to tense relations between neighbors. These simmer-
ing conflicts exploded with the 2003 insurgency and counterinsurgency.
In areas of North Darfur that came under the control of the SLA, the
tendency was to resolve ethnic tensions through a process of ethnic
cleansing—leading, at the very start of the conflict, to the expulsion of
Arabs belonging to Awlad Hamid and El Mahariyya, both sections of the
Abbala nomads of the Northern Rizeigat, compelling them to move, in
most cases to Kebkabiya. Following it, the sedentary "non-Arab" tribes
in the area claimed to be *kulu wahid* ("all one").[83]

Kebkabiya Province, which lies north of the Jebel Marra mountains
and includes some of the most fertile agricultural land in Darfur, illustrates the second type of outcome. Its capital, Kebkabiya, had a population of 21,000 residents and 49,264 IDPs in October 2004. A stream
of IDPs, "affected by drought rather than by conflict," came into
Kebkabiya. The province's system of governance divided the resident
population into two groups: the Fur and the Tama as natives, and the
Northern Rizeigat Arabs (Eraigat, Etifasta, Mahameed, Zabalad, Awlad-
Zeid, and Awlad-Rashid) and the Zaghawa as immigrants. A native
(Fur) *omdiya* headed the native administration of the province, with
sub-*omdas* from immigrant groups working under him. In Kebkabiya,
however, the local solution to the conflict was not ethnic cleansing but
a shift in Fur-Arab relations from a market-centered to a security-
centered focus. The result was a form of warlordism whereby the Fur
paid armed groups to protect them against incursions from other tribes:
"The groups who protect them wear military uniform and are armed
with guns, and are considered to be 'an army of the government.' Some
members of the Fur in this area have joined the government armed
forces themselves and some have left for Khartoum." Groups that
describe themselves as progovernment in Kebkabiya include various
Arab groups and non-Arab groups such as the Tama and the Gimir. The
Fur pay SP (Sudanese pound) 2,000 per person per day, about US$0.80
at the going exchange rate. One village had around ten to twelve armed
soldiers, who secured its farms and protected the routes to and from
other places. The result was to save the thirty to forty village councils
under this particular Fur *omda* from attack.[84]

The third type of outcome—establishing a middle ground—is illustrated by developments in Seraif town, which lies west of Kebkabiya Province and had a registered population of 39,000 in the 1993 census. The majority tribe here was the Beni Hussein, an Arab tribe, 25 percent pastoralist and 75 percent sedentary, while settler tribes included the Fur, Zaghawa, Tama, Gimir, Massalit, and other Arab groups. The Beni Hussein has had a homeland (Dar Seraif) and a native administration (*nazirate*) of its own for some time. The reason for this is political and goes back to the period of the Mahdiyya, when many Darfuri tribes were forced to move east to Omdurman to support the Mahdi. The Beni Hussein, however, refused and instead migrated westward to Dar Burgo in Chad. When they returned after the defeat of the Mahdi and settled in Jebel Elatasha in North Darfur, the British rewarded their loyalty with Dar Seraif as a homeland, in which they were granted their own native administration. Beni Hussein leaders still proudly display a pair of drums that they received as a gift from the British administration and that are supposed to symbolize their traditional status as rulers of a *dar*. After 2003, the Beni Hussein tribal administration was approached by both the government and the insurgency, each eager to secure its support. The Beni Hussein made it clear that they had no wish to "take sides" and wanted Dar Seraif to provide a safe haven for different communities and tribes. They have been left alone, at least for now, and represent a buffer zone between government troops in Kebkabiya and rebel groups to the north. Though the government trained members of the Beni Hussein as part of the Popular Defense Forces, the tribe secured an agreement with the government that such men would only be deployed locally to keep order within the *dar* and would be under the control of the local tribal authority. As a result, of all tribes, the Beni Hussein have been among the least affected by the crisis in Darfur.[85]

Abuja

By the time peace negotiations began in Abuja, the Nigerian capital, in 2005, banditry was a common practice in the ranks of both the insurgency and the counterinsurgency. The very anticipation of a peace deal led to a jostling for positions among insurgent movements: The SLA split along ethnic lines as the Zaghawa lined up behind Minni Minnawi and the Fur behind Abdel al-Nur. The more disciplined JEM stayed united behind Khalil Ibrahim. Most independent observers at Abuja agreed that the problem lay more with the haste with which the negotiations were conducted by those in charge than with a lack of urgency among the negotiating parties. According to one observer, "The problem lay less in the agreement itself—which even those who refused to sign said was 95% satisfactory—than with the process, which foreclosed prematurely."

As negotiations hopped from one monthly deadline to the next, a number of top officials from the United Nations, the African Union, and key Western governments jetted into Abuja, warning that negotiations were proceeding far too slowly and that funds for the mediation would dry up if there was no agreement: The "patience of the international community is running out," they said. Some threatened sanctions to bring the parties involved in the negotiations into line. The warnings came from high-ranking individuals: at first, Jack Straw, the British foreign secretary, then the Dutch prime minister, who told the parties in January that "the international community has poured a lot of money, time and effort into the talks," but "our patience is not unlimited." Then followed an ultimatum: "If the parties do not reach an agreement here soon, we, with the AU, will need to start looking at the alternatives."[86] When threats did not achieve the desired result, more pressure was added from other dignitaries: the U.K. secretary of state for international development, Hilary Benn, and finally, U.S. deputy secretary of state Robert Zoellick.[87]

There are two views of why the talks failed: One is based on an observation of the scene of negotiations; the other examines developments behind the scenes. Starting with the scene itself, the arrival of dignitaries created a sense of urgency, but one that was more of a reflection of the changed atmosphere in Abuja than of any change in the situation in Darfur. Collectively known as the donors, Western government representatives jointly pressured the parties to the conflict—mainly the insurgents—to reach an agreement without further delay. Meanwhile, the United Nations and the African Union played the good cops, intervening to get small last-minute extensions in the hope of further concessions. At one point, President Olusegun Obasanjo of Nigeria intervened to get Salim Ahmed Salim, the African Union–appointed chairperson of the mediation, to extend the deadline by forty-eight hours and then again by another forty-eight hours. As the pace of the talks changed from lethargic to feverish, "there was a frenzy of behind-the-scene deals, offers and threats as various leaders and officials [Obasanjo, Zoellick, Benn] endeavored to stave off collapse."[88]

A small number of Western donors underwrote the expenses for the negotiations. They warned repeatedly that funding would dry up if an agreement was not reached quickly. This put the negotiating parties—in particular, the rebels—and the AU mediators on a short leash. Salim complained to the U.N. Security Council in January 2006 that the funding situation was extremely precarious.[89] When he told mediators to wrap up by a given deadline, he cited lack of funds as the reason for it. Eventually, a series of deadlines was issued, one after another, by a number of authoritative parties. As they faced successive deadlines, both mediators and negotiating parties lost control of the process. Soon, the talks lurched to a halt. This is how one observer described the process:

> The ever-looming deadlines made it pointless to develop a comprehensive mediation strategy and plan. If the talks were always due to shut down in a matter of weeks, then there was no need to prepare a plan of action for the following six months. . . . For example, in late February and early March, confronted by the deadlock in Abuja and the fierce fighting in Darfur, the mediation team debated at length whether it was more likely to make progress by putting forward a comprehensive peace agreement aimed at addressing the root causes of the conflict or by tabling an enhanced humanitarian ceasefire agreement aimed at reducing the level of violence and improving the climate for negotiations. The debate was rendered moot by the Peace and Security Council's decree that the comprehensive agreement had to be concluded by the end of April. . . . The deadline diplomacy contributed indirectly to the absence of negotiations between the parties. In order to comply with the calls to speed up and meet unrealistic deadlines, the mediation team prepared position papers that moved far ahead of the parties as it tried to bridge the yawning gap between them. . . . To the great

> frustration of the mediation team, the parties' most strenu-
> ous efforts were directed at the mediators and not at each
> other. . . . The tight deadlines made it impossible for the
> mediators to communicate in a meaningful way with the
> people of Darfur and with important groups that were not
> represented at the talks. Similarly, the rebel negotiators
> were unable to brief and consult properly with their con-
> stituencies.[90]

Eventually, the rebels asked the mediators to give them three weeks to study and comment on the document. When they were turned down, they rejected the Darfur Peace Agreement (DPA).

The language of those directly involved in the talks began to reflect an acknowledgment of how rushed the process had become, so much so that it was no longer possible for the negotiating parties to claim owner-ship of it. If the chairperson of the mediation, Salim, began to refer to provisions in the DPA as the "mediators' proposals," "our proposals," and the "mediation's compromise," the Abdel al-Nur faction (which eventually did not sign the DPA) complained that the agreement was lit-erally being forced on it, asking "on what basis [did] the Movement have to sign an agreement [for] which it did not participate in its discussion?" As if to confirm this, there followed a three-thousand-word "Open letter to those members of the Movements who are still reluctant to sign" issued by six members of the mediation team, including its head, Sam Ibok, soon after the DPA had been signed by the government and Min-nawi. Addressing nonsignatory objections, they confirmed the worst: "Many of the suspicions about this Agreement are based on misunder-standing and the fact that many of you have not had the time to study the text in detail, and understand what it provides."[91]

But there is also another view of exactly what drove the process to a halt. This view is drawn from behind-the-scenes developments rather than those that could be observed during formal conference proceed-ings. Alex de Waal, a consultant to the African Union team, observed that rebel representatives seemed in no hurry to arrive at an agreement. Their demand that Western governments be involved in enforcing the agreement, as Western governments had indeed done with regard to Bosnia, seemed to reflect complacence born of a confidence that could come only from having friends in high places.[92] There is also the added, and curious, fact that Abuja—and, following it, Tripoli in 2007—must have been among the few negotiations in which sponsors actually expected to hammer out an agreement to end the conflict both piecemeal and in the public glare of media attention. Usually, international conferences are designed not as venues to reach agreements through protracted public negotiations but as ceremonial sites from which to ratify and announce the results of behind-the-scenes negotiations. What explains the incredible naïveté of the negotiators at Abuja in 2005–6 and Tripoli in 2007 that they gave the spoilers a field day, not once but twice?

When negotiations ended, fighting resumed. Many argued that the situation following the signing of the DPA was worse than that preceding it. For one, the rift between the rebels who signed the agreement and those who did not broke out into open warfare, as the Abdel al-Nur and Minnawi factions of the SLA confronted each other, each drawing support from a different ethnic faction.[93] The Minnawi faction, which had signed the agreement, turned on the civilian population in the areas it controlled, by replacing civilian with military courts and introducing extortionist practices in the name of taxation—claiming that it was the government of the place and so had the sovereign right to do anything it pleased.[94]

A cumulative result of these developments was the emergence of rogue commanders who answered to no one. Rogue units roamed the countryside and preyed on its residents. Minnawi's men in particular were said to combine looting with rape.[95] When Abdel al-Nur visited Jebel Marra in October 2005, after an eighteen-month absence, he professed to be "deeply shocked" by what he found: There were "quarrelling commanders"; one was "accused of killing many, many people"; others were accused of abuse of power, including imprisoning more than a hundred people without charge or trial, often for no reason other than a personal grudge; and last, there were "thousands of underage soldiers."[96] The U.N. DDR (disarmament, demobilization, and reintegration) unit estimated that 25 to 35 percent of twelve thousand rebels could be child soldiers.[97]

By March 2006, local people were calling the Minnawi faction "Janjawiid 2."[98] Both Amnesty International and the U.N. humanitarian chief, Jan Egeland, echoed these accusations: that Minnawi's men were killing and raping civilians and causing a new wave of displacement.[99] As more splinter groups emerged—not only from the SLA but also from the JEM—rebel banditry increased. Rebel bandits attacked commercial trucks for fuel, extorted cash from truckers, and looted livestock from nomads.[100] As SLA groups attacked humanitarian convoys and clashed with the JEM, the National Movement for Reform and Development (NMRD), a JEM splinter group, prepared to attack one and all, including AMIS (the African Union Mission in Sudan) and international NGOs, in an attempt to be recognized as a significant military player.[101]

If rebel groups began splintering during and after Abuja, nomadic Arab groups, too, began to reassess their nonparticipation after Abuja. The Arab camel nomads of the north, who had joined the government's counterinsurgency, began to consider the wisdom of casting their lot with the government. Many leaders felt betrayed by the DPA; not only were they not consulted, but the agreement did little to represent their interests.[102] If anything, Abuja made it clear that the government would not hesitate to ditch them should it consider that in its own interest. The government, too, began to assess the wisdom of an alliance with local militias that had their own agenda and whose ruthless pursuit of that agenda had tarnished the government's image internationally, perhaps irrevocably. There were reports of overtures between some of the Janjawiid and rebel commanders.

The Arab cattle nomads of the south who had abstained from the conflict concluded that they could not afford the widespread assumption among all concerned that the government represented Darfur's Arab groups against a rebellion supported by non-Arab groups. The trend became clear when some Darfuri Arabs, having publicly disassociated themselves from the Janjawiid, whom they termed mercenaries, announced the formation of their own rebel group—the Popular Forces Army—on December 6, 2006, and claimed that they had repulsed an assault by the Sudanese army at Kas-Zallingi only the previous day. There were also reports of other Arab groups' having signed political accords with rebel movements.[103]

.   .   .

As the post-Abuja situation settled down, one could discern two contrasting developments among the rebels: on the one hand, a spread in rebel banditry; on the other, an attempt by rebels and their allies to create a counter to Abuja, a rejection front. Those opposed to the DPA—the Abdel al-Nur faction of the SLM, the JEM, and the Sudan Federal Democratic Alliance (SFDA)—formed the National Redemption Front on June 30, 2006. Even as they united in opposition to the DPA, a jostling for power and positions went on inside the front. As individuals such as Ahmed Abdel Shafi challenged the leadership of Abdel al-Nur,[104] Abdel al-Nur drew his own lessons from the pre-Abuja phase of the rebellion, making overtures to all Arab tribes, including the Janjawiid: "If we make a movement without the Arabs, the government will move the Arabs against us."[105]

By late 2006, the Group of 19, also known as G-19, emerged as the strongest force on the ground in Darfur. It allied with the JEM and liaised with the Popular Forces Army, the first rebel group to be organized by Darfuri Arabs. But the Group of 19 also recognized the need to heal past rifts inside Darfur in order to build unity across ethnic divisions. So they urged a Darfur-Darfur dialogue "to lay the foundation for stability and development in Darfur" and proposed "to resolve the issue of Janjawiid by reintegrating them into society." As commanders from other factions joined G-19, the group changed its name to SLA-Unity.[106]

The changing position of the dominant leadership in the insurgency reflected a growing realization among sedentary tribes on the ground: that the problem was the government, not the Arab tribes of Darfur. The change in perspective made for a change in the interpretation of the violence: A displaced Fur *omda,* originally from an area southwest of Nyala, described how Arabs, both local and not, had attacked his village in March 2004, forcing him and most of his people, including many non-Fur, to flee. But he immediately stressed that "it was not a tribe fighting us, it was the government." He said the National Front government had, since the early 1990s, "fanned the flames, used the Arabs against the Africans. . . . Our problem is not with the Arabs, it is with the government. The government destroyed our area. Even if Arabs did take part, they are just poor people like us. The government is behind it."[107]

.   .   .

It is not just that the focus was shifting to the government as the source of the problem; there was also a deeper realization that the absence of government was an even greater problem. This distinction was echoed by displaced Hausa people in South Darfur: "The problem is not tribal, it is anarchy (*fawdha*)." *Fawdha* is a word loaded with meaning in Arabic. *Fawdha* is what happens when there is no government—at all. It is a state far worse than being under a repressive government (*zulm*). In other words, for the people of Darfur, the government had brought the worst kind of governance to Darfur: the absence of government.[108]

This point of view summed up the key lesson learned by the tribes that had been central to the insurgency: Without a united front among the major tribes of Darfur, sedentary and pastoralist, non-Arab and Arab, it would be difficult to engage the government effectively.

Peace, however, was wanted by all. But an exclusive focus on the question of peace risks ignoring the issues that divided the people of Darfur deeply: why the pressure of the ecological crisis had led them into the jaws of civil war in the first place. The main issue was the question of land and governance.

The consequence of a system that established distinctions among residents based on ethnic descent, labeling every resident as native or settler and turning this distinction into a basis for official action, was an institutionalized system of ethnic discrimination. The problem could only worsen with the passage of time. Whether the weight of immigrants was felt with the pressures of the market, the birth of successive generations over time, or was brought home by the environmental crisis moving entire groups in a short period, the net effect was an ethnic discrimination between "indigenes" and "settlers."[109] In such a context, struggles for equal rights appeared as so many ethnic conflicts.

Our analysis of the history of Darfur has shown that the practice of dividing subjects between "natives" and "settlers" was neither traditional nor natural. It was a mode of governance that allowed an alien colonial power to divide the colonized population, first into administrative units (homelands) and then the residents of each homeland into native and settler tribes. It is as if each homeland were organized as a microcosm of the larger colony. The mode of governance was ideally suited for an alien minority lording it over a colonized majority. Contrary to colonial claims, this had not been the "traditional" system in precolonial Darfur. Like most ruling lineages in the region of the Sahel, the Sultanate of Dar Fur had claimed to be of Arab origin. Yet the salient political distinction in the sultanate was not between Arab and non-Arab. Nor was it based on descent. Rather, it was between subjects of the sultanate who were not enslavable and the forest people who were enslavable and were collectively referred to as Fartit.

The roots of the Darfur conflict lie in the colonial and nationalist periods rather than in the sultanate. The 1987–89 civil war developed out of the formation of two tendencies in the postindependence period: one side organized as "native" tribes and the other as the "Quraish." The split between them was a mirror reflection of categories introduced into the colonial census—"native" and "settler" tribes—and animated through colonial administrative policies. A second influence in the formation of nativist organizations—from Sooni to the Darfur Development Front (DDF)—was that of early rebel movements in southern Sudan. The introduction of provincial autonomy, and the subsequent election of a Darfuri governor in 1981, accelerated the tension between the two tendencies, with the nativist tendency calling for autonomy and the Arab tribes looking to offset their numerical inferiority by building alliances with those in the central government.

The next big change came in 2002–3 and was mainly the result of shifting influences from the outside. The first was a major shift in the Darfuri movement, from a separatist to a nationalist orientation. It was, after all, John Garang who told the SLA leadership that they needed to change their name from Darfur Liberation Front to Sudan Liberation Front. A similar influence shaped the second major rebel movement, the Justice and Equality Movement, which came out of the split of the Islamist movement at the center. The irony is that the name change has not been accompanied by an equally decisive change in orientation, which is why rebel activism still employs the language of "native" or "indigenous" tribes of Darfur. In order to follow Garang's inspiration, the rebel movements would need to make their ideological orientation as well as their organizational thrust inclusive. The major challenge for the rebels is to resolve the civil war inside Darfur to create an alliance that cuts through the native-settler divide. Only then would the rebels be in a position to demand reform that would—in the words of John Garang—restructure the nature of power in Khartoum rather than a power sharing arrangement among its different parts as they were defined during the colonial period.

Conclusion:
Responsibility to Protect or
Right to Punish?

ON JULY 14, 2008, after much advance publicity and fanfare, the prosecutor of the International Criminal Court (ICC) applied for a warrant for the arrest of the president of Sudan, Omar Hasan Ahmad al-Bashir, on charges that included conspiracy to commit genocide along with other war crimes.[1] The application charges al-Bashir with (a) racially polarizing Darfur into "Arab" and "Zurga" or "Black," (b) turning the 2003–5 counterinsurgency into a pretext to expel "Zurga" ethnic groups from their *dars,* and (c) subjecting survivors to "slow death" from malnutrition, rape, and torture in the IDP camps.

None of these allegations can bear historical scrutiny. We have seen that the racialization of identities in Darfur had its roots in the British colonial period, when "Arab" and "Zurga" were incorporated in the census and provided the frame for government policy and administration. The spiral of land conflicts and land dispossession has been a consequence of four different causes: the land system that discriminated between "native" and "nonnative" tribes; environmental degradation that pushed northern tribes towards greener pastures in the south; the spillover of the four-decade-long civil war in Chad that militarized the intertribal conflict in Darfur; and the brutal counterinsurgency waged by the Bashir government in 2003–4. Similarly, to claim that ongoing rape in the camps is the result of official government policy is to ignore the simple fact that rape occurred in all camps, those controlled by the government and by the rebels. Indeed, as Andrew Natsios, the U.S. president's special envoy to Sudan, reminded the Senate Foreign Relations Committee on April 11, 2007: "The government has lost control of large parts of the province now. And some of the rapes, by the way, that are going on are by rebels raping women in their own tribes. We know in one of the refugee camps, it's now controlled by the rebels, formally. There have been terrible atrocities committed by the rebels against the people in the camps. . . . Some of the worst atrocities are being committed in Chad now, not in Darfur."

To make his case, the prosecutor presents two estimates of mortality. The first is the CRED / WHO estimate of 118,142 dead between September 2003 and January 2005. But the prosecutor presents what is a global tally, of *all* civilians ("Arabs" and "non-Arabs") who died from *all* causes—not just violence, but also drought and desertification—as if it were a tally of *only* "non-Arab" civilians who died from *only* violence. The second estimate is from John Holmes, U.N. undersecretary-general for humanitarian affairs, in April 2008: "A study in 2006 suggested that 200,000 had lost their lives from the combined effect of the conflict. That figure must be much higher now, perhaps half as much again." According to Reuters, "the United Nations cautioned reporters that the number was not a scientific estimate but a 'reasonable extrapolation.' "[2] But Holmes's extrapolation assumes constant mortality from 2003 to 2008—whereas the United Nations' own technical staff in Sudan spoke of a dip in mortality rates in Darfur, starting in early 2005, to as low as 200 per month, lower than the number that would constitute an emergency. The application goes on to break down the global figure of 300,000 into 35,000 killed "directly" and 80,000 to 265,000 "indirectly".[3] The assumption, once again, is that all deaths, "direct" or "indirect," are the result of a single cause—violence—coming from a single source: the government of Sudan.

Numbers aside, the charge of genocide does not rest on how many died in Darfur since 2003, but on establishing the *intention* to kill the rest: "The crime of genocide is a crime of intention. *AL BASHIR has the intention to destroy the target groups. We don't need to wait.*"[4] That intention, in turn, is derived from a narrative of history.

The conflict in Darfur began as a civil war in 1987–89. To acknowledge this, however, would be to recognize that the violent conflict in

Darfur began as an internal tribal civil war (1987–89) even *before* al-Bashir came to power in 1989.

In the prosecutor's mono-causal and one-dimensional version of history,[5] colonialism turns into a benign "tradition" and any attempt to reform the colonial legacy of tribal homelands is seen as a dress rehearsal building up to genocide, just as any part of the historical record that suggests that the violence in Darfur has multiple causes (the 1987–89 intertribal civil war, the environmental crisis, the Chadian civil war, and the "war crimes" attributed to rebel groups by the U.N. Commission on Darfur) and thus multiple responsibilities, is expunged from the record. Having assumed a single cause of excess deaths in Darfur—violence—the application goes on to ascribe responsibility to a single source: "What happened in Darfur is a consequence of Bashir's will."[6] This is demonization masquerading as justice.

The kernel of truth in the prosecutor's application concerns the period of 2003–4, when Darfur was the site of mass deaths. There is no doubt that the perpetrators of this violence should be held accountable, but when and how is a political decision that cannot belong to the ICC prosecutor. More than the innocence or guilt of the president of Sudan, it is the relationship between law and politics—including the politicization of the ICC—that poses a wider issue, one of greatest concern to African governments and peoples.

Humanitarian Intervention and Its Critics

When World War II broke out, the international order could be divided into two unequal parts, one privileged, the other subjugated: on the one hand, a system of sovereign states in the Western Hemisphere and, on the other, a colonial system in most of Africa, Asia, and the Middle East. Postwar decolonization recognized former colonies as states, thereby embracing state sovereignty as a global principle of relations among states. The end of the Cold War has led to another basic shift, heralding an international humanitarian order that promises to hold state sovereignty accountable to an international human rights standard. Many believe that we are in the throes of a systemic transition in international relations. The standard of responsibility is no longer international law but has shifted, fatefully, from law to rights. As the Bush administration made patently clear at the time of the invasion of Iraq, humanitarian intervention does not need to abide by the law. Indeed, its defining characteristic is that it is beyond the law. It is this feature that makes humanitarian intervention the twin of the War on Terror.

This new humanitarian order, officially adopted at the U.N.'s 2005 World Summit, claims responsibility for the protection of "vulnerable populations." That responsibility is said to belong to "the international community," to be exercised in practice by the United Nations and, in particular, by the Security Council, whose permanent members are the great powers.[7] This new order is sanctioned in a language that departs markedly from the older language of law and citizenship. It describes as "human" the populations to be protected and as "humanitarian" the crisis they suffer, the intervention that promises to rescue them, and the agencies that seek to carry out the intervention. Whereas the language of sovereignty is profoundly political, that of humanitarian intervention is profoundly apolitical and sometimes even antipolitical. Looked at closely and critically, what we are witnessing is not a global but a partial transition. The transition from the old system of sovereignty to a new humanitarian order is confined to entities defined as "failed" or "rogue" states. The result is once again a bifurcated system whereby state sovereignty obtains in large parts of the world but is suspended in more and more countries in Africa and the Middle East.

The Westphalian coin of state sovereignty is still the effective currency in the international system. It is worth looking at both sides of this coin: sovereignty and citizenship. If "sovereignty" remains the password to enter the passageway of international relations, "citizenship" still confers membership in the sovereign national political (state) community. Sovereignty and citizenship are not opposites but associates: The state, after all, embodies the key political right of citizens, the right of collective self-determination.

The international humanitarian order, in contrast, is not a system that acknowledges citizenship. Instead, it turns citizens into wards. The language of humanitarian intervention has cut its ties with the language of citizens' rights. To the extent that the global humanitarian order claims to stand for rights, these are the residual rights of the human and not the full range of rights of the citizen. If the rights of the citizen are pointedly political, the rights of the human pertain to sheer survival; they are summed up in one word: *protection*. The new language refers to its subjects not as bearers of rights—and thus active agents in their own emancipation—but as passive beneficiaries of an external "responsibility to protect." Rather than rights-bearing citizens, beneficiaries of the humanitarian order are akin to recipients of charity. Humanitarianism does not claim to reinforce agency, only to sustain bare life. If anything, its tendency is to promote dependency. Humanitarianism heralds a system of trusteeship.[8]

This language came into its own in 2006 when 150 heads of state and government met as the General Assembly of the United Nations in its sixtieth-anniversary year and unanimously resolved: "Each individual state has the responsibility to protect its populations from genocide, war crimes, ethnic cleansing and crimes against humanity. . . . We accept that responsibility and will act in accordance with it." They then went a step further, promising to surrender sovereignty should they fail to protect their populations from mass violence:

> The international community, through the United Nations, also has the responsibility to help to protect populations from genocide, war crimes, ethnic cleansing and crimes against humanity. In this context we are prepared to take collective action, in a timely and decisive manner, through the Security Council, in accordance with the Charter, including Chapter VII . . . , should peaceful means be inadequate and national authorities are manifestly failing to protect their populations from genocide, war crimes, ethnic cleansing and crimes against humanity.[9]

This declaration enshrined "the responsibility to protect" as a doctrine integral to the new post–Cold War international order. In a flush of enthusiasm, the new African Union (AU) overturned the principle of noninterference of its predecessor, the Organization of African Unity (OAU), declaring that Africans can no longer be "indifferent" to war crimes or gross abuses taking place on their continent and that claims of sovereignty should not be a barrier to addressing them.[10] Not surprisingly, there were afterthoughts, leading the president of the International Crisis Group to lament: "There has since 2005 been some back-sliding from this highpoint. One doesn't have to spend too much time in the UN corridors, or in some Asian capitals in particular, before hearing expressions of regret, or even denial, that so far-reaching a doctrine could possibly have been agreed to by national leaders."[11] What could have been the grounds for these afterthoughts?

It is not incidental that the "expressions of regret" arise in those parts of the world where states have increasingly developed the capacity to defend national sovereignty. It takes no great intellectual effort to recognize that the responsibility to protect has always been the sovereign's obligation. It is not that a new principle has been introduced; rather, its terms have been radically altered. To grasp this shift, we need to ask: *Who* has the responsibility to protect *whom* under *what conditions* and toward *what end*?

The era of international humanitarian order is not entirely new. It draws on the history of modern Western colonialism. At the outset of colonial expansion in the eighteenth and nineteenth centuries, leading Western powers—Britain, France, Russia—claimed to protect "vulnerable groups." When it came to countries controlled by rival powers, such as the Ottoman empire, Western powers claimed to protect populations they considered "vulnerable," mainly religious minorities such as specific Christian denominations and Jews. The most extreme political outcome of this strategy can be glimpsed in the confessional constitution bequeathed by France to independent Lebanon.[12]

When it came to lands not yet colonized, such as South Asia and large parts of Africa, they highlighted local atrocities and pledged to protect victims against rulers. It was not for lack of reason that the language of modern Western colonialism contraposed the promise of civilization against the reality of barbaric practices. In India, for example, the focus was on such practices as suttee, child marriage, and infanticide, whereas in Africa, it was on slavery in the nineteenth century, female genital mutilation (FGM) in the late twentieth century, and now genocide. The atrocities colonial archivists cataloged were not mere inventions but real and abhorrent practices. But all were cited to serve a particular political purpose. Whereas the crimes they denounced were real, the object of power was to turn the victims into so many proxies whose dilemma would legitimate colonial intervention as a rescue mission.

From this history was born the international regime of trusteeship exercised under the League of Nations. The league's trust territories were mainly in Africa and the Middle East. They were created at the end of World War I, when the colonies of the defeated imperial powers (the Ottoman empire, Germany, and Italy) were handed over to the victorious powers, who pledged to administer them as guardians would administer wards, under the watchful eye of the League of Nations.

One of these trust territories was Rwanda, administered as a trust of Belgium until the 1959 Hutu revolution.[13] It was under the benevolent eye of the League of Nations that Belgium hardened Hutu and Tutsi into racialized identities, using the force of law to institutionalize an official system of discrimination between them. Thereby, Belgian colonialism laid the institutional groundwork for the genocide that followed half a century later. The Western powers that constituted the League of Nations could not hold Belgium accountable for the way in which it exercised an international trust for one simple reason: To do so would have been to hold up a mirror to their own colonial record, for Belgian rule in Rwanda was but a harder version of the indirect rule practiced—to one degree or another—by all Western powers in Africa. This system did not simply deny sovereignty to its colonies; it redesigned their administrative and political life by bringing each under a regime of group identity and rights. Though one could argue that Belgian practice in Rwanda was an extreme case, it was certainly not exceptional.

Given the record of the League of Nations, it is worth asking how the new international regime of trusteeship would differ from the old one. What are the likely implications of the absence of citizenship rights at the core of this system? Why would a system of trusteeship not degenerate yet again into regimes that lack accountability and responsibility?

On the face of it, these two systems—one defined by sovereignty and citizenship, and the other by trusteeship and wardship—would seem to be contradictory rather than complementary. In practice, however, they are two parts of a single but bifurcated international system. One may ask how this bifurcated order can be reproduced without the contradictions being flagrantly obvious, without its appearing like a contemporary version of the old colonial system of trusteeship. A part of the explanation lies in how power has managed to subvert the language of violence and war, so as to serve its own claims.

War has long since ceased to be a direct confrontation between the armed forces of two states. As became clear during the clash between the Allied and the Axis powers in World War II, in America's Indochina War in the 1960s and 1970s, in its Iraq War in 1991, and then again in its 2003 invasion of Iraq, states do not target just the armed forces of adversary states; they target society itself: war-related industry and infrastructure, economy and workforce, and sometimes, as in the aerial bombardment of cities, the civilian population in general. The old distinctions enshrined in international law, especially the Geneva Conventions, are fading away. Few take these seriously as realistic. The trend is for political violence to become generalized and indiscriminate. Modern war is total war.

This particular development in the nature of modern war has tended to follow an earlier development of counterinsurgency in colonial contexts. Faced with insurgent guerrillas who were none other than armed civilians, colonial powers targeted the population of occupied territories. In reponse to Mao Zedong's dictum that guerrillas must be as fish in water, the American counterinsurgency theorist Samuel Huntington, writing during the time of the Vietnam War, responded that the object of counterinsurgency must be to drain the water and isolate the fish— that is, ethnic cleansing.

But the practice is older than post–World War II counterinsurgency. It dates back to the earliest days of modernity, to colonial era settler wars against Amerindians in the decades and centuries that followed 1492. Official and settler America pioneered the practice of interning entire civilian populations in what Americans called "reservations" and the British "reserves." It is this particular practice that the Nazis would later develop into an extreme form called "concentration camps." Often thought of as a British innovation during the late-nineteenth-century Boer War in South Africa, the origin of the practice of concentrating and interning populations in colonial wars was actually an American settler contribution to the development of modern war.

The regime identified with the international humanitarian order makes a sharp distinction between genocide and other kinds of mass violence. The tendency is to be permissive of insurgency (liberation war), counterinsurgency (suppression of civil war, or rebel/revolutionary movements), and interstate war as integral to the exercise of national sovereignty. Increasingly, these are taken as an inevitable if regrettable part of defending or asserting national sovereignty, domestically or internationally—but genocide is not.

Universal condemnation is reserved for only one form of mass violence—genocide—as the ultimate crime, so much so that counterinsurgency and war appear to be *normal* developments. It is genocide that is violence run amok, amoral, evil. The former is normal violence, but the latter is bad violence. Thus the tendency is to call for "humanitarian intervention" only where mass slaughter is named "genocide."

But what is genocide, and what are counterinsurgency and war? Who does the naming? The year 2003 saw the unfolding of two very different armed conflicts. One was in Iraq, and it grew out of war and invasion. The other was in Darfur, Sudan, and it grew as a response to an internal insurgency. The former involved a liberation war against a foreign occupation, the latter a civil war in an independent state. True, if you were an Iraqi or a Darfuri, there was little difference between the brutality of the violence unleashed in either instance. Yet much energy has been invested in the question of how to define the brutality in each case: whether as counterinsurgency or as genocide. We have the astonishing spectacle of the United States, which has authored the violence in Iraq, branding an adversary state, Sudan, which has authored the violence in Darfur, as the perpetrator of genocide. Even more astonishing, we have a citizens' movement in America calling for a humanitarian intervention in Darfur while keeping mum about the violence in Iraq. And yet, as we have already seen, the figures for the total number of excess dead are far higher for Iraq than for Darfur. The numbers of violent deaths as a proportion of excess mortality are also higher in Iraq than in Darfur.[14]

For anyone familiar with the documentation that came out of the debate between the United States and the United Nations / African Union on how to name the violence in Darfur, it is clear that the real disagreement was not over the scale of the violence and the destruction it had wrought but over what to call it.

It will help to look at the counterinsurgency against the Lord's Resistance Army (LRA) in northern Uganda,[15] to underline the politics of naming. The counterinsurgency in northern Uganda developed through different phases. The first phase opened with Operation North against insurgent groups connected with two regimes—those of Milton Obote II and Lutwa Okello—overthrown at different points in 1986. Operation North involved civilian massacres and other atrocities, now widely acknowledged in both official and civilian circles in Uganda.

A second phase began in 1996 with a new policy designed to intern practically the entire rural population of the three Acholi districts in northern Uganda. It took a government-directed campaign of murder, intimidation, bombing, and burning of whole villages to drive the rural population into IDP (internally displaced persons) camps, complete with enclosures guarded by soldiers. The government called the camps "protected villages"; the opposition called them "concentration camps." The camp population grew from a few hundred thousand by the end of 1996 to almost a million in 2002. By then, nearly the entire rural population of the three districts that comprised Acholiland had been interned in official camps. According to the government's own Ministry of Health, the excess mortality rate in these camps was approximately one thousand persons a week. Olara Otunnu, Uganda's ambassador to the United Nations under the former regime and later the U.N. secretary-general's special representative for children in armed conflict, himself an Acholi, broke his long public silence over the "war" in northern Uganda to point an accusing finger at the Yoweri Museveni government: genocide. In Otunnu's words:

> The human rights catastrophe unfolding in northern Uganda is a methodical and comprehensive genocide. An entire society is being systematically destroyed—physically, culturally, socially, and economically—in full view of the international community. In the sobering words of a missionary priest in the area: "Everything Acholi is dying." I know of no recent or current situation in which all the elements that constitute genocide under the Convention on the Prevention and Punishment of the Crime of Genocide (1948) have been brought together in such a comprehensive and chilling manner as in northern Uganda today.[16]

.   .   .

It is difficult to think of these three instances of mass internment and violence—Iraq, Darfur, and Acholiland—without noticing that only one is the subject of a debate as to whether or not it involves genocide, leading to a call for an internationally directed humanitarian intervention. Labeling is important, most obviously for legal reasons. Where mass slaughter is termed genocide, intervention becomes an international obligation; for the most powerful, the obligation presents an opportunity. But if genocide involves an international obligation to intervene, war and counterinsurgency do not, for they are understood to be part of the exercise of sovereignty by states. They are an expression of the *normal* violence of the state, said to be the reason why states have armies and armed forces. Labeling performs a vital function. It isolates and demonizes the perpetrators of one kind of mass violence and at the same time confers impunity on perpetrators of other forms of mass violence. What then is the distinguishing feature of genocide? It is clearly not extreme violence against civilians, for that is very much a feature of both counterinsurgency and interstate war in these times. Only when extreme violence tends to target a civilian population that is marked off as different "on grounds of race, ethnicity, or religion" is that violence termed genocide.

It is this aspect of the legal definition that has allowed "genocide" to be instrumentalized by big powers so as to target those newly independent states that they find unruly and want to discipline. Given that colonialism shaped the very nature of modern "indirect rule" and administrative power along "tribal" (or ethnic) lines, it is not surprising that both the exercise of power and responses to it tend to take "tribal" forms in these newly independent states. From this point of view, there is little to distinguish between mass violence unleashed against civilians in Congo, northern Uganda, Mozambique, Angola, Darfur, Sierra Leone, Liberia, Ivory Coast, and so on. Which one is to be named "genocide" and which ones not? Most important, who decides?

There is nothing new in the use of legal concepts to serve the expedience of great powers. What is new about the War on Terror is that the action against violence is simultaneously being moralized and legally deregulated. Is it then surprising that these very developments have tended to fuel processes that lead to violence gone amok, as in Iraq after 2003, or in Bashir's own little war on terror in Darfur in 2003–4? As the new humanitarian order does away with legal limits to preemptive war—thus, to the global War on Terror—it should not be surprising that counterinsurgency defines itself as a local War on Terror.

My point here is not to enter the debate around the definition of genocide but to show that the depoliticizing language of humanitarian intervention serves a wider function; "humanitarian intervention" is not an antidote to international power relations but its latest product. If we are to respond effectively to a humanitarian intervention, we need to understand its politics. The discourse on rights emerged historically as a language that claimed to define limits of power. Its political ambition was to turn victims into agents of resistance. Today, the overwhelming tendency is for the language of rights to enable power. The result is to subvert its very purpose, to put it at the service of a wholly different agenda, one that seeks to turn victims into so many proxies. It justifies interventions by big powers as an antidote to malpractices by newly independent small powers.

The International Criminal Court (ICC)

The emphasis on big powers as the enforcers of rights internationally is increasingly being twinned with an emphasis on the same big powers as enforcers of justice internationally. This conclusion is inevitable if we cast a critical eye on the short history of the International Criminal Court.[17]

The ICC was set up to try the world's most heinous crimes: mass murder and other systematic abuses. No sooner did discussions begin regarding the establishment of the court than Washington registered concern that an international criminal court could provide an opportunity to those with vindictive intentions to prosecute American soldiers or civilians. Washington's concerns were spelled out in detail in a scholarly article by its ambassador to the United Nations, John Bolton: "Our main concern should be for our country's top civilian and military leaders, those responsible for our defense and foreign policy." Bolton went on to ask "whether the United States was guilty of war crimes for its aerial bombing campaigns over Germany and Japan in World War II." From the viewpoint of the ICC statute, he had no doubt that the United States would in fact be guilty: "Indeed, if anything, a straightforward reading of the language probably indicates that the court *would* find the United States guilty. A fortiori, these provisions seem to imply that the United States would have been guilty of a war crime for dropping atomic bombs on Hiroshima and Nagasaki. This is intolerable and unacceptable." He also aired the concerns of the principal U.S. ally in the Middle East, Israel: "Thus, Israel justifiably feared in Rome that its preemptive strike in the Six-Day War almost certainly would have provoked a proceeding against top Israeli officials. Moreover, there is no doubt that Israel will be the target of a complaint concerning conditions and practices by the Israeli military in the West Bank and Gaza."[18]

Once it was clear that it would not be able to prevent the ICC from becoming a reality, the administration of George W. Bush made a different move. This was to sign bilateral agreements with individual countries whereby both signatories would pledge not to hand over each other's nationals—even those accused of crimes against humanity—to the ICC. By mid-June 2003, the United States had signed similar agreements with thirty-seven countries. Except for political clients such as Egypt, Israel, and the Philippines, as well as India, which had an ongoing counterinsurgency in Kashmir and thus its own reasons of state for not agreeing to international oversight, the others were small, poor countries, most of them heavily dependent on U.S. aid.

The Bush administration's next move was accommodation, made possible by the kind of political pragmatism practiced by the ICC's own leadership. The fact of mutual accommodation between the world's only superpower and an international institution struggling to get its bearings is clear if we take into account the four countries where the ICC has launched its investigations: Sudan, Uganda, Central African Republic, and Congo. All four are places where the United States has no objection to the course charted by ICC investigations. In Uganda, for example, where nearly a million people have been forcibly displaced in the throes of a government-executed counterinsurgency, the ICC has charged only the leadership of the LRA but not that of the pro–United States government. In Sudan, too, the ICC has charged officials of the Sudan government for what the U.N. Commission on Darfur alleged were "crimes against humanity" but not leaders of rebel movements for what the same commission alleged were "war crimes." In Congo, the ICC has remained mum about the links between the armies of Uganda and Rwanda—both pro–United States—and the ethnic militias that have been at the heart of the slaughter of civilians. The ICC's defense is that it used the principle of gravity in deciding whom to charge. This is how Luis Moreno-Ocampo justified his decision to charge the LRA but not the political leadership of the government: "The criteria for selection of the first case was gravity. We analyzed the gravity of all crimes in northern Uganda committed by the LRA and the Ugandan forces. Crimes committed by the LRA were much more numerous and of much higher gravity than alleged crimes committed by the UPDF [Uganda People's Defense Force]. We therefore *started with* an investigation of the LRA"[19] (italics added). That was in 2004. Five years have since passed. So far, the evidence suggests that, as in Darfur, the ICC's investigation did not start with just one side; it was in fact limited to investigating accusations against just one side. The ICC's attempted accommodation with the powers that be has changed the international face of the ICC. Its name notwithstanding, the ICC is rapidly turning into a Western court to try African crimes against humanity. Even then, its approach is selective: It targets governments that are adversaries of the United States and ignores U.S. allies, effectively conferring impunity on them.[20]

My point is not that those tried by the ICC have not committed crimes, including mass murder, but that the law is being applied selectively. Some perpetrators are being targeted and not others. The decision as to whom to target and whom not to is inevitably political. When the law is applied selectively, the result is not a rule of law but a subordination of law to the dictates of power.

Not only has the ICC stooped to embrace a partisan notion of justice, it has also not hesitated to do so at the expense of peace. The quest for peace in northern Uganda pitted the country's parliament against its president. In pursuit of peace, parliament passed a bill offering amnesty to the entire leadership of the LRA. Opposed to the amnesty offer, the president invited the ICC to charge the political leadership with crimes against humanity—even if the prerequisite was to declare Uganda a failed state unable to bring violators of human rights to justice. The ICC prosecutor obliged, joining the Ugandan president in bypassing both the legislature and the courts and thereby declaring both incompetent and Uganda a "failed" state![21] At the same time, it did so without holding the top government leadership responsible for arraigning practically the entire rural Acholi population. The terms of the resulting debate in Uganda on the role of the ICC pitted justice against peace. In this debate, the civilian population of Acholi districts often demanded peace, even if this would mean conferring immunity from prosecution on the LRA leadership. The president demanded justice—and wielded the ICC as a hammer.[22] The ICC, in turn, prioritized a particular form of justice—criminal justice.

If peace and justice are to be complementary, rather than conflicting, objectives, we need to distinguish victors' justice from survivors' justice: If one insists on distinguishing right from wrong, the other seeks to reconcile different rights. In a situation in which there is no winner and thus no possibility of victors' justice, survivors' justice may indeed be the only form of justice possible. If Nuremberg is being turned into the paradigm for victors' justice, the postapartheid transition in South Africa needs to be acknowledged as the paradigm for survivors' justice. The end of apartheid in South Africa was driven by two terms—forgive but do not forget—agreed upon at Kempton Park. The first part of the compact was that the new power will forgive all past transgressions of the law, as long as these are publicly acknowledged as wrongs. There will be no prosecutions. The second was that there will be no forgetting, which is why henceforth rules of conduct must change, thereby ensuring a transition to a postapartheid order. Clearly, if an ICC had existed then, we would *not* have had an antiapartheid transition in the mid-1990s.[23] It was South Africa's good fortune that its transition was in the main internally driven.

South Africa is not an isolated example. It is actually a prototype for conflicts raging across the African continent. Mozambique is another example in which peace and criminal justice appeared as alternatives. Had there been an ICC when the terms of the compromise were worked out in Mozambique, it is doubtful that these terms could ever have been implemented—for the ICC would surely have insisted that the place of the armed opposition backed by apartheid South Africa—Renamo—was not in parliament but in jail. Such, indeed, is the dilemma that bedevils the search for peace in northern Uganda: The main external obstacle to a peace agreement between the LRA and the government of Uganda is in fact the ICC's determination to criminalize the LRA's leadership in the name of pursuing justice. The challenge for Africa—as in

South Africa, Mozambique, Uganda, and Sudan—is not to shun justice but to explore forms of justice that will help end rather than prolong conflicts. The search for survivors' justice must be two-pronged: Prioritize peace over punishment, and explore forms of justice—not criminal but political and social—that will make reconciliation durable. If the terms of the transition from apartheid in South Africa embraced the first priority, it has yet to meet the second. From this point of view, the conflict in Darfur is not an exception to the African dilemma but an illustration of it.

Human rights fundamentalists argue for an international legal standard regardless of the political context of the country in question. Their point of view is bolstered by the widespread and understandable popular outrage, not just in the West but throughout Africa, against the impunity with which a growing number of regimes have been resorting to slaughter to brutalize their populations into silence. The realization that the ICC has tended to focus only on African crimes, and mainly on crimes committed by adversaries of the United States, has introduced a note of sobriety into the African discussion, raising concerns about a politicized justice and wider questions about the relationship between law and politics. The case of the ICC raises a more general question: that of the relationship between legal and political questions. In a democracy, the domain of the legal is defined through the political process. Even where there is a human rights regime, both the fact and the content of rights (for example, the Bill of Rights in the United States) are defined in the country's constitution—that is, in its foundational political act. At the same time, its actual operation in any given period is subject to political qualifications in light of the changing context (as, for instance, with the Homeland Security Act in the U.S. War on Terror).

What happens if one detaches the legal from the political regime? Two problems arise, both related to the question of political accountability. The only formal gathering of the global community today is the United Nations, in which the General Assembly is a fully representative body of states, but the Security Council is a congress of big powers that emerged from the ashes of World War II. To the extent that the ICC has any accountability, it is to the Security Council, not the General Assembly. It is this relationship that has made it possible for the only super-power of the post–Cold War era to turn the workings of the ICC to its advantage.

This problem was raised most directly by India. Like the United States and Sudan, India also refused to sign the Rome Statute. India's primary objection had to do with the relationship between the Security Council—of which India is not yet a permanent member—and the ICC. The Rome Statute gives the Security Council minimal powers of oversight over the ICC: The council has the power to require the ICC to look into particular cases and to forbid it from considering other cases. India's "basic objection was that granting powers to the Security Council to refer cases to the ICC, or to block them, was unacceptable, especially if its members were not all signatories to the treaty," for it "provided escape routes for those accused of serious crimes but with clout in the U.N. body." At the same time, India objected that "giving the Security Council power to refer cases from a non-signatory country to the ICC was against the Law of Treaties under which no country can be bound by the provisions of a treaty it has not signed."[24]

Yet another problem is that the absence of formal political accountability has created conditions for the informal politicization of the ICC. As summed up by an editorial in India's leading political daily, *The Hindu:* "The wheeling-dealing by which the U.S. has managed to maintain its exceptionalism to the ICC while assisting 'to end the climate of impunity in Sudan' makes a complete mockery of the ideals that informed the setting up of a permanent international criminal court to try perpetrators of the gravest of crimes against humanity."[25]

But the problem would still not be solved even if all members of the Security Council—including the United States—joined the ICC, for detaching the legal from the political regime poses a more general problem. In no country is the distinction between legal and political issues self-evident. In a democracy, the domain of the legal is defined through the political process. What would happen if we privileged the legal over the political, regardless of context? The experience of a range of transitional societies—post-Soviet, postapartheid, and postcolonial—suggests that such a fundamentalism would call into question their political existence. Several post-Soviet societies in Eastern Europe with a history of extensive informing, spying, and compromising have decided either not to fully open secret police and Communist Party files or to do so at a snail's pace. Societies torn apart by civil war, like post-Franco Spain, have chosen amnesia over truth, for the simple reason that they have prioritized the need to forge a future over agreeing on the past. The contrast is provided by Bosnia and Rwanda, where the administration of justice became an international responsibility and the decision to detach war crimes from the underlying political reality has turned justice into a regime for settling scores.

Every sovereign and independent country—witness the United States—reserves to itself the right to define the content of human rights, including the right to suspend these for reasons of national security. Those who face human rights as the language of an externally driven "humanitarian intervention" are required to contend with a legal regime in which the very notion of human rights law is defined outside of a political process—democratic or otherwise—that includes them as meaningful participants. Particularly for those in Africa, more than anywhere else, the ICC heralds a regime of legal and political dependency, much as the Bretton Woods institutions pioneered an international regime of economic dependency in the 1980s and 1990s. The real danger of detaching the legal from the political regime and handing it over to human rights fundamentalists is that it will turn the pursuit of justice into revenge-seeking, thereby obstructing the search for reconciliation and a durable peace. Does that mean that the very notion of justice must be postponed as disruptive to peace? No.

Conflict Resolution—Lessons from the Past

For an alternative to an externally imposed rescue and punishment, we need to look at the experience of Sudan. In Sudan, there are three different methods for resolving conflicts. The first, also the oldest, thus known as the traditional method, is society-driven. The second and the third, more recent, are both state-driven, the main distinction being between the internally driven Addis Ababa Agreement of 1972 and more externally driven agreements such as the Comprehensive Peace Agreement (CPA) that ended the civil war in the south in 2005 and the 2006 Abuja Agreement on Darfur.[26]

The basis of reconciliation systems in Darfur is *judia,* a grassroots process whereby belligerents agree to mediation by wise and respected men—the *ajwadi* (plural: *ajaweed*)—considered well versed in traditional rules for ending disputes. Researchers at Ahfad University for Women in Sudan described the process of traditional reconciliation in one such instance in 1986, a time when tension mounted between the Rizeigat and the Zaghawa, and each prepared a militia for a showdown. When provincial authorities failed to defuse the situation, the parties to the conflict turned to traditional methods, requesting Hesain Dawsa—a Zaghawa who was respected among the Rizeigat—to mediate between them. Dawsa defused the tense situation in "eight hours." His account may be idealized, but it points to the importance of operating in terms of local understandings.[27]

When I reached the Daein from Nyala, I demanded that each party be placed separately in a school building. I was accompanied by 8 ajawid.

I went to the Rezeigat camp first and rebuked them. "Do you want to betray your beloved late Nazir, who invited your Zaghawa brothers to come and live with you? Give me the names of those Zaghawa who cause trouble and I will take them with me, hand-cuffed, to Nyala!"

Then I went to the Zaghawa camp and started rebuking them. "Is this the way you behave to your hosts?" Then I asked them to write down on a piece of paper all that they demanded from the Rezeigat and to select 20 persons to represent them as spokesmen and grant them a mandate. Reading the list of demands, I tore the paper into pieces and threw them away.

I then went back to the Rezeigat camp and demanded the same thing. First of all, the Rezeigat demanded that the Zaghawa representatives be reduced to 15 and they wrote down 25 demands. When I read them, I commented, "I accept all your demands except two of them. Firstly, the demand for expelling the Zaghawa from your Dar because this is in contradiction of the constitution. Second, preventing Zaghawa from taking water from a water yard is inhuman. You can not cause your brothers to die of thirst."

They asked me, "Before we give you an answer, tell us about the Zaghawa demands!" I told them, "The Zaghawa have no demands to make. All the demands they made I rejected and tore their paper to pieces." Upon hearing this, they started shouting, "Give us back our paper! We have no demands as well."

I took the two delegates to the government authorities to document the reconciliation in writing and came back to enjoy the feast that the Rezeigat had prepared for us![28]

What are the lessons of this experience? The U.N. document that cited the experience was preoccupied with its Old World quaintness: (a) The mediator had learned the art of mediation from his father and combined experience (having mediated in twenty-six previous conferences) with a modern education, and (b) knew communal psychology ("Appease not your own people; demand that his own people be generous and thus get the others to be generous in turn"). But the document missed the real lesson: Reconciliation should preferably be an internal affair.

The tendency has been for mediation by wise persons to give way to institutional intervention.[29] Each of the three Darfur universities have now established Peace and Development Centers that offer a full menu of workshops, seminars, and training programs relevant to peace building. In all three Darfur states, there are also a number of Sudanese nongovernmental organizations (NGOs) and community-based organizations (CBOs) dedicated to promoting conflict resolution at the grass roots. When these groups were invited to a U.N. and AU-supported conference (the Darfur Joint Assessment Mission, or DJAM), the predominant view among them was that "the government should stop interfering in the affairs of the different tribal groups in Darfur and should leave them to sort out their problems on their own and by their own traditional methods." To make the point, they cited a Sudanese proverb: "Only a turtle knows how to bite another turtle."[30]

For *judia* to work, however, not only must the belligerents be local and identifiable, but they need to be neighbors with an interest in strengthening the system of local accountability.[31] The simple fact is that it is no longer just turtles who are involved in today's conflicts but all kinds of animals, local and not-so-local. As local conflicts have come to be incorporated into larger—national, regional, even global—processes, the limitation of the traditional system of mediation has become clear. For one thing, it lacks the capacity to reach many of the participants in such conflicts. Thus the demand that is most often made by those who turn to *judia* to solve local conflicts: Leave us alone!

It is the widening arena of conflict that has created room for state-led processes of reconciliation, starting with the Addis Ababa Agreement of 1972, which ended the first phase of the civil war in the south. The state-led agreement differed from traditional reconciliation in two respects: (1) There was minimal involvement of societal organizations; (2) in spite of this, the agreement was still internally driven, which is why those who supported the agreement were involved in its implementation and could be held accountable for that implementation.

The Addis Ababa Agreement held for nearly a decade. The main reason for its failure was that it introduced reforms in the structure of power in the south, but not in the north nor at the center. To the extent that there were reforms—from local elections to the devolution of power to make local accountability possible—these were introduced mainly in the south. If the Nimeiry government gained popularity, it was in the south, where it stood for reforms, but not in the north, where it symbolized autocracy. To hold, the Addis Ababa Agreement would have had to join power sharing with countrywide reforms.

The Comprehensive Peace Agreement of 2005 ended the second phase of the war in the south. Parties to the CPA had drawn their own lessons from 1972. For its part, the southern Sudan elite concluded that, without guaranteed access to resources, it would remain beholden to the northern elite at the center, as had indeed been the case after the 1972 agreement. So the southern elite called for a joining of power sharing with wealth sharing, whose terms would be guaranteed by the big powers internationally. At the same time, both leaderships decided against any internal reforms, including a process of democratization that would have gone beyond the holding of regular elections. Instead, each conferred impunity on the other in the name of reconciliation. Not surprisingly, the internal opposition in the north refused to be a party to the agreement.

The Darfur Peace Agreement (DPA) and the second leg of the same process in Libya unfolded under the overall influence of the big Western powers. The Abuja process was marked by several shortcomings. Since the negotiations were meant to bring government and insurgent representatives together, the Arab tribes were totally excluded from Abuja. This meant the *dar*less tribes were not represented in the Abuja process, which in fact demonized them by identifying them with the Janjawiid. The process departed from one key feature of the CPA: There would be no impunity, but this principle was applied selectively, only to the government side. By involving extraregional organizations such as the ICC, big powers were able to criminalize responsibility for human rights violations, thereby moving the focal point of the process away from the political to the criminal—at the same time feeding expectations on all sides that its object would be punishment, not reconciliation. This combination of African violations tried through non-African interventions introduced a conflict resolution mechanism whose consequences in the political domain were the same as those of the Cold War–era Structural Adjustment Programs (SAP) in the economic field: Those who made decisions did not have to live with their consequences, nor pay for them.

Ways Forward

Starting in 2003, I undertook several trips to Sudan, during which I made a conscious effort to meet and talk with as wide a range of academic and political leaders as possible. The first lesson I learned was that there was no neat division between internal and external forces when it came to the debate on Darfur. The only way I could make sense of the debate was to begin by focusing on the position rather than the location of the individual concerned: The key debate was between those who saw internal reform as the best way out of the crisis and those who called for an externally driven humanitarian intervention.

The most prominent among those calling for internal reform were John Garang and the Darfuri anthropologist Sharif Harir. Writing at the height of the north-south war, Harir tried to convince his fellow rebels that secession was not an answer, for a split would "only unravel the political order." Indeed, there was nothing unique about Sudan: "Many African states were suffering from the same types of conflicts that were taking place in the Sudan, e.g., Biafra in Nigeria, Eritrea as part of the Ethiopian empire etc." He reminded his comrades that "the SPLA was not at all for self-determination until the Nassir split occurred in 1991." But, even now, "the creation of two states one in the South and the other in the North . . . will not provide a short-cut to improving the present state of decay. It will, on the contrary, exacerbate the decay of both even before they have had a decent chance to have a run. It is, in short, a non-starter." Thus, Harir concluded: "The important point is that if Sudan is to be divided into two countries, there are no guarantees whatsoever that it might not end up as more than a dozen countries."[32]

As we have seen, John Garang went a step further to distinguish between two kinds of internal reform: (1) a superficial one that would share positions among regions and groups in the name of power sharing but would leave the institutional levers of power unreformed and (2) a deeper reform of the very nature of power.

> The method we have chosen in order to achieve the objective of a united Sudan is to struggle to restructure power in the centre so that questions as to what does . . . the south want do not arise. . . . I totally disagree with this concept of sharing power. . . . I use the words restructuring of political power in Khartoum rather than power-sharing because the latter brings to mind immediately the question, who is sharing power with whom? And the answer is usually North and South, Arabs and Africans, Christians and Muslims. It has the connotation of the old paradigm.[33]

The most important internal forces calling for an external intervention were the modernist parties, from the Islamists to the Communists. Some joined the call for an externally imposed "no-fly zone," whereas others advocated an outright external intervention in the form of U.N. forces. My Islamist rebel friend in Khartoum—whose name I cannot publish—had no doubt as to the future he hoped for: "I will celebrate if Americans impose a no-fly zone and if they hit selected targets."[34] Kamal el Juzuli, the secretary-general of the Writers' Union, a highly respected activist, was so desperate that he was even willing to consider a solution militarily imposed from the outside: "At first I was not in favor of American troops landing in Sudan, but then I went to the camps and found that is what the IDPs want. When I argued against it, they even doubted who I was. But I don't think Americans will come here; they will send others." I asked: "Do you think that Americans will solve your problem?" He answered, I thought desperately: "Not really. But what can we do? There is no other solution. We can't just do nothing."[35]

Yet others joined this call in the name of democracy. This is how a prominent intellectual in the Communist Party put it: "The key point is that the deployment of UN troops has become a general and essential demand of the people of Darfur, especially the inhabitants of the displaced persons camps, to protect them against the constant attacks of the Janjawiid. The AU troops have failed to provide such protection, and the government troops are considered as a party in the conflict with a very hostile attitude toward the people of Darfur."[36] The statement betrayed meager knowledge of developments in Darfur—of the forces that shape the views of IDPs and the constraints under which the African Union worked—as meager as that marshaled by an external force such as the Save Darfur Coalition in the United States.

The demand for further external intervention surfaced at the grassroots level in Darfur during a series of African Union–sponsored consultations that began under the auspices of Darfur-Darfur Dialogue and Consultation (DDDC). The consultations began in July 2006, starting with meetings in Nyala (South Darfur), Zalingei (West Darfur), and El Fasher (North Darfur). They brought together grassroots activists and leaders representing many different groups: the native administration regime in the rural areas, local voluntary organizations, political parties (both government and opposition), intellectuals and academics (each of the three states has a university), and the more than two million displaced people living in camps in Darfur.

The opening discussions in Nyala and Zalingei produced a consensus on one issue: The dialogue should include all political and ethnic affiliations, even groups implicated in providing recruits for the Janjawiid, and be independent of any political party or group (including the government).

For the African Union, these consultations produced a double shock. A large majority at the El Fasher meeting in July 2007 called for an external intervention by non-African forces. Most participants identified the African Union as the root cause of their problems and the United Nations as the most likely source of an effective solution. "The AU is like the Arab League," the representative from El Fasher Call, a voluntary organization, explained. "It responds to governments, not public pressure. All African governments are dictatorships, which is why people look at the AU with suspicion. The UN also represents governments, but most states in the UN are democratic." "We want the UN to come," the sultan of El Fasher added. "It has mercy."[37]

The naïveté of these assumptions was breathtaking. Just as they identified the United Nations with Western democracies, and talked as if democracies cannot be empires, every speaker who called for U.N. intervention seemed to assume that U.N. forces—unlike those of the African Union Mission in Sudan (AMIS)—would be white. They did not appear to have grasped that what will change in the transition from AMIS to UNAMID (the United Nations–African Union Mission in Darfur) is not really the troops on the ground but their overall command.

The discussion on U.N. intervention ended in a political cul-de-sac. On the one hand, the call for external intervention was backed by a strong feeling that all internal avenues (national and African) had been exhausted. On the other hand, those calling most vociferously for external intervention seemed to see the United Nations as a benign agency with no political agenda of its own—even though it is clear that a U.N. intervention would be guided by the big powers of the Security Council. In El Fasher, no one questioned the politics of an intervention driven by the major powers.

As the discussion proceeded, however, it became clear that the same local voluntary organizations that vociferously called for U.N. intervention were critical of the growing dependency of IDPs on international NGOs (INGOs). The representative from El Fasher Call made the point with some bitterness: "IDPs are trying to endear themselves to international NGOs but don't want to deal with national NGOs." "IDPs don't believe in anything Sudanese anymore," a representative from a Fur charity added. One participant from a construction NGO observed that the war had made people adopt a "consumer mentality." The disaffection with INGOs was shared by all local voluntary organizations, regardless of their ethnic affiliation or political inclination. "National NGOs lack the capacity to provide necessary services," a representative of Sudan Development Organisation explained, not least because they are excluded by INGOs: "They make no attempt to acknowledge that we know the ground better and also the demands of the people. No wonder most national NGOs have been rejected by the IDPs. If international NGOs gave us a chance, people might appreciate us more." Even those who claimed that "you would not have found any IDP alive in Darfur" without the INGOs agreed that INGOs had at least two problems—a short-term perspective and a limited agenda feeding that perspective: "Every organization has its own program for each place."

Hard as I found it to believe this, I could not deny the evidence of my own eyes and ears. The external intervention had produced an internal agency: IDPs demanding to be rescued. Desperately believing in another world, they remained innocent of the politics of this world. Faced with an IDP chorus calling for an external non-African intervention, the AU mediator, Salim Ahmed Salim, pointed out that an external intervention would work only if it reinforced an internal process, not if it was seen as a substitute for it. The critical thing about an intervention force is "not how large a force it is but what they have come to defend," since "without an agreement on peace, even a force of fifty thousand can't change the situation here radically." He meant to caution Darfuris that to pin all their hopes on an external intervention would be tantamount to abdicating their own responsibility. But he was in the minority.

Rather than think of the IDP view as some kind of a "false consciousness," it is more illuminating to think of the vantage point from which that view makes sense. As several Darfuri community organizers seemed to recognize, the IDP view was coming to personify a "consumer mentality." The consumer in this instance stands as the antithesis of the citizen. The fading of the citizen goes alongside the rise of the consumer. In this sense, consumer mentality is both a key element and an important product of humanitarian interventionism.

The dilemma of Darfur, unlike the south of Sudan, is that no internal force appears capable of effective leadership. Even the SPLA, which, under the terms of the separate Comprehensive Peace Agreement of January 2005, has been guaranteed 10 percent representation in every parliament in the northern states, lacks the human resources—and perhaps even the political will—necessary to provide effective leadership. Like the United Nations, the INGOs seem to have no patience with an internal political process. For them, the people of Darfur are not citizens in a sovereign political process as much as wards in an open-ended international rescue operation. They are there to "save" Darfur, not to "empower" it. This is why many of the big INGOs and some of the American and British staff at the U.N. offices in Khartoum are skeptical about the DDDC. They worry that bringing together political figures and representatives of civil society for an open discussion risks conveying a feeling that normalcy is returning to Darfur, when it is actually the depth of the crisis that should be emphasized. When I met the U.N. chief in Khartoum during my March 2008 visit and asked about the forthcoming 2009 elections, he looked worried. "The holding of elections is for the United Nations proof that there is no emergency here. We will have to fold up this operation and leave." The "humanitarian" effort is itself based on the conviction that both the crisis and its solution are military, not political; accordingly, there is little appetite for an internal political process designed to strengthen democratic citizenship.

Elections are indeed an alternative to negotiations when it comes to broadening the base of power in Khartoum. If negotiations open an opportunity to co-opt rebels into a national unity government, elections offer a chance to bring opposition parties into a national alliance. Given the lack of unity in a fragmented rebel movement, the electoral option that engages opposition parties may be a more realistic and promising bet for those in power. The Islamist regime split some time ago over how to resolve the war in the south. Those opposed to power sharing and wealth sharing left the government and formed their own rebel movement in Darfur: the JEM. The JEM has the strongest links with the regime in power in Chad and is reputedly also militarily the strongest among the rebel factions. Impatient to take power, the JEM drove to Omdurman in May 2008, confident of finding allies in the army. That fiasco should have driven home a lesson the governing faction should have learned in the south at the time of the CPA in 2002, that the only way for it to survive and stay in power is to continue to mobilize support behind a program that will lead to a broad-based government, and thereby, broaden its own base of support. If it does so, then its program has a strong chance of coinciding with the interests and aspirations of ordinary Sudanese. If it does not, Sudan will continue along the sorry road where none of those involved—the government, rebels, neighbors, and the international community—have the wisdom to forge a reconciliation that can take the people of Darfur and Sudan to a better tomorrow.

"What is the solution?" I asked General Henry Anyidoho, just after he had been appointed joint deputy special representative for the hybrid United Nations / African Union force. "Threefold," he replied, military fashion. "First, a complete cease-fire. Second, talks involving a cross section of Darfurians. They must agree. And third, the government has a big role to play. This is not a failed state; there is a sitting government." What about the Janjawiid? "They are nomadic forces on horseback; they have always been there. They are spread across Sahelian Africa: Niger, Sudan, Chad, the Central African Republic. The problem is that the AK-47 has replaced the bow and arrow. The Janjawiid should be disarmed before the rebels turn in their arms." Adam El Zain, who had been governor of South Darfur in 1982–83 and of North Darfur in 1983–85, and who is now a local administration expert at the University of Khartoum, disagreed: "The Mahamied [from whom many Janjawiid are recruited] have their problem: where to go. It is not necessary to disarm them; it is necessary to give them a solution."[38]

"What about the camps?" I asked General Anyidoho. "The camps are becoming militarized," he replied. "The objective should be to close the IDP camps." The camps are like so many time bombs ticking away. To begin with, many Darfuri residents are being forced into camps to access aid. In other words, not everyone in an IDP camp is there as a refugee from violence; many are there seeking shelter from drought and famine. Furthermore, camps are being militarized because all sides in the armed conflict see IDPs as a ready source of young cadres. The NGOs have joined the United States in seeking to build on the mandate of the new humanitarian regime. In a lecture delivered to the World Legal Forum's Seminar on International Use of Force, the president of the International Crisis Group, Gareth Evans, who had previously cochaired the 2001 Canadian government–sponsored International Commission on

Intervention and State Sovereignty, sought to broaden the interpretation of "responsibility to protect" to include preventive alongside curative measures, invoking a "responsibility to prevent, to react and to rebuild." It was a call for an international regime of total paternalism. Discounting the "backsliding" from certain quarters, "some Asian capitals in particular," Evans celebrated that "the language of the debate had changed . . . irreversibly," for it was "no longer possible to argue—as it was possible to argue centuries before—that sovereignty is a license to kill."[39] But Evans had overstretched his point. The real change is not that the license to kill no longer exists but that the ownership of that license has shifted, from particular national governments to big powers in the Security Council—who would be sovereign. As before, the sovereign would have the license to punish and to kill.

What about the American threat to "take steps"—a no-fly zone, sanctions? "It is not the way to go," said General Anyidoho, "Americans give deadlines all the time. The threat of sanctions is also not enough. They have lived under these for so long that they have become normal. They are used to living in seclusion. Now, they have oil. . . . We can't solve these problems through weapons. We have to sit and talk, which is why it is important to look at how Côte d'Ivoire was solved after four years of fighting. Outsiders can never solve the problem for us. It's a distant misery for them. We have to do it for ourselves." The real difference is not between disinterested outsiders and committed insiders, but between different kinds of outsiders and insiders—between interventions that tend to preclude the possibility of internal reform and those that reinforce it. That is the difference between intervention and solidarity.

To appreciate the choice between different kinds of outsiders, one need only compare the United Nations and the African Union. Setting aside what they have in common—inefficient and corrupt bureaucracies—and the extreme inequality of resources that the two command, the relevant difference here is between two dissimilar visions. In Darfur, at least, their respective visions were anchored in two contrasting paradigms: If the United Nations seemed to call for some form of victors' justice as exemplified by Nuremberg, the African Union stood for survivors' justice as represented by the transition to postapartheid South Africa. So marked was the difference between the two that one could say it represented a clear-cut choice, so much so that if one were asked to imagine the worst-case scenario—a crisis leading to a total breakdown of law and order in an African country—requiring an external intervention, I would have no hesitation in suggesting that the intervention be under the charge of the African Union and not the United Nations. The difference between the two is that—unlike the big powers that direct U.N. interventions—practically every country in the African Union can see itself in Darfur's shoes, and that makes a world of difference. It is noteworthy that the African Union did not see its work in Darfur as a purely humanitarian intervention from the outside but as an effort guided by humanitarian *and* political objectives. Speaking before the South African parliament, President Thabo Mbeki said the African Union's "strategic framework" was based on two considerations: "to protect the civilian population" and "to find an inclusive political solution."[40] The United Nations claimed to share the former objective but not quite the latter.

For Africa, a lot is at stake in Darfur. Foremost are two objectives, starting with the *unity* of Africa: The Save Darfur lobby in the United States has turned the tragedy of the people of Darfur into a knife with which to slice Africa by demonizing one group of Africans, African Arabs. For undergirding the claim that a genocide has occurred in Darfur is another, born of a colonial historiography, that Arabs in Sudan—and elsewhere in the African continent—are settlers who came in from the outside and whose rights must be subordinate to those of indigenous natives. This, and not the numbers killed, is what is said to differentiate the mass violence in Darfur from that in Congo and Angola and northern Uganda and other places. At stake is also the *independence* of Africa. The Save Darfur lobby demands, above all else, justice, the right of the international community—really the big powers in the Security Council—to punish "failed" or "rogue" states, even if it be at the cost of more bloodshed and a diminished possibility of reconciliation. More than anything else, "the responsibility to protect" is a right to punish but without being held accountable—a clarion call for the recolonization of "failed" states in Africa. In its present form, the call for justice is really a slogan that masks a big power agenda to recolonize Africa.

NOTES

Introduction

1. *Report of the International Commission of Inquiry on Darfur to the United Nations Secretary-General, Pursuant to Security Council Resolution 1564 of Sept. 18, 2004,* Geneva, Jan. 25, 2005, 131–32; see also, 160.

2. See www.iraqbodycount.org/database (accessed July 30, 2008); Nicolas J. S. Davies, "Estimating Civilian Deaths in Iraq—Six Surveys," (last updated Jan. 4, 2007), *Online Journal,* http://onlinejournal.com/artman/publish/article_643.shtml (accessed July 30, 2008); A. H. Alkhuzai, I. J. Ahmad, M. J. Hweel, T. W. Ismail, H. H. Hasan, A. R. Younis, O. Shawani, et al., "Violence-Related Mortality in Iraq from 2002 to 2006," *New England Journal of Medicine* 358, no. 2 (Jan. 31, 2008): 484–93; G. Burnham, R. Lafta, S. Doocy, and L. Roberts, "Mortality after the 2003 Invasion of Iraq: A Cross-Sectional Cluster Sample Survey," *Lancet* 368, no. 9545 (2006): 1421–28; Peter Beaumont and Joanna Walters, "Greenspan Admits Iraq Was about Oil, as Deaths Put at 1.2 Million," *Observer* (U.K.), Sept. 16, 2007, http://observer.guardian.co.uk/world/story/0,2170237,00.html.

3. Of Sudan's total area, 29 percent is classified as desert, 19 percent as semi-desert, 27 percent as low-rainfall savanna, 14 percent as high-rainfall savanna, 10 percent as a flood region (swamps and areas affected by floods), and less than 1 percent as true mountain vegetation. See United Nations Environment Programme, *Sudan: Post-conflict Environmental Assessment* (Nairobi, Kenya: UNEP, 2007), 42.

4. R. S. O'Fahey, *State and Society in Dar Fur* (London: C. Hurst & Co., 1980), 2.

5. Abduljabbar Abdalla Fadul, "Natural Resources Management for Sustainable Peace in Darfur," in "Environmental Degradation: Darfur," proceedings of the Environmental Degradation as a Cause of Conflict in Darfur conference (Khartoum, Dec. 2004), papers published by Africa Programme, University of Peace, Addis Ababa, Ethiopia, in Switzerland, 2006, 34, 16; M. W. Daly, *Darfur's Sorrow: A History of Destruction and Genocide* (Cambridge: Cambridge University Press, 2007), 6–7.

6. United Nations Environment Programme, *Sudan,* 48, 59; Abbas Abd Al

Mannan Hamid, "Local Authorities and Social Change with Reference to South Darfur Province" (master's thesis, Department of Political Science, University of Khartoum, 1979), 1–5.

7. Other writers have mapped in further detail five distinctive climactic and ecological zones in Darfur:

    A   A desert zone that lies between latitudes 16 and 20 north in which rainfall is less than 100 millimeters per year.

    B   A semidesert zone that lies between latitudes 12 and 16 north and receives an annual rainfall of 100 millimeters to 250 millimeters.

    C   A poor savanna zone that lies between latitudes 9 and 12 north and receives an average annual rainfall of 250 millimeters to 450 millimeters.

    D   A rich savanna zone that stretches between latitudes 8 and 9 north and receives an average annual rainfall of between 450 millimeters and 650 millimeters.

    E   The Jebel Marra highlands, which receive an annual rainfall up to 900 millimeters, especially in the southwestern parts.

See United Nations, Darfur Joint Assessment Mission, "Track 1—Darfur Early Recovery, Water Resources, Development and Utilization in Darfur States, War Affected Communities," Dr. Hamid Omer, water resources adviser (Oct. 2006), 2.

8. Ibid., 4; O'Fahey, *State and Society in Dar Fur,* 7.

9. Hassan Musa Daldoum, *The Dynamics of Ethnic Group Relations in Darfur: A Case of the Fur-Arab Relations in Western Darfur* (University of Khartoum, Faculty of Economic and Social Studies, May 2000), 65–66.

10. On the relation between ecology and social organization among the cattle nomads of the south, see Ian Cunnison, *Baggara Arabs: Power and the Lineage in a Sudanese Nomad Tribe* (Oxford: Clarendon Press, 1966), 25, 11–12, 168.

11. For a recent example, see Ruth Iyob and Gilbert M. Khadiagala, *Sudan: The Elusive Quest for Peace,* International Peace Academy Occasional Paper series (Boulder, Colo.: Lynne Rienner Publishers, 2006).

Chapter One

1. "Most African wars are all but ignored by mainstream British media. . . . When conflicts are reported, the attention comes in brief bursts, produced by non-specialist reporters, and focuses primarily on humanitarian aspects of the war, thus confirming the partial and paternalistic view that most Africans are helpless victims and their leaders unusually cruel and greedy." Lara Pawson, "Reporting Africa's Unknown Wars," chapter 3 in *Communicating War: Memory, Media and Military,* ed. Sarah Maltby and Richard Keeble (Bury Saint Edmunds, U.K.: Arima Publishing, 2007), 45.

2. Human Rights Watch Arms Project and Human Rights Watch: Africa, "Angola: Arms Trade and Violations of the Laws of War since the 1992

Elections" (New York: Human Rights Watch, 1992), quoted in Pawson, "Reporting Africa's Unknown Wars," 52.

3. On the Democratic Republic of the Congo, see UNICEF, "Child Alert: Democratic Republic of Congo—Martin Bell Reports on Children Caught in War" (July 2006), http://www.unicef.org/childalert/drc/content/Child _Alert_DRC_3n.pdf (accessed Apr. 30, 2008). *The Washington Post* claimed that 150,000 to 300,000 were killed between 1975 and 1991 and that "500,000 more died in renewed fighting from 1992 to 1994," Dec. 15, 1998. B. Coghlan, R. J. Brennan, P. Ngoy, D. Dofara, B. Otto, M. Clements, and T. Stewart, "Mortality in the Democratic Republic of Congo: A Nationwide Survey," *Lancet* 367, no. 9504 (2006): 44–51.

4. For information on the role of foreign companies in the DRC, see U.N. Security Council, "Final Report of the Panel of Experts on the Illegal Exploitation of Natural Resources and Other Forms of Wealth of the Democratic Republic of the Congo" (Oct. 2002), http://www.globalpolicy .org/security/issues/congo/2002/1015letter.pdf (accessed Aug. 25, 2006); Anneke Van Woudenberg, "Britain Must Confront Shameful Trade That Ruins Congolese Lives," *Independent*, Oct. 31, 2003, http://hrw.org/english/ docs/2003/10/31/uk12948.htm (accessed Aug. 25, 2006); "Mea Culpa: How Will the Blair Commission Change British Policy?" *Africa Confidential* (London), 46, no. 6 (Mar. 18, 2005); Human Rights Watch, "The Curse of Gold," New York, June 2005, http://hrw.org/reports/2005/drc0505/ (accessed Aug. 26, 2006); "Moral Choice," *Africa Confidential* 46, no. 6 (Mar. 18, 2005)—all cited in Pawson, "Reporting Africa's Unknown Wars."

5. On the politics of oil in Chad, see Roland Marchal, "The Unseen Regional Implications of the Crisis in Darfur," in *War in Darfur,* ed. Alex de Waal (Cambridge, Mass.: Harvard University Press, 2007), 185, 188.

6. Gal Beckerman, "US Jews Leading Darfur Rally Planning," *Jerusalem Post,* Apr. 27, 2006.

7. Rebecca Hamilton and Chad Hazlett, in *War in Darfur and the Search for Peace,* ed. Alex de Waal (Cambridge, Mass.: Harvard University Press, 2007), 344.

8. Save Darfur Coalition, search letter, undated, closes with note: "Inquiries should be addressed to: Sue Gambaccini, Isaacson, Miller, Washington, D.C., (703) 860-2462."

9. U.S. Department of State, "Interview on National Public Radio with Michele Norris," June 30, 2004, http://www.state.gov/secretary/former/ powell/remarks/34053.htm.

10. U.S. Department of State, "The Crisis in Darfur," Secretary Colin L. Powell, testimony before the Senate Foreign Relations Committee Washington, D.C., Sept. 9, 2004, http://www.state.gov/secretary/former/powell/remarks /36042.htm.

11. Coghlan, Brennan, Ngoy, Dofara, Otto, Clements, and Stewart, "Mortality in the Democratic Republic of Congo," 45.

12. The specific figures for the three states of Darfur were: 24 percent in North Darfur, 34 percent in West Darfur, and 42 percent in Kalma Camp, South

Darfur. See World Health Organization, "Retrospective Mortality Survey among the Internally Displaced Population, Greater Darfur, Sudan, August 2004" (Khartoum, Sudan: Sept. 15, 2004).

13. Ibid., iv.

14. WHO announced that it would conduct a follow-up study "to estimate the crude mortality rate . . . from 15th June to 15th August 2004" among fifty randomly selected clusters of IDPs "in each of the three states of Greater Darfur." Ibid., 1–2.

15. Coalition for International Justice, Apr. 2005, http://www.cij.org/publications/New_Analysis_Claims; see also "UN's Darfur Death Estimate Soars," BBC News, Mar. 14, 2005, http://news.bbc.co.uk/2/hi/africa/4349063.stm.

16. Russell Smith, "How Many Have Died in Darfur?" BBC, Feb. 16, 2005, http://news.bbc.co.uk/2/hi/world/africa/4268733.stm. For a tabulated presentation of WHO, CRED, and U.S. Department of State estimates, see United States Government Accountability Office, *Darfur Crisis: Death Estimates Demonstrate Severity of Crisis, but Their Accuracy and Credibility Could Be Enhanced,* Report to Congressional Requesters, GAO-07-24 (Nov. 2006), 15, 57–58, 60–61.

17. Reuters, Mar. 30, 2005, http://www.alertnet.org/thenews/newsdesk/L30582.

18. http://www.un.org/apps/news/story.asp?NewsID=19.

19. The United Nations itself speaks of "as many as 450,000 dead from violence and disease."

20. "Darfur's Real Death Toll," *The Washington Post,* editorial, Apr. 24, 2005 (no. 30), B06.

21. Ibid.

22. "Many more than 10,000," (Feb. 1, 2004), http://www.sudanreeves.org/Sections-article148-pl.html.

23. "More than 30,000 people may have already died in Darfur," (Feb. 5, 2004), http://www.sudanreeves.org/Sections-article150-pl.html.

24. "As many as fifty thousand or more may have died already," (May 12, 2004), http://www.sudanreeves.org/Sections-req-viewarticle-artid-191-allpages-1-theme-Printer.html.

25. "Very approximate figure of 80,000 dead," (Jun. 11, 2004), http://www.sudanreeves.org/Sections-req-viewarticle-artid-193-allpages-1-theme-Printer.html.

26. "Number of victims of genocide is already approaching (and has perhaps exceeded) 100,000," (Jun. 28, 2004), http://www.sudanreeves.org/Sections-article197-pl.html.

27. "Yield a total civilian mortality rate to date of approximately 120,000," (Jul. 6, 2004), http://www.sudanreeves.org/Sections-req-viewarticle-artid-199-allpages-1-theme-Printer.html.

28. "Approach to 150,000," (Jul. 21, 2004), http://www.sudanreeves.org/Sections-article201-pl.html.

29. "Estimated total of 180,000 deaths," (Aug. 13, 2004), http://www.sudanreeves.org/Sections-article207-pl.html.

30. "Total mortality figure is well over 200,000," (Aug. 27, 2004), http://www.sudanreeves.org/Sections-article210-pl.html.
31. "Deaths of as many as 300,000 human beings," (Oct. 12, 2004), http://www.sudanreeves.org/Sections-article221-pl.html.
32. "335,000 dead since February 2003," (Nov. 16, 2004), http://www.sudanreeves.org/Sections-article226-pl.html.
33. "Approximately 370,000 have died," (Dec. 12, 2004), http://www.sudan reeves.org/modules.php?op=modload&name=Sections&file=index&req=viewarticle&artid= 256&page=1.
34. "Total deaths number approximately 400,000," (Dec. 29, 2004), http://www.sudanreeves.org/Sections-article476-pl.html.
35. "340,000,"(Feb.10,2005),http://www.sudanreeves.org/Sections-article490-pl.html.
36. "Mortality is well in excess of 300,000," (Feb. 17, 2005). He then upped it to "approximately 380,000 human beings have died," (Mar. 11, 2005), "almost 400,000 have already perished," (Mar. 31, 2005), "conflict-related deaths now exceed 370,000," (Aug. 31, 2005), and "global mortality during the genocide in Darfur is roughly 400,000," (Dec. 23, 2005), http://www.sudanreeves.org/modules.php?op=modload&name=Sections&file=index&req=viewarticle&artid=491&page=1, http://www.sudanreeves.org/modules.php?op=modload&name=Sections&file=index&req=viewarticle&artid=497&page=1, http://www.sudanreeves.org/Sections-article499-p1.html,http://www.sudanreeves.org/Sections-article552-p1.html, and http://www.sudanreeves.org/Sections-article543-p1.html
37. He wrote that "total mortality, even when excepting the global mortality rate recently established by the UN World Health Organization for November 2004 to May 2005 still approximates to between 350,000 and 400,000," (Jul. 14, 2005), http://www.sudanreeves.org/Sections-article513-pl.htm. At the same time as he gave these absolute figures, Dr. Reeves also gave estimates of the weekly mortality rate: "civilians are dying at a rate of 1,000 per week," (Feb. 12, 2004), http://www.sudanreeves.org/Sections-article153-pl.html; "with more than 1,000 civilians dying weekly," (Feb. 17, 2004), http://www.sudanreeves.org/Sections-article154-pl.html; "the weekly civilian death toll is well above 2,000 human beings," (Jun. 1, 2004), http://www.sudanreeves.org/Sections-article184-pl.html. On July 28, Dr. Reeves reported that "present mortality exceeds 50,000 per month," http://www.sudanreeves.org/Sections-article202-pl.html, and then "2,000 who now die daily," (Aug. 9, 2004), http://www.sudanreeves.org/Sections-article206-pl.html. The mortality rate then came down to "over 1,000 human beings," (Oct. 25, 2004), http://www.sudanreeves.org/Sections-article223-pl.html, and climbed up to "approximately 35,000 per month," (Dec. 12, 2004), http://www.sudanreeves.org/Sections-article256-pl.html. The mortality rate for 2005 started at 15,000 a month: "current mortality rate in the larger humanitarian theatre is approximately 15,000 deaths per month," (Mar. 11, 2005), http://www.sudanreeves.org/modules.php?op=modload&name=Sections&file=index&eq=viewarticle&artid=497&page=1, declined to "approximately 10,000–15,000" per month," (May 7, 2005),

http://www.sudanreeves.org/Sections-article503-pl.html, and to "well over 6,000 people [are dying] every month," (Jun. 30, 2005) http://www.sudanreeves.org/Sections-article515-pl.html. Reeves gave only one estimate of the mortality rate during 2006 (Sept. 29, 2006): "very likely more than 10,000 conflict-related deaths per month." http://www.sudanreeves.org/Article126.html.

38. "human mortality that likely exceeds 400,000," (Jan. 14, 2006), http://www.sudanreeves.org/Sections-article539-pl.html.

39. "more than 450,000 deaths," (May 20, 2006), http://www.sudanreeves.org/Sections-article560-pl.html.

40. "as many as 500,000 have already died," (Jun. 24, 2006), http://www.sudanreeves.org/Sections-req-viewarticle-artid-572-allpages-1-theme-Printer.html.

41. "some 500,000 have already died," (Nov. 26, 2006), http://www.sudanreeves.org/Article136.html.

42. "400,000," (May 11, 2007), http://www.sudanreeves.org/Article166.html, a figure he quoted from Representative Frank Wolf, *Congressional Record,* May 2, 2007.

43. See the following op-eds by Nicholas Kristof in *The New York Times:* "Dare We Call It Genocide?," June 16, 2004; "The Secret Genocide Archive," February 23, 2005; "Day 113 of the President's Silence," May 3, 2005; "China and Sudan, Blood and Oil," April 23, 2006.

44. United States Government Accountability Office, *Darfur Crisis: Death Estimates Demonstrate Severity of Crisis, but Their Accuracy and Credibility Could Be Enhanced,* 26.

45. Ibid., 3, 26.

46. Ibid., 62.

47. Ibid., 42.

48. Ibid., 65.

49. Ibid., 10, 17, 15.

50. "Death in Darfur," *Science* 313, no. 5793 (Sept. 15, 2006): 1578–79.

51. See the discussion on the SSRC (Social Science Research Council) blog, "Making Sense of Darfur," http://www.ssrc.org/blogs/2007/08/16/deaths-in-darfur-keeping-ourselves-honest (accessed Aug. 5, 2008).

52. Fabienne Hara (director, political affairs, U.N. mission in Sudan), interview, Khartoum, May 5, 2007.

53. Ramesh Rajasingham (head of UN-OCHA in Sudan), interview, Khartoum, May 8, 2007.

54. Immanual de Solva (humanitarian coordinator for Sudan, assistant secretary-general, and head of the WFP), interview, Khartoum, May 7, 2007.

55. Rajasingham, interview.

56. Letter to the editor, *Financial Times,* Dec. 18, 2006.

57. Julie Flint and Alex de Waal, *Darfur: A New History of a Long War* (London and New York: Zed Books, 2008), 187.

58. Julie Flint, "All This Moral Posturing Won't Help Darfur," *Independent,* July 31, 2007.

59. Simon Tisdall, "Sudan Warns West of 'Iraq-Style Disaster' in Darfur," Mar. 12, 2008, http://www.guardian.co.uk/world/2008/mar/12/sudan.

60. Sudanreeves.org, http://www.sudanreeves.org/article126.htm.

61. Julie Flint, "In Sudan, Help Comes from Above," *New York Times,* op-ed, July 6, 2007.

62. "Darfur: A Plan B to Stop Genocide," hearing before the Foreign Relations Committee, United States Senate, April 11, 2007, http://www.senate.gov/~foreign/hearings/2007/hrg070411a.html (accessed Aug. 6, 2008).

63. Ibid.

64. South African Government Information, "Questions to the President at the National Assembly," May 17, 2007, http://www.info.gov.za/speeches/2007/07052112451002.htm (accessed Mar. 5, 2008).

65. Mahmood Mamdani, "Blue-Hatting Darfur," *London Review of Books* 29, no. 17 (Sept. 6, 2007).

66. The troops came from six countries—Nigeria, Rwanda, South Africa, Senegal, Gambia, and Kenya—and the police from Ghana. There were also military observers from Egypt and Libya, among other countries.

67. It called for the numbers of soldiers and police to be increased to a total of roughly eight thousand and for civilians to be brought in as humanitarian officers.

68. Major General Henry Anyidoho, interview, Khartoum, May 11, 2007.

69. Refugees International reported that "earlier in the year, AMIS had been able to provide some security and deterrence. Displaced persons were congregating near AMIS bases, the UN World Food Programme started parking its vehicles at AMIS sites, AMIS escorted humanitarian convoys, and helped victims of attacks get to hospitals. The round-the-clock presence of civilian police in some IDP [internally displaced person] camps has provided a greater sense of security to a population that is distrustful of the Sudanese police. AMIS forces have helped to restore order and provide security during the very difficult IDP re-registration process." Sally Chin and Jonathan Morgenstein, *No Power to Protect: The African Union Mission in Sudan* (Washington, D.C.: Refugees International, Nov. 2005). U.N. observers also agreed: Security in Kebkabiya has reportedly improved with the arrival of African Union monitors and more international NGO staff. Helen Young, Abdul Monim Osman, Yacob Aklilu, Rebecca Dale, Babiker Badri, and Abdul Jabbar Abdullah Fuddle, *Darfur—Livelihoods under Siege* (Medford, Mass.: Tufts University, Feinstein International Famine Center, June 2005), 40, http://fic.tufts.edu/downloads/darfur_livelihoods_under_siege.pdf (accessed Aug. 14, 2008).

70. Anyidoho, interview.

71. As early as 2005, when Refugees International sent a mission to assist AMIS in North Darfur, it noted that "all of AMIS's local interpreters were on strike because their salaries had been cut in half following a restructuring of salaries . . . for all AMIS personnel." Chin and Morgenstein, *No Power to Protect.*

72. There were other problems, too. AU soldiers were the focus of media attention. In September 2005, two AMIS soldiers died of AIDS-related illnesses,

sparking public anxieties. In March 2006, U.K. Channel 4 reported that women and girls as young as eleven at the Gereida IDP camp in South Darfur were claiming that AU soldiers had offered them money in exchange for sex. The African Union set up a committee to inquire into alleged "sexual misconduct including rape and child abuse" carried out by its forces. See Mamdani, "Blue-Hatting Darfur."

73. For quotes in this and the previous paragraph, see Chin and Morgenstein, *No Power to Protect.*

74. J. Millard Burr and Robert O. Collins, *Darfur: The Long Road to Disaster* (Princeton, N.J.: Markus Wiener Publishers, 2006), 305.

75. Warren Hoge, "African Union to Send Troops in Bid to Curb Sudan Violence," *New York Times,* Sept. 24, 2004.

76. *Report of the International Commission of Inquiry on Darfur for the United Nations Security-General Pursuant to Security Council Resolution 1564 of Sept. 18, 2004,* Geneva, Jan. 25, 2005: 158–61.

77. Ibid.

78. See Testimony of Colin Powell Before Senate Committee on Foreign Relations on September 9, 2004, "The Crisis in Darfur," U.S. Department of State, http://www.state.gov/secretary/former/powell/remarks/36042.htm (accessed on Aug. 5, 2008); also see, UN Security Council Resolutions 1590 (Mar. 24, 2005), 1591 (Mar. 29, 2005) and 1593 (Mar. 31, 2005), http://www.un.org/Docs/sc/unsc_resolutions05.htm (accessed Aug. 5, 2008).

79. U.N. Security Council Resolutions 1706 (Aug. 13, 2006) and 1769 (July 31, 2007), http://www.un.org/documents/scres.htm (accessed on Aug. 5, 2008).

80. "Obasanjo warns of 'near-genocide' in Darfur," Oct. 11, 2006, IRIN, http://www.alertnet.org/thenews/newsdesk/IRIN/2ea3314d173dd06dc482799b0c80b620.htm (accessed on Aug. 5, 2008).

81. Tisdall, "Sudan Warns West."

Chapter Two

1. Information on Save Darfur Coalition's domestic activities can be found on its website, http://savedarfur.org/pages/domestic_programs/ (accessed Aug. 5, 2008).

2. Stephanie Strom and Lydia Polgreen, "Publicity Campaign on Darfur Angers Relief Organisations," *International Herald Tribune,* June 1, 2007, http://www.iht.com/articles/2007/06/02/africa/02darfur-web.php (accessed Aug. 5, 2008).

3. In the same vein, a *New Republic* editorial on Darfur called for "force as a first-resort response." Quoted in Zuzanna Kobrzynski and Melanyce McAfee, "Force First," *The Washington Post,* May 1, 2006.

4. This discussion is based on Sam Dealey, "An Atrocity That Needs No Exaggeration," *New York Times,* op-ed, Aug. 12, 2007 (Sam Dealey reports on Africa for *Time* magazine); Flint, "All This Moral Posturing"; Flint, "In Sudan, Help Comes from Above."

5. Advertising Standards Authority (London), "ASA Adjudications" (Aug. 8, 2007), http://www.asa.org.uk/asa/adjudications/Public/TF_ADJ_42993.htm; see also Raphael G. Satter, "UK Advertising Regulator Says Ad Campaign's Darfur Deaths Claim Not Factual," *International Herald Tribune,* Aug. 15, 2007.

6. Chin and Morgenstein, *No Power to Protect* (see chap. 1, n. 69).

7. The global-level Save Darfur campaign was reproduced by some of its members at a more local level. Take, for example, a letter that Africa Action, a Save Darfur member organization, sent to its Listserv in December 2007, after the verdict by the U.K. advertising monitor, calling attention to "the genocide in Darfur," claiming that "more than 450,000 innocent lives have been lost" in "one of the most outrageous cases of disregard and contempt for human rights ever witnessed on the African continent," and calling "for U.S. leadership in support of a United Nations intervention to stop the genocide in Darfur." E-mail from Mobilize@africaaction.org. Africa Action letter titled "Please Act to End Genocide in Darfur on This Human Rights Day," Dec. 10, 2007.

8. Stephanie Strom and Lydia Polgreen, "Publicity Campaign on Darfur Angers Relief Organizations," *International Herald Tribune,* June 1, 2007, http://www.iht.com/articles/2007/06/02/africa/02darfur-web.php; "Darfur Advocacy Group Undergoes a Shake-up," *New York Times,* June 2, 2007, http://www.nytimes.com/2007/06/02/world/africa/02darfur.html.

9. Letter, 2, 3, 5.

10. David Rubenstein, "Act Now! Write and Op-Ed About a Plan B with Teeth!," Darfur Action—UC Davis, http://ucdstand.blogspot.com/ (accessed on Aug. 7, 2008).

11. *New York Times,* May 30, 2007; June 7, 2007.

12. Hamilton and Hazlett, " 'Not on Our Watch,' " 345, 354–55.

13. Ibid., 360.

14. E-mail from actionalerts@care2.com, Jan. 28, 2007.

15. Dan Glaister, "Not on Our Watch: How Hollywood Made America Care about Darfur," *Guardian,* May 19, 2007.

16. Hamilton and Hazlett, " 'Not on Our Watch,' " 360.

17. George Clooney, "United Nations Security Council Address on Darfur," delivered Sept. 14, 2006, New York City, http://www.americanrhetoric.com/speeches/georgeclooneyunitednations.htm (accessed Mar. 19, 2008).

18. Glaister, "Not on Our Watch."

19. Ibid.

20. Mary Riddell, "How Geldof Urged Writers to Go to War over Darfur," *Observer,* Mar. 25, 2007, http://observer.guardian.co.uk/world/story/0,2042211,00.html.

21. Quoted in Eichler-Levine and Hicks, " 'As Americans against Genocide,' " 719.

22. Ibid., 720.

23. Global Days for Darfur, "Christian Faith Action Packet," 8, http://www.savedarfur.org/globaldays.

24. Jodi Eichler-Levine and Rosemary R. Hicks, quoted in Rosemary R. Hicks, "Religion, Race, Rape and Rights: Building International Inter-religious Coalitions in Terms of Gender, Sexuality and Militarized Humanism" (working paper for the Columbia session of "After Pluralism," 2007), 7.

25. "Jewish Insert," http://www.savedarfur.org/faith (accessed May 2, 2006), quoted in Jodi Eichler-Levine and Rosemary R. Hicks, " 'As Americans against Genocide': The Crisis in Darfur and Interreligious Political Activism," *American Quarterly* 56, no. 3 (Sept. 2007): 717, 726.

26. "These selections imply that 'Save Darfur' means to activate the inherent impetus governing the religions of various member groups. While texts in the Christian and Jewish packets concentrate on motivating constructive activity (i.e., 'restoring' and rescuing), texts in the Muslim packet focus primarily on restraining activity (i.e., 'prevention')." Hicks, "Religion, Race, Rape and Rights," 11–14.

27. "While specific references to 'Arab' perpetrators were removed, the dichotomous narrative of 'systematic *ethnic* cleansing of African Darfuris by the Sudanese Government and their proxy militia—the Janjaweed' remained." Ibid., 8.

28. See www.savedarfur.org/faith (accessed Jan. 29, 2008).

29. See Nicholas Kristof, "Bush Points the Way," *New York Times,* May 29, 2004; "China and Sudan, Blood and Oil," *New York Times,* Apr. 23, 2006.

30. Nicholas Kristof on *Today* show, NBC, Nov. 13, 2006, NBC News Transcripts.

31. Eliot Weinberger, "Comment," *OCTOBER 123,* MIT (Winter 2008), 171.

32. From the outset, Kristof was clear that this was a contest between "Sudan's Arab rulers" and "black African Sudanese" in Darfur. He began by describing the government's response to the insurgency as "ethnic cleansing" (Mar. 24, 2004) but upped the ante only three days later, claiming that this was no longer ethnic cleansing but genocide. "Right now," he wrote on Mar. 27, "the government of Sudan is engaged in genocide against three large African tribes in its Darfur region." He continued: "The killings are being orchestrated by the Arab-dominated Sudanese government," and "the victims are non-Arabs: blacks in the Zaghawa, Massalliet and Fur tribes." See Nicholas D. Kristof, "Ethnic Cleansing, Again," *New York Times,* Mar. 24, 2004; and "Will We Say 'Never Again' Yet Again?" *New York Times,* Mar. 27, 2004.

33. Global Days for Darfur, "Jewish Faith Action Packet," 10, www.savedarfur .org/globaldays.

34. Nicholas D. Kristof, "Why Genocide Matters," *New York Times,* Sept. 10, 2006.

35. Gérard Prunier, letter to *London Review of Books,* Apr. 26, 2007.

36. Contrast this with the report of the International Commission of Inquiry on Darfur and its painstaking effort to make sense of the "Arab" and "African" identities. The commission's report concentrated on three related points. First, the claim that the Darfur conflict pitted "Arab" against "African" was facile. "In fact, the commission found that many Arabs in

Darfur are opposed to the Janjawiid, and some Arabs are fighting with the rebels, such as certain Arab commanders and their men from the Misseriya and Rizeigat tribes. At the same time, many non-Arabs are supporting the government and serving in its army." Second, the commission found that it has never been easy to sort different tribes into the categories "Arab" and "African": "The various tribes that have been the object of attacks and killings (chiefly the Fur, Massalit and Zeghawa tribes) do not appear to make up ethnic groups distinct from the ethnic groups to which persons or militias that attack them belong. They speak the same language (Arabic) and embrace the same religion (Muslim). In addition, also due to the high measure of intermarriage, they can hardly be distinguished in their outward physical appearance from the members of tribes that allegedly attacked them. Apparently, the sedentary and nomadic character of the groups constitutes one of the main distinctions between them." Finally, the commission put forward the view that political developments are driving the rapidly growing distinction between "Arab" and "African." On the one hand, "Arab" and "African" seem to have become political identities: "Those tribes in Darfur who support rebels have increasingly come to be identified as 'African' and those supporting the government as the 'Arabs.' A good example to illustrate this is that of the Gimmer, a pro-government African tribe that is seen by the African tribes opposed to the government as having been 'Arabised.' " On the other hand, this development was being promoted from the outside: "The Arab-African divide has also been fanned by the growing insistence on such divide in some circles and in the media." *Report of the International Commission of Inquiry on Darfur to the United Nations Secretary-General,* January 25, 2005, 130–31.

37. Quoted in Deborah Murphy, "Narrating Darfur: Darfur in the U.S. Press, March–September, 2004," in *War in Darfur and the Search for Peace,* ed. Alex de Waal (Cambridge, Mass.: Harvard University Press, 2007), 333–34, 322–23. See also the following op-eds by Nicholas Kristof in *The New York Times:* "Starved for Safety," March 31, 2004; "Dare We Call It Genocide?" June 16, 2004; and "Sudan's Department of Gang Rape," Nov. 22, 2005.

38. Available at http://www.savedarfur.org/pages/unity_statement (accessed Aug. 7, 2008).

39. Nompumelelo Motlafi, "Darfur Crisis Puts an Uncomfortable Spotlight on Arab and African Identity," *Cape Times,* Apr. 16, 2007.

40. The 2004 Unity Statement and Call to Action is available at the National Council of Churches site, http://www.ncccusa.org/news/04savedarfur coalition.html (accessed Aug. 7, 2008).

41. Nicholas D. Kristof, "Facing Down the Killers," *New York Times,* Dec. 18, 2004.

42. The Southern Sudan lobby comprised a coalition of religious and secular Zionist groups, mainly Christian Solidarity International (CSI) and the Sudan Coalition. See, J. Millar Burr and Robert O. Collins, *Darfur, The Long Road to Disaster,* 300–1; Hamilton and Hazlett, " 'Not on Our Watch,' " 342.

43. Murphy, "Narrating Darfur," 330.

Chapter Three

1. See T. F. Gossett, *Race: The History of an Idea in America* (New York: Oxford University Press), 5; R. Graves and R. Patai, *Hebrew Myths: The Book of Genesis* (New York: Doubleday, 1964), 121; Mahmood Mamdani, *When Victims Become Killers: Colonialism, Nativism, and the Genocide in Rwanda* (Princeton, N.J.: Princeton University Press, 2001), 79–87.

2. A. A. Arkell, *A History of the Sudan: From the Earliest Times to 1821* (London: Athlone Press, 1961), 113.

3. Ibn Khaldūn, *The Muqaddimah: An Introduction to History,* translated by Franz Rosenthal, abridged and edited by N. J. Dawood (London: Routledge and Kegan Paul, 1967), 60–61. For an extended discussion, see Abubaker Y. Ahmed Al-Shingietti, "Images of the Sudan: A Cultural Analysis of *The New York Times* and the London *Times* Coverage of Two Crises" (PhD diss., University of Massachusetts, May 1992).

4. Al-Shingietti, "Images of the Sudan," chap. 1. Al-Shingietti gives a genealogy of the name *Sudan,* which I have used as a guide for my own reading, though I am not wholly persuaded by his thesis that this led to "a universal cultural code—racism," ibid., 36.

5. W.E.B. Du Bois makes this point in *Africa and the World.* See Mahmood Mamdani, introduction to W.E.B. Du Bois, *Africa and the World.*

6. William Y. Adams, "Continuity and Change in Nubian Cultural History," *Sudan Notes and Records* 48 (1967): 21, in which he clearly advocates his theory about the history of Nubia. His more definitive work can be found in his book *Nubia: Corridor to Africa* (Princeton, N.J.: Princeton University Press, 1977).

7. Abdel Salam Mohamed Sidahmed, "State and Ideology in the Funj Sultanate of Sennar, 1500–1821" (MS thesis, Department of Political Science, University of Khartoum, June 1983), 22–23.

8. Winston S. Churchill, *The River War: An Account of the Reconquest of the Sudan* (first published 1899; New York: Carroll & Graf Publishers, 2000), 7–8. Page references are to the 2000 edition.

9. H. A. MacMichael, *A History of the Arabs in the Sudan,* 2 vols. (Cambridge: Cambridge University Press, 1922), 1:114–15.

10. This account begins with the Guhayna: "The Guhayna, prior to their immigration into Africa, had been settled in the Hegaz from south of Yanbu' to north of el Haurá." It ends with a racial observation on the Nubians: "Thus the settlement of Nubia by the Arabs proceeded to all intents undisturbed, and by the fifteenth century the racial characteristics of the population in the neighborhood of the first two cataracts, and perhaps as far south as Dongola, had become substantially what they are today." This is how MacMichael sums up his "general impression of four tides of Arab immigration into the Sudan" in volume 2:

> The first flowed through Egypt in the seventh and eighth centuries and was a natural sequel to the conquest of that country. . . . The

second immigration took place in the eighth century across the Red Sea by way of Abyssinia as a result of the overthrow of the Omayyads by the 'Abbasids, and eventually resulted in the foundation of the Arab-Fung hegemony in the Gezira. . . . Then in the thirteenth and fourteenth centuries the conquest of the mamluk Sultans broke down the barrier which had been for so long presented by the Christian kingdom of Dongola and opened the way for a fresh inflow of Arabs into the Sudan. . . . The fourth great immigration followed the foundation of the Fung kingdom and the conquest of Egypt by Selim I.

Ibid., 1:138–39, 1:188, 2:10–11.

11. MacMichael was obsessed with color and race as clues to a people's potential. Here is an example: "The GAWAMA'A. The history of the Gawama'a, in so far as they are Arabs, is similar to that of the Bedayria, but they are even less homogenous than the latter, and the fact that taken as a whole *they are darker in color and more debased in manners* suggests that the original Arab nucleus of the tribe was small, and that in consequence it became more merged in the negro" (italics added). Ibid., 1:223.

12. Harold MacMichael, "Notes on the History of Kordofan before the Egyptian Conquest," including appendix on "The Funj," 2, 3, 4, 5, 10–11, 27–28. See Sudan Archive at Durham University, U.K., SAD 281/3/1-30.

13. In "The Coming of the Arabs to the Sudan," Burton Memorial Lecture, delivered to the Royal Asiatic Society, July 20, 1928, MacMichael claimed that "in Darfur, in the great range of Gebel Marra, we hear of another Arab chieftain as marrying into the royal house of the Fur, and so becoming the first of a line of negroid Sultans claiming Arab descent, of whom the last ceased to reign only twelve years ago." SAD E/5/11, 5, 6.

14. MacMichael, "Notes on the History of Kordofan before the Egyptian Conquest," 5, 27–28. In the 1928 lecture, MacMichael continued his story beyond the fall of the Nubian kingdom to the Mamluks in 1276, turning to the Arab "wise stranger" to explain the founding of both the Sultanate of Funj and that of Dar Fur. MacMichael, "The Coming of the Arabs to the Sudan," 14.

15. S. Hillelson, "David Reubeni: An Early Visitor to Sennar," *Sudan Notes and Records* 16:55–56, cited in Yusuf Fadl Hasan, *Studies in Sudanese History* (Khartoum: Sudatek Limited, 2003), 47–48.

16. Ibid.

17. R. S. O'Fahey and J. L. Spaulding, *Kingdoms of the Sudan* (London: Methuen, 1974), 31, quoted in Dr. Albaqir Alafif Mukhtar, "On the Fringes of Northern Identity: What's Missing in the Darfur Peace Process?" (report, United States Institute for Peace, Washington, D.C., May 24, 2006), 18.

18. Yusuf Fadl Hasan, *The Arabs and the Sudan from the Seventh to the Early Sixteenth Century* (1st ed., Edinburgh University Press, 1969; Khartoum: Sudatek Limited, 2005), 174.

19. MacMichael, *History of the Arabs in the Sudan,* 2:62–63. Another genealogy provided to MacMichael (genealogy ABC in MacMichael) was composed

by al-Siddiq Hadra, a Mahasi faki from Khartoum North, using a similar method.

20. Fergus Nicoll, *The Mahdi of Sudan and the Death of General Gordon* (Gloucestershire, U.K.: Sutton Publishing, 2004), 16.

21. MacMichael, "Coming of the Arabs to the Sudan," 5, 6.

22. MacMichael, *History of the Arabs in the Sudan*, 2:3–4.

23. Ian Cunnison, "Classification by Genealogy: A Problem of the Baggara Belt," in *Sudan in Africa*, ed. Yusuf Fadl Hasan (Khartoum: Institute of African and Asian Studies, University of Khartoum, 1971).

24. "For example, in a genealogy given by MacMichael, the Humr Falayta claim that Falayt had four sons—'Gibrin, Hasabu Salam, Sunan and Masnan'—and that each was founder of one of the four branches of the tribe (the Jubarat, Salamat, Awlad Surur, and Metaniyn). Humr call these last two Sonan and Mutnan. But it is well known that the Jubarat and the Salamat are strangers who sought shelter among the Humr, and not kin at all. No Gibrin was ever son of Falayt." Ibid.

25. P. L. Shinnie, "The Culture of Medieval Nubia and Its Impact on Africa," in *Sudan in Africa*, ed. Yusuf Fadl Hasan, 47.

26. MacMichael, *History of the Arabs in the Sudan*.

27. Neil McHugh has elaborated these to five lines of descent that "have had political, social or religious importance in Sudan." The fifth and final line of descent is the *Umawwi*. Associated with Banu Umayya, who established the first caliphal dynasty, this line was claimed by the Funj royal house. Neil McHugh, *Holymen of the Blue Nile: The Making of an Arab Islamic Community in the Nilotic Sudan, 1500–1850* (Evanston, Ill.: Northwestern University, 1994), 9–10.

28. The former are the great majority of the historically sedentary riverine peoples (the Ja'aliyyin proper, the Shayqiyya, the Bidayriyya, etc.) and the latter most of the nomadic groups that occupy the river's hinterland (the Juhayna proper, the Rufa'a, the Shukriyya). McHugh has argued that the fact that they so clearly encapsulate the divide between sedentary and nomadic Arabs points to "a process of genealogical standardization that had much less to do with literal migration than with political and economic associations, possibly including clientage and slavery." Ibid.

29. Nadia Khalaf, "British Policy Regarding the Administration of the Northern Sudan, 1899–1951" (PhD diss., Political Science Department, Duke University, 1965; University Microfilms International, Ann Arbor, Mich.), 42–44.

30. Neil McHugh identifies four idioms: northern (Berber and Dongola), central (the Gezira and points east), western (the White Nile, Kordofan, and Darfur), and the Baggara (cattle herders of the southern portion of the Gezira, White Nile, Kordofan, and Darfur). The Arabic of transhumant pastoralists "differs significantly from that of continuous sedentary cultivators." McHugh, *Holymen of the Blue Nile*, 8.

31. MacMichael, "The Coming of the Arabs to the Sudan," 9–13. MacMichael's explanation of why Sudan so attracted Arab nomads that they stayed has at best the whiff of an educated guess:

Egypt is not an ideal country for the nomad. Its rainfall is negligible, and there is a superfluity of cultivation. The Sudan, on the other hand, excluding the southern provinces, has much in common with Arabia. To anyone with a knowledge of the Sudan, there is hardly a description given by Palgrave or Doughty, or indeed by any other Arabian traveler, of the desert grazing grounds, the bleak sun-blackened hills of wasted sandstone, or the more kindly valley fed by springs or rainfall, that might not be applied, almost word for word, to some part of the country lying inland from the Nile, on either side of it, to the north of Khartoum. The same trees occur, the same grasses, the same barren outcrops of rock, the same sandy wastes. The Red Sea is, in fact, no more than an accidental rift which some convulsion of nature has interposed between two parts of the same country, though the western part has been more fortunate in that the Nile has forced its way through it from the mountains of Abyssinia and the Great Lakes, providing, in its northern reaches, the riverain cultivator with heaven-sent means of cultivating the banks by pump or water-wheel.

. . .

One can see what happened. As the Arabs gravitated southward through Egypt they heard of wide pasture lands eminently suited to their camels and sheep—at this time they probably owned no cattle—and when they were able to sample the promised land they found themselves upon familiar ground among familiar conditions. Most of them therefore stayed there with their beasts; but others, pressing further ahead, acquired cattle—the tsetse fly would not have let the camel live, even were other conditions favorable—and took up their abode between the negroes of the south and the camel and sheep-owners of the north.

32. Ibid., 7, 8.
33. Hasan, *The Arabs and the Sudan*, 21–33; Hasan, *Studies in Sudanese History*, 135, 174–75.
34. See Hasan, *The Arabs and the Sudan*, 20–49, 62, 72–73, 100–111.
35. Hasan, *The Arabs and the Sudan*, 18–49. Hasan tells us that Arabs constituted a privileged minority in Egypt in the days of the Umayyad and the early 'Abbāsid caliphate. Its members received pensions from the treasury and did not pay the land tax—initially not at all, and later only in part. Since 'Umar b. al-Khattāb feared that involvement in agriculture would corrupt their fighting abilities, he prohibited them from owning land. Even when this restriction was eliminated, Arabs continued to live in the cities. Only toward the end of Umayyad rule did Arabs begin to mix with the Egyptians.
36. Arabs were tribes, some of which had briefly conquered Egypt and many others of which lived in various parts of the lower Nile Valley with varying degrees of independence from the power in Cairo. Most settled inhabitants

of the lower Nile were gradually "Arabized" peasants—but not Arabs. I am grateful to Tim Mitchell for this observation. Personal communication.

37. See Hasan, *The Arabs and the Sudan,* 20–21, 26–27; also Hasan, *Studies in Sudanese History,* 12–13, 29. "With the passage of centuries, various Islamic intellectuals, eager to forget the initial Nubian victory, devised increasingly elaborate and fanciful accounts that undertook to construe baqt shipments as payment of tribute." See also Jay Spaulding, "Precolonial Islam in the Eastern Sudan," in Nehemiah Levtzion and Randall L. Pouwels, eds., *The History of Islam in Africa* (Athens: Ohio University Press, 2000), 117.

38. Official Mamluk relations with Sudanese lands to the north were confined to Beja and Nubia. In both cases, treaties required each to pay a regular tribute to the Mamluk sultan. According to the Beja treaty drawn up after their eighth-century defeat, the Beja agreed to pay a tribute of three hundred young camels annually and to grant Mamluks the privilege of entering Beja country as traveling merchants, without the right to stay as residents. The treaty with Nubia, drawn up later, was more exacting. Article 5 stated: "Every year you shall deliver three hundred sixty slaves to the Imam of the Muslims. They shall be slaves of good quality of your country, without defect both male and female, neither extremely old nor children under age. Those you shall deliver to the governor of Aswan." The treaty was superseded in A.D. 1276, when dissident Arabs fled to Nubia and Mamluks responded with an invasion. See Hasan, *The Arabs and the Sudan,* 21.

39. The numbers of Arab migrants were already being taken note of in the early decades of the ninth century. Arab immigration took three main forms. First, there are records of Arab immigrants buying land from Nubians during the Umayyad and early 'Abbāsid period. As early as the reign of al-Ma'mūn in the tenth century, the Nubian king complained that Arabs had begun to buy the lands of his subjects in the region between Aswan and Bajrash, where they were not supposed to settle, but his complaint did not stop Arab encroachment in that area. Second, following the discovery of gold and emeralds in the eastern desert in the ninth century, there are records of a stream of Arabs moving to the mines of the Beja, already well known because they had in the past been a fabled source of wealth for the pharaohs. The third destination that attracted Arab immigrants was the port of Aydhab in Beja country. A town of five hundred inhabitants with a Friday mosque, Aydhab became "one of the busiest ports in the Muslim world" toward the end of the twelfth century.

Except for a few limestone buildings, the majority of Aydhab's houses were huts. Shipbuilding materials were imported from Yemen and India, but ships were built locally to suit the Red Sea waters. Cargo unloaded from Indian and Chinese ships at Aden was taken by Red Sea dhows to Aydhab. From there, the goods were carried to a town in Upper Egypt. Aydhab was sacked in A.D. 1183, during the war between the Ayyūbids and the Crusaders, but the Crusaders were finally put to flight by an army sent from Egypt. The prosperity of Aydhab depended on the eastern trade and the pilgrim traffic, and the port was run under dual control: The ruler of Egypt sent a governor (*wali*), and he shared the revenue with the local Beja chief. When Ibn Battūtah visited Aydhab, two-thirds of the revenue went to the Beja chief al-Hadarabi and one-third to the Mamluk sultan. See Hasan, *The Arabs and the Sudan,* 69–73.

40. Here is how Yusuf Fadl Hasan quotes Ibn Khaldūn:

> At their [the Nubians'] conversion [to Islam] payment of *Jizya* ceased. Then several clans of the Arab tribe of Juhayna dispersed throughout their country and settled there. They assumed power and filled the land with disorder and chaos. The kings of Nubia, at first, tried to drive them out by force. They failed, so they changed their tactics and tried to win them over by offering their daughters in marriage. Thus it was that their kingdom disintegrated, for it passed to the sons of the Juhayna from their Nubian mothers in accordance with the non-Arab practice of inheritance by the sister and her sons. So their kingdom fell to pieces and their country was inherited by the Arabs of the Juhayna. And there remains no trace of central authority in their lands because of the change wrought in them by the influence of Arab beduinization through intermarriage and alliance.

Hasan, *The Arabs and the Sudan,* 127–28.

Ibn Khaldūn's views have also been criticized by Jay Spaulding as unsupported by any historical evidence from Nubia and thus to be understood "as supporting evidence for his general theory of the role of nomads in the course of history": "While this theoretical preoccupation does not necessarily invalidate his account of events in Nubia, it does constitute a conspicuous bias, and should have inspired a critical attitude among scholars. It is most surprising that although Ibn Khaldun's similarly colorful and emphatic views concerning the role of nomadic Arab invaders in his own homeland have long since been tested and found wanting, no serious challenge has been offered to his vision of Nubian history." Jay Spaulding, "The End of Nubian Kingship in the Sudan, 1720–1762," in *Modernization in the Sudan: Essays in Honor of Richard Hill,* ed. M. W. Daly (New York: Lilian Barber Press, 1985), 22–23.

41. "From Ibn Khaldun's statement on other grounds there is no doubt that in the 14th century, after the barrier of the Christian kingdom of Dongola had been swept away that is, large bodies of nomads, chiefly Guhayna, pushed westwards from the Nile into Kordofan, Darfur and Wadai with their herds, and became progenitors of the camel owning nomads of the North and the Baggara of the South." MacMichael then went on to speculate of the Baggara of South Darfur: "Of the details of this great race-movement there is little known but it is sufficiently obvious that those Arabs who pushed Southwards and took to cattle-breeding inter-married freely with the negroid tribes whom they to some extent supplanted; but succeeded at the same time in preserving the free and independent spirit, the language and the clearcut features of the Arab, while acquiring from the negro many cus-

toms and superstitions, a somewhat heavier physique and a darker complexion." And then, of the camel owners of the north, he wrote: "The camel owners in the North, roaming further afield, naturally kept more aloof from alien influences and preserved the purity of their Arab blood to a greater extent than did their bretheren in the South. Most of the negroid characteristics noticeable among them are derived from the slaves brought by their fathers and forefathers from the South." See H. A. MacMichael, "Notes on the Tribes of Darfur," Oct. to Dec. 1915, SAD 110/6/1-99.

P. M. Holt, author of many editions of a history of modern Sudan in English, also relied on Ibn Khaldūn to conclude that "the Arabization of the northern Sudan resulted from the penetration of the region by tribes who had already migrated from Arabia to Upper Egypt." See P. M. Holt and M. W. Daly, *The History of the Sudan from the Coming of Islam to the Present Day*, 3rd ed. (Boulder, Colo.: Lynne Rienner, 1979), 3, 23.

42. Ibn Khaldūn, *Muqaddimah*, 118.

43. Hasan, *Studies in Sudanese History*, 13.

44. Hasan, *The Arabs and the Sudan*, 143 (Nubia), 139 (Beja).

45. For an account of immigrants from West Africa, see Hasan, *Studies in Sudanese History*, 89, 197–98, 200; O'Fahey, *State and Society in Dar Fur*, 4–5, 118 (see intro., n. 4).

46. MacMichael, *History of the Arabs in the Sudan*, 1:83–84.

47. In all, West African immigration comprised a variety of peoples, including the Fulbe, Kanuri, Kanembu, Kotoko, and Maba. O'Fahey, *State and Society in Dar Fur*, 5; see also Abd al-Rahman Abubaker Ibrahim, "Development and Administration in Southern Darfur" (MS thesis, Political Science Department, Faculty of Economics and Social Studies, University of Khartoum, Dec. 1977), 333ff.

48. Al-Naqar, *The Pilgrimage Tradition in West Africa*, 91; Bawa Yamba, *Permanent Pilgrims*; Birks, *Across the Savannas to Mecca*, 62; cited in Gregory Mann and Baz Lecocq, "Between Empire, Umma, and Muslim Third World: The French Union and African Pilgrims to Mecca, 1946–1958," *Comparative Studies of South Asia, Africa, and the Middle East* 27, no. 2 (2007): 367–83.

49. O'Fahey, *State and Society in Dar Fur*, 4–5.

50. O'Fahey has observed that West African migration has been "unobtrusive" though "continuous." One may ask, Unobtrusive to whom? Presumably to the historian.

51. O'Fahey, *State and Society in Dar Fur*, 74.

52. He gives three examples to illustrate this development: the kingdom of Taqali in Kordofan, the Keira dynasty in Dar Fur, and a Muslim dynasty established in Wadai in the seventeenth century A.D. Hasan, *The Arabs and the Sudan*, 153–54.

53. "Many of the 19th c explorers and anthropologists oriented their knowledge of Africa from a background of the discovery of Ancient Egypt and it is not surprising that various theories . . . were formulated to indicate the links which may have existed between the civilizations of the Nile Valley

and East Africa prior to 1500 A.D." M. Posnansky, "Pre-nineteenth Century Contacts between the Sudan and East Africa, and the Nile Valley in Early Times," in *Sudan in Africa,* ed. Yusuf Fadl Hasan (Khartoum: Institute of African and Asian Studies, University of Khartoum, 1971), 51.

54. "The spread of Arabic flowed not only from the dispersion of Arabs but from the unification of the Nile by a government, the Funj Sultanate, that utilized Arabic as an official means of communication, and from the use of Arabic as a trade language." McHugh, *Holymen of the Blue Nile,* 9.

55. William Y. Adams, *Nubia: Corridor to Africa* (London: Allen Lane, 1977), 666, 667. Similarly, Bruce Trigger concluded on the basis of his archeological field study of lower Nubia: "The study of settlement patterns indicated greater continuity in the human occupation of lower Nubia than the cultural-historical approach had done, and suggested that cultural change frequently had occurred without major changes in ethnicity." Bruce G. Trigger, "Paradigms in Sudan Archaeology," *International Journal of African Historical Studies* 27, no. 2 (1994): 332, quoted in Mohamed A. Abusabib, "Art, politics, and cultural identification in Sudan," *Aesthetica Upsaliensia,* no. 8 (Uppsala: Uppsala Universitet, 2004): 49–50.

56. Bryan G. Haycock, "The Place of the Napatan-Meroitic Culture in the History of the Sudan and Africa," in Hasan, *Sudan in Africa,* 26–41.

57. B. G. Haycock, "Some Reflections on W. Y. Adams, 'Continuity and Change in Nubian Cultural History,' " *Sudan Notes and Records* 52 (1977): 116, 118; Abdel Salam Mohamed Sidahmed, "State and Ideology in the Funj Sultanate of Sennar, 1500–1821" (master's thesis, Department of Political Science, University of Khartoum, 1983), 23–24.

58. Adams, *Nubia,* 550–56, 584, 568, cited in Abdullahi Ali Ibrahim, "Breaking the Pen of Harold MacMichael: The Ja'aliyyin Identity Revisited," *International Journal of African Historical Studies* 21, no. 2 (1988): 225.

59. Adams, *Nubia,* 666–67.

60. McHugh, *Holymen of the Blue Nile,* 4.

61. Jay Lloyd Spaulding, "Kings of Sun and Shadow: A History of the Abdallab Provinces of the Northern Sinnar Sultanate, 1500–1800 A.D." (PhD diss., Columbia University, 1971), 55. Spaulding's position with regard to Arab migration into Sudan has remained consistent since the publication of O'Fahey and Spaulding, *Kingdoms of the Sudan,* although his strongest statement is contained in "End of Nubian Kingship," where he concludes (p. 23) that the "immigrant hordes of Bedouin Arabs" who allegedly overthrew Nubia in the thirteenth century should be "stricken from the historical record" in light of the Nubian character of the Funj monarchy.

62. Jay Spaulding, *The Heroic Age in Sinnar* (Trenton, N.J.: Red Sea Press, 2007), xvii; McHugh, *Holymen of the Blue Nile,* 4–5; Spaulding, "Kings of Sun and Shadow."

63. Sidahmed, "State and Ideology," 60.

64. Spaulding, *Heroic Age,* 81, 87, 67, 68. See also Jairus Banaji, "Islam, the Mediterranean and the Rise of Capitalism," *Historical Materialism* 15 (2007): 47–54.

65. Ibid., 167–68.
66. Ibid., 75, 124, 87.
67. Socially, a feature of the "new middle class" was constant "use of slaves as household servants." It became customary for bride wealth in a middle-class family to include a slave. As domestic slavery spread among the middle classes, there was "a gradual change in the role of women, who found themselves relieved of their traditional contributions to production." Symbolic of the changing status of middle-class women was the rise of a new social fiction, that women cannot swim, whereas swimming had been a skill "vital to rural folk in a land where cultivated islands were numerous but boats were few." The new respectability of middle-class women was accompanied by the adoption of a new dress, "the modern *tob,* an enveloping robe which covered not only the lower body but also the torso and head, a strikingly beautiful garment, but expensive and awkward, rendering most forms of physical labor impossible." In addition to domestic service, slaves were also set to work in their masters' fields. Spaulding, *Heroic Age,* 108.
68. Almost all the commodities merchants offered for exchange, "including gold, ivory, slaves, civet, and rhinoceros horn," came from the southern Funj kingdom. Even before the rise of the new middle class, the lion's share of nonagricultural commodities produced by the southern commoners passed directly to the nobility as feudal dues and, through them, as tribute to the central government: "For example, a subject who killed a leopard or who found an unusually large cache of gold dust must turn his bonanza over to the local lord, who would reward him with more modest gifts appropriate to his station." Spaulding, *Heroic Age,* 68, 59.
69. Ibid., 60.
70. Ibid., 203.
71. Ibid.
72. Even MacMichael was constrained to acknowledge this in his 1928 lecture:

> Those who settled at an early date in the riverain districts without displacing the earlier inhabitants *en bloc,* would tend to become absorbed racially and culturally by them; but away from the river, tribal life survived to a far greater extent. . . . Briefly, it may be said, the main feature of the ethnic history of the northern and central Sudan from the end of the 13th century onwards has been the gradual coalition of Arab and black (and, in the northern riverain districts, Berberine), into a series of groups, the justification for whose universal claim to be Arabs varies widely. It is really strong among the sallow camel and sheep-owning nomads of the north, and even among the dark, hawk-eyed cattle and horse-breeding Baggara and certain of the northern riverain groups, but it is slight among most of the sedentary villagers. To speak in very general terms, these latter are the offspring of mixed marriages, whereas the darker strain often noticeable among the nomads is due to concubinage.

A bizarre notion this, which makes ancestral distinctions based on whether union was the result of intermarriage or concubinage. MacMichael, "Coming of the Arabs to the Sudan," 16–17.

73. Wendy R. James, "Social Assimilation and Changing Identity in the Southern Funj," in *Sudan in Africa,* ed. Yusuf Fadl Hasan (Khartoum: Institute of African and Asian Studies, University of Khartoum, 1971), 198–208.

74. The second group to maintain cultural independence from the Arab-Funj complex are the Uduk-speaking people, who number about ten thousand. The Uduk combine a remote location, virtual economic self-sufficiency, and a different system of values based on matrilineal organization with a historical assertion of autonomy in the face of severe slave-raiding.

75. James, "Social Assimilation," 210.

76. This discussion of cattle nomads is based on Cunnison, *Baggara Arabs,* 19–20, 25, 11–12, 168, 2 (see intro., n. 10).

77. Ibid., 2.

78. Ibid., 1.

79. Jay Spaulding, personal communication.

80. Quoted in the Save Darfur Coalition's video, *Darfur: A 21st Century Genocide,* cited in Eichler-Levine and Hicks, " 'As Americans against Genocide,' " 725 (see chap. 2, n. 25).

81. When the Baggara associate ancestral names with an ancient cradleland such as Arabia of the Prophet's time, says Cunnison, "the effect is to produce respectability out of antiquity." The difference between literate and nonliterate societies for Cunnison is that the latter claim a more immediate connection, whereas the former take the trouble to elaborate a longer journey: "With pagan tribes the connection is often immediate—the founder of a major significant contemporary group may be said to have been only one generation removed from some divinity. The Arabs, however, belong to a culture in which learned men keep genealogies and take more stock of the passing of generations: to suggest that the founder of a contemporary lineage was actually the son of a man of the Prophet's time would lead only to disbelief on the part of the people who are to be impressed by the claim." Cunnison, "Classification by Genealogy," 194, 189.

82. Ibrahim, "Breaking the Pen of Harold MacMichael," 221.

83. Branislaw Malinowski, in *Myth in Primitive Psychology* (Westport, Conn: Negro Universities Press, 1971, c. 1926), argued against older anthropological theories that claimed that myth was a primitive form of speculation about the natural world or a confused recollection of history. Malinowski maintained that myths must be regarded as charters—claims to territorial ownership and thus justifications of social and political hierarchy in the present. This line of reasoning was followed by E. E. Evans-Pritchard, who argued in his classic *The Nuer* (New York: Oxford University Press, 1969, c. 1940) that lineages were not historical facts but structural indicators of different group relationships in the present. Paul Bohannan, who worked among the Tiv in West Africa, wrote quite explicitly in the 1950s on "genealogical charters," making the same argument about origin claims.

See his *Justice and Judgment Among the Tiv* (New York: Oxford University Press, 1957). I am grateful to Talal Asad for this insight.

84. Talal Asad, personal communication, June 2, 2008.

85. Hasan, *The Arabs and the Sudan,* 176.

86. Sudan People's Liberation Army (SPLA) / Sudan People's Liberation Movement (SPLM), Dept. of Information, Feb. 1989, in Abdul Ghaffar M. Ahmed, 83–90. What many Sudanese object to are the chauvinistic claims made by the power elite about the content of Sudanese Arabism that transcends culture into race. See Sharif Harir, "Recycling the Past in the Sudan: An Overview of Political Decay," in *Short-Cut to Decay: The Case of the Sudan,* ed. Sharif Harir and Terje Tvedt, 10–68 (Uppsala: Scandinavian Institute of African Studies, 1994), 21, 18–19.

87. MacMichael, *History of the Arabs in the Sudan,* 1:84; A. B. Theobald, *Ali Dinar: Last Sultan of Darfur, 1898–1916* (London: Longman, 1965), 7.

88. Theobald, *Ali Dinar,* 7, 9; Daldoum, *The Dynamics of Ethnic Group Relations in Darfur,* 24–25 (see intro., n. 9).

89. Daldoum, *Dynamics of Ethnic Group Relations in Darfur,* 25; Theobald, *Ali Dinar,* 9.

90. Daldoum, *Dynamics of Ethnic Group Relations in Darfur,* 26.

91. "The claim to an Arab identity," writes Jérôme Tubaina, "has less to do with the above [cultural] criteria than it does with often-fictional patrilineal lineages that lead back to mythical Arab forbearers." As Neil McHugh notes, "Arab identity signified, above all, an Arab genealogy (*nasab*)." See Jérôme Tubaina, "Darfur: A War for Land?" in *War in Darfur and the Search for Peace,* ed. Alex de Waal (Cambridge, Mass.: Harvard University Press, 2007), 70.

92. As Ian Cunnison has noted, "The study of people after people shows that genealogies are altered to make them suitable reflections of group arrangements at any given time. These alterations may take the form of elision of generations, the merging together of collateral branches, the incorporation of total strangers, and the exclusion of groups who, having moved away, are no longer relevant." Cunnison, "Classification by Genealogy," 192.

93. Abdullahi Ali Ibrahim has pointed out that William Adams understood genealogies in a nonliteral manner, as "indicating the segmentary lineage system of the Arabs which functions as a structure of non-government; that is, the fiction of universal kinship takes the place of formal government institutions." Adams, *Nubia,* 564–65, quoted in Ibrahim, "Breaking the Pen of Harold MacMichael," 219.

Chapter Four

1. On the Sudanic states, see Roland Oliver and J. D. Fage, *A Short History of Africa* (New York: Penguin, 1962), 44, 33, 31. Tor Irstam, *The King of Ganda* (Stockholm: Ethnographical Museum of Sweden, 1944), discusses the main ritual aspects of "sacral kingship" in Africa, including Darfur. See also "Executive Summary," in *Environmental Degradation: Darfur,* proceedings

of the Environmental Degradation as a Cause of Conflict in Darfur conference, Khartoum, Dec. 2004 (Addis Ababa, Ethiopia: University for Peace,
Africa Programme, 2006), 20.

2. Irstam, *King of Ganda,* 36–37.
3. Spaulding, "End of Nubian Kingship in the Sudan," 18 (see chap. 3, n. 40).
4. Jay Spaulding and Lidwein Kapteijns, "Land Tenure and the State in the
   Pre-colonial Sudan," *Northeast African Studies* 9, no. 1 (2002): 4, 36, 38–39.
5. Oliver and Fage, *Short History of Africa,* 32.
6. See *The Encyclopaedia Britannica,* 667, cited in Daly, *Darfur's Sorrow,*
   22–23 (see intro., n. 5).
7. H. G. Balfour-Paul, *History and Antiquities of Darfur,* museum pamphlet
   no. 3 (Khartoum: Sudan Antiquities Service, 1955), 3.
8. Convention points to a king prior to Sulayman, a descendant of an Arab
   named Ahmed al-Ma'Qur who married the Fur king's daughter. It is
   through the system of matrilineal descent that the first Muslim king, Sultan
   Daali, is said to have been born. Al-Tunisi, *Tuslhidh,* 143, cited in Hamid,
   "Local Authorities and Social Change," 11 (see intro., n. 6). O'Fahey has
   suggested that the impetus to change from tribal chiefdom to the supratribal sultanate of Dar Fur probably came from the long-distance caravan
   trade. The agent of that transformation was "an Arab or Arabized Muslim
   who intermarried with the chiefly family." Their son, Sulayman Solon-
   dungo (Sulayman the Arab), appears in various traditional accounts as the
   person who drove out the Tunjur and whose rule is associated with the
   establishment of Islam as a court cult. He is described as uniting the Fur
   and non-Fur peoples of the Jebel Marra region and conquering the area
   around the mountain range. R. S. O'Fahey, "Religion and Trade in the
   Kayra Sultanate of Dar Fur," in *Sudan in Africa,* ed. Yusuf Fadl Hasan
   (Khartoum: Institute of African and Asian Studies, University of Khartoum, 1971), 88. Theobald, *Ali Dinar,* 17 (see chap. 3, n. 87).
9. O'Fahey, *State and Society in Dar Fur,* 11 (see intro., n. 4).
10. Ibid., 8, 35.
11. A number of Fur sultans were born of Zaghawa mothers (ibid., 14–28),
    and a number of Fur princesses were married out of the royal clan. See
    Sharif Harir, " 'Arab Belt' vs. 'African Belt': Ethno-Political Conflict in Dar-
    fur and the Regional Political Factors," in *Short-Cut to Decay: The Case of
    the Sudan,* ed. Sharif Harir and Terje Tvedt (Uppsala: Scandinavian Insti-
    tute of African Studies, 1994), 152.
12. O'Fahey, *State and Society in Dar Fur,* 146.
13. Hamid, "Local Authorities and Social Change," 11.
14. "When the sultanate was restored in 1898 by Ali Dinar, he spent most of
    his reign driving the nomads back, until he was killed by the British in
    1916. They then discovered that they had no alternative but to continue
    his policy." R. S. O'Fahey, "Darfur: A Complex Ethnic Reality with a Long
    History," *International Herald Tribune,* May 15, 2004. See also Atta
    El-Battahani, "Towards a Typology and Periodization Scheme of Conflicts
    in Darfur Region in Sudan," in *Understanding the Crisis in Darfur: Listen-
    ing to Sudanese Voices,* ed. Abdel Ghaffar M. Ahmed and Leif Manger

(Bergen, Norway: University of Bergen, Centre for Development Studies, 2006), 37; R. S. O'Fahey, "Conflict in Darfur: Historical and Contemporary Perspectives," in *Environmental Degradation: Darfur,* proceedings of the Environmental Degradation as a Cause of Conflict in Darfur conference, Khartoum, Dec. 2004 (Addis Ababa, Ethiopia: University for Peace, Africa Programme, 2006), 25. See Harir, " 'Arab Belt' vs. 'African Belt,' " 153.

15. O'Fahey, "Conflict in Darfur," 25.

16. O'Fahey, *State and Society in Dar Fur,* 49–50, 58–59.

17. "The estate system . . . was a patron-client relationship defined by land or community rather than a thorough-going exploitative system comparable to the irrigation-based systems of the Middle East." Ibid., 49.

18. United Nations, Darfur Joint Assessment Mission, Track 1, Musa Adam Abdul-Jalil with Gert Ludeking, "Situation Analysis of Land Tenure Issues: Problems and Implications of Darfur Early Recovery" (Dec. 2006), 3; Musa Adam Abdul-Jalil, "Land Tenure, Land Use and Inter-ethnic Conflicts in Darfur," in *Understanding the Crisis in Darfur: Listening to Sudanese Voices,* ed. Abdel Ghaffar M. Ahmed and Leif Manger (Bergen, Norway: University of Bergen, Centre for Development Studies, 2006), 24–25; O'Fahey, *State and Society in Dar Fur,* 54–55.

19. Quoted in Jay Spaulding, "Conflict in Dar Fur: A View from the Old Sudan," *Sudan Studies Association Newsletter* 24, no. 2 (Feb. 2006): 21.

20. O'Fahey, *State and Society in Dar Fur,* 53, 54, 57–58.

21. Yagoub Abdalla Mohamed, "Land Tenure, Land Use and Conflicts in Darfur," in *Environmental Degradation: Darfur,* proceedings of the Environmental Degradation as a Cause of Conflict in Darfur conference, Khartoum, Dec. 2004 (Addis Ababa, Ethiopia: University for Peace, Africa Programme, 2006), 59.

22. O'Fahey, *State and Society in Dar Fur,* 65, 57–58.

23. Take, for example, the two types of landed estates that existed in Borno. The first was a type of estate held by a class of religious notables (the *fuqara*), populated and cultivated by their followers. The rulers of Songhai on the Middle Niger granted estates and privileged status to Muslim holy men in the fifteenth and sixteenth centuries, as did the rulers of Kanem/Borno when they granted *mahrams,* or immunities, to a number of *faqih* clans. The second type of landed estate was cultivated by slaves. These *abidiyya* (royal slave) settlements were similar to the Fulani *rumada,* or the princely estates, of Songhai, as described in a French report of about 1798. Many Dar Fur documents refer to estates, *hawakir,* with their slaves, where the actual social position of slaves is more serflike. Slaves were given some land to cultivate; they married and lived on the land and paid an annual tribute to the king, in whose domain lay the land. The tribute consisted of a certain number of children born from their marriages and *dhurra,* or millet grain, from their cultivations. See Hasan, *Studies in Sudanese History,* 64 (see chap. 3, n. 15); and O'Fahey, *State and Society,* 108.

24. O'Fahey, *State and Society in Dar Fur,* 50–51.

25. Donald Crummy has argued that the Ethiopian peasant was not a serf, for he was not bound to the land, nor to the master, nor was he subject to for-

mal disabilities before the law, nor prohibited from advancing himself socially, including through marriage into the elite. In the kingdom of Funj, however, the producer was akin to a serf: Called a *masakin,* he could not demonstrate any sign of opulence in public; his testimony was worth only a fraction of that of a nobleman; he could not seek justice except through a nobleman; he was legally barred from marrying into the nobility; and, finally, he could not buy or sell land. His only right was to petition the lord to transfer his dues and services to another master. See Spaulding and Kapteijns, "Land Tenure and the State," 47, 49, 50.

26. Abdul-Jalil, "Land Tenure, Land Use and Inter-ethnic Conflicts in Darfur," 24; see also O'Fahey, *State and Society in Dar Fur,* 61.

27. It is noteworthy that the sultans of Dar Fur and Wadai claimed the title *amir al-mu'minin* ("commander of the faithful") as claimed by the first four caliphs of Islam, but the king of the Funj did not. Spaulding, "Precolonial Islam in the Eastern Sudan," 120 (see chap. 3, n. 37).

28. Alex de Waal, "Who Are the Darfurians? Arab and African Identities, Violence and External Engagement," *African Affairs* 104 (Apr. 2005): 184.

29. O'Fahey, *State and Society in Dar Fur,* 148.

30. Yusuf Fadl Hasan, "External Influences and the Progress of Islamization in the Eastern Sudan between the 15th and 18th Centuries," in *Sudan in Africa,* ed. Yusuf Fadl Hasan (Khartoum: University of Khartoum, Institute of African and Asian Studies, 1971), 73.

31. O'Fahey, *State and Society in Dar Fur,* 120.

32. Ahmed Kamal el-Din, "Islam and Islamism in Darfur," in *War in Darfur and the Search for Peace,* ed. Alex de Waal (Cambridge, Mass.: Harvard University Press, 2007), 94, 95; see also O'Fahey, *State and Society in Dar Fur,* 121.

33. *Fuqara* is plural for *faqir* (literally, "the poor one" and more poetically "he who is in spiritual need") or *faqi* which can refer to sufi sheikhs as a humble recognition. In more contemporary times, it has come to refer to the followers of these sheikhs and not really the sheikhs themselves.

34. Sharif Harir, "Re-cycling the Past in the Sudan: An Overview of Political Decay," in *Short-Cut to Decay: The Case of the Sudan,* ed. Sharif Harir and Terje Tvedt (Uppsala: Scandinavian Institute of African Studies, 1994), 29.

35. Spaulding, "Precolonial Islam in the Eastern Sudan," 124.

36. There was the *zawiya* associated with the Qadiriyya order, traced to the influence of Sheikh Taj al-Din al-Bahari, the Sufi leader and follower of the Qadiriyya order (after 'Abd al-Qadir al-Jilani, 1077–1166) who met Dawud b. 'Abd al-Jalil, a Sudanese merchant from Arbaji, during the pilgrimage in Mecca about 1577 and was invited to visit the Funj kingdom. There he stayed for seven years, during which he initiated a number of prominent Sudanese into the Qadiriyya order. Another zawiya, associated with the Khatmiyya, is traced to the influence of Hejaz-based Muhammad Uthman al-Mirghani (1793–1853), disciple of the great Moroccan mystic Ahmad b. Idris al-Fasi. The Khatmiyya, however, did not come into its own until the colonial period. The Qadiriyya order was later rivaled by a *zawiya* linked to the Tijaniyya order, founded by Ahmad al-Tijani (1737–1815) at Ayn Madi in Algeria. Although the Tijaniyya order was introduced in the Sudan from

Egypt, by Muhammad al-Mukhtar al-Shankiti, who traded in Egypt and the Sudan, most Tijaniyya followers came from communities of "westerners" in Dar Fur, Kordofan, and along the Blue Nile. Though a North African order, the Tijaniyya spread across the Sahara into Hausaland at the time of the jihad of al-Hajj Umar. From Hausaland, it took an easterly direction. Other orders, such as Shadhiliyya and Sammaniyya, were also introduced into the Funj Sultanate. Hasan, "External Influences and the Progress of Islamization," 79; McHugh, *Holymen of the Blue Nile,* 131; Hasan, "External Influences and the Progress of Islamization," in *Sudan in Africa,* 80; see also Hasan, *Studies in Sudanese History,* 197.

37. O'Fahey, *State and Society in Dar Fur,* 115.
38. Hasan, *Studies in Sudanese History,* 38.
39. McHugh, *Holymen of the Blue Nile,* 18.
40. Ibid., 10.
41. First came "Shaykh Mahmud al-Araki from Egypt and taught the people to observe the laws of the *Idda;* then came A. H. Shaykh Ibrahim al-Bulad, also from Egypt, in the second half of the 10th (16th) c., moving to the Shayqiyya country where he taught Khalil and the Risala, spreading learning and knowledge of the law to the Gezira. After a short time, there followed Shaykh Taj al-Din al-Bahari from Baghdad. He introduced Tariq al-Qawm, the path of the Sufis into the Funj country." Another religious reformer was Ibrahim al-Bulad b. Jabir, born on the island of Taranj in the Shayqiyya country, who read Muslim law under the leader of the Maliki school in Cairo. With the completion of his studies, he returned to his country about 1570, where he began teaching the two Maliki textbooks: the *Risala* of Abu Zayd al-Qayrawani (d. 996) and the *Mukhtasar* of Khalil b. Ishaq (d. 1563). He was the first scholar to introduce the teaching of the *Mukhtasar* in the Funj kingdom. Hasan, *Studies in Sudanese History,* 32, 33.
42. Hasan, *Studies in Sudanese History,* 41, 33; Hasan, "External Influences and the Progress of Islamization," 82.
43. Hasan, "External Influences and the Progress of Islamization," 84.
44. O'Fahey, *State and Society in Dar Fur,* 118.
45. Hasan, "External Influences and the Progress of Islamization," 85; de Waal, "Who Are the Darfurians?" 185–86.
46. J. S. Tirmingham places Darfur and Wadai within his eastern, or Nilotic, cycle of Islamic penetration, which is distinguished by profound Arabization and the widespread influence of the Sufi *tariqas.* Despite considerable political and religious influence emanating from the west, he argues that the main impetus toward Islamization came from the Nile Valley. See J. S. Tirmingham, *Islam in West Africa* (Oxford: Clarendon Press, 1959), 46. Yet there appear to be no references to *tariqas* in Dar Fur before the nineteenth century; O'Fahey, "Religion and Trade," 91.
47. O'Fahey, "Religion and Trade," 88; Burr and Collins, *Darfur: The Long Road to Disaster,* 17–18 (see chap. 1, n. 74).
48. Hasan, "External Influences and the Progress of Islamization," 84.
49. Hasan, *The Arabs and the Sudan,* 44 (see chap. 3, n. 18); Hasan, *Studies in Sudanese History,* 64.

50. The demand was not restricted to Egypt; the Hejaz in Saudi Arabia was also an important market. Ibid., 192–93.

51. Ibid., 44, 43; Hasan, *Studies in Sudanese History,* 17.

52. This paragraph and the next three are based on Hasan, *The Arabs and the Sudan,* 44, 47, 124.

53. Hasan, *Studies in Sudanese History,* 73, 65, 62; see also O'Fahey, "Religion and Trade," 94.

54. Father Krump writes: "In all of Africa, as far as the Moorish lands are concerned, Sinnar is close to being the greatest trading city. Caravans are continually arriving from Nubia, from across the Red Sea from India, Ethiopia, Dar Fur, Borno, from Cairo, Dunqula, Fezzan and other kingdoms. . . . Furthermore, every day at the public market, slave-men and women of every age are sold like cattle." Quoted in Hasan, *Studies in Sudanese History,* 68.

55. Ibid., 91.

56. O'Fahey, *State and Society in Dar Fur,* 11.

57. Hasan, *Studies in Sudanese History,* 72; O'Fahey, *State and Society in Dar Fur,* 144.

58. Jay Spaulding, "Pastoralism, Slavery, Commerce, Culture and the Fate of the Nubians of Northern and Central Kordofan under Dar Fur Rule, ca. 1750–ca. 1850," *International Journal of African Historical Studies* 39, no. 3 (2006): 408.

59. O'Fahey, "Religion and Trade," 92.

60. Ibid., 93; Umar A. Al-Naqar, "The Historical Background to the 'Sudan Road,' " in *Sudan in Africa,* ed. Yusuf Fadl Hasan (Khartoum: University of Khartoum, Institute of African and Asian Studies, 1971), 98.

61. Al-Naqar, *Pilgrimage Tradition in West Africa,* 137, 152–63, cited in Gregory Mann and Baz Lecocq, "Between Empire, Umma and Muslim Third World: The French Union and African Pilgrims to Mecca, 1946–58," *Comparative Studies of South Asia, Africa, and the Middle East* 27, no. 2 (2007).

62. Young, Osman, Aklilu, Dale, Badri, and Fuddle, *Darfur—Livelihoods under Siege,* 3–4 (see chap. 1, n. 69). See also O'Fahey, *State and Society in Dar Fur,* 135; 33; Al-Naqar, "The Historical Background," 99.

63. O'Fahey, *State and Society in Dar Fur,* 44–45.

64. Ibid., 139.

65. For example, there was a policy of taking the sons of important tribal chiefs to court, first to be socialized and become accustomed to royal traditions, and second to be trained in the contemporary art of government. This policy served not only to inculcate loyalty in future tribal leaders but also to ensure that these young boys were kept as hostages under the control of the sultan just in case their tribes revolted. Abd al-Rahman Abubaker Ibrahim, "Development and Administration in Southern Darfur" (master's thesis, Political Science Department, Faculty of Economics and Social Studies, University of Khartoum, Dec. 1977), 29. For similar reasons, the British district commissioner in Nyala had followed the same policy of bringing the sons of tribal chiefs under their supervision. The British administrators called them "the Green Hat Boys."

66. Few of the titles that signified the administrative structure created by the Keira sultans—titles such as *mayram, habboba,* and *takanawi* as well as *fashir*—were Fur in origin. Rather, they suggest "a floating stock of central Sudanic titles and ideas that were inherited and adapted by the Keira to their own needs." On the *magdume,* see O'Fahey, *State and Society in Dar Fur,* 70–71, 87; Hamid, "Local Authorities and Social Change," 13 (see intro., n. 6).

67. During the reign of Sultan Muhammad al-Fadl, one of these provincial governors (Abu Sheikh Dali), named Kurra Gabr al Dar, had revolted. A. A. Arkell, "The History of Darfur, 1200–1700," *Sudan Notes and Records* 33 (1952), 201. (Arkell's study was published in volumes 32 and 33 of *Sudan Notes and Records.*)

68. O'Fahey, *State and Society in Dar Fur,* 69, 90, 81–83.

69. Fines provided a constant source of revenue for the chiefs. They remained the linchpin of Fur customary law, grounded in a tradition that traces its beginning to the quasi-legendary sultan Daali, who, in the late fifteenth or early sixteenth century, is said to have codified it in the so-called *kitab* or *qanun dali.* Ibid., 109.

70. Daly, *Darfur's Sorrow,* 26–27.

71. Kurra was the only slave in Dar Fur's history to achieve a quasi-independent position of power, but the brevity of his hold on it demonstrated the inherent fragility of the slave's position. Free notables held and inherited office by right and had kin connections to sustain them, slaves at the pleasure of their masters; . . . Gifted individuals from the slave caste were raised up by the sultans precisely because they were more tractable than the hereditary nobility, which drew its strength from ethnic bonds and the possession of great estates. And the Keira sultans had particular cause to be wary of the later power of their chiefs since two of their number, Umar Lel and Abu'l-Qasim, had met their deaths indirectly at the hands of the chiefs.

See O'Fahey, *State and Society in Dar Fur,* 39–40, 41.

72. The figures for Sinnar are from Jay Spaulding, "Slavery, Land Tenure and Social Class in the Northern Turkish Sudan," *International Journal of African Historical Studies* 15, no. 1 (1982): 8–9. During Sinnar's heyday, the sultan had the exclusive right to caravanning. He did so through the royal merchants and had trade relations with countries such as Arabia, Ethiopia, and India. Sidahmed, "State and Ideology," 71 (see chap. 3, n. 7). On slavery in Darfur, see O'Fahey, "Religion and Trade," 95. Walz reckoned that the camel trade constituted 25 percent of the total value of goods imported from Dar Fur. Hasan, *Studies in Sudanese History,* 90–91, 95.

73. Spaulding, "Slavery, Land Tenure and Social Class," 12.

74. This paragraph and the next are based on O'Fahey, *State and Society in Dar Fur,* 45, 18, 12.

75. Nachtigal, 1971, 70–71, cited in O'Fahey, *State and Society in Dar Fur,* 12.

76. O'Fahey, *State and Society in Dar Fur,* 93–94.

77. On slavery in the Funj Sultanate, see O'Fahey and Spaulding, *Kingdoms of the Sudan* (London: Methuen, 1974), 56; Sidahmed, "State and Ideology," 65–66; Spaulding and Kapteijns, "Land Tenure and the State," 51.

78. Ibid.

79. Ibid.

80. This paragraph is based on Hasan, *Arabs and the Sudan,* 47, 46; O'Fahey, "Conflict in Darfur," 31; O'Fahey, "Religion and Trade," 92–93.

81. de Waal, "Who Are the Darfurians?" 183.

82. Turkish colonial rule in southern Sinnar, particularly in those districts governed directly, greatly stimulated the spread of the slave trade. From a legal perspective, slaves in Turkish Sinnar were classified as beasts along with other livestock, or occasionally "talking animals." These brutes in human form were given bizarre and derogatory names: "Slaves of the Master." The European officers attempted to justify their own active collaboration in the colonial slave system by advancing the theory—historically incorrect—that domestic and agricultural slavery had always been an integral part of northern Sudanese society and could therefore be eradicated only very, very slowly. From these apologetics have emerged different historiographical traditions on slavery: If Europeans blame the *Jallaba* (native merchants), the Sudanese tend to see the *Jallaba* as the carriers of civilization. Spaulding, *The Heroic Age in Sinnar,* 157, 158; O'Fahey, *State and Society in Dar Fur,* 12, 100.

83. M. W. Daly and Jane R. Hogan, *Images of Empire: Photographic Sources for the British in the Sudan* (Boston: Brill, 2005), 8–9.

84. Spaulding, "Slavery, Land Tenure and Social Class," 4–8.

85. "Sudan Days and Ways," quoted in Al-Shingietti, "Images of the Sudan," 76–77 (see chap. 3, n. 3).

86. Ahmed Mohammed Kani, *The Intellectual Origin of Islamic Jihad in Nigeria* (London: Al Hoda, 1988); de Waal, "Who Are the Darfurians?" 188, 189–90.

87. The Turco-Egyptian rule is described as the most brutal and exacting of the periods of colonial rule (1821–85) that have dominated the Sudan. As early as the first years the Jaaliyyin tribes of the Matamma area, under the leadership of Mac Nimir, were to revolt, reacting to humiliation by Ismail Pasha, the son of the viceroy of Egypt Ismail Pasha, and burning him along with his troops. The brother-in-law of the deceased, the Difterdar, who was in Kordofan at the time, upon hearing the news went on a rampage scourging the White Nile area and devastating the Hassaniyyia tribes among others. The levels of dissent were already high when the Mahdi started calling for a revolt in 1880 and, coincidentally, from the Aba Island in the White Nile. Adam Ardaib Idris, "Political Culture and Cultural Hegemony: Questions of Identity and National Integration in the Sudan" (MS thesis, Political Science Department, University of Khartoum, Mar. 1996), 50–51; O'Fahey, *State and Society in Dar Fur,* 12.

88. John Iliffe, *A Modern History of Tanganyika* (Cambridge and New York: Cambridge University Press, 1979) and Terence O. Ranger, *African Voice in*

Southern Rhodesia; both cited in T. Hodgkin, "Mahdism, Messianism and Marxism in an African Setting," in *Sudan in Africa,* ed. Yusuf Fadl Hasan (Khartoum: Institute of African and Asian Studies, University of Khartoum, 1971), 121.

89. Burr and Collins, *Darfur: Long Road to Disaster,* 9.
90. Both quoted in Al-Shingietti, "Images of the Sudan," 96.
91. Churchill, *River War,* 34 (see chap. 3, n. 8).
92. Burr and Collins, *Darfur: Long Road to Disaster,* 11, 18.
93. Noah Salomon, personal communication.
94. Ibrahim, "Development and Administration in Southern Darfur," 36 (see chap. 3, n. 47).
95. This paragraph is based on C.A.G. Wallis, private papers (provided personally to the author in London, Apr. 1964); Sir James Robertson, "Local Government in the Sudan" (lecture, Middle East School, Jerusalem, July 10, 1945), 1; Khalaf, "British Policy," 44–45, 46–47 (see chap. 3, n. 29); MacMichael, *History of the Arabs in the Sudan,* 2:315 (see chap. 3, n. 9).
96. Young, Osman, Aklilu, Dale, Badri, and Fuddle, *Darfur—Livelihoods under Siege,* 5–6.
97. Harold MacMichael, "The Problem of the Anglo-Egyptian Sudan" (speech, Royal Empire Society, Mar. 12, 1913, Sudan Archive: SAD 723/13/1).
98. Daly and Hogan, *Images of Empire,* 13–14.

Chapter Five

1. See Samir Amin, *Accumulation on a World Scale: A Critique of the Theory of Underdevelopment,* trans. Brian Pearce (New York: Monthly Review Press, 1974); Walter Rodney, *How Europe Underdeveloped Africa* (Washington, D.C.: Howard University Press, 1974).
2. Rome redefined itself as an empire immediately after conquering the world as a republic/city. A distinction thereafter emerged in the way in which the eastern and western halves of the empire were ruled. In so far as the east had been ruled by Hellenized dynasties (originally established by Alexander), it was ruled through intermediaries, like Herod in Palestine or Cleopatra in Egypt, or through individuals or groups (potential intermediaries) on whom Rome conferred the rights of a citizen. In contrast, the western empire (e.g., Roman Britain) was all about conquering and civilizing barbarians and about literally establishing Roman colonies in their midst. (I am indebted to Bob Meister for this clarification.) The distinction between Roman and "provincial" law after A.D. 200 is not quite that between civil and "customary" law in the British empire. Whereas the Romans reproduced the law of the provinces for pragmatic reasons, the British combined this pragmatism with an active shaping of customary laws to give it a specific content and boundary (in Africa, "tribal" and "racial").
3. H. A. MacMichael, "Tribes of the Sudan," Sudan Archive, SAD 403/10/29-40.

4. Part 1, Background and Method, 15; Methods, vol. 1, 15, 259; *Census of Sudan, 1953.* In the final report, the number of "races or people" was increased to nine. These were: Arab, Beja, Nubiyin, "mainly Nilotic," "mainly Nilo-Hamitic," "mainly Sudanic," "Westerners," "foreigners with Sudanese status," and "foreigners with non-Sudanese status." Background and Methods, vol. 1, 160–61. The category "foreigners" excluded West Africans: "It is extremely difficult to find out the nationality of 'Westerners'—i.e., of persons from Nigeria and French Equatorial and West Africa. Many have lived in Sudan for years without having applied to the Ministry of the Interior for Sudanese citizenship. Moreover, answers to questions about whether a person or his parents arrived in the Sudan before 1898 are not in the least likely to be reliable: firstly, because they often would not know; and, secondly, because even if they did, their ardour for Sudanese citizenship might induce them to distort the facts. Of necessity, they were recorded as Sudanese if they answered 'Sudanese.'" Part 1, Background and Method, 16, *Census of Sudan, 1953.*

5. For all figures, see "Ninth Report of the Preliminary Findings of the Census," table 4: "Language Spoken at Home," and table 7: "Tribal Group or Nationality Group," 7–10, 23–24. *Census of Sudan, 1953.*

6. Gunnar Haaland, "Nomadism as an Economic Career among the Sedentaries of the Sudan Savannah Belt," in *Essays in Sudan Ethnography,* ed. Ian Cunnison and Wendy James, presented to Sir Edward Evans-Pritchard (London: C. Hurst & Co., 1972), 151–52, 162–63, 168. This source is the basis of the discussion in this and the following paragraph. The Baggara are sometimes referred to as the Baqqara in the literature.

7. For a fuller discussion, see Mamdani, *When Victims Become Killers,* chap. 2 (see chap. 3, n. 1).

8. In all, the population of Sudan was divided into five races: "Arab," "Beja and Small Hamitic Groups," "Nubians," "Negroes," and "Other Negroid 'Westerners.'" The last race was divided into three groups: "Darfurian Negroids," "French Equatorials," and "Nigerians" living in Darfur.

9. *Census of the Sudan, 1953.*

10. Dr. Elshafie Khidir Saeid, "Darfur: The Crisis and the Tragedy," Communist Party of Sudan (mimeo, Khartoum, Sudan), 1.

11. Burr and Collins, *Darfur: Long Road to Disaster,* 18 (see chap. 1, n. 74).

12. Ali Dinar's attempted restoration of a Fur monarchy led to a chaotic situation, one of continuous civil war, and this underlined the urgent need to restore order. It is this imperative that explained the elements of continuity between Ali Dinar's rule and that of the old sultanate. Ali Dinar set about ruling through slaves, generals, and confidants sent out with war bands on an ad hoc basis. O'Fahey, *State and Society in Dar Fur,* 90 (see intro., n. 4). At the same time, he fell back on Mahdist officials to run his state administration: To take but two examples, he kept Arabi Dafallah, the former Mahdist general, with him at court and retained Hamad Abd al-Qadir in the same post as he had held under the Mahdiyya, that of the deputy judge (*na'ib shari*). O'Fahey, *State and Society in Dar Fur,* 126. At the same time,

he sought to control the *fuqara* (holy men) by organizing them formally, district by district, parallel to the local administration, under *muqaddams* who were held responsible for their group's behavior and discipline. Ibrahim, "Development and Administration in Southern Darfur," 36 (see chap. 3, n. 47); O'Fahey, *State and Society in Dar Fur,* 90, 126, 127–28; United Nations, "Dimensions of Challenge for Darfur," working draft, Dec. 30, 2006, 4; United Nations, Darfur Joint Assessment Mission—Track 1, "Darfur Early Recovery, Darfur Conflict Analysis," draft report, chap. 2, Dec. 19, 2006, 3.

13. Ibrahim, "Development and Administration in Southern Darfur," 103–4.

14. M. Abd al-Rahim, *Imperialism and Nationalism in the Sudan* (Oxford: 1969), 41–51; Ibrahim, "Development and Administration in Southern Darfur," 104–5, 107–8.

15. Ronald Robinson, "Non-European Foundations of European Imperialism: Sketch for a Theory of Collaboration," in *Studies in the Theory of Imperialism,* ed. R. F. Owen and B. Sutcliffe (London: Longman, 1966), 135.

16. G.M.A. Bakheit, "British Administration and Sudanese Nationalism, 1919–1939" (PhD diss., St. John's College, Cambridge University, 1965), 23–24.

17. Ibid., 29.

18. Ibid., 26.

19. M. Shibeika, *The Independent Sudan* (New York: Robert Speller & Sons, 1959), 476.

20. Bakheit, "British Administration and Sudanese Nationalism," 33.

21. Khalaf, "British Policy," 102–3 (see chap. 3, n. 29).

22. "Sir Harold MacMichael, an Outstanding Colonial Administrator" (obituary), *Times,* Sept. 22, 1969.

23. Harold MacMichael, "Indirect Rule for Pagan Communities," Sudan Archive, SAD 586/1/1. All quotes in this paragraph are from this source.

24. Cd. 5467 of 1911, p. 47, quoted in Lugard, *The Dual Mandate in British Tropical Africa,* 216, cited in MacMichael, "Indirect Rule." There followed a question: "Are they not, it may be asked, so deeply imbued with elements of blind savagery, treachery and ignorance that, if those elements were removed, no appreciable value would attach to what was left?" The answer came by way of another quotation, this time from a Cambridge professor, Pollard, author of *The Cambridge Modern History* (vol. II, chapter 6): what makes for stable government is "not reason . . . not law . . . still less is it force; it is mainly custom and habit. Without a voluntary and unreasoning adherence to custom and deference to authority, all society and all government would be impossible." MacMichael stressed the importance of "unreasoning adherence" when it came to "pagan character," which he claimed was "essentially feudal in [his] instincts," why it is "useless to approach him with abstract ideas of Liberty, Fraternity, Equality."

25. *The Cambridge Modern History,* vol. 2, chap. 6, cited in MacMichael, "Indirect Rule."

26. For a detailed discussion of the debate, see Bakheit, "British Administration and Sudanese Nationalism," 131–35.

27. Director of intelligence to civil secretary, Jan. 22, 1925, "Note on Native

Administration," Northern Governors Meeting, 1925, item 17 S. G. A. /C.S./SCR/32-A-9, cited in Bakheit, ibid.

28. Bakheit, "British Administration and Sudanese Nationalism," ibid.

29. Governor-general, "Annual Report for 1921," cmd. 1837, London: H.M.O., 6.

30. Governor-general, "Annual Report for 1923," cmd. 2281, London: H.M.O., 6.

31. Khalaf, "British Policy," 110.

32. Governor-general, "Annual Report for 1926," cmd. 2291, 7.

33. Sudan Archive, J. L. Maffey, "Minute, His Excellency the Governor General," Khartoum, Jan. 1, 1927. SAD 695/8/3-5.

34. Ibrahim, "Development and Administration in Southern Darfur," 110–11.

35. Khalaf, "British Policy," 91–92.

36. Bakheit, "British Administration and Sudanese Nationalism," 78.

37. See Harold MacMichael, CS, to governor of Kordofan, Mar. 23, 1929, NRO I CIVSEC I/33/92, cited in Justin Willis, "Hukm: The Creolization of Authority in Condominium Sudan," *Journal of African History* 46 (2005): 38.

38. Idris, "Political Culture and Cultural Hegemony," 55 (see chap. 4, n. 87).

39. Sudan government, "Report of the De La Warr Commission" (Khartoum, 1937), 6.

40. Khalaf, "British Policy," 157.

41. Abd al-Rahim Muddathir, "Arabism, Africanism and Self-identification in the Sudan," in *Sudan in Africa,* ed. Yusuf Fadl Hasan (Khartoum, Institute of African and Asian Studies, University of Khartoum, 1971), 236.

42. Among the adherents to and supporters of British indirect rule, its older form—the more conservative form known as native authority or indirect rule—is sharply distinguished from its reformed version, known as native administration. If indirect rule is identified with the person of Sir Frederick Lugard, the reformed version, native administration, is identified with Sir Donald Cameron, a British governor in Tanganyika and other colonies in the interwar period. This is how G.M.A. Bakheit, later to be Gaafar al-Nimeiry's minister of local government, defined the difference between the older system and its reformed version: Bakheit claimed that "as a method of administration the system of Indirect Rule had been developed to consist of a Native Authority normally single and autocratic," even if it was part of the larger machinery of colonial government. "Native Administration, on the other hand, emerged from another school of 'Indirect Rule,' and that is local administration associated with the name of Sir Donald Cameron. To him, a local authority meant more than an autocratic chief. It covered chiefs, chiefs in councils, councils of chiefs and non-chiefs. The emphasis of the system was shifted from the preservation of chieftainship and stereo-typing their institutions, into the evolution towards representative local govt. Native Authorities were to be gradually but persistently transferred into institutions deriving their legitimacy, not from any inherited right, but from being acceptable to the people." G.M.A. Bakheit, "Native Administration in the Sudan and Its Significance to Africa," in

Sudan in Africa, ed. Yusuf Fadl Hasan (Khartoum: Institute of African and Asian Studies, University of Khartoum, 1971), 258.

43. Hamid, "Local Authorities and Social Change," 58 (see intro., n. 6).
44. Ibrahim, "Development and Administration in Southern Darfur," 114.
45. Bakheit, "Native Administration in the Sudan," 260.
46. Sudan Archive, SAD 797/1/1-51: "Draft Minute on Traditional Authorities Bill" (undated, but between 1951 and 1956), see 38-42; Musa Abdul-Jalil, Adam Azzain Mohammed and Ahmed Yousuf, "Native Administration and Local Governance in Darfur: Past and Future," in *War in Darfur and the Search for Peace,* ed. Alex de Waal (Cambridge, Mass.: Harvard University Press, 2007), 45.
47. De Waal, "Who Are the Darfurians?" 191 (see chap. 4, n. 28).
48. Willis, "Hukm," 37.
49. Ibid., 40.
50. Ibid.
51. O'Fahey, "Conflict in Darfur," 25 (see chap. 4, n. 14).
52. Quoted in Daly, *Darfur's Sorrow,* 107 (see intro., n. 5).
53. Ibid., 134–35.
54. Governor-general, "Annual Report for 1933," cmd. 4387, 77; governor-general, "Annual Report for 1926," cmd. 2991, 71; governor-general, "Annual Report for 1930," cmd. 3935, 92; governor-general, "Annual Report for 1936," cmd. 5575, 87 (London: H.M.O.); Khalaf, "British Policy," 107–9.
55. Young, Osman, Aklilu, Dale, Badri, and Fuddle, *Darfur—Livelihoods under Siege,* 11.
56. Ibrahim, "Development and Administration in Southern Darfur," 250.
57. O'Fahey, "Conflict in Darfur," 25.
58. See, for example, the following table:

Disparities in Regional Income (in U.S. dollars)

REGION	INCOME 1967/68	INCOME 1982/83
Khartoum	236	283
Middle (including the Blue Nile)	183	201
Eastern (including Port Sudan and Kassala)	180	195
Kordofan (including Southern Kordofan)	153	164
Northern Region	124	130
Darfur	98	102
Standard Deviation	44.5	57

SOURCE: Young, Osman, Aklilu, Dale, Badri, and Fuddle, *Darfur—Livelihoods Under Siege,* 13, also 12; see also, United Nations, "Dimensions of Challenge for Darfur," 21.

59. Here is a table compiled by the ILO:

Average Income of Households by Province, 1967–68 (in U.S. dollars)

PROVINCE PRE-1974 BOUNDARIES	AVE. INCOME
Northern Province	124
Khartoum	236
Kassala and Red Sea	183
Blue Nile	180
Kordofan	153
Darfur	98

SOURCE: International Labour Organization, *Growth, Employment and Equity: A Comprehensive Strategy for the Sudan* (Geneva: ILO, 1976), 19.

60. Valerie Kozel and Patrick Mullen, "Estimated Poverty Rates across Northern Sudan" (Washington, D.C.: World Bank, 2003), cited in United Nations, "Dimensions of Challenge for Darfur," 33.

61. According to Sudanese government figures:

Federal Transfers to Northern States, 2000–2006 (Jan.–March)

	2000	2001	2002	2003	2004	2005	2006 JAN—MAR
USD IN MILLIONS	$ 80.36	231.62	287.57	408.18	561.38	829.49	245.01
IN % OF TOTAL TRANSFERS							
N. Darfur	6.4	6.3	5.1	5.2	5.5	5.7	4.7
S. Darfur	5.3	4.5	4.2	4.6	4.9	4.6	4.4
W. Darfur	4.7	4.0	2.9	2.9	3.0	3.1	2.7
Greater Darfur	16.3	14.7	12.3	12.7	13.4	13.5	11.8
Khartoum	6.4	19.4	23.2	24.2	21.4	20.1	14.5
Gezira	22.9	16.9	18.0	16.6	18.1	18.0	14.0
Other States (11)	54.5	49.4	46.5	46.5	47.1	48.5	59.7

SOURCE: National State Support Fund (NSSF), cited in United Nations, "Dimensions of Challenge for Darfur," Table 4, 33.

62. United Nations, "Dimensions of Challenge for Darfur," 27.

63. Ibid., 22.

64. The main piece of land legislation previously enacted by the colonial authorities was the Titles to Land Ordinance, passed in 1899. Under it, the colonial government designated the rain lands of central, eastern, and western Sudan as unsettled areas where land was classified as government-owned and then divided into two categories: government land subject to no rights and government land subject to rights vested in a community, such as a tribe, section, or village.

65. Newcomers were also required to produce written recommendations from native administrators in their own homelands, a practice designed to screen out troublemakers. African Union, Darfur Joint Assessment Mission—Track 1, "Darfur Early Recovery, Peace and Security" (draft interim cluster report, Dec. 18, 2006), 8.

66. United Nations, Darfur Joint Assessment Mission—Track 1, Abdul-Jalil with Ludeking, "Situation Analysis of Land Tenure Issues: Problems and Implications of Darfur Early Recovery" (Dec. 2006) 4.

67. In fact, Darfuri elites, both non-Arab and Arab, often refer to Dar Beni Hussein as proof that land-poor groups can gain access to resources through negotiations—proof that the traditional system can be amended to accommodate new realities. Jérôme Tubiana, "Darfur: A War for Land?" in *War in Darfur,* 80–81; Khalaf, "British Policy," 37–38, 44.

68. "Just as hukm became expressive of the expected relationship between nazir and subject, dar—again a word long in use, but acquiring new significance—came to assert a unique claim to the resources of a territory, associated with the powers of hukm." Willis, "Hukm," 45; see also de Waal, "Who Are the Darfurians?" 192.

69. This is how one author has summed up colonial land and governance policy:
    - Use rights predominate, and such rights tend to be inclusive rather than exclusive.
    - Rights lapse if land is not used for a certain period (three years in the goz). [*Goz* means "sandy soil cultivation."]
    - Land remains within the clan or tribe and can rarely, if ever, be sold to outsiders, although outsiders may have use rights.
    - The political solidarity of a tribe (with the exception of the camel nomads) is related to its power to control and manage the territory designated as its homeland (dar).
    - A native authority chief has the power to allocate land, e.g. to newcomers, and to adjudicate disputes.
    - Women have restricted land rights . . . through their husbands or fathers. . . .

    African Union, Darfur Joint Assessment Mission—Track 1, "Darfur Early Recovery: Peace and Security," 7.

70. The argument is made in Talal Asad, *The Kababish Arabs: Power, Authority and Consent in a Nomadic Tribe* (London: C. Hurst & Co., 1969).

71. The Fur conquest of Kordofan took place in two waves during the eighteenth century. At both times, the Fur invaders looked to pastoralist allies to clear their way: The first wave extended patronage to a group called the Beni Jerrar, whereas the second wave created a new elite of pastoral clients, the Kababish. Until the late nineteenth century, the Kababish was the name of a loose confederation of tribes. Talal Asad has shown that the Kababish identity developed only with the British conquest of 1898, when Sheikh Ali el Tom, the first British-appointed *nazir,* distributed the offices in the native administration to his first cousins and their sons, thereby creating the political dominance of the new Awlad Fadlallah lineage and indeed the Kababish as a unit for colonial administration—i.e., a tribe. Ibid., 158–59, 207–8.

72. "I beg to forward the proceedings of a 'Meglis' of the Beni-Helba held at Nyala on 6. 2. 1926 when the amalgamation of the two sections Gabir and Gubara was finally accomplished. . . . It would appear from DC's [district commissioner's] meeting that the Alawna on the following day adopted a somewhat truculent attitude and that they have declined to come under Nazir Dabaka. As the large majority of this section are at present living in Dars other than Dar Beni-Helba the solution of the difficulty becomes simple. . . . In this instance they will be under the shartai of the Bergid and the Sultan of the Dago respectively both of whom are of 'Zurug' origin." Governor, Darfur Province, quoted in Ibrahim, "Development and Administration in Southern Darfur," appendix 1, 456–59; see also Ibrahim, "Development and Administration in Southern Darfur," 175–77.

73. Governor-general, "Annual Report for 1927," cmd. 3284, 7, cited in Khalaf, "British Policy," 124.

74. Ibrahim, "Development and Administration in Southern Darfur," 122.

Chapter Six

1. Bakheit, "Native Administration in the Sudan and Its Significance to Africa," in Hasan, *Sudan in Africa,* 262 (see chap. 5, n. 42).

2. Harir, "Recycling the Past in the Sudan," 40 (see chap. 3, n. 86).

3. United Nations, Darfur Joint Assessment Mission—Track 1, "Darfur Early Recovery, Darfur Conflict Analysis," draft report, chap. 2, Dec. 19, 2006.

4. On Britain's southern policy, see Francis Deng, *War of Visions: Conflict of Identities in the Sudan* (Washington D.C.: Brookings Institution, 1995). 57–58.

5. Harold A. MacMichael, Sudan Archive, SAD 586/1/52, 10.3.28.

6. Ibid.

7. Harir, "Recycling the Past in the Sudan," 331.

8. Al-Rahim, "Arabism, Africanism and Self-identification in the Sudan," in Hasan, ed., *Sudan in Africa,* 236.

9. Sudan government, "Report of the Committee on the Sudanization of the Civil Service," Khartoum, Sudan Archive, SAD 425/1/1-20. June 17, 1948.

10. Deng, *War of Visions*, 51.

11. Ibid., 57–58.

12. Khalid Mansour, *The Government They Deserve: The Role of the Elite in Sudan's Political Evolution* (London: Kegan Paul International, 1990), 199.

13. Jago Salmon et al., "Drivers of Change: Civil Society in Northern Sudan" (unpublished, DFID Department for International Development, United Kingdom, Khartoum, July 22, 2007), 8.

14. Hamid, "Local Authorities and Social Change," 81 (see intro., n. 6).

15. Burr and Collins, *Darfur: Long Road to Disaster*, 70 (see chap. 1, n. 74).

16. Adam Mohammed, "The Comprehensive Peace Agreement and Darfur," in *War in Darfur and the Search for Peace*, ed. Alex de Waal (Cambridge, Mass.: Harvard University Press, 2007), 201.

17. Young, Osman, Aklilu, Dale, Badri, and Fuddle, *Darfur—Livelihoods Under Siege*, 11 (see chap. 1, n. 69).

18. M. A. Mohamed Salih, *Understanding the Conflict in Darfur* (Centre of African Studies, University of Copenhagen, May 2005), 4–5.

19. Hamid, "Local Authorities and Social Change," 132.

20. Harir "Recycling the Past in the Sudan," 39.

21. Hamid, "Local Authorities and Social Change," 82.

22. Harir, " 'Arab Belt' vs. 'African Belt,' " 156 (see chap. 4, n. 11).

23. Hamid, "Local Authorities and Social Change," 85–86.

24. Ibid., 86–88.

25. Ibid., 89.

26. Ibid., 89.

27. Ibid., 84.

28. United Nations, "Dimensions of Challenge for Darfur," 5.

29. Harir, " 'Arab Belt' vs. 'African Belt,' " 156–57.

30. Burr and Collins, *Darfur: Long Road to Disaster*, 72.

31. Ibid., 81.

32. Harir, " 'Arab Belt' vs. 'African Belt,' " 158; Daldoum, *Dynamics of Ethnic Group Relations in Darfur*, 82 (see intro., n. 9).

33. On the face of it, the 1981 Regional Development Act joined North and South Darfur as one region.

34. Harir, " 'Arab Belt' vs. 'African Belt,' " 160.

35. Harir, "Recycling the Past in the Sudan," 47; Salih, *Understanding the Conflict in Darfur*, 6, 7.

36. Morton, in Young, Osman, Aklilu, Dale, Badri, and Fuddle, *Darfur—Livelihoods under Siege*, 25.

37. Hamid, "Local Authorities and Social Change," 63.

38. United Nations, "Dimensions of Challenge for Darfur," 8–9, 12.

39. E.S.M. Ateem lists sixteen different rural council border disputes and conflicts in southern Darfur Province alone that occurred soon after the implementation of this act. "All these conflicts were over the right to own tribal land or 'hakura.' " E.S.M. Ateem, "Tribal Conflicts in Darfur: Causes and Solutions" (seminar on The Political Problems of the Sudan, July 9–11, 1999, AKE-Bildungswerk Institute of Development Aid and Policy,

Vlotho/NRW, Germany, 1999), 4; Young, Osman, Aklilu, Dale, Badri, and Fuddle, *Darfur—Livelihoods under Siege,* 22; Musa Abdul-Jalil, Adam Azzain Mohammed, and Ahmed Yousuf, "Native Administration and Local Governance in Darfur," 50 (see chap. 5, n. 46).

40. For an analysis of the 1971 law, I have relied on Ibrahim, "Development and Administration in Southern Darfur," 326–27, 339–42, 412 (see chap. 3, n. 47).

41. Salmon et al., "Drivers of Change," 8–9.

42. Harir, "Recycling the Past in the Sudan," 17.

43. Young, Osman, Aklilu, Dale, Badri, and Fuddle, *Darfur—Livelihoods under Siege,* 9.

44. Salih, *Understanding the Conflict in Darfur,* 7–8.

45. All quotations from Hassan al-Turabi in Mohamed Elhachmi Hamdi, *Conversations with Hassan al-Turabi* (Boulder, Colo.: Westview Press, 1998), 13, 45, 89, 46, 87, 91.

46. Burr and Collins, *Darfur: Long Road to Disaster,* 270.

47. Chap. 3c in Young, Osman, Aklilu, Dale, Badri, and Fuddle, *Darfur—Livelihoods under Siege,* 42.

48. Chap. 6, in *Understanding the Crisis in Darfur: Listening to Sudanese Voices,* ed. Abdel Ghaffar M. Ahmed and Leif Manger (Bergen, Norway: University of Bergen, Centre for Development Studies, 2006), 67.

49. Fadul and Tanner, in *War in Darfur and the Search for Peace,* ed. Alex de Waal (Cambridge, Mass.: Harvard University Press, 2007), 302.

50. Douglas Johnson, *The Root Causes of Sudan's Civil Wars* (Oxford: James Currey, 2003), 140–41; Prunier, letter to *London Review of Books,* 5 April, 2007 (see chap. 2, n. 35); Flint and de Waal, *Darfur: New History of a Long War,* 57–61 (see chap. 1, n. 57); Burr and Collins, *Darfur: Long Road to Disaster,* 287; Young, Osman, Aklilu, Dale, Badri, and Fuddle, *Darfur—Livelihoods under Siege,* 23.

51. Many Darfuri Massalit fled to Chad for safety during this period. One such group in Chagawa village had spent two years (1996 to 1998) in Chad. See Young, Osman, Aklilu, Dale, Badri, and Fuddle, *Darfur—Livelihoods under Siege,* 3.

52. This reform was passed by the Neema Congress of the NIF in 1995. Abdul-Jalil, Mohammed, and Yousuf, "Native Administration and Local Governance," 51.

53. Abdel Ghaffar M. Ahmad and Leif Manger, "Reflections on the meeting 'Understanding the Darfur Conflict: An Attempt at an Analysis, Addis Ababa, July 25–26, 2005,' " in *Understanding the Crisis in Darfur,* ed. Ahmed and Manger, 56.

54. Saeid, "Darfur: The Crisis and the Tragedy," 5 (see chap. 5, n. 10).

55. United Nations, Darfur Joint Assessment Mission—Track 1, "Darfur Early Recovery, Darfur Conflict Analysis," 9.

56. Abdalla Osman El Tom and M. A. Mohamed Salih, review of *The Black Book of Sudan, Review of African Political Economy* 30, no. 97 (Sept. 2003): 511–30.

57. Abdullahi Osman El-Tom, "The Arab Congregation and the Ideology of Genocide in Darfur, Sudan," *Citizen,* Sept. 2, 2007, 4 (sent from USAAfricaDialogue@googlegroups.com, on Jan. 27, 2008).

58. United Nations, Darfur Joint Assessment Mission—Track 1, "Darfur Early Recovery, Darfur Conflict Analysis," 6.

59. This paragraph and the next are based on Mohamed Abusabib, *Art, Politics and Cultural Identification in Sudan* (Uppsala, Sweden: Uppsala University, 2004), 62–63, 97, 72–73.

60. Idris, "Political Culture and Cultural Hegemony," 63–64 (see chap. 4, n. 87).

61. Mansour Khalid, Nimeiry's foreign minister at the time of the Addis Ababa Agreement of 1972 and after, who split with Nimeiry and joined the SPLA upon its formation, put it this way in his introduction to a book by John Garang: "The SPLM began as an all-embracing national movement, open to all Sudanese, and particularly those of the marginalized regions of the country: Nuba, Beja, Fur and Ingessana. All those ethnic groups happen to be of non-Arab stock. Instead of taking this all-embracing approach as evidence of SPLA/M's national vocation, it was taken as yet another proof of the SPLM's 'racism.' " Mansour Khalid, "Introduction," in John Garang, *The Call for Democracy in Sudan,* edited with an introduction by Mansour Khalid (London and New York: KPI, 1992), 15.

62. Idris, "Political Culture and Cultural Hegemony," 112.

63. John Garang, "Statement by John Garang at Koka Dam, 20 March, 1986," in Garang, *Call for Democracy in Sudan,* 127.

64. Garang, *Call for Democracy in Sudan,* 55. This is how Mansour Khalid put it in his introduction:

> The Sudan, anthropologically, is not a country of Arabs and Africans but that of Arabicized Africans or Africanized Arabs and pure Africans; racial purity is alien to it. On the other hand the pre-eminence of Arab culture has never been challenged by the non-Arabs, except those driven by reactive inferiority complexes, like the secessionists of Anyanya I and Anyanya II. In fact the entrenchment of Arabo-Islamic culture in the Sudan was the great achievement of two purely African Sudanese kingdoms: the Funj and the Fur. However, the bottom line, we argued, is political and economic power and political phenomena cannot be explained away by anthropology, less so by zoology.

Khalid, "Introduction" to Garang, *Call for Democracy in Sudan,* 3.

In his introduction to Garang's 1987 collection, Mansour Khalid wrote: "What the SPLM is challenging, therefore, is not Arabism as a cultural identity but as a political supremacy based on racial heredity. Also the ethnic diversity advocated by the SPLM is nothing but respect for cultural specificities rather than the perpetuation of ethnicity as a source of dissension." Mansour Khalid, "Introduction," in John Garang, *John Garang*

Speaks, edited with an introduction by Mansour Khalid (London and New York: KPI, 1987), xii.

65. John Garang, "First Statement to the Sudanese People on 10 August 1989, Following the Military *Coup d'Etat* of 30 June, 1989," in Garang, *Call for Democracy in Sudan,* 258.

66. "Seminar with John Garang de Mabior at the Brookings Institution, Washington D.C., 9 June 1989," and "Excerpts from the Speech of John Garang to the Media and the Sudanese Community in London (Africa Hall), June 1989," in Garang, *Call for Democracy in Sudan,* 214, 205.

Chapter Seven

1. Ahmed Abdel Rahman Al-Bashir, "Problems of Settlement of Immigrants and Refugees in Sudanese Society," (PhD diss., University of Oxford, 1978), 38; cited in Flint and de Waal, *Darfur: New History of a Long War,* 43 (see chap. 1, n. 57).

2. United Nations Environment Programme, *Sudan: Post-conflict Environmental Assessment,* 48, 59 (see intro., n. 3).

3. Ibid., 11.

4. Ibid., 62.

5. Ibid., 60. There is a vigorous debate on the causes of ongoing environmental degradation, in Darfur and in other parts of the Sahel: To what extent is degradation the result of global factors ("global warming"), and to what extent is it a product of short-term local strategies that have tended to magnify the problem in the longer term? Scholarly work has traced the causes of degradation in Darfur to multiple factors, from low rainfall (38 percent) to overcutting/deforestation (32 percent), overcultivation (15 percent), overgrazing (3 percent), and an assortment of other causes, including fires (12 percent). One side points out that well over 60 percent of the causes of environmental degradation can be traced to human activity, and the other side argues that these activities need to be seen as a response of disempowered groups to global trends such as lower rainfall, even if the response has in turn exacerbated the crisis by further contributing to the decline in rainfall.

   Among the most important of the local causes of environmental degradation is deforestation and the destruction of water systems. Preconflict studies on forestry and fuel wood consumption in Darfur (see the following table) indicate a conservative annual deforestation rate of 4,000–6,000 square kilometers. In North Darfur, traditional industries (fired brick, lime kilns, and bakeries) consume huge amounts of firewood, which are transported over long distances. In West Darfur, both armed nomadic groups and armed forces of the state have commonly resorted to extensive tree felling, not only to supply camel browse but also to deter farmers from returning to cultivate the land. The annual loss of forestland in Darfur has increased geometrically, nearly seven times in fifty years, from 818 square kilometers in 1956 to 5,600 in 2006.

Estimated Annual Deforestation in Relation to Increasing Population

YEAR	POPULATION	DENSITY PERSON/KM^2	ANNUAL PER CAPITA CONSUMPTION OF FUELWOOD (MT)	ESTIMATED ANNUAL DEFORESTATION (KM^2)
1956	1,080,000	3	572,400	818
1973	1,340,000	4	710,200	1,015
1983	3,500,000	10	1,855,000	2,650
1993	5,600,000	15	2,968,000	4,240
2003	6,480,000	18	3,434,400	4,906
2006	7,395,000	20	3,919,350	5,600

SOURCE: Compiled from Track 2 workshop on natural resource management, cited in United Nations, Darfur Joint Assessment Mission—Track 1, "Darfur Early Recovery, War Affected Communities," Dec. 15, 2006, Table 3, 11.

According to UNEP, the international relief community, "a major customer for the bricks, particularly to build the two-meter high compound walls required by international security standards . . . has become a significant factor in the deforestation process." Not only has brick making "become an important source of income for IDPs in Darfur," but it "has also caused considerable environmental damage around the camps."

Here is how bricks are made: "The water necessary for the manufacturing process is obtained either from watercourses or from deep boreholes with submersible pumps installed by the aid community. The rate of extraction from such boreholes is not monitored, and may in some cases not be sustainable. Finally, trees are needed to fire the bricks in temporary kilns—local studies have found that one large tree is needed to fire 3000 bricks." United Nations Environment Programme, *Sudan: Post-conflict Environmental Assessment,* 107.

Whereas deforestation preceded the present conflict, the destruction of water systems has been a result of the conflict. Observers point to an "extensive, systematic and deliberate destruction of water systems during the conflict." The destruction has led, on the one hand, to contamination of domestic wells, which will have to be redug before they can be reused, and, on the other, to damage to or looting of pumps and boreholes and destruction of water-harvesting systems. Rapid degradation of the environment has gone hand in hand with widespread destruction of assets: "Houses have been burned, cattle and livestock have been looted, crops have been deliberately damaged, seeds have been stolen, irrigation pumps have been looted, and water systems destroyed." Livestock markets have also been reduced to less than half their previous number, as major traders from Omdurman have stopped coming due to growing insecurity. The range of scholarly studies is summed up in a U.N.-sponsored report. One comment captures the author's own point of view: "For the fragile and vulnerable environment of Darfur, the human impact must be considered even more significant." United Nations, Darfur Joint Assessment Mission—Track 1, "Darfur Early Recovery, War Affected Communities," draft interim cluster report, Dec. 15, 2006, 4, 5, 12, 14.

6. This paragraph is based on Burr and Collins, *Darfur: Long Road to Disaster,* 65, 92–93, 66, 5 (see chap. 1, n. 74).

7. Ibid.

8. This paragraph and the preceding one are based on ibid., 27, 36, 37.

9. This paragraph and the preceding one are based on ibid., 102–3, 38, 40, 63–64.

10. Ibid., 44, 46.

11. Ibid., 25–26.

12. Ibid., 176.

13. It generated 20 percent of the national foreign exchange earnings before the discovery of oil in the last decade, and below 8 percent after it. Darfur accounts for 21 percent of the cattle, 22 percent of the sheep and goats, 24 percent of the camels, 31 percent of the donkeys and 63 percent of the horses in Sudan. Along with Egypt, Libya was a key market for live camel exports, as Saudi Arabia was for live sheep. 18 percent of these exports were from the Greater Darfur region. By 2003, Darfur alone was annually exporting 30,000 camels to Libya and about 50,000 camels to Egypt. Young, Osman, Aklilu, Dale, Badri, and Fuddle, *Darfur—Livelihoods under Siege,* 51, 53, 5 (see chap. 1, n. 69).

14. This was a relatively mature and skilled labor force with responsibilities in Darfur. More than half were over thirty years of age, about 75 percent were married and the literacy rate was double that found in Darfur. Ibid., 85.

15. The system depends on a personal contact between the agent and the migrant, so that the worker would trust that the money will be handed over to the right people and promptly too. There is no charge for sending a *hawala* and it is quicker than using the banking system. Sending money through a bank is more difficult since it requires documents (ID or a passport). The *hawaldars* make their money by the differential in the exchange rates between the two currencies. Ibid., 95–98.

16. This paragraph is based on Burr and Collins, *Darfur: Long Road to Disaster,* 77–78, 83, 51, 75; and Ali Haggar, "The Origins and Organization of the Janjawiid in Darfur," in *War in Darfur and the Search for Peace,* ed. Alex de Waal (Cambridge, Mass.: Harvard University Press, 2007), 120.

17. Daly, *Darfur's Sorrow,* 217–18 (see intro., n. 5).

18. Burr and Collins, *Darfur: Long Road to Disaster,* 107–8.

19. Ibid., 138, 152, 44.

20. Ibid., 166–67.

21. Ibid., 224–25.

22. Ibid., 227; see also "The Case against Hissène Habré, an 'African

Pinochet,' " Human Rights Watch, http://hrw.org/justice/habre/intro_web2.htm (accessed Aug. 1, 2008).

23. Burr and Collins, *Darfur: Long Road to Disaster,* 183, 236.

24. To be sure, Libya had begun organizing proxies as early as the 1970s, but always as supplements to the Libyan army itself. After successive defeats at the hands of Habre's troops (with support from the Americans and French), Libya shifted to proxies as its main form of military involvement in the region. Haggar, "The Origins and Organization of the Janjawiid in Darfur," 121–22, 125.

25. UN, "Dimensions of Challenge for Darfur," 14.

26. Burr and Collins, *Darfur: Long Road to Disaster,* 192.

27. Haggar, "The Origins and Organization of the Janjawiid in Darfur," 118.

28. For details, see Mamdani, *When Victims Become Killers,* chap. 6 on Congo (see chap. 3, n. 1).

29. Ibrahim, "Development and Administration in Southern Darfur," 336 (see chap. 3, n. 47).

30. Daldoum, *Dynamics of Ethnic Group Relations in Darfur,* 66 (see intro., n. 9).

31. Ibid., 67.

32. The majority of the nomadic Arab groups that lined up behind the Beni Helba to wage war against the Fur originated from Chad. Harir, " 'Arab Belt' vs. 'African Belt,' " 181 (see chap. 4, n. 11).

33. A. Mohamed, *Police* magazine, 21.

34. Daldoum, *Dynamics of Ethnic Group Relations in Darfur,* 81.

35. Harir, " 'Arab Belt' vs. 'African Belt,' " 166.

36. Haggar, "The Origins and Organization of the Janjawiid in Darfur," 121–23.

37. Harir, " 'Arab Belt' vs. 'African Belt,' " 164–65; Burr and Collins, *Darfur: Long Road to Disaster,* 286.

38. Haggar, "The Origins and Organization of the Janjawiid in Darfur," 126.

39. Burr and Collins, *Darfur: Long Road to Disaster,* 37, 56, 58.

40. On the link between Chadian groups and the Abbala in North Darfur, see Haggar, "The Origins and Organization of the Janjawiid in Darfur," 124, 125, 126.

41. Ibid., 217.

42. Alex de Waal, "Refugees and the Creation of Famine: The Case of Dar Masalit, Sudan," *Journal of Refugee Studies* 1, no. 2 (1988): 127–40; Young, Osman, Aklilu, Dale, Badri, and Fuddle, *Darfur—Livelihoods under Siege,* chap. 3, p. 3.

43. Burr and Collins, *Darfur: Long Road to Disaster,* 205; J. Morton, "The History and Origins of the Current Conflict in Darfur," 17; United Nations, Darfur Joint Assessment Mission—Track 1, "Darfur Early Recovery, Darfur Conflict Analysis," 13 (see chap. 5, n. 12).

44. Flint and de Waal, *New History of a Long War,* 48–49; Harir, " 'Arab Belt' vs. 'African Belt,' " 165.

45. See Theobald, *Ali Dinar* (see chap. 3, n. 87); Harir, "Recycling the Past in the Sudan," 15 (see chap. 3, n. 86).

46. Burr and Collins, *Darfur: Long Road to Disaster,* 286.

47. Ushari Ahmed Mahmud and Suleyman Ali Baldo, *Human Rights Abuses in the Sudan 1987: The Dhein Massacre: Slavery in the Sudan* (London: Sudan Relief and Rehabilitation Commission, 1987).

48. Amnesty International 1989, cited in Alex de Waal, in *War in Darfur and the Search for Peace,* ed. Alex de Waal (Cambridge, Mass.: Harvard University Press, 2007), 6.

49. M. A. Mohamed Salih and Sharif Harir, "Tribal Militias: The Genesis of National Disintegration," in *Short-Cut to Decay: The Case of the Sudan,* ed. Sharif Harir and Terje Tvedt (Uppsala: Scandinavian Institute of African Studies, 1994), 186.

50. Harir, "Recycling the Past in the Sudan," 59.

51. De Waal, "Sudan: The Turbulent State," 19.

52. African Rights, 1995; de Waal, "Sudan: The Turbulent State," 6.

53. "Case against Hissène Habré."

54. See Alex de Waal, "Making Sense of Chad," *Pambuzka News* 342, Feb. 5, 2008.

Chapter Eight

1. Harir, " 'Arab Belt' versus 'African Belt,' " (see chap. 4, n. 11).

2. Ironically, the letter exaggerated the presence and role of Arabs in Darfur, thereby downplaying their marginality.

3. Harir, " 'Arab Belt' versus 'African Belt,' " 165.

4. Daldoum, *Dynamics of Ethnic Group Relations in Darfur,* 99 (see intro., n. 9).

5. Harir, " 'Arab Belt' versus 'African Belt,' " 149–50.

6. Ibid., 146–47.

7. Ibid., 147; see also Daldoum, *The Dynamics of Ethnic Group Relations in Darfur,* 95, 108.

8. Ibid., 148.

9. The first, in 1924, was between the Rizeigat cattle nomads and the Dinka, their neighbors to the south; the second, in 1932, was between the camel nomads of northern Kordofan, the Kababish and the Kawahla, and their neighbors in northern Darfur, the Zayyadiyya, Berti, and Meidob. See Zuhair Mohamadi Bashar, "Mechanisms for Peaceful Coexistence Among Tribal Groups in Darfur" (in Arabic, MA thesis, IAAS, University of Khartoum, 2003) cited in Adam A. Mohamed, "Indigenous Institutions and Practices Promoting Peace and/or Mitigating Conflicts: The Case of Southern Darfur," in "Environmental Degradation: Darfur," 69 (see intro., n. 5). Many writers have claimed an intrinsic relationship among nomadism, a raiding economy, and violence.

In his *Muqaddimah* (Introduction), Ibn Khaldūn attributed the rise and fall of leaderships and kingdoms in North Africa to wars in which nomads were the main actors. Others have made the point that even the Great Wall of China was built to stop nomads from attacking settled farmers. Mohamed, "Indigenous Institutions and Practices," 68. Writers on Darfur have also observed a relationship between nomads and tribal conflict: Of the thirty-nine major tribal conflicts that took place in Darfur during the 1923–2003 period, nomadic groups were involved in twenty-nine. Adam A. Mohamed, "Intergroup Conflicts and Customary Mediation: Experiences from Sudan," *African Journal on Conflict Resolution,* no. 1 (2002); Adam A. Mohamed, "The Rezaiga Camel Nomads of Darfur Region: From Cooperation to Confrontation," *Nomadic Peoples* (forthcoming); A. I. Wadi, *Perspectives on Tribal Conflict in the Sudan* (IAAS, University of Khartoum, 1998); all cited in "Environmental Degradation: Darfur," 69.

Based on the available data, the period before the 1970s showed only five conflict resolutions in Darfur, while from the 1970s onward, many conflict resolution agreements have been signed. The following table shows that there were 3 conflicts from 1932 to 1969 and 19 from 1974 to 1999, with 11 small ones 1990–91. For details, see Daldoum, *Dynamics of Ethnic Group Relations in Darfur,* 78–79.

NO.	TRIBAL GROUPS INVOLVED	YEAR	MAJOR CAUSE OF CONFLICT
1	Kababish, Kawahla, Berti and Medoub	1932	grazing and water rights
2	Kababish, Medoub and Zayyadia	1957	grazing and water rights
3	Rizeigat, Baggara and Maaliya	1968	local politics and administration
4	Rizeigat, Baggara, Maaliya and Dinka	1975	grazing and water rights
5	Beni Helba, Zayyadia and Mahariya	1976	grazing and water rights
6	Northern Rizeigat (Abbala) and Dago	1976	grazing and water rights
7	Northern Rizeigat and Bargo	1978	grazing and water rights
8	Northern Rizeigat and Gimir	1978	grazing and water rights
9	Northern Rizeigat and Fur	1980	grazing and water rights
10	Northern Rizeigat and Bargo	1980	grazing and water rights
11	Taaisha and Salamat	1980	local politics and administration
12	Kababish, Berti and Zayyadia	1981	grazing and water rights
13	Rezeigat Baggara and Dinka	1981	grazing and water rights
14	Northern Rizeigat and Beni Helba	1982	grazing and water rights
15	Kababish, Kawahla, Berti and Medoub	1982	grazing and water rights
16	Rezeigat and Misiriya	1983	grazing and water rights

NO.	TRIBAL GROUPS INVOLVED	YEAR	MAJOR CAUSE OF CONFLICT
17	Kababish, Berti and Medoub	1984	grazing and water rights
18	Rezeigat and Misiriya	1984	grazing and water rights
19	Gimir and Fellata (Fulani)	1987	administrative boundaries
20	Kababish, Kawahla, Berti and Medoub	1987	grazing and water rights
21	Fur and Bidayat	1989	armed robberies
22	Arab and Fur	1989	grazing, cross-boundary politics
23	Zaghawa and Gimir	1990	administrative boundaries
24	Zaghawa and Gimir	1990	administrative boundaries
25	Taaisha and Gimir	1990	land
26	Bargo and Rezeigat	1990	grazing and water rights
27	Zaghawa and Maaliya	1991	land
28	Zaghawa and Marareit	1991	grazing and water rights
29	Zaghawa and Beni Hussein	1991	grazing and water rights
30	Zaghawa v. Mima and Birgid	1991	grazing and water rights
31	Zaghawa and Birgid	1991	grazing and water rights
32	Zaghawa and Birgid	1991	grazing and water rights
33	Fur and Turgum	1991	land
34	Zaghawa and Arab	1994	grazing and water rights
35	Zaghawa Sudan v. Zaghawa Chad	1994	power and politics
36	Massalit and Arab	1996	grazing, administration
37	Zaghawa and Rezeigat	1997	local politics
38	Kababish Arabs and Medoub	1997	grazing and water rights
39	Massalit and Arab	1996	grazing, administration
40	Zaghawa and Gimir	1999	grazing, administration
41	Fur and Arab	2000	grazing, politics, armed robberies

10. De Waal, "Who Are the Darfurians?" 197 (see chap. 4, n. 28).
11. Yousif Takana, "Darfur Conflict Mapping Analysis" (unpublished report, *Darfur-Darfur Dialogue and Consultation,* Khartoum, Nov. 2007), 40–41.

12. The details are in the table below:

Number of Migrants from North to South Darfur, 1986

AREA COUNCIL	NO. OF MIGRANTS FROM NORTH DARFUR
Nyala (central area)	108,976
El Dien (eastern area)	72,849
Buram (southern area)	95,240
Zalengei (western area)	64,593
Ed el Ganam (southwestern)	42,352
TOTAL	384,010

13. Takana, "Darfur Conflict Mapping Analysis," 8–9.
14. Ibid., 15–16.
15. Ibid., 25.
16. Ibid., 13–14.
17. The Salamat, for example, began by asking for a separate native administration from the Ta'aisha in 1982 but, after a fierce fight, settled for one *omda* to represent them in the Ta'aisha administration. Ibid., 14.
18. Ibid., 39.
19. Flint and de Waal, *Darfur: New History of a Long War,* 58–59 (see chap. 1, n. 57).
20. Hasan, *Studies in Sudanese History,* 61–63 (see chap. 3, n. 15).
21. Takana, "Darfur Conflict Mapping Analysis," 47–48.
22. Ibid., 45–47.
23. Ibid., 57–60.
24. Ibid., 60.
25. Burr and Collins, *Darfur: Long Road to Disaster,* 204–5 (see chap. 1, n. 74).
26. Young, Osman, Aklilu, Dale, Badri, and Fuddle, *Darfur—Livelihoods under Siege,* 67–70 (see chap. 1, n. 69).
27. Musa Adam Abdul-Jalil, "Land Tenure, Land Use and Inter-ethnic Conflicts in Darfur," in *Understanding the Crisis in Darfur: Listening to Sudanese Voices,* ed. Abdel Ghaffar M. Ahmed and Leif Manger (Bergen, Norway: University of Bergen, Centre for Development Studies, 2006), 27. A few new ones were added in the interim, but they nowhere near made up for the overall decline. After the outbreak of the current civil war in 2003, President al-Bashir issued a decree authorizing the formation of a high committee for the demarcation of eleven livestock migration routes in the three states of Darfur. United Nations, Darfur Joint Assessment Mission, Track 1, Abdul-Jalil with Ludeking, "Situation Analysis of Land Tenure Issues," 10 (see chap. 4, n. 18).

28. Young, Osman, Aklilu, Dale, Badri, and Fuddle, *Darfur—Livelihoods under Siege,* chap. 4, 19–20.
29. Ibid., chap. 4, 26.
30. Harir, " 'Arab Belt' versus 'African Belt,' " 162, 174.
31. De Waal, "Who Are the Darfurians?" 193.
32. Harir, " 'Arab Belt' versus 'African Belt,' " 149–50.
33. "Minister of Interior Lays Emphasis on Role of Chad in Darfur," *Sudan Times,* May 24, 1989; "Sudan Rural Solidarity on Darfur Problem," *Sudan Times,* June 20, 1989.
34. Burr and Collins, *Darfur: Long Road to Disaster,* 244.
35. United Nations, Darfur Joint Assessment Mission—Track 1, "Darfur Early Recovery, Darfur Conflict Analysis," 5 (see chap. 5, n. 12).
36. Harir, " 'Arab Belt' versus 'African Belt,' " 180.
37. Daldoum, *Dynamics of Ethnic Group Relations in Darfur,* 104.
38. Into this bloody and scourged field entered a body of profiteers that rustled both Fur and Arab livestock. Harir, " 'Arab Belt' versus 'African Belt,' " 170.
39. Ibid. This became clear during a protest demonstration organized by the National Council for the Salvation of Dar Fur in Khartoum on March 12, 1988. The dominant coalition partner—i.e., the Umma Party—not only instructed its thirty-four parliamentary deputies not to join the demonstration but also tried to get an injunction from the judiciary to outlaw the demonstration. Deputies from the DUP—i.e., the junior coalition partner—marched in the demonstration.
40. Harir, " 'Arab Belt' versus 'African Belt,' " 145.
41. Ibid., 176.
42. Ibid., 183.
43. According to Abusin and Takana, the whole system must be reconsidered if security, resource management, tax assessment and collection, and ethnic tensions are to be eased. Young, Osman, Aklilu, Dale, Badri, and Fuddle, *Darfur—Livelihoods under Siege,* chap. 3, 3. See also United Nations, Darfur Joint Assessment Mission—Track 1, "Darfur Early Recovery, Darfur Conflict Analysis," 5.
44. Daldoum, *Dynamics of Ethnic Group Relations in Darfur,* 81. The nomadic tribes had demanded traditional and political rights in both Wadi Azum and Wadi Salih. Ibid., 92.
45. Ibid., 95.
46. Estimate of Massalit Losses (1995–97) in the Tribal Wars with the Arabs

YEAR	NO. KILLED	NO. INJURED	VILLAGES BURNED	LIVESTOCK LOOTED	HUTS BURNED
1995/96	312	84	13	2743	607
1996/97	374	85	37	6060	2226
TOTAL	686	169	50	8803	2833

Details of Livestock Looted from the Massalit (1995–97)

YEAR	CATTLE	CAMELS	HORSES	DONKEYS	GOATS	SHEEP	TOTAL
1995/96	758	142	80	61	1546	156	2743
1996/97	1791	47	36	25	4011	150	6060
TOTAL	2549	189	116	86	5557	306	8803

Young, Osman, Aklilu, Dale, Badri, and Fuddle, *Darfur—Livelihoods under Siege,* chap. 3, annex, "Livelihoods in El Geneina Area," Tables 1 and 2.

47. United Nations, Darfur Joint Assessment Mission—Track 1, "Darfur Early Recovery, Darfur Conflict Analysis," 5.
48. Young, Osman, Aklilu, Dale, Badri, and Fuddle, *Darfur—Livelihoods under Siege,* chap. 3, 3.
49. Ibid.; Abdul-Jalil, "Land Tenure, Land Use and Inter-ethnic Conflicts in Darfur," 29–30.
50. Burr and Collins, *Darfur: Long Road to Disaster,* 288–89.
51. On Abd al-Wahid and the SLA, see Julie Flint, "Darfur's Armed Movements," in *War in Darfur and the Search for Peace,* ed. Alex de Waal (Cambridge, Mass.: Harvard University Press, 2007), 160, 148, 152, 147, 143.
52. The SLA draws its support largely from the Fur, Zaghawa, and Massalit, although it is by no means confined to these groups, and some of its fighters and commanders have been drawn from Arab groups. The JEM is smaller, mainly Zaghawa and Islamist in orientation. JEM split in 2004, and a number of fighters went off to form the National Movement for Reform and Development (NMRD). The SLA split into two factions in 2006, SLA/Minnawi (predominantly Zaghawa) and SLA/Abd al-Wahid (predominantly Fur).
53. Flint, "Darfur's Armed Movements," 151.
54. Other sources speak of the formation of a "secret 25-man committee from the 6 states of Sudan to collect information about political and economic marginalization." Ibid., 150.
55. Burr and Collins, *Darfur: Long Road to Disaster,* 290–91.
56. Dr. Albaqir Alafif Mukhtar, "On the Fringes of Northern Identity: What's Missing in the Darfur Peace Process?" (Washington D.C.: United States Institute for Peace, working paper, May 24, 2006), 7; Flint and de Waal, *Darfur: A New History of a Long War,* 99–103, 110–11.
57. Salih, *Understanding the Conflict in Darfur,* 18 (see chap. 6, n. 18); Flint, "Darfur's Armed Movements," 148.
58. Burr and Collins, *Darfur: Long Road to Disaster,* 309.
59. Flint and de Waal, *Darfur: New History of a Long War,* 81–85, 92–96; Roland Marchal, "The Unseen Regional Implications of the Crisis in Darfur," 76, 81–82, 88, 112–13, and Jérôme Tubiana, "Darfur: A War for

Land?," 72, in *War in Darfur and the Search for Peace,* ed. Alex de Waal (Cambridge, Mass.: Harvard University Press, 2007), 72.

60. Marchal, in *War in Darfur and the Search for Peace,* ed. Alex de Waal (Cambridge, Mass.: Harvard University Press, 2007), 193, 194–95.

61. Quoted in Flint and de Waal, *Darfur: New History of a Long War,* 124.

62. International Crisis Group, *Darfur Rising,* report, no. 76, March 25, 2004; United Nations, Darfur Joint Assessment Mission—Track 1, "Darfur Early Recovery, Darfur Conflict Analysis," 5–6.

63. United Nations, Darfur Joint Assessment Mission—Track 1, "Darfur Early Recovery, Darfur Conflict Analysis," 6.

64. Ibid.

65. Burr and Collins, *Darfur: Long Road to Disaster,* 285.

66. Flint and de Waal, *Darfur: New History of a Long War,* 33–70.

67. Flint and de Waal, "The Janjawiid," in *Darfur: A Short History,* chap. 3.

68. Ibid.; African Union, Darfur Joint Assessment Mission—Track 1, "Darfur Early Recovery, Peace and Security," 2 (see chap. 5, n. 65).

69. Haggar, "The Origins and Organization of the Janjawiid in Darfur," 113, 115.

70. Burr and Collins, *Darfur: Long Road to Disaster,* 288.

71. Key informant 4. Interview with AO, HY, and RD. Kebkabiya, Oct. 5, 2004. Key informant 9. Interview with AO. Kebkabiya, Oct. 6, 2004. Key informant 10. Interview with AO. Kebkabiya, 2004. Young, Osman, Aklilu, Dale, Badri, and Fuddle, *Darfur—Livelihoods under Siege,* 38, cited in notes 28, 29, and 30 in chap. 2, "The History and Origins of the Current Conflict in Darfur."

72. Ariel Zellman, "The Janjaweed in the Sudan: A Case of Chronic Paramilitarism" (paper presented at the ISA Annual Convention, San Diego, Calif., Mar. 23, 2006), 24–25.

73. De Waal, "Who Are the Darfurians?", 190.

74. Haggar, "The Origins and Organization of the Janjawiid in Darfur," 113, 115.

75. Ibid., 128.

76. Hilal M. Interview with AO and BB, Khartoum Elriyad, Oct. 2004, Young, Osman, Aklilu, Dale, Badri, and Fuddle, *Darfur—Livelihoods under Siege,* chap. 2, note 31.

77. Key informant 10. Interview with AO. Kebkabiya, 2004, ibid., cited in note 30.

78. "Islam, Democracy, the State and the West: Roundtable with Dr. Hasan Turabi," *Middle East Policy* 1, no. 3 (1992): 49–61; Salih, *Understanding the Conflict in Darfur,* 9; Burr and Collins, *Darfur: Long Road to Disaster,* 285.

79. Haggar, "The Origins and Organization of the Janjawiid in Darfur," 129.

80. Key informant 8. Interview with HY and AO. Kebkabiya, Oct. 7, 2004, Young, Osman, Aklilu, Dale, Badri, and Fuddle, *Darfur—Livelihoods under Siege,* chap. 2, note 32.

81. Key informant 1. Interview with HY and AO. Kebkabiya, Oct. 4 and 5, 2004, ibid., cited in note 33.

82. Key informant 6. Interview with BB, AM, and HY. El Fasher, Sept. 29, 2004, ibid., cited in note 34.

83. Ibid., see Annex 6, "Livelihoods in el Geneina," 161–73.

84. However, the local agreement does not protect their livestock, and other Arab groups who were not party to it have taken their animals. In addition, if individual families cannot pay, they are left unprotected. This paragraph on Kebkabiya is based on Annex 2, "Livelihoods in Kebkabiya," in ibid., 122, 125, 127–28.

85. Yet the indirect impact of insecurity on access to markets, the availability of goods in local markets, and mobility (of both livestock and labor) have significantly affected their livelihoods. The relative importance of cultivation has increased as that of livestock has declined. This paragraph on el Seraif is based on Annex 4, "Livelihoods in el Seraif," in ibid., 146–52.

86. Laurie Nathan, "The Making and Unmaking of the Darfur Peace Agreement," in *War in Darfur and the Search for Peace,* ed. Alex de Waal (Cambridge, Mass.: Harvard University Press, 2007), 248–49.

87. Danit Toga, "The African Union Mediation and the Abuja Peace Talks," in ibid., 241.

88. Nathan, "The Making and Unmaking of the Darfur Peace Agreement," 250.

89. Cited in ibid.

90. Ibid., 250, 260.

91. Ibid., 262–63; Alex de Waal, "Sudan: The Turbulent Strategy," in *War in Darfur and the Search for Peace,* ed. Alex de Waal (Cambridge, Mass.: Harvard University Press, 2007), 276.

92. Abdel al-Nur asked for American and British guarantees regarding implementation "like in Bosnia." De Waal, "Darfur's Deadline," in *War in Darfur and the Search for Peace,* 276.

93. African Union, Darfur Joint Assessment Mission—Track 1, "Darfur Early Recovery, Peace and Security," 5.

94. Julie Flint, "Fresh Hopes for North Darfur," BBC News, June 14, 2007; United Nations, Darfur Joint Assessment Mission—Track 1, "Darfur Early Recovery, Darfur Conflict Analysis," 15.

95. Flint, "Darfur's Armed Movements," 154.

96. Ibid., 155; African Union, Darfur Joint Assessment Mission—Track 1, "Darfur Early Recovery, Peace and Security," 5.

97. UN/AU Technical Assessment Mission, June 2006; 4.

98. Flint, "Darfur's Armed Movements."

99. Flint, "Darfur's Armed Movements," 170–71.

100. United Nations, S/205/650, Oct. 14, 2005, cited in United Nations, Darfur Joint Assessment Mission—Track 1, "Darfur Early Recovery, Darfur Conflict Analysis," 7.

101. Ibid.

102. Fadul and Tanner, "Darfur After Abuja: A View from the Ground," 291 (see chap. 6, n. 49).

103. Flint, "Darfur's Armed Movements," 167.

104. United Nations, Darfur Joint Assessment Mission—Track 1, "Darfur Early Recovery, Darfur Conflict Analysis," 8.

105. Flint, "Darfur's Armed Movements," 161.

106. Ibid., 168, 169.

107. Fadul and Tanner, "Darfur After Abuja: A View from the Ground," 295.

108. Ibid.

109. Many scholars are convinced that ethnic conflict is a result of tensions between pastoralists and farmers. They argue for a development policy that will observe pastoralist rights in the context of mixed farming strategies:

> The paper strongly argues that equity, efficiency and environmental sustainability strongly suggest that much can be gained from the restoration of non-exclusive property rights to pastoralists, and from the reestablishment of property regimes that allow for the exploitation of the comparative advantage of different production techniques in a regional context. This can only be achieved by avoiding policies that call for the territorialisation of pastoralists together with the adoption of policies that foster the integration of pastoralism and farming. How to achieve this in practice requires in-depth social scientific study as well as technical research.

Understanding the Crisis in Darfur: Listening to Sudanese Voices, ed. Abdel Ghaffar M. Ahmed and Leif Manger (Bergen, Norway: University of Bergen: Centre for Development Studies, 2006), 52.

Conclusion

1. Office of the Prosecutor, ICC, *Situation in Darfur, The Sudan*, Public Document, No. ICC-02/05, July 14, 2008, 26–27.

2. Louis Charbonneau, "UN says Darfur dead may be 300,000; Sudan denies," Reuters, April 22, 2008, http://www.alertnet.org/thenews/newsdesk/N22308543.htm.

3. Office of the Prosecutor, ICC, *Situation in Darfur, The Sudan*, 14.

4. *Prosecutor's Statement on the Prosecutor's Application for a Warrant of Arrest under Article 58 Against Omar Hassan Ahmad AL BASHIR*, The Hague, July 14, 2008, 5.

5. Ibid., 96–98, 101–102.

6. International Criminal Court, "ICC Prosecutor presents case against Sudanese President, Hassan Ahmad AL BASHIR, for genocide, crimes against humanity and war crimes in Darfur," The Hague, July 14, 2008, ICC-OTP-20080714-PR341-ENG, http://www.icc-cpi.int/press/pressreleases/406.html.

7. The British Labour Party's spokesperson, John Lloyd, has argued for the West, ideally the United Nations, to intervene in Africa, even if it smacks of neoimperialism. John Lloyd, "Cry, the Benighted Continent," *FT* magazine, Aug. 5–6, 2006, 10; Pawson, "Reporting Africa's Unknown Wars," 42–54 (see chap. 1, n. 1).

8. The U.N. Security Council's response to mass violence in Darfur has been to pass Resolutions 1590 and 1591. Even if not realized in practice, these resolutions have the effect of placing Sudan under foreign trusteeship. Res-

olution 1593 charged the ICC with responsibility for trying the perpetrators of human rights abuses in Darfur.

9. Quoted in Gareth Evans, president, International Crisis Group, "The
Responsibility to Protect and the Use of Military Force" (presentation to
Seminar on International Use of Force, World Legal Forum, The Hague,
Dec. 11, 2007), 1–2, http://www.crisisgroup.org/home/index.cfm?id=5209
&1=1 (accessed Dec. 14, 2007).

10. David Mepham and Alexander Ramsbotham, *Safeguarding Civilians:
Delivering on the Responsibility to Protect in Africa* (London: Institute for
Public Policy Research, 2007), 6–7.

11. Evans, "Responsibility to Protect," 2.

12. For a detailed account, see Ussama Makdisi, *The Culture of Sectarianism,
Community, History, and Violence in Nineteenth-Century Ottoman Lebanon*
(Berkeley and Los Angeles: University of California Press, 2000).

13. See Mamdani, *When Victims Become Killers* (see chap. 3, n. 1).

14. A. H. Alkhuzai, I. J. Ahmad, M. J. Hweel, T. W. Ismail, H. H. Hasan, A. R.
Younis, O. Shawani, et al., "Violence-Related Mortality in Iraq," 484–93 (see
intro., n. 2); G. Burnham, R. Lafta, S. Doocy, and L. Roberts, "Mortality
after the 2003 Invasion of Iraq," 1421–28 (see intro., n. 2); "Greenspan
Admits Iraq was about Oil" (see intro., n. 2).

15. Adam Branch, "Uganda's Civil War and the Politics of ICC Intervention,"
Ethics & International Affairs 21, no. 2 (Summer 2007): 179–98.

16. Otunnu went on to compare the situation in northern Uganda to that in
Darfur:

> The situation in northern Uganda is far worse than that of Darfur, in
> terms of its situation, its magnitude, the scope of its diabolical com-
> prehensiveness, and its long-term impact and consequences for the
> population being destroyed. For example, Darfur is 17 times the geo-
> graphic size of northern Uganda and 4 times the size of its popula-
> tion, yet northern Uganda has had 2 million displaced persons for 10
> years, the same as the number of displaced persons in Darfur today.
> The situation in Darfur has lasted for 2½ years now; the tragedy in
> northern Uganda has gone on for 20 years now, with the forced dis-
> placement and concentration camps having lasted now for 10 years.
> I applaud the attention and mobilization being focused by the inter-
> national community on the abominable situation in Darfur. But
> what shall I tell the children of northern Uganda when they ask: how
> come the same international community has turned a blind eye to
> the genocide in their land?

Finally, he called for a United Nations intervention in northern Uganda on
the grounds of "the responsibility to protect":

> The genocide in northern Uganda presents the most burning and
> immediate test case for the solemn commitment made by world
> leaders in September. Will the international community on this

occasion apply "Responsibility to Protect" objectively, based on the facts and gravity of the situation on the ground, or will action or inaction be determined by "politics as usual"?

Olara Otunnu, "Saving Our Children from the Scourge of War" (Sydney Peace Prize lecture, Sydney, Australia, Nov. 9, 2005), http://www.usyd.edu.au/news/84.html?newscategoryid=4&newsstoryid=764 (accessed Apr. 28, 2008).

17. On the ICC, see Evelyn Leopold, "Bitter Fight with U.S. Leads to Compromises on Court," *Sunday News* (Dar es Salaam), July 14, 2002; "Amnesty Criticizes U.S., Sierra Leone Impunity Deal," *Monitor,* Kampala, Uganda, May 10, 2003, 6; Chalmers Johnson, *Blowback: The Costs and Consequences of American Empire* (New York: Henry Holt, 2000), 12–13. For a detailed discussion, see Mahmood Mamdani, *Good Muslim, Bad Muslim: America, the Cold War, and the Roots of Terror* (New York: Pantheon, 2004), chap. 4.

18. John R. Bolton, "The Risks and Weaknesses of the International Criminal Court from America's Perspective," *Law and Contemporary Problems* 167 (Winter 2001): 6, 3.

19. Quoted in Branch, "Uganda's Civil War," 194.

20. If the ICC is turning into a Western court to try African perpetrators of mass crimes, genocide, too, is becoming a non-Western crime. The official genealogy of genocide excludes the crimes perpetrated against Native Americans, against Africans in the course of modern transatlantic slavery and the colonial era that followed it, as well as those perpetrated by the United States during the Indo-Chinese and Iraqi wars and counterinsurgencies.

21. This is what the ICC had to say in a press release about the Amnesty Act in Uganda: "In a bid to encourage the members of the LRA to return to normal life the Ugandan authorities have enacted an amnesty law. President Museveni has indicated to the Prosecutor his intention to amend this amnesty so as to exclude the leadership of the LRA, ensuring that those bearing the greatest responsibility for the crimes against humanity committed in northern Uganda are brought to justice." One wonders which is worse: that the ICC had no idea that the amnesty law was passed by parliament in the teeth of presidential opposition or that it knew this but did not care about constitutional niceties? ICC Press Release, "President of Uganda Refers Situation Concerning the Lord's Resistance Army (LRA) to the ICC," The Hague, Jan. 29, 2004; see http://www.icc-cpi.int/pressrelease_details&id=16&1=en.html, cited in Branch, "Uganda's Civil War," 184. Branch questions "whether the Uganda case was legally admissible according to the principle of complementarity enshrined in the Rome Statute . . . that the ICC only take cases in which national courts are 'unable' or 'unwilling' to undertake investigation and prosecution."

22. The collaboration between the ICC prosecutor and the Ugandan president came to an end when their objectives no longer coincided. Once the demand for peace became overwhelming, Museveni turned away from the ICC and asked it to drop criminal charges against the LRA leadership: "What we have agreed with our people is that they should face traditional

justice, which is more compensatory than a retributive system." "Uganda Defies War Crimes Court over Indictments," *Guardian,* Mar. 12, 2008.

23. This is not to ignore the fact that in the specific instance of Darfur, the ICC got involved because the matter of Darfur was referred to it by the U.N. Security Council. When the Security Council refers any matter to it, the court has no option but to take it up. Indeed, Darfur is the first test of the Security Council's power to refer a case to the ICC.

24. India's case is summed up in "Duplicity on Darfur," *Hindu,* Apr. 12, 2005, http://www.thehindu.com/2005/04/12/stories/2005041204151000.htm (accessed Mar. 19, 2008).

25. Ibid.

26. The Eastern Sudan Peace Agreement (ESPA), concluded in October 2006, brought an end to the twelve-year insurgency of the Beja Congress and its smaller ally, the Rashaida Free Lions, organized under the banner of the Eastern Front. De Waal, "Darfur's Elusive Peace," 385.

27. A. A. Mohamed and B. Y. Badri, "Intercommunal Conflicts in Sudan— Causes, Resolution, Mechanism and Transformation: A Case Study of the Darfur Region" (Khartoum, Ahfad University for Women, 2002).

28. African Union, Darfur Joint Assessment Mission—Track 1, "Darfur Early Recovery, Peace and Security," 13 (see chap. 5, n. 65).

29. See, for example, Mohamed and Badri, "Intercommunal Conflicts in Sudan," in relation to Nyala in 1990 and interviews for the Darfur Joint Assessment Mission (DJAM) in relation to more recent efforts.

30. African Union, Darfur Joint Assessment Mission—Track 1, "Darfur Early Recovery, Peace and Security," 14.

31. Ibid. There is also a time-honored practice of using tribal festivals as occasions with manifest community goodwill that may be harnessed for mediation. Such, for example, is the Zaffa, an annual gathering for all the leaders of the tribes in an area such as a district, involving dance, music, displays of horsemanship, etc. African Union, Darfur Joint Assessment Mission— Track 1, "Darfur Early Recovery, Peace and Security," 12.

32. Harir, "Recycling the Past in the Sudan," 61, 63, 65 (see chap. 3, n. 86).

33. "Seminar with John Garang" and "Excerpts from the Speech of John Garang to the Media and the Sudanese Community," in Garang, *Call for Democracy in Sudan,* 214, 205 (see chap. 6, n. 61).

34. Interview with anonymous source, Khartoum, May 3, 2007.

35. Interview with Kamal el Juzuli, secretary-general, Sudanese Writers' Union, Khartoum, May 7, 2007.

36. Saeid, "Darfur: The Crisis and the Tragedy," 7 (see chap. 5, n. 10).

37. All quotes from the El Fasher meeting are taken verbatim from my own notes.

38. Interview with Professor Adam El Zain, Khartoum, May 7, 2007.

39. Evans, "Responsibility to Protect," 2.

40. "Questions to the President at the National Assembly," South African Government Information, May 17, 2007, http://www.info.gov.za/speeches/2007/07052112451002.htm (accessed Mar. 5, 2008).

SELECT BIBLIOGRAPHY

Archives

The following sources were found in the Sudan Archive, Durham University:

"Draft Minute on Traditional Authorities Bill." 1951–56. SAD 797/1/1–51.
MacMichael, Harold. SAD 586/1/52, 10.3.28.
———. "The Coming of the Arabs to the Sudan." July 1928. SAD E/5/11, 5, 6.
———. "Indirect Rule for Pagan Communities." SAD 586/1/1.
———. "Notes on the History of Kordofan before the Egyptian Conquest & Appendix." SAD 281/3/1–30.
———. "Notes on the Tribes of Darfur." October–December 1915. SAD 110/1/1–99 & SAD 403/10/29–40.
———. "The Problem of the Anglo-Egyptian Sudan." Royal Empire Society. March 12, 1913. SAD 723/13/1.
Maffey, J.L. "Minute, His Excellency the Governor-General." Khartoum, Sudan. January 1, 1927. SAD 695/8/3–5.
"Report of the Committee on the Sudanization of the Civil Service." Khartoum, Sudan. June 1948. SAD 425/1/1–20.

Conference Papers

Ateem, E.S.M. "Tribal Conflicts in Darfur: Causes and Solutions." Paper presented at Political Problems of the Sudan Conference. Vlotho/NRW, Germany, 1999.
Evans, Gareth. "The Responsibility to Protect and the Use of Military Force." Paper presented at the Seminar on International Use of Force, The Hague, 2007.
"Executive Summary of Environmental Degradation: Darfur." In *Environmental Degradation as a Cause of Conflict in Darfur*. Khartoum, Sudan: University of Peace, 2004.
Fadul, Abduljabbar Abdalla. "Natural Resources Management for Sustainable

Peace in Darfur." In *Environmental Degradation as a Cause of Conflict in Darfur*. Khartoum, Sudan: Unversity of Peace, 2004.

Hicks, Rosemary R. "Religion, Race, Rape and Rights: Building International Inter-Religious Coalitions in Terms of Gender, Sexuality and Militarized Humanism." In *After Pluralism*. New York: Columbia University, 2007.

Mohamed, Adam Azzain. "Indigenous Institutions and Practices Promoting Peace and/or Mitigating Conflicts: The Case of Southern Darfur." In *Environmental Degradation as a Cause of Conflict in Darfur*. Khartoum, Sudan: University of Peace, 2004.

Mohamed, Yagoub Abdalla. "Land Tenure, Land Use and Conflicts in Darfur." In *Environmental Degradation as a Cause of Conflict in Darfur*. Khartoum, Sudan: University for Peace, 2004.

O'Fahey, R. S. "Conflict in Darfur: Historical and Contemporary Perspectives." In *Environmental Degradation as a Cause of Conflict in Darfur*. Khartoum, Sudan: University of Peace, 2004.

Zellman, Ariel. "The Janjaweed in the Sudan: A Case of Chronic Paramilitarism." In *ISA Annual Convention*. San Diego, Calif., 2006.

Government Hearings/Documents

Government of South Africa. May 17, 2007. "Questions to the President at the National Assembly." In *South African Government Information*.

Governor-general of Sudan. "Annual Report for 1921." London: H.M.O, 1921. cmd. 1837.

———. "Annual Report for 1923." London: H.M.O., 1923. cmd. 2281.

———. "Annual Report for 1926." London: H.M.O., 1926. cmd. 2291,7.

———. "Annual Report for 1927." London: H.M.O., 1927. cmd. 3284, 7.

———. "Annual Report for 1930." London: H.M.O., 1930. cmd. 3935, 92.

———. "Annual Report for 1933." London: H.M.O., 1933. cmd. 4387, 77.

———. "Annual Report for 1936." London: H.M.O., 1936. cmd. 5575, 87.

United Nations Security Council. New York, 2006. "United Nations Security Council Address on Darfur—George Clooney."

U.S. Government Accountability Office. November 2006. "Darfur Crisis: Death Estimates Demonstrate Severity of Crisis, but Their Accuracy and Credibility Could Be Enhanced."

U.S. Senate Committee on Foreign Relations. 2004. "The Crisis in Darfur—Secretary Colin L. Powell Testimony."

U.S. Senate Committee on Foreign Relations. April 11, 2007. "Darfur: A Plan B to Stop Genocide."

Interviews/Personal Communications

Abdelghani, Adil. March 25, 2004.

Akol, Lam. July 6, 2006.

Aldehaib, Amel. May 3, 2007.

al-Gaddal, Mohammed. March 27–28, 2004.

Anonymous. May 3, 2007.

Anyidoho, Major General Henry. May 11, 2007.

Asad, Talal. June 2, 2008.

Assal, Manzul A.M. March 18, 2004.

Bahaddin, Dr. July 7, 2007.

Bolad, Yagoub. March 18 & May 3, 2004.

Bowden, Mark. May 7, 2007.

Dass, Dr. July 5, 2007.

de Solva, Immanual. May 7, 2007.

el-Asfia, Taj. May 3, 2007.

el-Atiya, Tayib. August 18, 2007.

El-Battahani, Atta. March 17, 18, 27, 28, 2004.

El-Hardallu, Adlan A. March 24–25, 2004.

el-Juzuli, Kamal. May 7, 2007.

el-Juzuli, Majdi. May 9, 2007.

el-Mahdi, Sadig. March 27, 2004.

el-Tom, Mohamed el-Amin. March 25, 2004 & May 3, 2007.

El Tybe, Yusuf. May 5, 2007.

el-Zain, Adam. May 7, 2007.

Fadil, Abdel Fadil. March 28, 2004.

Hamed, Ustaz Adam Mohamed. May 7, 2007.

Hamza, Amal. March 24, 2004.

Hara, Fabienne. May 5, 2007.

Hasan, Yusuf Fadl. March 20, 21, 2004 & May 6, 2007.

Hassan, Nasredeen Hussein. March 18, 22, 2004.

Honwana, Joao. July 5, 2007.

Huad. May 3, 2007.

Husein, M.A. August 18, 2007.

Ibrahim, Farouk M. March 18, 20, 27, 2004.

Katuntu, Abdu. August 7, 2007.

Khalid, Mansour. May 7 & July 5, 2007.

Kristof, Nicholas. November 13, 2006.

Majid, Saleh Abdel. May 3, 2007.

Mantier, Akeldo. March 23, 2004.

Mekki, Hassan. March 23–25, 2004.

Minawi, Minni. February 26, 2008.

Mitchell, Tim. April 23, 2008.

Mohamed, Abdul. July 6, 2007.

Mohamed, Walaa Salah. May 11, 2007.

Mumtaz. July 6, 2007.

Otunnu, Olara. November 9, 2005.

Rajasingham, Ramesh. May 8, 2007.

Rajkundalia, Jyoti. March 19, 2004.

Salomon, Noah. May 10, 2007.

Spaulding, Jay. E-mail correspondence December 2007; January–May 2008.

Turabi, Hasan. May 10, 2007.

Umbadda, Siddig. May 3, 2007.
Youssouf, Ibrahim. February 24, 2008.
Zainulabedeen, El-Tayeb. March 22, 28, 2004 & May 7, 2007.
Zakaria, Abdullah. February 29, 2008.
Zerihoun, Taye-Brook. February 24, 2008.
Zyd, Abdelrahman Abu. March 19, 22, 2004.

Newspapers

Beckerman, Gal. "U.S. Jews Leading Darfur Planning." *The Jerusalem Post,* April 27, 2006.

Dealey, Sam. "An Atrocity That Needs No Exaggeration." *The New York Times,* August 12, 2007.

El-Tom, Abdullahi Osman. "The Arab Congregation and the Ideology of Genocide in Darfur, Sudan." *Citizen,* September 2, 2007.

Debarrati Guha-Sapir. *Financial Times.* "Letter to the Editor." May 7, 2005.

Flint, Julie. "All This Moral Posturing Won't Help Darfur." *The Independent* (London), July 2, 2007.

———. "Fresh Hopes for North Darfur." BBC News, June 14, 2007.

———. "In Sudan, Help Comes from Above." *The New York Times,* July 6, 2007.

Glaister, Dan. "Not on Our Watch—How Hollywood Made America Care About Darfur," *The Guardian* (U.K.), May 19, 2007.

The Guardian (U.K.). "Uganda Defies War Crimes Court over Indictments." March 12, 2008.

The Hindu. "Duplicity on Darfur." April 12, 2005.

Hoge, Warren. "African Union to Send Troops in Bid to Curb Sudan Violence." *The New York Times,* September 24, 2004.

IRIN. "Obasanjo Warns of 'near-Genocide' in Darfur." October 11, 2006.

Kristof, Nicholas D. "Bush Points the Way." *The New York Times,* May 29, 2004.

———. "China and Sudan, Blood and Oil." *The New York Times,* April 23, 2006.

———. "Dare We Call It Genocide?" *The New York Times,* June 16, 2004.

———. "Day 113 of the President's Silence." *The New York Times,* May 3, 2005.

———. "Ethnic Cleansing, Again." *The New York Times,* March 24, 2004.

———. "Facing Down the Killers." *The New York Times,* December 18, 2004.

———. "The Secret Genocide Archive." *The New York Times,* February 23, 2005.

———. "Starved for Safety." *The New York Times,* March 31, 2004.

———. "Sudan's Department of Gang Rape." *The New York Times,* November 22, 2005.

———. "Why Genocide Matters." *The New York Times,* September 10, 2006.

———. "Will We Say 'Never Again' yet Again?" *The New York Times,* March 27, 2004.

Leopold, Evelyn. "Bitter Fight with U.S. Leads to Compromises on Court." *Sunday News,* July 14, 2002.

Lloyd, John. "Cry, the Benighted Continent." *FT Magazine,* August 5–6, 2006.

The Monitor. "Amnesty Criticizes U.S., Sierra Leone Impunity Deal." May 10, 2003.

Motlafi, Nompumelelo. "Darfur Crisis Puts an Uncomfortable Spotlight on Arab and African Identity." *Cape Times,* April 16, 2007.

The New York Times. Advertisements published May 30, 2007; June 7, 2007

The New York Times. "Sir Harold MacMichael, an Outstanding Colonial Administrator (obituary)." September 22, 1969.

The Observer. Beaumont, Peter and Joanna Walters. "Greenspan Admits Iraq Was About Oil, as Deaths Put at 1.2 Million." September 16, 2007.

O'Fahey, R.S. "Darfur: A Complex Ethnic Reality with a Long History." *International Herald Tribune,* May 15, 2004.

Prunier, Gerard. Letter to the editor. *London Review of Books,* April 27, 2007.

Riddell, Mary. "How Geldof Urged Writers to Go to War over Darfur." *The Observer,* March 25, 2007.

Satter, Raphael G. "U.K. Advertising Regulator Says Ad Campaign's Darfur Deaths Claim Not Factual." *International Herald Tribune,* August 15, 2007.

Smith, Russell. "How Many Have Died in Darfur." BBC News, February 16, 2005.

Strom, Stephanie, and Lydia Polgreen. "Darfur Advocacy Group Undergoes a Shake-Up." *The New York Times,* June 2, 2007.

———. "Publicity Campaign on Darfur Angers Relief Organizations." *The International Herald Tribune,* June 1, 2007.

Sudan Times. "Minister of Interior Lays Emphasis on Role of Chad in Darfur." May 24, 1989.

Sudan Times. "Sudan Rural Solidarity on Darfur Problem." June 20, 1989.

Tisdall, Simon. "Sudan Warns West of Iraq-Style Disaster in Darfur." *The Guardian* (U.K.), March 12, 2008.

Van Woudenberg, Anneke. "Britian Must Confront Shameful Trade That Ruins Congolese Lives." *The Independent* (London), October 31, 2003.

The Washington Post. "Darfur's Real Death Toll." April 24, 2005.

Published Sources

Abdul-Jalil, Musa. "Land Tenure, Land Use and Inter-Ethnic Conflicts in Darfur." In *Understanding the Crisis in Darfur: Listening to Sudanese Voices,* edited by Abdel Ghaffar Muhammad Ahmad and Leif O. Manger. Bergen, Norway: BRIC, University of Bergen, 2006.

Abdul-Jalil, Musa, Adam Azzain Mohammed, and Ahmed Yousuf. "Native Administration and Local Governance in Darfur: Past and Future." In *War in Darfur and the Search for Peace,* edited by Alex de Waal. Cambridge, Mass.: Harvard University Press, 2007.

Abdel-Rahim, Muddathir. *Imperialism and Nationalism in the Sudan: A Study in Constitutional and Political Development, 1899–1956, Oxford Studies in African Affairs.* Oxford: Clarendon Press, 1969.

Abusabib, Mohamed A. *Art, Politics, and Cultural Identification in Sudan.* Uppsala, Sweden: Uppsala University, 2004.

Adams, William Yewdale. "Continuity and Change in Nubian Cultural History." *Sudan Notes and Records* 48 (1967).

———. *Nubia: Corridor to Africa.* Princeton, N.J.: Princeton University Press, 1977.

Ahmad, Abdel Ghaffar Muhammad, and Leif O. Manger. "Reflections on the Meeting 'Understanding the Darfur Conflict: An Attempt at Analysis, Addis Ababa, July 25–26.'" In *Understanding the Crisis in Darfur: Listening to Sudanese Voices,* edited by Abdel Ghaffar Muhammad Ahmad and Leif O. Manger. Bergen, Norway: BRIC, University of Bergen, 2006.

Alkhuzai, A.H., I.J. Ahmad., M.J. Hweel,T.W. Ismail, H.H. Hasan, A.R. Younis, O. Shawani, et al. "Violence-Related Mortality in Iraq from 2002 to 2006." *New England Journal of Medicine* 358, no. 5 (January 2008).

Al-Naqar, Umar Abd al-Razzaq. "The Historical Background to the Sudan Road." In *Sudan in Africa,* edited by Yusuf Fadl Hasan. Khartoum, Sudan: University of Khartoum, 1971.

Al-Naqar, Umar Abd al-Razzaq. *The Pilgrimage Tradition in West Africa: A Historical Study with Special Reference to the Nineteenth Century.* Khartoum, Sudan: University of Khartoum Press, 1972.

Amin, Samir. *Accumulation on a World Scale: A Critique of the Theory of Underdevelopment.* Translated by Brian Pearce. New York: Monthly Review Press, 1974.

Arkell, A. A. "The History of Darfur, 1200–1700." *Sudan Notes and Records* 32–33 (1952).

———. *A History of the Sudan: From the Earliest Times to 1821.* London: University of London, Athlone Press, 1961.

Asad, Talal. *The Kababish Arabs: Power, Authority and Consent in a Nomadic Tribe.* London: C. Hurst & Co., 1970.

Bakheit, G.M.A. "Native Administration in the Sudan and Its Significance to Africa." In *Sudan in Africa,* edited by Yusuf Fadl Hassan. Khartoum, Sudan: University of Khartoum Press, 1971.

Balfour-Paul, H. G. "History and Antiquities of Darfur." *Sudan Antiquities Service,* no. 3 (1955).

Banaji, Jairus. "Islam, the Mediterranean and the Rise of Capitalism." *Historical Materialism* 15 (2007).

Bawa Yamba, Christian. *Permanent Pilgrims: The Role of Pilgrimage in the Lives of West African Muslims in Sudan.* Washington, D.C.: Smithsonian Institution Press, 1995.

Birks, J. S. *Across the Savannas to Mecca: The Overland Pilgrimage Route from West Africa.* London: C. Hurst, 1978.

Bohannan, Paul. *Justice and Judgment Among the Tiv.* London, New York: Oxford University Press, 1957.

Bolton, John R. "The Risks and Weaknesses of the International Criminal Court from America's Perspective." *Law and Contemporary Problems* 167 (Winter 2001).

Branch, Adam. "Uganda's Civil War and the Politics of ICC Intervention." *Ethics & International Affairs* 21 (Summer 2007).

Burnham, Gilbert, Riyadh Lafta, Shannon Doocy, and Les Roberts. "Mortality

After the 2003 Invasion of Iraq: A Cross-Sectional Cluster Sample Survey." *The Lancet* 368, no. 9545 (2006).

Burr, Millard, and Robert O. Collins. *Darfur: The Long Road to Disaster.* Princeton, N.J.: Markus Wiener, 2006.

Churchill, Winston. *The River War: An Account of the Reconquest of the Sudan.* New York: Carroll and Graf Publishers, 2000.

Coghlan, Benjamin, Richard Brennan, Pascal Ngoy, David Dofara, B. Otto, M. Clements, and T. Steward. "Mortality in the Democratic Republic of Congo: A Nationwide Survey." *The Lancet* 367, no. 9504 (2006).

Cunnison, Ian. "Classification by Genealogy: A Problem of the Baggara Belt." In *Sudan in Africa: Studies Presented to the First International Conference Sponsored by the Sudan Research Unit, February 7–12, 1968,* edited by Yusuf Fadl Hassan. Khartoum, Sudan: University of Khartoum Press, 1971.

———. *Baggara Arabs: Power and the Lineage in a Sudanese Nomad Tribe.* Oxford: Clarendon Press, 1966.

Daldoum, Hassan Musa. *The Dynamics of Ethnic Group Relations in Darfur: A Case of the Fur-Arab Relations in Western Darfur.* Khartoum, Sudan: University of Khartoum Press, 2000.

Daly, M. W. *Darfur's Sorrow: A History of Destruction and Genocide.* Cambridge, U.K.: Cambridge University Press, 2007.

Daly, M. W., and Jane Hogan. *Images of Empire: Photographic Sources for the British in the Sudan.* Boston: Brill, 2005.

de Waal, Alex. "Darfur's Deadline: The Final Days of the Abuja Peace Process." In *War in Darfur and the Search for Peace,* edited by Alex de Waal. Cambridge, Mass.: Harvard University Press, 2007.

———. "Making Sense of Chad." *Pambuzka News* 342 (2008).

———. "Refugees and the Creation of Famine: The Case of Dar Masalit, Sudan." *Journal of Refugee Studies* 1 (1988).

———. "Sudan: The Turbulent State," and "Sudan: The Turbulent Strategy." In *War in Darfur and the Search for Peace,* edited by Alex de Waal. Cambridge, Mass.: Harvard University Press, 2007.

———. "Who Are the Darfurians? Arab and African Identities, Violence and External Engagement." *African Affairs* 104 (April 2005).

Deng, Francis. *War of Visions: Conflict of Identities in the Sudan.* Washington, D.C.: Brookings Institution, 1995.

Du Bois, W. E. B. *The World and Africa.* New York: Oxford University Press, 2007.

Eichler-Levine, Jodi, and Rosemary R. Hicks. "As Americans Against Genocide: The Crisis in Darfur and Interreligious Political Activism." *American Quarterly* 56, no. 3 (September 2007).

el-Battahani, Atta. "Towards a Typology and Periodization Scheme of Conflicts in Darfur Region in Sudan." In *Understanding the Crisis in Darfur: Listening to Sudanese Voices,* edited by Abdel Ghaffar M. Ahmed and Leif O. Manger. Bergen, Norway: BRIC, University of Bergen, 2006.

el-Din, Ahmed Kamal. "Islam and Islamism in Darfur." In *War in Darfur and the Search for Peace,* edited by Alex de Waal. Cambridge, Mass.: Harvard University Press, 2007.

El-Tom, Abdullahi Osman, and M. A. Mohamed Salih. "Review of the Black

Book of Sudan." *Review of African Political Economy* 30, no. 97 (September 2003).

Evans-Pritchard, E. E. *The Nuer: A Description of the Modes of Livelihood and Political Institutions of a Nilotic People.* New York: Oxford University Press, 1969.

Fadul, Abdul Jabbar and Victor Tanner. "Darfur After Abuja: A View from the Ground." In *War in Darfur and the Search for Peace*, edited by Alex de Waal. Cambridge, Mass.: Harvard University Press, 2007.

Flint, Julie, and Alex de Waal. *A New History of a Long War.* London & New York: Zed Books, 2008.

Flint, Julie, and Alex de Waal. *Darfur : A Short History of a Long War.* London & New York: Zed Books, 2005.

Flint, Julie. "Darfur's Armed Movements." In *War in Darfur and the Search for Peace*, edited by Alex de Waal. Cambridge, Mass.: Harvard University Press, 2007.

Garang, John. *John Garang Speaks,* edited and introduced by Mansour Khalid. London & New York: Kegan, Paul International, 1987.

———. *The Call for Democracy in Sudan*, edited and introduced by Mansour Khalid. London & New York: Kegan, Paul International, 1992.

Gossett, Thomas F. *Race: The History of an Idea in America.* New York: Oxford University Press, 1997.

Graves, Robert, and Raphael Patai. *Hebrew Myths: The Book of Genesis.* Garden City, N.Y.: Doubleday, 1964.

Haaland, Gunnar. "Nomadism as an Economic Career among the Sedentaries of the Sudan Savannah Belt." In *Essays in Sudan Ethnography*, edited by Ian Cunnison and Wendy James. London: C. Hurst & Co., 1972.

Hagan, John, and Alberto Palloni. "Death in Darfur." *Science* 313, no. 5793 (September 2006).

Haggar, Ali. "The Origins and Organization of the Janjawiid in Darfur." In *War in Darfur and the Search for Peace*, edited by Alex de Waal. Cambridge, Mass.: Harvard University Press, 2007.

Hamdi, Mohamed Elhachmi. *Conversations with Hasan Al-Turabi.* Boulder, Colo.: Westview Press, 1998.

Hamilton, Rebecca, and Chad Hazlett. "Not on Our Watch, the Emergence of the American Movement for Darfur." In *War in Darfur and the Search for Peace*, edited by Alex de Waal. Cambridge, Mass.: Harvard University Press, 2007.

Harir, Sharif. "Arab Belt vs. African Belt: Ethno-Political Conflict in Darfur and the Regional Political Factors," and "Re-Cycling the Past in the Sudan: An Overview of Political Decay." In *Short-Cut to Decay: The Case of the Sudan*, edited by Sharif Harir and Terje Tvedt. Uppsala: Nordiska Afrikainstitutet, 1994.

Hassan, Yusuf Fadl. *The Arabs and the Sudan: From the Seventh to the Early Sixteenth Century.* Edinburgh, U.K.: Edinburgh University Press, 1967.

———. "External Influences and the Progress of Islamization in the Eastern Sudan Between the 15th and 18th Centuries." In *Sudan in Africa; Studies Presented to the First International Conference Sponsored by the Sudan*

Research Unit, February 7–12, 1968, edited by Yusuf Fadl Hassan. Khartoum, Sudan: University of Khartoum Press, 1971.

———. *Studies in Sudanese History.* Khartoum, Sudan: Sudatek Limited, 2003.

Haycock, Bryan G. "The Place of the Naptan-Meroitic Culture in the History of the Sudan and Africa." In *Sudan in Africa; Studies Presented to the First International Conference Sponsored by the Sudan Research Unit, February 7–12, 1968,* edited by Yusuf Fadl Hassan. Khartoum, Sudan: University of Khartoum Press, 1971.

———. "Some Reflections on W. Y. Adams, 'Continuity and Change in Nubian Cultural History.' " *Sudan Notes and Records* 52 (1977).

Hillelson, S. "David Reubeni: An Early Visitor to Sennar." *Sudan Notes and Records* 16 (1933).

Hodgkin, T. "Mahdism, Messianism and Marxism in an African Setting." In *Sudan in Africa,* edited by Yusuf Fadl Hassan. Khartoum, Sudan: University of Khartoum, 1971.

Holt, P. M., and M.W. Daly. *The History of the Sudan from the Coming of Islam to the Present Day.* London: Weidenfeld and Nicolson, 1979.

Ibrahim, Abdullahi Ali. "Breaking the Pen of Harold MacMichael: The Ja'aliyyin Identity Revisited." *International Journal of African Historical Studies* 21, no. 2 (1988).

Iliffe, John. *A Modern History of Tanganyika.* Cambridge, U.K. & New York: Cambridge University Press, 1979.

Irstam, Tor. *The King of Ganda; Studies in the Institutions of Sacral Kingship in Africa.* Westport, Conn.: Negro University Press, 1970 (originally published by Hakan Ohlssons Boktryckeri, Lund, Sweden in 1944).

"Islam, Democracy, the State and the West: Roundtable with Dr. Hasan Turabi." *Middle East Policy* 1, no. 3 (1992).

Iyob, Ruth, and Gilbert M. Khadiagala. *Sudan: The Elusive Quest for Peace, International Peace Academy Occasional Paper Series.* Boulder, Colo.: Lynne Rienner Publishers, Inc., 2006.

James, Wendy R. "Social Assimilation and Changing Identity in the Southern Funj." In *Sudan in Africa; Studies Presented to the First International Conference Sponsored by the Sudan Research Unit, February 7–12, 1968,* edited by Yusuf Fadl Hassan. Khartoum, Sudan: University of Khartoum Press, 1971.

Johnson, Chalmers A. *Blowback: The Costs and Consequences of American Empire.* New York: Metropolitan/Owl Books, 2004.

Johnson, Douglas H. *The Root Causes of Sudan's Civil Wars, African Issues.* Bloomington: Indiana University Press, 2003.

Khaldun, Ibn. *The Muqaddimah: An Introduction to History.* Translated by Frank Rosenthal. Edited by N.J. Dawood. Princeton, N.J.: Princeton University Press, 1967.

Khalid, Mansour. "Introduction." In *John Garang Speaks,* edited and introduced by Mansour Khalid. London & New York: Kegan, Paul International, 1987.

———. *The Government They Deserve: The Role of the Elite in Sudan's Political Evolution.* London: Kegan, Paul International, 1990.

———. "Introduction." In *The Call for Democracy in Sudan,* edited and introduced by Mansour Khalid. London & New York: Kegan, Paul International, 1992.

Khani, Ahmed Mohammed. *The Intellectual Origin of Islamic Jihad in Nigeria.* London: Al Hoda, 1988.

Lugard, Frederick John Dealtry. *The Dual Mandate in British Tropical Africa.* Hamden, Conn.: Archon Books, 1965.

MacMichael, Harold A. *A History of the Arabs in the Sudan and Some Account of the People Who Preceded Them and of the Tribes Inhabiting Dárfur.* Cambridge, U.K.: The University Press, 1922.

Mahmud, Ushari Ahmed and Suleyman Ali Baldo. *Human Rights Abuses in the Sudan 1987: The Dhein Massacre; Slavery in the Sudan.* London: Sudan Relief and Rehabilitation Commission, 1987.

Makdisi, Ussama Samir. *The Culture of Sectarianism: Community, History, and Violence in Nineteenth-Century Ottoman Lebanon.* Berkeley: University of California Press, 2000.

Malinowski, Bronislaw. *Myth in Primitive Psychology.* Westport, Conn.: Negro University Press, 1971.

Mamdani, Mahmood. "Blue-Hatting Darfur." *London Review of Books* 29, no. 17 (September 2007).

———. *Good Muslim, Bad Muslim: America, the Cold War, and the Roots of Terror.* New York: Pantheon Books, 2004.

———. *When Victims Become Killers: Colonialism, Nativism, and the Genocide in Rwanda.* Princeton, N.J.: Princeton University Press, 2001.

Mann, Gregory, and Baz Lecocq. "Between Empire, Umma, and Muslim Third World: The French Union and African Pilgrims to Mecca, 1946–1958." *Comparative Studies of South Asia, Africa, and the Middle East* 27, no. 2 (2007).

Marchal, Roland. "The Unseen Regional Implications of the Crisis in Darfur." In *War in Darfur and the Search for Peace,* edited by Alex de Waal. Cambridge, Mass.: Harvard University Press, 2007.

McHugh, Neil. *Holymen of the Blue Nile : The Making of an Arab-Islamic Community in the Nilotic Sudan, 1500–1850.* Evanston, Ill.: Northwestern University Press, 1994.

"Mea Culpa: How Will the Blair Commission Change British Policy?" *Africa Confidential* 46, no. 6 (March 2005).

Mepham, David, and Alexander Ramsbotham. *Safeguarding Civilians: Delivering on the Responsibility to Protect in Africa.* London: Institute for Public Policy Research, 2007.

Mohamed, Adam Azzain. "The Comprehensive Peace Agreement and Darfur." In *War in Dafur and the Search for Peace,* edited by Alex de Waal. Cambridge, Mass.: Harvard University Press, 2007.

———. "Intergroup Conflicts and Customary Mediation: Experiences from Sudan." *African Journal on Conflict Resolution,* no. 1 (2002).

Mohamed, Adam Azzain, and B. Y. Badri. *Intercommunal Conflicts in Sudan—Causes, Resolution, Mechanism, and Transformation: A Case Study of the Darfur Region.* Khartoum, Sudan: Ahfad University for Women, 2002.

"Moral Choice." *Africa Confidential* 46, no. 6 (March 2005).

Morton, J. "The History and Origins of the Current Conflict in Darfur." In

Darfur—Livelihoods under Siege, edited by Helen Young, Abdul Monim Osman, Yacob Aklilu, Rebecca Dale, Babiker Badri and Abdul Jabbar Abdullah Fuddle. Medford, Mass.: Feinstein International Famine Center, Tufts University, 2005.

Muddathir, Abd al-Rahim. "Arabism, Africanism and Self-Identification in the Sudan." In *Sudan in Africa,* edited by Yusuf Fadl Hassan. Khartoum, Sudan: University of Khartoum Press, 1971.

Murphy, Deborah. "Narrating Darfur: Darfur in the U.S. Press, March–September 2004." In *War in Darfur and the Search for Peace,* edited by Alex de Waal. Cambridge, Mass.: Harvard University Press, 2007.

Nachtigal, Gustav. *Sahara and Sudan.* London: C. Hurst & Humanities Press International, 1971.

Nathan, Laurie. "The Making and Unmaking of the Darfur Peace Agreement." In *War in Darfur and the Search for Peace,* edited by Alex de Waal. Cambridge, Mass.: Harvard University Press, 2007.

Nicoll, Fergus. *Sword of the Prophet: The Mahdi of Sudan and the Death of General Gordon.* Stroud, U.K.: Sutton, 2004.

O'Fahey, R. S. "Religion and Trade in the Kayra Sultanate of Dar Fur." In *Sudan in Africa,* edited by Yusuf Fadl Hassan. Khartoum, Sudan: University of Khartoum Press, 1971.

———. *State and Society in Dar Fur.* London: C. Hurst, 1980.

O'Fahey, R. S., and Jay Spaulding. *Kingdoms of the Sudan.* London & New York: Methuen 1974.

Oliver, Roland Anthony, and J. D. Fage. *A Short History of Africa, Penguin African Library.* Harmondsworth & Baltimore: Middlesex, Penguin Books, 1962.

Owen, Roger, and Robert B. Sutcliffe, ed., *Studies in the Theory of Imperialism.* London: Longman, 1972.

Pawson, Lara. "Reporting Africa's Unknown Wars." In *Communicating War: Memory, Media and Military,* edited by Sarah Maltby and Richard Keeble. Burry Saint Edmunds, U.K.: Arima Publishing, 2007.

Posnansky, M. "Pre-Nineteenth Century Contacts between the Sudan and East Africa, and the Nile Valley in Early Times." In *Sudan in Africa; Studies Presented to the First International Conference Sponsored by the Sudan Research Unit, February 7–12, 1968,* edited by Yusuf Fadl Hassan. Khartoum, Sudan: University of Khartoum Press, 1971.

Ranger, T. O. *The African Voice in Southern Rhodesia, 1898–1930.* London: Heinemann Educational, 1970.

Robinson, Ronald. "Non-European Foundations of European Imperialism: Sketch for a Theory of Collaboration." In *Studies in the Theory of Imperialism,* edited by Roger Owen and Robert B. Sutcliffe. London: Longman, 1972.

Rodney, Walter. *How Europe Underdeveloped Africa.* Washington, D.C.: Howard University Press, 1974.

Salih, M.A. Mohamed, and Sharif Harir. "Tribal Militias: The Genesis of National Distintegration." In *Short-Cut to Decay: The Case of the Sudan,* edited by Sharif Harir and Terje Tvedt. Uppsala: Nordiska Afrikainstitutet, 1994.

Salih, M. A. Mohamed. *Understanding the Conflict in Darfur*. Copenhagen: Centre of African Studies, University of Copenhagen, 2005.

Shibikah, Makki. *The Independent Sudan*. New York: R. Speller, 1959.

Shinnie, P. L. "The Culture of Medieval Nubia and Its Impact on Africa." In *Sudan in Africa; Studies Presented to the First International Conference Sponsored by the Sudan Research Unit, February 7–12, 1968*, edited by Yusuf Fadl Hassan. Khartoum, Sudan: University of Khartoum Press, 1971.

Spaulding, Jay. "Conflict in Dar Fur: A View from the Old Sudan." *Sudan Studies Association Newsletter* 24, no. 2 (February 2006).

———. "The End of Nubian Kingship in the Sudan, 1720–1762." In *Modernization in the Sudan*, edited by M. W. Daly. New York: L. Barber Press, 1985.

———. *The Heroic Age in Sinnar*. Trenton, N.J.: Red Sea Press, 2007.

———. "Pastoralism, Slavery, Commerce, Culture and the Fate of the Nubians of Northern and Central Kordofan under Dar Fur Rule " *International Journal of African Historical Studies* 39, no. 3 (2006).

———. "Precolonial Islam in the Eastern Sudan." In *The History of Islam in Africa*, edited by Nehemia Levtzion and Randall Lee Pouwels. Athens: Ohio University Press, 2000.

———. "Slavery, Land Tenure and Social Class in the Northern Turkish Sudan." *International Journal of African Historical Studies* 15, no. 1 (1982).

Spaulding, Jay, and Lidwein Kapteijns. "Land Tenure and the State in Pre-Colonial Sudan." *Northeast African Studies* 9, no. 1 (2002).

Theobald, A. B. *Ali Dinar: Last Sultan of Darfur, 1898–1916*. London: Longman, 1965.

Toga, Dawit. "The African Union Mediation and the Abuja Peace Talks." In *War in Darfur and the Search for Peace*, edited by Alex de Waal. Cambridge, Mass.: Harvard University Press, 2007.

Trigger, Bruce G. "Paradigms in Sudan Archaeology." *International Journal of African Historical Studies* 27, no. 2 (1994).

Trimingham, J. Spencer. *Islam in West Africa*. Oxford: Clarendon Press, 1959.

Tubaina, Jérôme. "Darfur: A War for Land?" In *War in Darfur and the Search for Peace*, edited by Alex de Waal. Cambridge, Mass.: Harvard University Press, 2007.

Wadi, A. I. *Perspectives on Tribal Conflict in the Sudan*. Khartoum, Sudan: IAAS University of Sudan, 1998.

Weinerger, Eliot. "Comment." *October 123, MIT* (Winter 2008).

Willis, Justin. "Hukm: The Creolization of Authority in Condominium Sudan." *Journal of African History* 46 (2005).

Reports

Abdul-Jalil, Musa, and Gert Ludeking. "Track 1—Situation Analysis of Land Tenure Issues: Problems and Implications of Darfur Early Recovery." In *Darfur Joint Assessment Mission*. United Nations, December 2006.

Angola: Arms Trade and Violations of the Laws of War Since the 1992 Elections. New York: Human Rights Watch and Human Rights Watch Arms Project, 1992.

Bell, Martin. *Child Alert: Democratic Republic of Congo.* UNICEF, 2006.

Chin, Sally, and Jonathan Morgenstein. *No Power to Protect: The African Union Mission in Sudan.* Refugees International, November 2005.

Curse of Gold. Human Rights Watch, 2005.

Darfur Rising. International Crisis Group, 2004.

Dimensions of Challenge for Darfur. United Nations, December 2006.

Final Report of the Panel of Experts on the Illegal Exploitation of Natural Resources and Other Forms of Wealth of the Democratic Republic of Congo. Global Policy, 2002.

Final Report of the Panel of Experts on the Illegal Exploitation of Natural Resources and Other Forms of Wealth of the Democratic Republic of Congo. U.N. Security Council, October 2002.

Growth, Employment and Equity: A Comprehensive Strategy for the Sudan. Geneva: International Labour Organization, 1976.

Kozel, Valerie, and Patrick Mullen. *Estimated Poverty Rates Across Northern Sudan.* Washington, D.C.: World Bank, 2003.

Omer, Hamid. "Track 1—Darfur Early Recovery, Water Resources, Development and Utilization in Darfur States, War Affected Communities." In *Darfur Joint Assessment Mission,* United Nations, October 2006.

Report of the De La Warr Commission. Khartoum, Sudan, 1937.

Report of the International Commission of Inquiry on Dafur for the United Nations Security-General Pursuant to Security Council Resolution 1564. Geneva: United Nations, 2005.

Retrospective Mortality Survey among the Internally Displaced Population, Greater Darfur, Sudan. Geneva: World Health Organization, August 2004.

Sudan: Post-Conflict Environmental Assessment. Nairobi, Kenya: United Nations Environment Programme, 2007.

"Track 1—Darfur Early Recovery, Darfur Conflict Analysis." In *Darfur Joint Assessment Mission.* United Nations, December 2006.

"Track 1—Darfur Early Recovery, Peace and Security." In *Darfur Joint Assessment Mission.* African Union, December 2006.

"Track 1—Darfur Early Recovery, War Affected Communities." In *Darfur Joint Assessment Mission.* United Nations, December 2006.

UN/AU Technical Assessment Mission. United Nations and African Union, 2006.

Young, Helen, Abdul Monim Osman, Yacob Aklilu, Rebecca Dale, Babiker Badri and Abdul Jabbar Abdullah Fuddle. *Darfur—Livelihoods under Siege.* Medford, Mass.: Feinstein International Famine Center, Tufts University, 2005.

Theses and Dissertations

Al-Bashir, Ahmed Abdel Rahman. "Problems of Settlement of Immigrants and Refugees in Sudanese Society." PhD diss., Oxford University, 1978.

Al-Shingietti, Abubaker Y. Ahmed. "Images of the Sudan: A Cultural Analysis of the New York Times and the London Times Coverage of Two Crises." PhD diss., University of Massachusetts, 1992.

Bakheit, G.M.A. "British Administration and Sudanese Nationalism, 1919–1939." PhD diss., St. John's College, Cambridge University, 1965.

Bashar, Zuhair Mohamadi. "Mechanisms for Peaceful Coexistence Among Tribal Groups in Darfur." MA thesis, University of Khartoum, 2003.

Daldoum, Hassan Musa. "The Dynamics of Ethnic Group Relations in Darfur: A Case of the Fur-Arab Relations in Western Darfur." MSc thesis, Faculty of Economic and Social Studies, University of Khartoum, 2000.

Hamid, Abbas Abd Al Mannan "Local Authorities and Social Change with Reference to South Darfur Province." MA thesis, University of Khartoum, 1979.

Ibrahim, Abd al-Rahman Abubaker. "Development and Administration in Southern Darfur." MSc thesis, University of Khartoum, 1977.

Idris, Adam Ardaib. "Political Culture and Cultural Hegemony: Questions of Identity and National Integration in the Sudan." MSc thesis, University of Khartoum, 1996.

Khalaf, Nadia. "British Policy Regarding the Administration of the Northern Sudan, 1899–1951." PhD diss., Duke University, 1965.

Sidahmed, Abdel Salam Mohamed. "State and Ideology in the Funj Sultanate of Sennar, 1500–1821." MSc thesis, University of Khartoum, 1983.

Spaulding, Jay. "Kings of Sun and Shadow: A History of the Abdallab Provinces of the Northern Sinnar Sultanate, 1500–1800." PhD diss., Columbia University, 1971.

Unpublished Works

Mohamed, Adam Azzain. "The Rezaiga Camel Nomads of Darfur Region: From Cooperation to Confrontation." Nomadic Peoples. N.d.

Mukhtar, Albaqir Alafif. "On the Fringes of Northern Identity: What's Missing in the Darfur Peace Process?" Washington, D.C.: United States Institute for Peace, 2006.

Saeid, Dr. Elshafie Khidir "Darfur: The Crisis and the Tragedy." Khartoum, Sudan: Communist Party of Sudan. N.d.

Salmon, Jago et al. "Drivers of Change: Civil Society in Northern Sudan." Khartoum, Sudan: DFID Department for International Development, July 2007.

Takana, Yousif. "Darfur Conflict Mapping Analysis." In Darfur—Darfur Dialogue and Consultation. Khartoum, 2007.

Wallis, C.A.G. "Private Papers." London, April 1964.

UN Resolutions

"U.N. Security Council Resolution 1590." March 24, 2005.

"U.N. Security Council Resolution 1591." March 29, 2005.

"U.N. Security Council Resolution 1593." March 31, 2005.

"U.N. Security Council Resolution 1706." August 13, 2006.

"U.N. Security Council Resolution 1769." July 31, 2007.

Websites

"ASA Adjudications." Advertising Standards Authority (accessed August 8, 2007). Available from www.asa.org/UK/asa/adjudications/Public/TF_ADJ _42993.htm.

BBC News. "UN's Darfur Death Estimate Soars." March 14, 2005.

"The Case Against Hissene Habre, An African Pinochet." Human Rights Watch (accessed August 1, 2008). Available from http://hrw.org/justice/habre/ intro_web2.htm.

"Christian Faith Action Packet. Global Days for Darfur." Available from www .savedarfur.org/globaldays.

Davies, Nicolas J S. *Estimating Civilian Deaths in Iraq—Six Surveys* January 4, 2008 (accessed July 30, 2008). Available from http://onlinejournal.com/ artman/publish/article_643.shtml.

"Iraq Body Count." (accessed July 30 2008). Available from www.iraqbodycount .org/database.

"Jewish Faith Action Packet." Global Days for Darfur. Available from www .savedarfur.org/globaldays.

"Making Sense of Darfur." Social Science Research Council 2007 (accessed August 5, 2008). Available from www.ssrc.org/blogs/2007/08/16/deaths-in -darfur-keeping-ourselves-honest.

Reeves, Eric. *Sudan Reeves.* Available from www.sudanreeves.org.

———. "many more than 10,000." (February 1, 2004). Available from http:// www.sudanreeves.org/Sections-article148-p1.html.

———. "more than 30,000 people may have already died in Darfur." (February 5, 2004). Available from http://www.sudanreeves.org/Sections-article150 -p1.html.

———. "as many as fifty thousand or more may have died already." (May 12, 2004). Available from http://www.sudanreeves.org/Sections-req-viewarticle- artid-191-allpages-1-theme-Printer.html.

———. "very approximate figure of 80,000 dead." (June 11, 2004). Available from http://www.sudanreeves.org/Sections-req-viewarticle-artid-193 -allpages-1-theme-Printer.html.

———. "number of victims of genocide is already approaching (and has perhaps exceeded) 100,000." (June 28, 2004). Available from http://www .sudanreeves.org/Sections-article197-p1.html.

———. "yield a total civilian mortality rate to date of approximately 120,000." (July 6, 2004). Available from http://www.sudanreeves.org/Sections-req -viewarticle-artid-199-allpages-1-theme-Printer.html.

———. "approach to 150,000 thousand deaths." (July 21, 2004). Available from http://www.sudanreeves.org/Sections-article201-p1.html.

———. "estimated total of 180,000 deaths." (August 13, 2004). Available from http://www.sudanreeves.org/Sections-article207-p1.html.

———. "total mortality figure is well over 200,000." (August 27, 2004). Available from http://www.sudanreeves.org/Sections-article210-p1.html.

———. "deaths of as many as 300,000 human beings." (October 12, 2004). Available from http://www.sudanreeves.org/Sections-article221-p1.html.

———. "335,000 dead since February 2003." (November 16, 2004). Available from http://www.sudanreeves.org/Sections-article226-p1.html.

———. "approximately 370,000 have died." (December 12, 2004). Available from http://www.sudanreeves.org/modules.php?op=modload&name=Sections &file=index&req=viewarticle&artid=256&page=1.

———. "total deaths number approximately 400,000." (December 29, 2004). Available from http://www.sudanreeves.org/Sections-article476-p1.html.

———. "340,000. "(February 10, 2005). Available from http://www.sudanreeves .org/Sections-article490-p1.html.

———. "mortality is well in excess of 300,000" (February 17, 2005). Available from http://www.sudanreeves.org/modules.php?op=modload&name= Sections&file=index&req=viewarticle&artid=491&page=1.

———. "approximately 380,000 human beings have died." (March 11, 2005). Available from http://www.sudanreeves.org/modules.php?op=modload& name=Sections&file=index&req=viewarticle&artid=497&page=1.

———. "almost 400,000 have already perished." (March 31, 2005). Available from http://www.sudanreeves.org/Sections-article499-p1.html.

———. "conflict-related deaths . . . now exceed 370,000." (August 31, 2005). Available from http://www.sudanreeves.org/Sections-article552-p1.html.

———. "global mortality during the genocide in Darfur is roughly 400,000." (December 23, 2005). Available from http://www.sudanreeves.org/Sections -article543-p1.html.

———. "total mortality . . . still approximates to between 350,000 and 400,000." (July 14, 2005). Available from http://www.sudanreeves.org/Sections -article513-p1.html.

———. "civilians are presently dying at a rate of 1,000 per week." (February 12, 2004). Available from http://www.sudanreeves.org/Sections-article153-p1 .html.

———. "with more than 1,000 civilians dying weekly." (February 17, 2004). Available from http://www.sudanreeves.org/sections-article154-p1.html.

———. "more than 1,000 people are dying every week." (March 31, 2004). Available from http://www.sudanreeves.org/Sections-article162-p1.html.

———. "evidence now suggests that a thousand people are dying every week." (April 13, 2004). Available from http://www.sudanreeves.org/Sections -article167-p1.html.

———. "The weekly civilian death toll is well above 2,000 human beings." (June 1, 2004). Available from http://www.sudanreeves.org/Sections -article184-p1.html.

———. "present mortality exceeds 50,000 per month." (July 28, 2004). Available from http://www.sudanreeves.org/Sections-article202-p1.html.

———. "2,000 who now die daily." (August 9, 2004). Available from http://www .sudanreeves.org/Sections-article206-p1.html.

———. "increases daily mortality in Darfur to over 1,000 human beings." (October 25, 2004). Available from http://www.sudanreeves.org/Sections-article223-p1.html.

———. "current mortality rate has increased to approximately 35,000 per month." (December 12, 2004). Available from http://www.sudanreeves.org/Sections-article256-p1.html.

———. "current mortality rate in the larger humanitarian theater is approximately 15,000 deaths per month." (March 11, 2005). Available from http://www.sudanreeves.org/modules.php?op=modload&name=Sections&file=index&req=viewarticle&artid=497&page=1.

———. "current monthly mortality is approximately 10,000–15,000." (May 7, 2005). Available from http://www.sudanreeves.org/Sections-article503-p1.html.

———. "well over 6,000 people are dying every month." (June 30, 2005). Available from http://www.sudanreeves.org/Sections-article515-p1.html.

———. "very likely more than 10,000 conflict-related deaths per month." (September 29, 2006). Available from http://www.sudanreeves.org/Article126.html.

———. "human mortality that likely exceeds 400,000." (January 14, 2006). Available from http://www.sudanreeves.org/Sections-article539-p1.html.

———. "more than 450,000 deaths." (May 20, 2006). Available from http://www.sudanreeves.org/Sections-article560-p1.html.

———. "as many as 500,000 have already died." (June 24, 2006). Available from http://www.sudanreeves.org/Sections-req-viewarticle-artid-572-allpages-1-theme-Printer.html.

———. November 26, 2006. "some 500,000 have already died." (November 26, 2006). Available from http://www.sudanreeves.org/Article136.html.

———. "400,000." (May 11, 2007). Available from http://www.sudanreeves.org/Article166.html.

Rubenstein, David. "Act Now! Write an Op-Ed About a Plan B with Teeth!," (accessed August 7, 2008). Available from http://ucdstand.blogspot.com/

"Save Darfur Coalition" (accessed January 29, 2008). Available from www.savedarfur.org/faith.

"The 2004 Unity Statement and Call to Action." National Council of Churches (accessed August 7, 2008). Available from www.ncccusa.org/news/04savedarfur-coalition.html.

"Unity Statement." Save Darfur Coalition (accessed August 7, 2008). Available from www.savedarfur.org/pages/unity_statement.

INDEX

Mahmood Mamdani, a third-generation East African of Indian descent, grew up in Kampala, Uganda, and received his PhD from Harvard in 1974. A political scientist and an anthropologist, he is Herbert Lehman Professor of Government in the Departments of Anthropology and Political Science and the School of International and Public Affairs at Columbia University. He was the president of the Council for the Development of Social Science Research in Africa (1999–2003). He was also a founding director of the Centre for Basic Research in Kampala, Uganda's first nongovernmental research organization. He has taught at the University of Dar es Salaam (1973–79), Makerere University in Kampala (1980–93), the University of Cape Town (1996–99), and Princeton University (1995–96). His previous books include *Good Muslim, Bad Muslim; Citizen and Subject* (which won the Herskovits Prize of the African Studies Association of the United States); and *When Victims Become Killers.* He lives in New York City and Kampala with his wife and son.

A NOTE ON THE TYPE

This book was set in Minion, a typeface produced by the Adobe Corporation specifically for the Macintosh personal computer, and released in 1990. Designed by Robert Slimbach, Minion combines the classic characteristics of old-style faces with the full complement of weights required for modern typesetting.

Composed by North Market Street Graphics, Lancaster, Pennsylvania
Printed and bound by Berryville Graphics, Berryville, Virginia
Designed by Wesley Gott

Printed in the United States
by Baker & Taylor Publisher Services